D1596001

SHAKESPEARE'S LITERARY AUTHORSHIP

Re-situating Shakespeare historically as an early modern professional, Patrick Cheney views him not simply as a man of the theatre, but also as an author with a literary career. Cheney argues that Shakespeare's genius for disappearing into 'character' within the collaborative work of the theatre counters Elizabethan England's dominant model of authorship. Rather than present himself as a national or laureate poet, as Edmund Spenser does, Shakespeare conceals his authorship through dramaturgy, rendering his artistic techniques and literary ambitions opaque. Accordingly, recent scholars have attended more to his innovative theatricality or his indifference to textuality than to his contribution to modern English authorship. By tracking Shakespeare's 'counter-laureate authorship', Cheney demonstrates the presence throughout the plays of sustained intertextual fictions about the twin media of printed poetry and theatrical performance. These fictions speak to Shakespeare's standing as a new European author of poems and plays, and to his fascination with a literary afterlife, on page as on stage. By challenging Spenser as England's National Poet, Shakespeare reinvents English authorship as a key part of his legacy.

PATRICK CHENEY is Distinguished Professor of English and Comparative Literature at Pennsylvania State University. He is the author of *Shakespeare, National Poet–Playwright* (Cambridge, 2004), and is editor of a number of publications on early modern English drama and poetry, including *The Cambridge Companion to Shakespeare's Poetry* (2007), *The Cambridge Companion to Christopher Marlowe* (2004), and, with Brian J. Striar, *The Collected Poems of Christopher Marlowe* (2006).

WILLIAM SHAKESPEARE

Frontispiece: *William Shakespeare*, Jacques Wagrez. By permission of the
Folger Shakespeare Library.

SHAKESPEARE'S LITERARY AUTHORSHIP

PATRICK CHENEY

Pennsylvania State University

CAMBRIDGE UNIVERSITY PRESS

Cambridge, New York, Melbourne, Madrid, Cape Town, Singapore, São Paulo, Delhi

Cambridge University Press
The Edinburgh Building, Cambridge CB2 8RU, UK

Published in the United States of America by Cambridge University Press, New York

www.cambridge.org
Information on this title: www.cambridge.org/9780521881661

First published 2008

Printed in the United Kingdom at the University Press, Cambridge

A catalogue record for this publication is available from the British Library

ISBN 978-0-521-88166-1 hardback

For Robert R. Edwards
Scholar, critic, colleague, friend, youth soccer coach

Contents

Figures

Preface

How are we to classify 'Shakespeare' today? In our editions of his works, in our literary criticism and biographies, in our classrooms, in the media, and even in our playbills, how are we to describe William Shakespeare as a professional figure in early modern culture?

Nearly unanimously, we have come to speak of him as a playwright or dramatist, and thus as a consummate man of the theatre, a working dramatist or jobbing playwright. Recent work from two important fields – theatre criticism and bibliographical criticism[1] – coheres in solidifying this professional classification: Shakespeare wrote his plays for performance in the new commercial theatre, taking no interest in their publication; when his plays did reach print, as they started doing in 1594 and continued to do for the remainder of his career, he had no hand in their publication. According to this classification, the play scripts and printed texts that have come down to us are products of early modern collaborative culture, with its actors, businessmen, scribes, printers, and so forth, not of an individuated author with a literary career. Modern scholarship, then, posits that we are to classify Shakespeare in terms of *collaborative theatricality*.

While the theatrical, collaborative Shakespeare has generated a vast wealth of scholarship and criticism, controlling the editions from which we teach, write, and perform, it is too narrowly circumscribed to serve as an accurate *historical* classification. Two recent groups of Shakespeareans, working largely independently of each other, have turned up mutually reinforcing complications. Leading bibliographical critics have argued that Shakespeare wrote his plays both for performance and for print, and thus that we need to classify him as a 'literary dramatist', an author who wrote plays exhibiting not simply consummate theatrical acumen but also a print-culture interest in literary fame.[2] Previous to this revolutionary finding,

---

[1] For definition of these terms, see the Introduction.
[2] Erne, *Shakespeare as Literary Dramatist*. See also Peters, *Theatre of the Book*.

leading literary critics reminded us that in addition to his plays Shakespeare wrote and published freestanding poems, such as *Venus and Adonis* or the Sonnets, thereby supplying 'strong grounds for putting the poems at the front of our thinking about Shakespeare, and perhaps even at the front of collected editions of his works'.[3] While this second group tends to 'ask why we do not think of Shakespeare as primarily a non-dramatic poet' (C. Burrow, 'Life and Work in Shakespeare's Poems' 17), the first marginalizes the poems by speaking of Shakespeare as simply a 'dramatic' author.

What seems required, then, is a fuller, more historically accurate classification, one that sees Shakespeare as a collaborative man of the theatre who wrote plays for both page and stage alongside his freestanding poems, and who ended up bridging the divide between the professional exigencies of the bustling commercial theatre and the longer-term goals of literary immortality, producing works important to London's mercantile development, to England as a developing nation, and to the advent of modern English authorship. In short, missing in modern criticism is a figure I call 'Shakespeare, national poet-playwright'.

In a 2004 book by this title, also published by Cambridge University Press, I tried to re-classify Shakespeare in these terms. In particular, I argued that we need to account for the presence of freestanding poems in Shakespeare's predominantly dramatic career by reference not only to the plague that closed the theatres but also to a fundamentally new institution of authorship emergent in the sixteenth century: for the first time since antiquity, all around Europe writers began to combine poems with plays as part of their literary career. In England, the pioneer of this classical model of authorship was Christopher Marlowe, who inherited it from Ovid, the Augustan author who wrote not simply elegiac and epic poetry but also a play titled *Medea*, extant in two lines and famed in antiquity as the mark of Ovid's genius. Marlowe used a three-genre 'Ovidian *cursus*' of poems and plays – erotic verse, epic, and tragedy – to counter the strictly poetic career of England's Virgil, Edmund Spenser, who wrote pastoral, courtly verse, epic, and hymn. At stake in this 1590s rivalry was the way leading Elizabethan authors were to write the nation: Spenser penned a nationhood of royal power (leaning toward a nationhood of aristocratic power); while Marlowe penned a 'counter-nationhood', which asserted the leadership of

---

[3] C. Burrow, 'Life and Work in Shakespeare's Poems' 17. See also Burrow's 2002 Oxford edition, *The Complete Sonnets and Poems*.

the author himself.[4] Shakespeare, I posited, inherited the national rivalry between Spenser and Marlowe, and made it the defining frame of his art. In poems and plays alike, he rehearsed complex cultural conflicts from the spheres of politics, religion, and sexuality in terms of this literary dynamic, revealing his commitment not simply to commercialism and professionalism but also to nationalism and fame.

To support this argument, I relied on four principal forms of evidence. First, I took the publishing record of Shakespeare's poems and plays to heart, noting that between 1593 and 1612 his poems appeared – and reappeared through subsequent editions – alongside quarto editions of his plays (see Figure 1). Second, I discovered that Shakespeare's contemporaries tended to see him more often as either the author of poems or as the author of both poems and plays than as simply a man of the theatre. Third, I found that Shakespeare's poems and plays record a fiction about the cultural dialogue between poetry and theatre, including print-poetry and stage performance. And fourth, I observed that the history of Shakespeare editions after his death gradually led to an (anachronistic) privileging of the plays over the poems, from Heming and Condell's 1623 First Folio of the plays and John Benson's 1640 edition of the poems up through the 1790 edition of Edmond Malone's *The Plays and Poems of William Shakespeare*, the foundation of standard editions today (see Figure 2). For reasons of space, however, I divided my study into two volumes, with the first specifying the argument through individual chapters on the poems, and the second specifying the argument through chapters on representative plays.

Shakespeare's Literary Authorship both is and is not the planned follow-up to *Shakespeare, National Poet-Playwright*. Strictly speaking, the new book is not a sequel; if it were one, it would simply depend on the general argument outlined in Part I of the earlier study, and remain content with analyses of representative plays. This is not the case. Rather, I have picked up an idea introduced only in the Epilogue to *Poet-Playwright*, 'Shakespeare's counter-laureate authorship', and used it as a foundation here. Consequently, Spenser becomes even more important than he was previously. I also decided to track the presence in Shakespeare's plays of a discourse about books, poetry, and theatre more formally than I did for the poems. The results of both decisions shape Part I here, which aims to introduce a relatively new model of Shakespearean authorship. Part II then selects one play from each of Shakespeare's four dramatic genres – history, comedy,

---

[4] The terms and concepts derive from Cheney, *Marlowe's Counterfeit Profession*, responding (gratefully) to Helgerson, *Forms of Nationhood*.

Year	Plays	Poems
1593		Q1 *VA*
1594	Q1 *Tit*, Q1 *2H6*	Q1 *RL*
		Q2 *VA*
1595	O1 *3H6*	O1 *VA* (?)
1596	Q1 *E3*	O2 *VA*
1597	Q1 *LLL*, Q1 *R2*, Q1 *R3*, Q1 *RJ*	
1598	Q1, Q2 *1H4*, Q2 *LLL*, Q2, Q3 *R2*, Q2 *R3*	O1 *RL*
1599	Q2 *RJ*, Q3 *1H4*, Q2 *E3*	O1, O2 *PP*, O3, O4 *VA*,
1600	Q1 *H5*, Q *2H4*, Q1 *MA*, Q1 *MND* Q2 *2H6*, Q1 *3H6*, Q2 *Tit*, Q1 *MV*	O2, O3 *RL*
1601		Q1 *Love's Martyr*
1602	Q1 *MW*, Q3 *R3*, Q2 *H5*	O5 *VA* (?)
1603	Q1 *Ham*	
1604	Q2 *Ham*, Q4 *1H4*	
1605	Q4 *R3*	
1606		
1607		O6 *VA* (?), O4 *RL*
1608	Q1 *KL*, Q4 *R2*, Q5 *1H4*	O7 *VA* (?)
1609	Q1 *TC*, Q1, Q2 *Per*, Q3 *RJ*	Q Son
1610		O8 *VA* (?)
1611	Q3 *Tit*, Q3 *Ham*, Q3 *Per*	Q1 Reissue of *Love's Martyr* as *Britain's Annals*
1612	Q3 *Tit*, Q3 *Ham*, Q3 *Per*, Q5 *R3*	O3 *PP*
1613	Q6 *1H4*	
1614		
1615	Q5 *R2*	
1616		O5 *RL*
1617		O9 *VA*
1618		
1619	Q3 *2H6*, Q2 *3H6*, Q4 *Per*, Q2 *MW*, Q2 *MV*, Q2 *KL*, Q3 *H5*, Q2 *MND*	
1620		O10 *VA*
1621		
1622	Q1 *Oth*, Q6 *R3*, Q7 *1H4*, Q1 *RJ* (?), Q4 *Ham* (?)	
1623	FF	

Figure 1. Shakespeare's poems and plays in print, 1593–1623

Notes

(1) The present book concentrates on the years 1593 to 1612.

(2) All editions that advertise Shakespeare's authorship are underlined. When the title page contains Shakespeare's initials, dotted lines are used. Dotted lines also indicate works where there are two title pages (one of which contains Shakespeare's name) or an entire edition is lost.

Date	Editor	Title	Contents	
1623	Heminge and Condell	*Mr. William Shakespeares Comedies, Histories, & Tragedies*	Plays	
1640	Benson	*Poems: Written By Wil. Shake-speare. Gent*		Poems: Sonnets rearranged; poems from *Passionate Pilgrim* spliced in; 'Phoenix and Turtle' and *A Lover's Complaint*; but not *Venus* or *Lucrece*
1709	Rowe	*The Works of Mr. William Shakespear*, 6 vols.	Plays	
1709	Lintott	A Collection of Poems, viz.: I. Venus and Adonis; II. The Rape of Lucrece; III. The Passionate Pilgrim; IV. Sonnets to Sundry Notes of Musick, by Mr. William Shakespeare		Poems: *Venus*; *Lucrece*; *Passionate Pilgrim*; 'Phoenix and Turtle'
1710	Lintott	Same, with Sonnets added.		Poems: *Venus*; *Lucrece*; *Passionate Pilgrim*; 'Phoenix and Turtle'; *A Lover's Complaint*; 1609 Sonnets
1710	Curll-Gildon	*The Works of Mr. William Shakespear, Volume the Seventh, containing Venus and Adonis, Tarquin and Lucrece and His Miscellany Poems*		Poems: *Venus*; *Lucrece*; *Passionate Pilgrim*; 'Phoenix and Turtle'; *A Lover's Complaint*; Benson Sonnets
1714	Rowe	*The Works of Mr. William Shakespear*, expanded to 8 vols.	Plays	

Figure 2. Benson to Malone: The publication of Shakespeare's poems and plays

Date	Editor	Title	Contents	
1714	Gildon	*The Works of Mr. William Shakespear, Volume the Ninth*		Poems: *Venus*; *Lucrece*; *Passionate Pilgrim*; 'Phoenix and Turtle'; *A Lover's Complaint*; Benson Sonnets
1725	Pope	*The Works of Shakespeare*, 6 vols.	Plays	
1725	Sewell	*The Works of Mr. William Shakespear, the Seventh Volume, containing Venus and Adonis, Tarquin and Lucrece and Mr. Shakespear's Miscellany Poems*		[see title]
1728	Pope	2nd edn of 1725 edn	Plays	
1728	Sewell	2nd edn of 1725 edn		Poems [same as 1st edn]
1733	Theobald	*The Works of Shakespeare*, 7 vols.	Plays	
1744	Hanmer	*The Works of Shakespeare*, 6 vols.	Plays	
1747	Pope and Warburton	*The Works of Shakespeare*, 8 vols.	Plays	
c. 1760	[Based on Sewell 1728]	*Poems on Several Occasions. By Shakespeare*		Poems [same as Sewell 1728]
1765	Johnson	*The Plays of William Shakespeare*, 8 vols.	Plays	
1766	**Steevens**	***Twenty of the Plays of Shakespeare***	**Plays**	**Poems: 1609 Sonnets**
1767–68	Capell	*Mr. William Shakespeare his Comedies, Histories, and Tragedies*, 10 vols.	Plays	
1771	Hanmer	2nd edn of Hanmer edition	Plays	
1771	Ewing	*Shakespeare's Poems*		Poems: *Venus, Lucrece, Passionate Pilgrim*, Benson Sonnets

Figure 2. (cont.)

Date	Editor	Title	Contents	
1773	Johnson and Steevens	*The Plays of William Shakespeare*, 10 vols.	Plays	
1773–74	**Bell**	***Bell's Edition of Shakespeare's Plays, 9 vols.***	Plays	Poems: *Venus; Lucrece; Passionate Pilgrim;* 'Phoenix and Turtle'; *A Lover's Complaint;* Benson Sonnets
1775	Evans	*Poems Written by Mr. William Shakespeare*		Poems: *Venus; Lucrece; Passionate Pilgrim;* 'Phoenix and Turtle'; *A Lover's Complaint;* Benson Sonnets
1780	Bathurst and Malone	*Supplement to the Edition of Shakespeare's Plays Published in 1778,* 2 vols.	Plays	Poems: *Venus; Lucrece; Passionate Pilgrim;* 'Phoenix and Turtle'; *A Lover's Complaint;* 1609 Sonnets
1785	Bathurst and Malone	3rd edn of Johnson and Steevens	Plays	
1786	Rann	*The Dramatic Works of Shakspeare, in Six volumes,* 6 vols.	Plays	
1790	**Malone**	***The Plays and Poems of William Shakspeare,*** **10 vols.**	Plays	Poems: *Venus; Lucrece; Passionate Pilgrim;* 'Phoenix and Turtle'; *A Lover's Complaint;* 1609 Sonnets

Figure 2. (cont.)

Note

The figure shows the complex evolution of the printing of Shakespeare's poems alongside his plays. (For the purpose of economy, the lists of plays are not included.) The right-hand column charts the distinction between the printing of Benson's poems, especially the Sonnets, and the printing of Shakespeare's poems from the earliest editions, especially the 1609 Sonnets. Most importantly, perhaps, the figure charts the way in which the printing solely of Shakespeare's plays recurrently produced a response volume on the poems, with Benson responding to Heminge and Condell, both Lintott and Curll-Gildon to Rowe, Sewell to Pope, and perhaps Evans to Capell, untill Steevens, Bell, and Malone individually began to combine plays and poems in a single edition (bold type). Significantly, the first two editions to include plays and poems together (Steevens, 1766; Bell, 1773–4) are advertised as editions only of '*Plays*'.

tragedy, and romance – to specify the argument as it develops from early in his career till late: the early history play *2 Henry VI*; the mid-career comedy *Much Ado about Nothing*; the mid-career tragedy *Hamlet*; and the late romance *Cymbeline*. The outcome, I believe, is a book that remains consistent with the first book while offering an independent approach.

The title *Shakespeare's Literary Authorship* is the preferred title of the Press, replacing the working title, *Shakespeare's Counter-Laureate Authorship*. In speaking of Shakespeare's 'literary authorship', I do not seek to occlude alternative models. Rather, I wish to draw attention to certain parts of Shakespeare's works that we may construe in part as 'literary', by which I mean 'of or pertaining to, or of the nature of, literature' (*OED*, Def. 2), or what Shakespeare and his age called 'poesie'. In emphasizing Shakespeare's literary authorship, I hope both to challenge and to complement recent work on his collaborative authorship, and to highlight literary authorship within collaborative practice.[5]

Although I intend the argument here to stand on its own, I also try to indicate when I have already discussed a certain topic, by parenthetically supplying page or chapter numbers for an abbreviated title to *Poet-Playwright* (*SNPP*). Readers who wish to find details about my classification of Shakespeare as a sixteenth-century Ovidian poet-playwright writing in competition with Marlowe and Spenser may consult especially chapters 1 and 2 of the earlier book.

One essay published elsewhere might help explain the relative absence of *The Winter's Tale* in the pages following: 'Perdita, Pastorella, and the Romance of Literary Form: Shakespeare's Counter-Spenserian Authorship', forthcoming in *Shakespeare and Spenser*, edited by Julian B. Lethbridge (Manchester: Manchester University Press, 2008).

For helping shape *Shakespeare's Literary Authorship*, I am grateful to colleagues, students, friends, and family. Colleagues who have offered support or conversation include Tim Arner, James Bednarz, Jane Bellamy, Catherine Belsey, Mike Bristol, Georgia Brown, Martin Butler, Dympna Callaghan, Jonathan Crewe, Margreta de Grazia, Heather Dubrow, Katherine Duncan-Jones, Richard Dutton, Lynn Enterline, Mary Floyd-Wilson, Elizabeth

---

[5] In particular, I seek to enter critical space opened by Bristol, *Big-Time Shakespeare*: 'The romantic valorization of literary authorship as an embattled practice of solitary creativity is almost certainly inaccurate, at least for the early modern period . . . Shakespeare was undoubtedly the author of these works. It is far from certain, however, that any narrower, more contemporary sense of literary authorship was active in his own self-understanding . . . Certainly . . . Ben Jonson, Edmund Spenser, and Michael Drayton . . . went to considerable lengths to establish their identity as literary authors through the medium of printed works. It is not clear, however, whether William Shakespeare did or did not aspire to the status of author' (52–5).

Fowler, Kenneth Gross, Philip Hardie, Richard Helgerson, Jeff Knapp, David Loewenstein, Joe Loewenstein, Laurie Maguire, Willy Maley, Larry Manley, Russ McDonald, David Lee Miller, Louis Montrose, Simon Palfrey, Gail Paster, Curtis Perry, Anne Prescott, the late Sasha Roberts, Katherine Rowe, Tiffany Stern, Margaret Tudeau-Clayton, Stephen Wheeler, Richard Wilson, and Henry Woudhuysen. I am grateful to Georgiana Ziegler of the Folger Shakespeare Library for finding the image of Shakespeare appearing on the cover of this book, by Jaques Wagrez; and to Bettina Smith for helping to process the image for publication.

Those who have generously read portions of the manuscript include a series of very good colleagues indeed: Colin Burrow, Ewan Fernie, Heather James, Bill Kennedy, William Kuskin, Mike Schoenfeldt, Charlotte Scott, John Watkins, and Valerie Wayne. Andrew Hadfield, Laura Knoppers, and Richard McCabe have been a constant source of help, personal and professional.

In Oxford, I am grateful for the care of Mick and Karen Foley, Tish Francis and Douglas Barrie, and Mark Fricker.

I am also grateful to the following colleagues for convening conferences, panels, or lectures allowing me to present my project: Katherine Eggert, for the International Spenser Society at the MLA; Philip Hardie and Helen Moore, the third Passmore Edwards Symposium on literary careers, Corpus Christi, Oxford; David Norbrook and Bart van Es, the early modern seminar, Merton College, Oxford; Charlie Ross and John Watkins, the early modern seminar, Newberry Library, Chicago; Lukas Erne, both at the University of Neuchatel, Switzerland, and at the meeting of the Shakespeare Association of America, Bermuda; Thomas Herron and Hannibal Hamlin, SAA, Philadelphia; and Marica Tacconi, Director of Penn State's Institute for the Arts and Humanities.

Parts of the present book appear (or will appear) in the following publications: part of chapter 1 in *Classical and Counter-Classical Literary Careers*, edited by Philip Hardie and Helen Moore; part of chapter 3 in *The Cambridge Companion to Shakespeare's Poetry*, edited by Patrick Cheney; part of chapter 4 in *Shakespeare's Book: Essays on Writing, Reading, and Reception*, edited by Richard Wilson; and part of chapter 6 in *The Companion to Shakespeare's Sonnets*, edited by Michael Schoenfeldt. I am grateful for permission to reprint material from these pages.

Over the past few years, I have benefited from the expert work of several research assistants: Giuseppina Iacono; LeAnne Kline, Nicholas Repsher, and Dustin Stegner. A sturdy group of undergraduate interns also helped: Eric Brune, Matt Dailey, and Dana Helsel. Matt Dailey did a great job of preparing the index and Lesley Owens of proofing the entire book. My thanks to all.

Also at Penn State, I would like to thank my former and current English Department Heads, Robert Caserio and Robin Schulze, and my Comparative Literature Department Head, Caroline D. Eckhardt, for their generous support. Also instrumental has been the Institute for the Arts and Humanities, along with its Director, Marica Taconni, who supplied a Resident Scholars Grant that released me from teaching during fall 2006, when I completed the book.

Readers for the Press include Raphael Lyne and Lukas Erne, as well as an anonymous reader. The detailed reports helped shape the final script in immeasurable ways, and I deeply appreciate the work and help. Throughout the process, Lukas Erne has especially been a constant source of information, dialogue, and advice.

At the Press, I wish to thank Sarah Stanton for generously encouraging my work over many years, and for presiding over the review process with judicious commitment. I would also like to thank Rebecca Jones, Jo Breeze, and Christopher Hills for their help during the publication process, and Jo Bramwell for her help in copy-editing the typescript.

At Penn State, Garrett A. Sullivan Jr read the entire script and offered countless suggestions for improvement, and provided constant dialogue over many years – and many runs.

The book is dedicated to Robert R. Edwards, who for nearly twenty years has been my mentor and close friend. Bob has read a good deal of the book, offered scrupulous advice, and been the best colleague I could hope for.

Once again, I wish to thank Debora, Evan, and Kelton for their love and support.

Note on texts and reference

All quotations from Shakespeare's poems and plays come from *The Riverside Shakespeare*, ed. G. Blakemore Evans *et al.* (Boston, MA: Houghton, 1997), unless otherwise indicated. Square brackets enclosing words and passages in quotations from the text signal either the editorial emendations of copy-text or additions to it.

Quotations from Chaucer's poetry come from *The Riverside Chaucer*, ed. Larry D. Benson *et al.* (Boston, MA: Houghton, 1987), based on *The Works of Geoffrey Chaucer*, ed. F. N. Robinson, 2nd edn. (Boston, MA: Houghton, 1957).

Quotations from Spenser's poetry come from *The Poetical Works of Edmund Spenser*, ed. J. C. Smith and Ernest De Sélincourt, 3 vols. (Oxford: Clarendon, 1909–10).

Quotations from Marlowe's plays come from *Christopher Marlowe: The Complete Plays*, ed. Mark Thornton Burnett, Everyman Library (London: Dent; Rutland, VT: Tuttle, 1999), while quotations from Marlowe's poems come from *The Collected Poems of Christopher Marlowe*, ed. Patrick Cheney and Brian J. Striar (New York: Oxford University Press, 2006), unless otherwise noted.

Quotations from Milton's works come from *John Milton: Complete Poems and Major Prose*, ed. Merritt Y. Hughes (Indianapolis: Odyssey, 1957).

Quotations from Petrarch come from *Petrarch's Lyric Poems: The 'Rime sparse' and Other Lyrics*, ed. Robert M. Durling (Cambridge, MA: Harvard University Press, 1976).

Quotations from Ovid come from *Ovid in Six Volumes*, Loeb Classical Library, trans. Grant Showerman, 2nd edn., rev. G. P. Goold, 6 vols. (Cambridge, MA: Harvard University Press; London: Heinemann, 1977–89), with the exception of the *Amores*, where I use Marlowe's translation (*Ovid's Elegies*), unless otherwise noted. The numbering of the *Amores* elegies in the Loeb volume differs from that in Marlowe's translation, because the Loeb prints 3.5 on Ovid's dream vision, which Marlowe does not translate, since it did not appear in the edition he was using. Thus those poems in *Ovid's Elegies* after 3.4 differ in numbering from the Loeb volume. Similarly, the line numbering in the Cheney and Striar edition of *Ovid's Elegies*, which begins with the four-line prologue to the work, differs from that in the Loeb, which begins with 1.1.

Unless otherwise noted, quotations and translations from other classical authors – including Virgil – come from the Loeb Classical Library. As the 'Works cited' list at the end reveals, major exceptions include Homer's *Iliad* and *Odyssey*, which come from the translations of Richmond Lattimore; Plato's dialogues, from the edition of Edith Hamilton and Huntington Cairns; Aristotle's works, from the edition of Richard McKeon; and the Bible, from the facsimile of the Geneva edition of 1560 published by the University of Wisconsin Press.

Throughout, I modernize the archaic i-j and u-v of Renaissance texts, as well as other obsolete typographical conventions such as the italicizing of names and places.

For citation, I rely on the 'works cited' format from *The MLA Style Manual* (1985); this format depends on a system of abbreviation in the text and the notes, and thus it includes full citations only in the list of 'Works cited' at the end. Cambridge University Press has brought certain features of the text into conformity with house style, such as including titles (often abbreviated) for all first citations (except for editions of primary sources).

Abbreviations

Per	Pericles
PP	The Passionate Pilgrim
R2	Richard II
R3	Richard III
RL	The Rape of Lucrece
RJ	Romeo and Juliet
Son	Sonnets
TC	Troilus and Cressida
Tem	The Tempest
TGV	Two Gentlemen of Verona
Tim	Timon of Athens
Tit	Titus Andronicus
TN	Twelfth Night
TNK	The Two Noble Kinsmen
TS	The Taming of the Shrew
VA	Venus and Adonis
WT	The Winter's Tale

OTHER WORKS AND ABBREVIATIONS

Aen	Aeneid
Am	Amores
AS	Astrophil and Stella
Ch	Chorus
FF	First Folio of Shakespeare's plays
FQ	The Faerie Queene
HL	Hero and Leander
Met	Metamorphoses
MC	Mutabilitie Cantos
MS	manuscript
Norton	Norton Shakespeare
OE	Ovid's Elegies
OED	Oxford English Dictionary
Oxford	Oxford Shakespeare
Pr	Prologue
'PS'	'The Passionate Shepherd to His Love'
Q	quarto
Riverside	Riverside Shakespeare
RS	Rima sparse

SC	*The Shepheardes Calender*	
	Apr	*Aprill*
	Aug	*August*
	Dec	*December*
	Jan	*Januarye*
	Oct	*October*
	Nov	*November*
SD	stage direction	
SNPP	*Shakespeare, National Poet-Playwright,* by Patrick Cheney (Cambridge University Press, 2004)	
1 Tamb	*Tamburlaine the Great Part 1*	
2 Tamb	*Tamburlaine the Great Part 2*	
Tr	*Tristia*	

Introduction:
'Printless foot': finding Shakespeare

Toward the end of *The Tempest*, Prospero lets slip the enigmatic phrase 'printless foot' during his famous valedictory speech on the theatricality of magic art. In doing so, he speaks deftly to the fundamental paradox about Shakespeare's authorship addressed in this book: that William Shakespeare would produce a dramatic art on the early seventeenth-century London stage written through with a discourse of print culture.

Prospero's speech has long been recognized to derive from Ovid's *Metamorphoses*, where the witch Medea addresses Hecate and other demons of the night, as she gathers herbs when preparing to reverse the aging process of her father-in-law, Aeson. Prospero's incantation begins,

> Ye elves of hills, brooks, standing lakes, and groves,
> And ye that on the sands with printless foot
> Do chase the ebbing Neptune, and do fly him
> When he comes back; you demi-puppets that
> By moonshine do the green sour ringlets make.
>
> (*The Tempest* 5.1.33–7)

Here Shakespeare presents his dramatic artist-figure self-consciously imitating the author of a printed poem from antiquity, yet he represents the metaphysical agents invoked, thosc elvish spirits of nature, as theatrically performing the invisible action of their own erasure. Effectively, Prospero's 'demi-puppets' dance on the sands with 'printless foot'.

Prospero's speech has been widely discussed, but, to my knowledge, never in quite these terms. Scholars agree that Shakespeare carefully imitates Ovid, both the original Latin and Arthur Golding's 1567 translation, relying on paraphrase and on improvization, in the process turning up his 'most sustained Ovidian borrowing'.[1] While inescapably Prospero's valediction to

---

[1] J. Bate, *Shakespeare and Ovid* 249.

magic continues to be identified as Shakespeare's farewell to the theatre, I wish to draw attention to three neglected features as points of entry for the present discussion (we shall return to the speech at the end of chapter 2). First, while the opening line invoking the 'elves of hills, brooks, standing lakes, and groves' fairly accurately renders the corresponding line in both Ovid and Golding, the next four lines form Shakespeare's invention.[2] According to Jonathan Bate, the 'earlier part of [Prospero's] ... speech seems to be a lightening of the [Ovidian] original: the playful spirits chasing the tide as it ebbs and running from it as it comes back are like children on the beach' (251). Second, the most striking set of terms for Shakespeare's improvization, 'printless foot' and 'demi-puppets', elegantly evokes and brings into conjunction the 'two different and in some sense fundamentally opposed forms of production [in Shakespeare's professional career]: theatrical performances and printed books'.[3] Third, Shakespeare presents Prospero conjoining theatre and book in an unusual yet precise formulation, first using language to erase the evidence of print, as the elves chase the ebbing ocean with 'printless foot', and then drawing attention to the agency of performance, as the elves 'make' their fairy rings in the moonlight.

While modern editions of *The Tempest* recognize the 'theatrical overtone' of 'demi-puppets',[4] annotation on 'printless foot' remains scant. For instance, John Dover Wilson, Frank Kermode, Anne Barton, Stephen Orgel, and David Lindley do not provide any gloss at all. In their Arden 3 edition, Virginia Mason Vaughan and Alden T. Vaughan usefully gloss the phrase as 'leaving no print or trace (first occurrence in *OED a.*). Because the elves are not corporeal, they leave no footprints. Cf. *VA* 147–8, where nymphs dance on the sands without leaving footprints' (ed. 265). In *Shakespeare's Words*, David Crystal and Ben Crystal gloss 'printless' as simply 'making no print, leaving no trace', citing *The Tempest*.[5]

Similarly, criticism on 'printless foot' in recent important discussions of Prospero's speech remains negligible. Bate can label the speech an 'extremely skilfully managed ... piece of Renaissance imitation' but neglect it as a model of Shakespearean authorship, instead emphasizing the 'deeply disturbing' collision between 'pagan' and 'Christian' systems of ethics (251–3). In a follow-up to Bate, Raphael Lyne does transpose Prospero's speech to

[2] Golding translates Ovid's Latin ('auraeque et venti montesque amnesque lacusque') as 'Ye Ayres and windes: ye Elves of Hilles, of Brookes, of Woods alone' (7.197). As we shall see, in 1839 Maginn first noticed the presence of two words not accounted for in either Golding or Ovid (Furness, ed. *Temp* 235): 'elves' and 'alone'.

[3] Bristol, *Big-Time Shakespeare* 30.   [4] Orgel, ed., *Temp* 189.

[5] Crystal and Crystal, *Shakespeare's Words* 346.

Shakespeare's authorship, suggesting that the most disturbing anomaly, Prospero's sudden evocation of black magic, might show the playwright confidently 'putting Ovid in his place' – that is, 'renouncing' Ovid's *literary* magic *in his poetry*. Yet Lyne skips over both 'printless foot' and 'demi-puppets', and thus misses the specific professional context for Shakespeare's allusive Ovidian speech.[6] For, as the Vaughans report, the *OED* cites *The Tempest* as the first use of the word 'printless', suggesting that it might be not simply rare in English but a Shakespearean coinage, with only two other examples cited, the first by Milton in *Comus*, clearly indebted to Shakespeare: 'Whilst from off the waters fleet / Thus I set my printless feet / O'er the Cowslip's Velvet head' (896–8).[7] This brief history helps mark the word 'printless', in conjunction with 'demi-puppets', as a rather fine metonym for the peculiar early modern signature that I call 'Shakespeare's literary authorship'.

More specifically, the emergence of the word 'printless' at the very time that print culture is becoming established, along with the way 'printless' modifies the word 'foot', encourages us to view Shakespeare's phrase in terms not simply of print culture but more precisely of printed poetry. According to Stephen Hinds, 'Few word-plays are more familiar in Latin poetry than the one between the bodily and metrical senses of the word *pes* [foot]'.[8] Shakespeare's use of 'printless foot' in a speech clearly revising his favorite (Latin) author evokes print poetry and manifestly erases it. Especially when juxtaposed with 'demi-puppets', 'printless foot' comes to stand for an unusual phenomenon neglected in modern Shakespeare scholarship: an invisible poetic authorship produced within the London commercial theatre.

Thus, Shakespeare puts the representation of printed poetry into immediate conjunction with staged theatre, as if to draw attention to the material conditions of his own authorial predicament: he is the consummate 'man of the theatre' paradoxically engaged with the art of print-poetry.[9] While some might take the peculiar form of the conjunction between poetic book and

---

[6] Lyne, 'Ovid, Golding and the "rough magic" of *The Tempest*' 160–1. See also Barkan, *Gods Made Flesh* 288; S. A. Brown, *Metamorphoses of Ovid* 70–6; Baldwin, *William Shakspere's Small Latine and Lesse Greeke* 2: 448–51.

[7] Neither Early English Books Online (EEBO) nor the Chadwyk-Healy database for poetry, drama, and prose records an earlier use of the word 'printless' than that in Shakespeare's late romance.

[8] Hinds, *Metamorphoses of Persephone* 16. Hinds cites Ovid, *Met* 5.264, *Am* 3.1.8, *Tr* 1.1.15–16; Catullus, *Odes* 14.21–3; and Horace, *Ars poetica* 80. While Ovid did not invent the pun, his wide use of it might have led Shakespeare to attach 'Ovidian' significance to it. For the concept of *ebbing verse*, see *WT* 5.1.101–3.

[9] The phrase 'man of the theatre' comes from (e.g.) *The Oxford Shakespeare* (xxxvi). In an important 1986 essay, Levin identifies the major accomplishment of the twentieth century: 'Our century … has

performed theatre to verify Shakespeare's standing as an arch-theatrical man eschewing print along with poetry, I shall argue to the contrary: Shakespeare's authorial representation brings theatre decisively into play with printed poetry, inventing arguably his most enduring (yet today, perplexing) legacy. The self-conscious character of the representation might lead us to classify Shakespeare's seminal English authorship as fundamentally (but never merely) 'literary', and further, to locate printed books, the art of poetry, and staged theatre as historic components of the Shakespearean literary imaginary.[10]

THE CRITICAL CONTEXT: AUTHORSHIP ON 'PAGE' AND 'STAGE'

Prospero's discourse of 'printless foot' and 'demi-puppets' bridges a historic divide in Shakespeare studies: between what we might call *theatre criticism* and *bibliographical criticism*. Theoretically, these two forms of criticism seem to have little to do with each other, for indeed the expertise required for each tends to be quite different. Theatre criticism is more diverse and complex, but those who practice it tend to be concerned with questions of theatre history, with performance, with metatheatre, and thus with viewing Shakespeare as a consummate playwright, actor, and shareholder in the Chamberlain's Men and later the King's Men, committed to the new economy of the London commercial theatre.[11] In contrast, the much more recent bibliographical criticism, not as diverse but nonetheless complex, tends to focus on the history of the book, on print culture, and on a material model of cultural collaboration that underwrites the production of printed books by William Shakespeare.[12]

restored our perception of him to his genre, the drama, enhanced by increasing historical knowledge alongside the live tradition of the performing arts' ('Critical Approaches to Shakespeare from 1660 to 1904' 228).

[10] I derive this latter concept in response to Montrose, 'Spenser's Political Imaginary', subsequently central to his *The Subject of Elizabeth*.

[11] See Gilbert, 'Performance Criticism'; and its companion piece, Tastpaugh, 'Performance History'. On metatheatre, see Dubrow, 'Twentieth-Century Shakespeare Criticism' 41. By grouping metatheatre with performance, I am yoking two potentially separate forms of criticism in order to emphasize a broader, shared branch devoted exclusively to Shakespearean drama.

[12] A recent issue of *Shakespeare Quarterly* opens with a superb model of this criticism: Stallybrass, Chartier, Mowery, and Wolfe, 'Hamlet's Tables and the Technologies of Writing in Renaissance England'. This form of criticism is so new that it does not show up in *An Oxford Guide*, ed. Wells and Orlin, which inventories twelve forms of criticism, ranging from 'Humanist Interpretations' to 'Performance Criticism'. The ninth form, 'Materialist Criticisms', discusses only the 'three most influential strands – Marxism, new historicism, and cultural materialism'; see Harris, 'Materialist Criticisms' 472. In settling on the term 'bibliographical' to designate this broad form of criticism, in part to offset theatre criticism, I am grateful for conversations with Lukas Erne.

Despite differences with theatre criticism, bibliographical criticism none-theless grows out of, bonds itself with, and remains complicit in the dominant twentieth-century model of Shakespeare as 'the working drama-tist'.[13] In the words of one of its leading practitioners, 'Shakespeare had no obvious interest in the printed book. Performance was the only form of publication he sought for his plays.'[14] In its emphasis on collaboration and the material production of art, bibliographical criticism thus joins theatre criticism not simply in denying the status of 'author' to William Shakespeare but in rejecting the 'literary' as a category.[15]

For the majority of critics today, the divide between theatre and biblio-graphical criticism may exist in practice (as perhaps in training), but during the past few years a new field has sought to cross the divide: 'stage-to-page' criticism. According to a recent practitioner, 'As a movement ... the stage-to-page field, combin[es] ... theatre history and book history, reaching towards a "Shakespeare" defined by multiple contexts rather than authorial intention ... [This] critical movement ... concentrates not on "Shakespeare" the individual author but on the collaborative, multilayered, material, histor-ical world that fashioned the Shakespeare canon.'[16] As this formulation makes clear, stage-to-page criticism joins bibliographical and theatre criticism in benefiting from recent historicism to respond to the traditional model of Shakespeare famously articulated by Milton in *L'Allegro*: 'sweetest Shakespeare, fancy's child', 'Warbl[ing] ... his native Wood-notes wild' (133–4). Recent historical criticism in all three forms – theatre, biblio-graphical, page-to-stage – rightly resists this *poetic* view of Shakespeare for being fanciful and thus unhistorical.

---

[13] Greenblatt, ed., *Norton* 1.
[14] Kastan, *Shakespeare and the Book* 6. Kastan voices the received wisdom; see *Pelican Shakespeare*, ed. Orgel and Braunmuller 1; J. Bate, ed. 97. For other important bibliographical criticism, see Orgel, 'What Is a Text?'; de Grazia and Stallybrass, 'Materiality of the Shakespearean Text'; Maguire, *Shakespearean Suspect Texts*; Blayney, 'Publication of Playbooks'; Masten, *Textual Intercourse*; Murphy, ed., *Renaissance Text*, and *Shakespeare in Print*. One origin lies in McKenzie, 'Printers of the Mind'.
[15] On how bibliographical criticism differs from performance criticism, see Kastan 6–9; for his critique of the 'literary' as a category, see esp. 14–49. However, on how 'the autonomy of the author and of the work are the most celebrated casualties of the newer historical criticism', see Keilen, *Vulgar Eloquence* 8, including a spirited defense of the 'literary' (esp. 4–12).
[16] Stern, *Making Shakespeare* 5–6. Stern cites two 'recent books' as 'principal' instigators of the new field: *New History of Early English Drama*, ed. Cox and Kastan; *A Companion to Shakespeare*, ed. Kastan. Two older books (cited by Orgel, 'What Is a Text?' 83) are Honigmann, *The Stability of Shakespeare's Text*; Bentley, *Profession of Dramatist in Shakespeare's Time*. More recently, see Worthen, *Shakespeare and the Authority of Performance*; Weimann, *Author's Pen and Actor's Voice*; D. A. Brooks, *From Playhouse to Printing House*.

The present book joins an even newer, or fourth field of criticism; this field acknowledges the revisionist principle of social collaboration in the production of Shakespeare's plays but simultaneously grants *individuated literary authorship* to 'Shakespeare' himself. No doubt the origins trace to the early and mid-1990s; in Richard Helgerson's succinct formulation, Shakespeare 'helped make the world that made him'.[17] Louis Montrose is more specific when discussing Edmund Spenser, in a thrilling indictment of Michel Foucault, who powerfully advanced Roland Barthes's 'death of the author' with the concept of the 'author function':[18]

Foucault's own anti-humanist project is to anatomize the subject's subjection to the disciplinary discourses of power. I find this aspect of Foucault's social vision – his apparent occlusion of a space for human agency – to be extreme. In other words, my intellectual response is that his argument is unconvincing, and my visceral response is that it is intolerable.[19]

Montrose does not 'seek to restore to the individual the illusory power of self-creation'; nor does he wish to 'remystify the social production of the text, to reassert its status as an expression of the autonomous author's singular creative genius'. Rather, 'Any meaningful response to Foucault's provocative concept of the "author function" will commence, not by rejecting it, but rather by expanding and refining it, by giving greater historical and cultural specificity and variability both to the notion of Author and to the possible functions it may serve' (92). Like many critics today, Montrose rejects the exaggeration of Foucault's model of 'social construction', calling for a model that allows for the author's individual agency.

While Montrose does not specify the details, among Shakespeare critics Michael Bristol most lucidly crystallizes what we might call a post-revisionist model of authorship:

Authorship need not be understood as a sovereign and proprietary relationship to specific utterances. It is perhaps more fully theorized in terms of dialogue and ethical sponsorship. The author is both debtor and trustee of meaning rather than sole proprietor; authority is always ministerial rather than magisterial. (Bristol, *Big-Time Shakespeare* 58)

According to Bristol, 'Shakespeare labored in his vocation at the selection, composition, and verbal articulation of scripts intended for production in the

---

[17] Helgerson, *Forms of Nationhood* 215.
[18] See Barthes, 'Death of the Author'; Foucault, 'What Is an Author?'
[19] Montrose, 'Spenser's Domestic Domain' 92.

theatre. But Shakespeare did not work in conditions of sovereign independence and artistic isolation … He was in continual dialogue with other writers, including both his literary sources and his immediate contemporaries.' Thus, Bristol concludes that 'Shakespeare's vocation can … be interpreted both as the practice of a craft and as the production of a commodity in the context of a nascent show business' (58).

To my knowledge, we have not improved upon Bristol's formulation, which carefully embeds Shakespeare's 'authorship' in the material culture of his time yet grants to him a 'vocation' that is 'literary', dependent on 'dialogue with other writers', both those in his own literary system (such as Spenser and Christopher Marlowe) and those in systems other than his own (such as Virgil, Ovid, Petrarch, and Chaucer). While Bristol's phrasing inclines toward a social construction of the author, he makes possible a criticism that grants authorial individuation. In today's post-revisionist climate, perhaps we need no longer fear attending to the agency of the author, as long as we allow for his social embededness.[20]

In *Troilus and Cressida*, Shakespeare seems to anticipate a post-revisionist model of authorship, when Achilles asks Ulysses, 'What are you reading?' (3.3.95), and Ulysses reports on the contents of his book, twice using the theatrical concept of the actor's 'part':[21]

> A strange fellow here
> Writes me that man, how dearly ever parted,
> How much in having, or without or in,
> Cannot make boast to have that which he hath,
> Nor feels not what he owes, but by reflection;
> …
> I do not strain at the position –
> It is familiar – but at the author's drift,
> Who in his circumstance expressly proves
> That no man is the lord of any thing,
> Though in and of him there be much consisting,
> Till he communicate his parts to others.
>
> (*Troilus and Cressida* 3.3.95–117)

---

[20] In *Patterns of Intention*, Baxandall writes of 'posited purposefulness' for visual artists: 'The account of intention is not a narrative of what went on in the painter's mind but an analytical construct about his ends and means, as we infer from them the relation of the object to identifiable circumstances' (109; used by Montrose, *Subject of Elizabeth* 257n8). In Shakespeare studies, the assignment of intentionality requires that we rely on bibliographical scholarship to determine as accurately as possible that indeed Shakespeare wrote a given passage, and not, say, George Peele, or that his text is not affected in a substantive way by a compositor or other collaborative agent.

[21] On the word 'part' in Shakespeare's acting vocabulary, see *SNPP* 120, 123–4, 141, 170.

We do not know who the 'strange fellow' or 'author' is (Plato has been the main candidate), and the topic being discussed is the nature of perception – 'that the eye could not see itself except by reflection'[22] – but the 'drift' that Ulysses reads into his author's text bears usefully on the question of authorial agency. Especially in the last three lines, Ulysses anticipates a post-revisionist model when he locates agency in the reciprocity between self and other: 'man' cannot own (be 'lord of') 'any thing', 'though' he himself possesses much value ('consisting').[23]

As illustrated in Ulysses' phrase 'author's drift', Shakespeare occasionally uses the word 'author' and its cognates in his works: a total of twenty-four times, across both poems and plays, from the beginning of his career to the end. Half of these instances appear to refer to a nonliterary cause or agency, as when Ursula in *Much Ado about Nothing* says, 'Don John is the author of all' (5.2.98–9), meaning the cause of the civic turmoil in Messina.[24] But the other half of the instances clearly refer to a literary 'author' – whether the author of a printed book, as in Ulysses' phrase, or the author of a staged play, as in the final Chorus to *Henry V*: 'Thus far, with rough and all-unable pen, / Our bending author hath pursu'd the story' (Epilogue 1–2). As such, Shakespeare's own definition of authorship is divided, not merely between the conceptual and the literary (the causal and the creative), but between the print-author and the play-author. As we shall see, even though Shakespeare uses the word 'author' to emphasize a character's agency and intention, inside his fictions he tends to represent authorship itself more obliquely. In effect, his works stage a historic dialogue about the meaning of the 'author'; in the process, they open up a story about Shakespearean literary authorship itself.

The leading spokesman for the post-revisionist 'return of the author' in Shakespeare criticism has become Lukas Erne.[25] Erne's groundbreaking 2003 monograph, *Shakespeare as Literary Dramatist*, relies on post-revisionist

---

[22] Muir, ed. 126.

[23] In *Shakespeare and the Poets' War*, Bednarz uses the Ulysses speech to identify Shakespeare's theory of 'authorial self-reflection' (264), in opposition to Jonson's theory (51; see 263). In *Censorship and Sensibility*, Shuger also selects Ulysses' speech to illustrate the social character of subjectivity in early modern identity: 'for early modern persons identity was, and was felt to be, relationally constructed. Selfhood – one's sense of identity and value – seems, that is, to have been experienced as radically dependent on the image of oneself seen in the eyes of others' (160).

[24] In chapter 6, I show the extent to which the details of *Much Ado* encourage us to see Don John as a 'literary' author; this villain dangerously rejects poetry in favor of theatre.

[25] The phrase 'return of the author' comes from the title of the conference held in 2004 at the University of Leicester, which aimed to create a dialogue between Erne and editors of the *Oxford Shakespeare*, Wells and Taylor. The conference was organized by Richard Wilson. The dialogue between recent authorship criticism and theatre criticism is complicated; for instance, Wells discusses the nineteenth- and twentieth-century division over seeing *King Lear* as 'a work of literature' or as 'an actable drama',

notions of authorship to resist the conclusions of bibliographical, theatre, and stage-to-page criticism, and thus to find space for the individuated literary author:

> Shakespeare, 'privileged playwright' that he was, could afford to write plays for the stage *and* the page … From the very beginning, the English Renaissance plays we study had a double existence, one on stage and one on the printed page … Printed playbooks became respectable reading matter earlier than we have hitherto supposed, early enough for Shakespeare to have lived through and to have been affected by this process of legitimation … The assumption of Shakespeare's indifference to the publication of his plays is a myth.[26]

By seeing Shakespeare as a 'literary dramatist' composing scripts *both* for performance *and* for publication within his own moment, Erne constructs a historical model that coalesces the best energies of poetical, theatrical, and bibliographical criticism; most emphatically, he alters 'stage to page' to 'stage *and* page'.

As one of Erne's forerunners, Julie Stone Peters, puts the case rather forcefully in her 2001 *Theatre of the Book*,

> The printing press had an essential role to play in the birth of the modern theatre at the turn of the fifteenth century. As institutions they grew up together … In the English-speaking world, Shakespeare's career has helped to produce one of those enduring lies so convenient to the history of progress: that Renaissance dramatists were unconcerned with the circulation of their work on the page; that the press kept aloof from the stage and the early stage kept aloof from the press. But nearly a century before Shakespeare was born, there began, in fact, to develop a relationship that would help create the theatre for which he wrote. Printing, far from being marginal to the Renaissance theatre, was crucial at the outset … Drama was understood to play itself out in two arenas – on the stage and on the page.[27]

Following the historical and bibliographical research of Peters and Erne, criticism is starting to abandon the simplicity of either a strictly theatrical or a strictly bibliographical criticism, or even page-to-stage criticism, in an attempt to render more accurately the relationship between the two media in the early modern era. During the past five years, a sobering piece of

---

to offer a model both related to and different from the one presented here: '*King Lear* has come to be seen as the height of its author's achievement as a dramatist and as a poet: a poetic drama whose poetry can be fully apprehended only through performance' (ed., *KL* 2–3).

[26] Erne, *Shakespeare as Literary Dramatist* 20, 23, 25–6. As a major progenitor of his project, Erne cites Berger, *Imaginary Audition*, who aims to demonstrate the way in which the language of Shakespeare's plays demands a literary interpretation. In 'Shakespeare for Readers', Erne supports his argument for viewing 'Shakespeare's rise to prominence as print-published dramatic author' (MS 1) by discussing stage directions in the early printed texts as sites 'where we may … hope to observe him speaking in his own voice' (MS 8).

[27] Peters, *Theatre of the Book* 1–8.

news has awakened some from the pleasures of performance intoxication: if we seek historical accuracy, no longer can we separate theatre from book, performance from print, in criticism on William Shakespeare.[28]

While embracing Erne's and Peters's post-revisionist model, I suggest nonetheless that the formulation of a 'literary dramatist' is not quite accurate, since it remains unconsciously circumscribed by the 'dramatic' terms of the previous phases, and thus neglects to account for the five freestanding poems that this author saw published during his own lifetime.[29] In 1593 and 1594, Shakespeare published two Ovidian narrative poems, complete with dedicatory epistles to the Earl of Southampton: *Venus and Adonis* and *The Rape of Lucrece*. By 1599, Shakespeare's reputation as a nondramatic author was so marketable that William Jaggard, who in 1623 would bring out the First Folio of the plays, printed *The Passionate Pilgrim*, whose title page falsely ascribed the collection of lyric poems to 'W. Shakespeare'. Then in 1601 Shakespeare himself contributed a 67-line philosophical hymn, known today as 'The Phoenix and Turtle', to Robert Chester's *Love's Martyr*, which also printed poems by Ben Jonson, John Marston, and George Chapman. Finally, in 1609 *Shake-speares Sonnets* appeared, printing both the Sonnets and a third narrative poem, *A Lover's Complaint*, although we still do not know whether Shakespeare authorized the volume or not. In 1640, when John Benson printed the first collected edition of Shakespeare's *Poems*, modeled carefully on the Folio plays, he suggested that the 'excellent and sweetly composed poems' deserve 'proportionable glory' with the plays. Benson even intimates that only the author's 'death' (*2ʳ) prevented Shakespeare from publishing his poems in a volume companionate with the plays.[30]

Ever since Charles Gildon in 1710, critics have been trying to account for the fact that the world's most famous playwright ended up producing a

---

[28] In 'Shakespeare and the Bibliophiles', Nelson recently surveys book owners of Shakespeare's poems and plays before 1616: 'I conclude, against the grain of much modern criticism, that Shakespeare's poems and plays ought to be approached, if we are to respect history, not as documents of politics, theology, religious controversy, philosophy, or anthropology, but as "poesy": that is to say, as objects of delight, as verbal and dramatic art, as – dare I think it? – English Literature' (70). In a personal communication, Lawrence Manley reminds me that in 1602 the Countess of Bridgewater's library included 'Diuers Playes by Shakespeare', as recorded in the inventory supplied by Hackel, *Reading Material in Early Modern England*, who comments: 'Perhaps a volume in which diverse separate quartos were bound together, the first of which was printed in 1602' (266; see 248–9).

[29] Recently, Erne has mended this breach; see 'Print and Manuscript'.

[30] On Benson, and for chapters on all five poems and *The Passionate Pilgrim*, see *SNPP* (on the question of the Sonnets' authorization, see ch. 8).

substantial body of poetic verse in print.[31] By benefiting from the pioneering work of Erne and others, we may re-classify Shakespeare as an early modern author: he is a *literary poet-playwright*. As a result, we might say that the chief legacy of late sixteenth- and early seventeenth-century literary culture becomes the emergence of a hybrid form of authorship articulated through the medium of both printed poetry and staged theatre, legibly registered in the Shakespearean poet-playwright author-figure.[32] As the quite different careers of Ulysses and Prospero intimate, we may find supporting evidence for this revised classification, not simply in bibliographical scholarship, but also in the discourse of the plays themselves.

Shakespeare's Literary Authorship will be the first study to examine just how the literary poet-playwright recurrently puts his model of hybrid authorship center stage. From early in his career till late, across the genres of comedy, history, tragedy, and 'romance', he rehearses a discourse of the book and a discourse of the theatre, and, most importantly, he combines the two discourses together, letting the concepts of *book* and *theatre* jostle in historically telling ways. Like Ulysses' speech on the 'author's drift' at the midpoint of Shakespeare's career, Prospero's valediction to magic at the end supplies a compact example, intimating how often Shakespearean author-ship interlaces the language of books, including poetic books, with the language of theatre.

SHAKESPEARE'S 'SELF-CONCEALING' AUTHORSHIP

Primarily, then, this book aims to contribute to a foundational conversation in Shakespeare studies: just how we are to understand the mystery of Shakespeare's authorship. In the next three sections, we shall look into the nature of this mystery, attempting to formulate a fresh model, before ending with a forecast of the book's structure.

The mystery of Shakespearean authorship exists because, unlike nearly every major author from Virgil to Spenser, Shakespeare rarely *presents himself*. Stephen Greenblatt's critically acclaimed 2004 biography, *Will in the World: How Shakespeare Became Shakespeare*, demonstrates our continuing fascination with this elusive phantom. When Greenblatt writes, 'Shakespeare was a master of double consciousness ... [H]e contrived ... to hide

---

[31] Gildon, *Works of Mr William Shakespear. Volume the Seventh*. See Cannan, 'Early Shakespeare Criticism'.

[32] Cf. C. Burrow, 'Sixteenth Century', who limits the 'chief legacy' to the 'development of a form of authorship which was located in London life and articulated through the medium of print' (26).

himself from view ... Shakespeare's signature characteristic [was] his astonishing capacity to be everywhere and nowhere, to assume all positions and to slip free of all constraints' (155, 242), he essentially updates the famous model of authorship that we have subscribed to since the nineteenth century.

According to this model, Shakespeare's genius lies in *hiding his authorship* in order to foreground his characters, to privilege his actors, and to submit himself genially to the authorial anonymity of the theatrical medium.[33] Samuel Taylor Coleridge first spoke of 'myriad-minded Shakespeare', and said that 'Shakspere never promulgates any party': he is 'Self-sustained – deriving his genius immediately from heaven – independent of all earthly or rational influence ... Least of all poets ancient or modern does Shakespeare appear to be coloured or affected by the age in which he lived – he was for all times – & countries.'[34] Following Coleridge, John Keats coined the phrase '*Negative Capability*' to designate this model of authorship: 'that is[,] when man is capable of being in uncertainties, Mysteries, doubts, without any irritable reaching after fact & reason'.[35]

In the 1960s, Norman Rabkin built on Keats when introducing his influential model of *complementarity* – what he calls the 'true constancy' of 'the dialectical dramaturgy', which does not choose 'between conflicting ethical systems'.[36] In 1995, Alvin B. Kernan could generalize this tradition lucidly: 'Shakespeare was not an autobiographical poet, at least not in any simple, direct sense. Anything but. He remains, in fact, the most anonymous of our great writers – we seem always to glimpse only the back of his head just as he slips around the corner.'[37] As recently as 2002, Harold Bloom can say, 'Shakespeare ... does not portray himself anywhere in his plays ... He provides us with an almost infinite range of surmise.'[38]

In another acclaimed book from 2004, *Shakespeare After All*, Marjorie Garber resurrects the Keatsian formulation that '"The poetical Character"

---

[33] In *Will in the World*, Greenblatt emphasizes Shakespeare's career-long habit of hiding his authorship in opacity (see, e.g., 155, 324, 355, 372–3). On Shakespeare's 'genius', see J. Bate, *Genius of Shakespeare* viii; Bloom, *Genius* xii, 15–30.

[34] According to A. Patterson, Coleridge becomes 'the critic who single-handedly created for the English-speaking world the credo of Shakespeare's disinterestedness, or transcendental freedom from the historical conditions of his time' (*Shakespeare and the Popular Voice* 7; Coledridge quoted from 6 and from 164n13).

[35] E. Cook, ed., *John Keats* 370.   [36] Rabkin, *Shakespeare and the Common Understanding* 11.

[37] Kernan, *Shakespeare, the King's Playwright* 179.

[38] Bloom, *Genius* 16–17. Even more recently, see Wells, 'Current Issues in Shakespeare Biography': 'Shakespeare is the supreme ventriloquist. He can enter into the hearts and minds of a vast range of characters, often expressing diametrically opposed opinions, leaving us with no certainty as to which of the points of view he might have agreed with' (14).

avoids the "egotistical sublime" ', and reminds us just how often we conclude that Shakespeare's 'plays do not reflect the personal opinions, or the moral or political attitudes, of their author'.[39] In 1987, Garber had published *Shakespeare's Ghost Writers*, using Freud's theory of the uncanny to argue that if we wish to find 'Shakespeare' in his plays we will have to track the figure of the ghost: when Shakespeare 'write[s] … ghosts', he literally conjures up the spirit of the past, but this event constitutes a 'transference' that uncannily 'write[s] … *us*'.[40] Working from such post-structuralist theorists as Derrida, with his model of deconstruction, Garber locates 'a critique of the concept of authorship' in Shakespearean dramatic texts because authorship in this man's hands is finally 'undecidabl[e]' (26): 'It is as though Shakespeare *is* beyond authorship … "Shakespeare" is present as an absence – which is to say, as a ghost. Shakespeare as an author is the person who, were he more completely known, would not be the Shakespeare we know' (11; her emphasis). Like many today, Garber retains a vested interest in preserving Shakespearean authorship as a mystery; uncannily, deconstruction does not simply become the most accurate model for such a preservation project; it also qualifies as a post-modern version of Negative Capability: the author remains unknowable; his text, undecidable.

In a final psychoanalytically inflected essay important to mention, titled 'Personal Shakespeare', William Kerrigan identifies 'three clues' to what he calls 'the personality of the author': 'a deep attunement to acting, a fascination with improbable couples, and an uneasy vulnerability to a peculiarly sexual or genital form of misogyny'.[41] In particular, Kerrigan singles out the late play *Antony and Cleopatra* as 'a tragedy in which acting and improbable love triumph over sexual disillusionment, which turned out to be the same thing as staging a counterepic that absorbs and subordinates the imperial drives of his age' (190). Kerrigan's hermeneutic is notable for the slippage it allows between the 'person' and the 'author', the flesh-and-blood-man and the pen-and-print-writer; like Greenblatt in *Will in the World*, Kerrigan aims to use the works of the author to understand the man. At the same time, his insertion of the word 'counterepic' into the profile raises the possibility of adding a fourth 'clue' to Shakespeare's literary authorship: his deep attunement to poetry and in particular to the intriguing phenomenon of 'counter-epic' – a topic we shall return to in chapter 1. For now, we need add only that Shakespeare's interest in poetry extends from epic to lyric and to narrative poetry.

---

[39] Garber, *Shakespeare After All* 17.   [40] Garber, *Shakespeare's Ghost Writers* xiv–xv; her emphasis.
[41] Kerrigan, 'Personal Shakespeare' 185.

While occasionally attending to the intrigue of 'personal Shakespeare', I try to concentrate on something more palpable: not the personal man in his works – or what Greenblatt calls 'the actual person who wrote the most important body of imaginative literature of the last thousand years' (12) – but the author represented in his works. Not William Shakespeare, from Stratford-upon-Avon, born 1564, died 1616, but that man's representations of the author-figure in his fictions. I take the cue of Timon of Athens, when Shakespeare presents his tragic hero ridiculing a figure named The Poet, not simply because this author seeks a wealthy patron to support his literary career, but more particularly because he 'Stand[s] for a villain in [his] ... own work': 'Wilt thou', Timon adds, 'whip thine own faults in other men?' (5.1.38–9). While admittedly the hermeneutic of an author-based (as opposed to a person-based) criticism may not shed new light on the husband of Anne Hathaway, the father of Susanna Shakespeare (later Susanna Hall), or the respected shareholder of the King's Men, it does rely on the fictions within the plays to illuminate the kind of author that William Shakespeare was, the form of authorship that he penned in response to the pressures of his cultural system, and above all the version of authorship that Renaissance print culture ended up stamping as 'Shakespeare's'.

SHAKESPEARE'S COUNTER-AUTHORSHIP: EXTEMPORAL
INTERTEXTUALITY

If Shakespeare is the first major author in the Western tradition who conspicuously avoids presenting himself, we might come to speak of his 'counter-authorship'.[42] Counter-authorship is an oblique literary form of self-representation that allows the author to hide behind the veil of his fictions, while allowing us to follow him, through tracks he himself leaves – in his diction, images, myths, and so forth – some of them presumably 'conscious' but hardly all of them. While we may occasionally glimpse the man behind the works, more palpably we can attend to the textual character of his authorship. Perhaps it is because Shakespeare writes a counter-authorship that we have had so much difficulty following his practice.[43]

---

[42] I borrow the concept of 'counter' from W. R. Johnson in his seminal essay 'The Problem of the Counter-Classical Sensibility', which chooses 'counter' over 'anti' because it is 'essentially positive: its renunciations exist only for the sake of new affirmations' (124n3). My use of the term does differ from Johnson's; whereas he classifies Virgil and Spenser as 'classical' authors and Ovid as 'counter-classical', I would observe that all three engage in self-presentation, whereas Shakespeare does not. As used in this book, then, the word *counter* means both *in opposition to* and *in reciprocation with*.

[43] For instance, in both *Venus* and *Lucrece* Shakespeare veers from the Elizabethan epyllion practice – established by Lodge, Daniel, and Marlowe – of using the first-person voice, and he does so again in

To get at Shakespeare's self-concealing counter-authorship, I rely throughout on a methodology that the previous approaches inventoried above largely ignore: a paradoxical methodology in which an 'absent' Shakespearean authorship is visibly 'present' through intertextuality. In Shakespeare's hands, intertextuality becomes a technique and principle of authorship.[44] By isolating moments of intertextuality, in which the Shakespearean text relates to other identifiable texts, we get as close to Shakespearean authorship as we are likely to get. In passages such as Prospero's Ovidian farewell to magic or Ulysses' speech on the 'author's drift', we can see the author at work, crafting his text out of the texts of other authors, reading those authors and rewriting them through pressures from his own literary environment. Such a methodology ascribes agency to Shakespearean authorship, and complicates it, through awareness of the social constructedness of literary works.

Yet the term 'intertextuality' alone might not always be the most accurate one for describing this author's mysterious practice. In its original formulation, Julia Kristeva uses 'intertextuality' to mean a purely textual phenomenon accessible to the reader but independent of the intentions of the author and of the historical circumstances of production: 'each word (text) is an intersection of word (texts) where at least one other word (text) can be read ... [A]ny text is constructed as a mosaic of quotations; any text is the absorption and transformation of another. The notion of *intertextuality* replaces that of intersubjectivity, and poetic language is read as at least *double*.'[45] Following up on Kristeva, Roland Barthes privileges an intertextual phenomenon that consists of countless anonymous traces designed to 'disperse ... the author as the centre, limit, and guarantor of truth, voice and pre-given meaning': 'Any text is a new tissue of past citations. Bits of codes, formulae, rhythmic models, fragments of social languages, etc. .... [T]he intertext is a general field of anonymous formulae whose origin can scarcely ever be located; of unconscious or automatic

---

his only freestanding, printed lyric poem (another genre traditionally relying on the personal 'I'), 'The Phoenix and Turtle'. Consequently, in the only work he pens that does rely on the personal voice, the Sonnets, Shakespeare creates the greatest controversy of all. See Bloom, *Genius*: 'Where shall Shakespeare be found in Shakespeare? We all want to find him in the Sonnets, but he is too cunning for us, and you have to be the Devil himself to find Shakespeare there' (25).

44 The closest I have seen to this principle comes from Barkan, 'What Did Shakespeare Read?': 'Shakespeare finds the stories that replicate his personal obsessions; the stories give those obsessions certain shapes; he in turn re-shapes them by producing ever-varying adaptations; in the end he becomes a reader of, and source for, himself'(44). Barkan ends his essay by specifying the principle with respect to Ovid in *Titus* and *The Tempest*: 'When Shakespeare's characters have their fullest experience reading, they turn to Shakespeare's favourite source' (46).

45 Kristeva, 'Word, Dialogue, and Novel' 37.

quotations, given without quotation-marks.'[46] By de-centering the author, and centering the reader and the 'text', revisionists like Barthes and Kristeva seek to erase the traditional notion of an individuated author, who self-consciously relies on classical principles of 'echo', 'allusion', or 'borrowing' when imitating verifiable literary sources, often of canonical standing.[47] Despite the concerted efforts of revisionists, however, the term 'intertextuality' has recently mutated beyond their control to acquire a more flexible meaning as both a *text-centered* and an *author-centered* concept – handy, for instance, when a critic wishes to refer to the relationship between two texts by known authors.[48]

Recently, we have been seeing signs of a new way to overcome the limitations of both traditional and revisionist methodologies. In a 2006 study of Milton, for instance, Gordon Teskey silently leaps over the top of intertextuality, but he innovatively substitutes 'allusion' with what he calls 'improvization', by which he means a poet's imposition of 'an outward order, a *schema*, on things and events as they emerge unpredictably in time'.[49] For Teskey, the notion of allusion is 'inadequate for two reasons: because it implies a conscious, isolated act of reference rather than a relatively unconscious process of improvisation, and because it has the direction of movement backwards'. In fact, often for Milton 'Things in the past are captured, torn free of their contexts in previous works, and brought forward in time to be worked into something new' (116). We might think of Teskey's principle of 'improvization' as a post-revisionist concept applicable to Shakespeare's dramatic practice, but it remains a bit oblique, and we might wish to resist Teskey's psychological emphasis (exhibited, for instance, in words like 'unconscious' and 'unpredictable').

As an alternative to the traditional 'allusion', the revisionist 'intertextuality', and the post-revisionist 'improvization', we might posit a concept well suited to William Shakespeare, his works, and what we can tell about his literary practice: *extemporality*. The word as used here derives from Shakespeare's plays and poems, from early till late, across comedy, history, tragedy, romance, and Ovidian narrative poem. He uses *extempore* five times (*1H4* 2.4.280, 316; *TS* 2.1.263; *MND* 1.2.68; *WT* 4.4.677), *extemporal*

---

[46] Barthes, 'Theory of the Text' 31, 39.

[47] For traditional methodologies, see Pigman, 'Imitation and the Renaissance Sense of the Past' and 'Versions of Imitation in the Renaissance'; Ricks, 'Allusion'; above all Bloom, *Anxiety of Influence*. For a recent overview of revisionist theory with respect to traditionalism, see Allan, *Intertextuality*.

[48] For details, see Still and Worton, 'Introduction', *Intertextuality*; Clayton and Rothstein, 'Figures of Corpus'. Throughout, I try to let the Shakespearean *text* direct the form that a particular instance of intertextuality takes, from pure Kristeva to pure Bloom, with much in between.

[49] Teskey, *Delirious Milton* 116–17; his emphasis.

three times (*1H6* 3.1.6; *LLL* 1.2.183, 4.2.50), and *extemporally* two more (*AC* 5.2.217; *VA* 836), bringing the total to ten. From these instances, we learn a good deal about a particular artistic process that clearly mattered to this author.

Without question, Shakespeare imagines the concept of extemporality as a theatrical technique of performance. For instance, Cleopatra fears that if she submits to Caesar he will parade her back in Rome, where 'the quick comedians / Extemporally will stage us' (5.2.216–17). Seven of the ten instances pertain to an actor's improvization of his speech; as the Bishop of Winchester puts it to Humphrey, Duke of Gloucester, in *1 Henry VI*, 'Do it without invention, suddenly, / As I with sudden and extemporal speech / Purpose to answer what thou canst object' (3.1.5–7). Yet Winchester's insertion of the word 'invention' – one of the cardinal principles of Renaissance poetics – complicates the definition, implying a bridge between an actor's extemporal speech and a poet's crafted intention. In *Love's Labour's Lost*, Don Armado constructs the bridge more directly when he exclaims, 'Assist me, some extemporal god of rhyme, for I am sure I shall turn sonnet. Devise, wit, write, pen, for I am for whole volumes in folio' (1.2.183–5). The superbly comical confusion of the boundaries between lyric poetry and theatrical performance also emerges in Holofernes' remark to Nathaniel, 'will you hear an extemporal epitaph on the death of the deer' (*LLL* 4.2.50–1), as it does in *Venus and Adonis*, when the goddess 'sings extemporally a woeful ditty' (836), which Shakespeare associates with Orphic 'echo' (840; *SNPP* 82–4).

In the present book, *echo, borrowing, allusion, influence, intertextuality,* and even *improvisation* all prove instrumental at various times, but Shakespearean *extemporal intertextuality* proves useful when trying to get at this author's practice of rehearsing another literary text obliquely, 'without invention, suddenly'. By extemporal intertextuality, then, we may designate Shakespeare's impromptu evocation of either a past or contemporary text as a disciplined 'apprehension', rather an intentional 'comprehension' (to borrow Theseus' famous terms from *A Midsummer Night's Dream* [5.1.19–20]). Extemporal intertextuality grants agency to both the author and the cultural field within which the author works; it also draws attention to performance and theatricality, vital to the literary art of Shakespeare in both his plays and poems, as the examples above indicate.

Although recent bibliographical, theatre, and stage-to-page criticism emphasize how Shakespeare *became* the 'National Poet' after his death, I recall that he actively participates in his own historical making.[50] During

---

[50] Cf. esp. Dobson, *Making of the National Poet*; de Grazia, *Shakespeare Verbatim*.

the past few decades, we have had invaluable studies of Shakespeare's literary relationship with such authors as Ovid, Virgil, Chaucer, Petrarch, Sidney, Marlowe, and Jonson, as well as of the principles of influence and intertextuality underwriting these relationships, and even of the author's acute literary language; such studies form a composite challenge to any criticism that tries to view Shakespeare as simply a man of the theatre.[51] Shakespeare *is* a man of the theatre, but he is much more: he is an arch-theatrical man who, in plays and poems alike, engages fully the major canonical authors of Western literature.

SHAKESPEARE'S COUNTER-LAUREATE AUTHORSHIP: SPENSER

To extend work done on the nature of Shakespearean intertextuality, let us take the specific cue of Jonson, in his famed memorial poem to Shakespeare from the First Folio:

> My Shakespeare, rise; I will not lodge thee by
> Chaucer, or Spenser.   (lines 19–20; repr. *Riverside* 97)

Jonson does not clarify why he will not 'lodge' Shakespeare by either the Old Poet, Dan Chaucer, or Spenser, the self-proclaimed New Poet, but Jonson implies that he understands Shakespeare to be a quite different kind of author from Spenser ('or' Chaucer).[52] The context of Jonson's distinction suggests that he views the great Elizabethan author, like the great Ricardian one, as an English national *poet*, the author of *poems* important to the nation, and Shakespeare alternatively as a *playwright*, the author of plays in the Western dramatic tradition stemming from the Greeks and Romans and leading up to 'our Lily', 'sporting Kyd', and 'Marlowes mighty line' (29–30).

---

[51] On Ovid, see J. Bate, *Ovid*. On Virgil, see Bono, *Literary Transvaluation*; D. B. Hamilton, *Virgil and 'The Tempest'*; Tudeau-Clayton, *Jonson, Shakespeare, and the Early Modern Virgil*. On Ovid and Virgil, see James, *Shakespeare's Troy*. On Chaucer, see Thompson, *Shakespeare's Chaucer*; Donaldson, *Swan at the Well*. On Petrarch, see Enterline, *Rhetoric of the Body*. On Sidney, see Duncan-Jones, *Ungentle Shakespeare*. On Marlowe, see Shapiro, *Rival Playwrights*; Cartelli, *Marlowe, Shakespeare, and the Economy of Theatrical Experience*. On Jonson, see Bednarz, *Shakespeare and the Poets' War*. On intertextuality, see Bruster, *Quoting Shakespeare*. And on literary language, see Kermode, *Shakespeare's Language*; Freinkel, *Reading Shakespeare's Will*; Russ McDonald, *Shakespeare and the Arts of Language*.

[52] In *The Shepheardes Calender*, Spenser calls Chaucer 'the old famous Poete' and himself the 'new Poete' (*Dedicatory Epistle* 1, 19). For 'Dan Chaucer', see *FQ* 4.3.32 (and *MC* 7.7.9). Jonson's architectural metaphor, *lodge*, may participate in a traditional metaphor for poetry as *space, building, house, room*; see, e.g., Marlowe, *OE* 3.1.39–40; Donne, 'The Canonization' 32. In his 2004 article on 'William Shakespeare' in *The Dictionary of National Biography*, Peter Holland says that Jonson uses the metaphor to refer to the memorial poem of William Bass, where Bass says that Shakespeare should be given space in Westminster Abbey by Chaucer, Spenser, and Beaumont (39).

While Jonson does not mention Shakespeare's five printed poems, and neglects an important origin of Shakespeare's self-concealing authorship in Chaucer, Jonson allows for an idea worth exploring: we may not *lodge* Shakespeare *by* Spenser, but we need to house the authorship of Shakespeare in the neighborhood of Spenser. While editors and critics since the eighteenth century have turned up intriguing details regarding the literary relation between these two giants of the Elizabethan era (most of it confined to editorial annotation and short critical notes), we still lack a comprehensive study, including a frame that reveals why this relation matters.[53]

To accomplish its primary aim, *Shakespeare's Literary Authorship* argues that Shakespeare invents his famed authorship – self-concealment, complementarity, undecidability, negative capability – by *countering* the idea of the laureate or national poet established in antiquity by Virgil and rehearsed most momentously during the English Renaissance by the author whom Thomas Nashe proclaimed in 1592 to be 'the Virgil of England', Edmund Spenser.[54]

To perform his role as national poet, Spenser eschewed the new commercial theatre, instead choosing to author such poetic works as the pastoral *Shepheardes Calender* (1579) and the epic *Faerie Queene* (1590, 1596).[55] In the *October* eclogue of the *Calender*, however, Spenser includes the 'stately stage', especially the 'Bacch[ic]' tragic genre of 'bus-kin fine' (106–13), as an important genre for the Elizabethan author to pen, in a passage that proved important for the tragedies of Marlowe. During the middle of his career, Spenser appears to have changed his mind about the stage, for he wrote recurrent fictions critiquing the theatre, most notably *The Tears of the Muses* but also the Busirane episode in the Legend of Chastity (*FQ* 3.11–12) and the Cambina episode in the Legend of Friendship (*FQ* 4.3).

Yet late in his career (1596) Spenser quietly suggests an analogy between his visionary poetry and the specular operation of theatre, when Calidore witnesses Colin Clout's vision of the Graces on Mount Acidale (*FQ* 6.10),

---

[53] In addition to *SNPP*, see Cheney, 'Shakespeare's Sonnet 106'. For a full bibliography on the Shakespeare-Spenser connection, which I drafted, see the volume of essays, *Spenser and Shakespeare*, edited by Julian Lethbridge, to be published by Manchester University Press.

[54] Nashe, in McKerrow, ed., *Works of Thomas Nashe* 1: 299. Cf. the received wisdom: whereas Shakespeare 'uniformly disparage[es]' poets, Jonson unwisely praises them, so that in Shakespeare's plays we 'are spared the embarrassment that Jonson sometimes gives us when he crowns his own head with laurel' (Muir, *Shakespeare the Professional* 40). Cf. also E. R. Hunter, *Shakspere and the Common Sense* 133.

[55] Gabriel Harvey mentions Spenser's *Nine Comedies* (Letter 3, in G. G. Smith, ed., *Elizabethan Critical Essays* 1: 115), but critics doubt whether they ever existed (Oruch, 'Works, Lost').

and asks the shepherd, 'Whether it were the traine of beauties Queene, / Or Nymphes, or Faeries, or enchaunted show' (17): 'Tell me, what mote these dainty Damzels be, / Which here with thee doe make their pleasant playes?' (19). Back in the Proem to the 1590 *Faerie Queene*, Spenser had used the metaphor of the theatrical 'maske' to identify himself as the anonymous author of *The Shepheardes Calender*: 'Lo I the man, whose Muse whilome did maske, / As time her taught, in lowly Shepheards weeds, / Am now enforst a far unfitter taske, / For trumpets sterne to chaunge mine Oaten reeds' (1.Pr.1). In response, I suggest, Shakespeare plots his famed invention of *theatrical character* along Spenser's Virgilian grid of pastoral and epic, precisely to affect national sentiment.[56]

According to Richard Helgerson, the laureate author uses a religiously sanctioned masculine art to write the nation, and presents himself as doing so.[57] Self-presentation becomes the hallmark of the laureate: he advertises his artistic selfhood as divine authority for fashioning national identity affectively.[58] Helgerson identifies Spenser as Renaissance England's 'first laureate poet', and compares him with two other classes of writers (*Laureates* 100): the 'amateur', such as Sir Philip Sidney; and the 'professional', such as Marlowe. Whereas the amateur sees his art as an escape from national service and marks his literary career with repentance, and the professional sees his work as a way largely to make a living, the laureate makes literature his public contribution to the state throughout his adult life. The 'something of great constancy at the center of the laureate's work', Helgerson writes, is 'the poet himself' (40): 'His laureate function requires that he speak from the center' (12). From this internalized command center, the laureate communicates his religious authority within the political arena: 'A laureate could not be a timeserver. Rather, he was the servant of eternity' (8). In Spenser's case, nonetheless, the laureate's sense of duty to the nation, coupled with his self-adopted vatic role (74), repeatedly conflicts with the call to amorous desire: 'only Spenser could construct a fiction that set forth this exalted vision of love and beauty without losing hold of the world of Elizabethan political reality' (66).

---

[56] Cf. Alpers, *What is Pastoral?*: 'All the court figures in *As You Like It* can be seen as playing out Spenser's metaphor for himself as a pastoral poet: "Lo I the man, whose Muse whilome did maske"' (74).

[57] Helgerson, *Self-Crowned Laureates* 1–20. The following account is an abbreviated version of Helgerson's influential model. The concept of writing the nation more formally organizes Helgerson's *Forms of Nationhood* (on Shakespeare, see 195–245).

[58] On the importance of affective energy to Spenser's epic project, see Campana, 'On Not Defending Poetry'. On the passions in Shakespeare, see esp. Paster, *Humoring the Body*.

According to Helgerson, Jonson succeeds Spenser as England's great laureate, self-consciously replacing the New Poet's Virgilian persona with his own Horatian one (103). To transact his Horatian status, Jonson relies on satire rather than romance, presenting himself as 'A Laureate Satirist' (122–4), and he takes Horace's interest in theatre from the *Ars poetica* and elsewhere to present himself as 'A Laureate Dramatist' (144–65). Yet, as is well known, Jonson grounds his laureate practice of writing plays in the publication of his poems.[59] While no doubt feeling the professional tension between composing poems and producing plays, Jonson prints both forms in his monumental edition of his *Works* the year Shakespeare died (1616). By doing so, Jonson institutionalizes the practice that will become important to subsequent authors, like Milton and Dryden.[60]

Even though Jonson and Spenser introduce different laureate personae and write in different genres, both turn to the printing press to present themselves, relying on such self-conscious strategies as the first-person composition of prefatory material and the clearly marked self-representation of authorial character, such as Colin Clout in *The Shepheardes Calender* or Horace in *Poetaster*. Thus, for all its complexity, English Renaissance laureateship had both a specific portraiture and a direct genealogy.

If this sounds familiar, perhaps it is because we have produced a relatively stable narrative about the historical emergence of modern English authorship during the early modern period. Yet in the standard versions of this narrative Shakespeare receives little part, if any, to play.[61] According to this narrative, Spenser and Jonson, not Shakespeare (or Marlowe), transact the large-scale cultural shift from the older notion of authorship to the one held widely today: the individuated author as a self-shaping agent in the production of his own literary oeuvre and fame.[62] Most importantly, Spenser emerges as England's inaugural laureate author who uses the literary

---

[59] In the words of Yachnin, Jonson really 'wanted to be a poet rather than a playwright' (*Stage-Wrights* 12).

[60] Both Gascoigne and Daniel precede Jonson in producing collected editions of works that include both poems and plays. Nonetheless, Jonson is the first to make the poetry-theatre rubric structural to his edition, to include more than a few plays, and to print plays produced for the new commercial theatre.

[61] Notably, see Wall, 'Authorship and the Material Conditions of Writing', who maps Helgerson's model of the laureate on to more recent work on authorship and print culture, to tell the story this way: 'When Spenser and Jonson used the book format to generate the author's laureate status … they produced … modern and familiar images of literary authority – classically authorized writers who serve as the origin and arbiter of a literary monument that exceeds its place in everyday cultural transactions' (86).

[62] Wall refers to Shakespeare and to Marlowe only once each in passing (83, 71). Similarly, in *Laureates* Helgerson makes only intermittent remarks about Shakespeare (e.g., 4, 10, 39–40, 48–9) and Marlowe (36, 112, 147, 217). Thus, both critics miss an opportunity to slot these authors into a fuller story about the emergence of the English laureate author.

monuments of print and book to extricate himself from 'everyday cultural transactions' and thus to present himself as England's national poet.[63] Oddly, our language's greatest writer lies outside the pale of modern authorship because he is thought to have absented himself from the institution on which this authorship was founded: that of print, and especially print-poetry.[64]

In this book, I suggest that Shakespeare is an alert reader of Spenser's laureate self-fashioning, and organizes his own art in opposition to it.[65] We might say that the blank at the heart of Shakespearean authorship is a self-erasure that opposes the very *presence* of Spenserian self-*writing*. Instead of writing poems in such Virgilian national genres as pastoral and epic, Shakespeare organizes his professional career around the new theatre, but significantly he uses drama to respond to the Spenserian national project, and he produces an interleaving career in the art of poetry, including some of the most extraordinary poems in English. The presence of Shakespeare as an author of printed poetry, everywhere on display in reports by contemporaries (such as Richard Barnfield, Francis Meres, Gabriel Harvey, and Thomas Freeman [*SNPP* 49–50, 64–7]), was much more conspicuous to Elizabethan and Jacobean culture than it is to us today.[66] One reason is that Shakespeare's first two narrative poems were reprinted numerous times

---

[63] In a series of essays, Montrose influentially follows up on Helgerson on Spenser's invention of 'a new Elizabethan author function': Spenser's '"Laureate" authorial persona ... not only professionalizes poetry, it authenticates through print the subjectivity of a writer whose class position might otherwise have rendered him merely the anonymous functionary of his patron. In claiming the originative status of an "Author", a writer claims the authority to direct and delimit the interpretive activity of that elite community of readers by whom he himself is authorized to write' ('Elizabethan Subject and the Spenserian Text' 319).

[64] Like Wall and Helgerson, C. Burrow in 'Sixteenth Century' foregrounds Spenser (22) and Jonson (25–6) in a narrative about 'the emergence of a dignified profession of literary authorship which worked in collaboration with the medium of print' (25–6). When Burrow mentions 'Shakespeare', he speaks rather of 'the name of Shakespeare', which 'by 1598 ... was frequently appearing on the title pages of the printed versions of his plays' (22). Burrow links his discussion with Wall (22) and Helgerson (28n27).

[65] Cf. G. Taylor, 'Forms of Opposition': the 'blank' underwriting 'Shakespeare' and Negative Capability is an 'illusion' – a 'self-erasure' (313). See also R. Wilson, *Secret Shakespeare*: 'it will be the theme of *Secret Shakespeare* that while it may have been historically determined and perpetuated, this author's vanishing act was a deliberate function of his work: that Shakespeare wrote his plays with the conscious intention of secreting himself' (10–11).

[66] Two recent studies provide new evidence for thinking about Shakespeare as a literary poet-playwright. In 'By the Placing of His Words', Wells discusses a manuscript found in 2003, written by William Scott during Shakespeare's lifetime, which refers to and quotes from both *Lucrece* and *Richard II*. In 'Frances Meres and the Cultural Contexts of Shakespeare's Rival Poet Sonnets', M. P. Jackson demonstrates that Shakespeare responded to Meres's celebration of him in the 1598 *Palladis Tamia* – including by relying on Meres's discourse about Marlowe, Chapman, Jonson, Drayton, and even Spenser to create a 'composite creation' known today as the Rival Poet (244).

during his lifetime: *Venus* in 1594, 1595, 1596, 1599, 1602, 1607, 1608, and 1610; *Lucrece* in 1598, 1600, 1607, and 1616 (see Figure 1). In other words, these poems did not simply appear and then disappear; they became a visible feature of Elizabethan and Jacobean literary culture. Consequently, we may need to replace our yardstick for measuring literary reception, with one that includes subsequent editions and evidence of contemporary reaction. (No wonder that in 1599 Jaggard published his volume of poetry by printing William Shakespeare as its author on the title page.)

Instead of self-consciously using the printing press to advance his authorial status to the nation, Shakespeare established a much more nebulous relation to the new print medium, so that today many believe he created an authorship that eschewed commercial publishing and thus literary fame. While Shakespeare's relation to the printing press did differ from Spenser's, we might speculate that the myth about Shakespeare's aversion to print was itself a successful strategy of counter-laureate authorship.[67]

Spenser may organize his art around self-presentation, and Shakespeare around self-concealment, yet the man from Stratford did not simply conceal his authorship. He theorized self-concealment as a political strategy of national leadership. According to Helgerson, in *2 Henry IV* 'Shakespeare does not get rid of Falstaff; Hal does. Judgment comes from within the play as a function of Hal's kingly office, not from without as a function of Shakespeare's poetic one. Shakespeare is simply not there. The laureates are' (*Laureates* 10). It is this principle that leads Helgerson to classify Shakespeare as a 'professional' writer, concerned with making a living, not a laureate, concerned with shaping the nation. Yet such an account forgets the Reconciliation Scene in *1 Henry IV*, when King Henry chastises Hal for debauching himself in public and reveals his own strategy of political leadership, relying on theatrical metaphors, and thereby bringing his political strategy into alignment with the author's own literary one: 'By being seldom seen, I could not stir / But like a comet I was wond'red at ... / And then I stole all courtesy from heaven, / And dress'd myself in such humility / That I did pluck allegiance from men's hearts' (3.2.46–52). Yet to the audience, Shakespeare ironizes the authority of the father, for back in Act 1,

---

[67] By this last phrase, I mean a specific version of counter-authorship, in which Shakespeare counters the art of the laureate, especially its primary principle of national self-presentation, its operation from a centralizing 'self', its crown in the genre of epic, and its commitment to literary immortality. When Shakespeare responds to Spenser in particular, we may specify his version of counter-laureate authorship as distinctly 'counter-Spenserian'. Not all counter-authorship is counter-laureate, nor is all counter-laureate authorship counter-Spenserian, but throughout I concentrate on counter-laureate authorship of the Spenserian variety: on the way in which Shakespeare's authorship counters the laureate poetics exhibited in Spenser's literary career.

scene 2, the wastrel son, in his 'I know you all' soliloquy (1.2.195–217), reveals that he has taken from his father the political ploy of theatrical self-concealment, and overgone it. Hal's strategy recalls that of Spenser, who presented himself as a lowly shepherd, Colin Clout, only suddenly to appear as the 'sovereigne of song' (*Nov* 25): Hal has been concealing himself, not through absence but through presence, donning the costume of a sporting clown so as to emerge suddenly as a shining sovereign: 'Being wanted, he may be more wond'red at' (201).[68] Accordingly, Shakespeare invests a famous icon from this play, Hal's mounting of his horse for battle at Shrewsbury, with reference to Spenser (chapter 2).

While Shakespeare's 'theatre of wonder' has been much discussed of late,[69] to my knowledge critics have not yet traced the idea to Spenser's poetics, where, as readers of Spenser will remember, *wonder* is also everywhere on display, including over 300 times as a word in cognate form. Shakespeare's theatre of wonder may be the most renowned in English literature, but we might recall that it is perhaps best approached as a counter-Spenserian phenomenon. For Shakespeare, unlike for Spenser, wonder is not simply the poet's expression of spiritual rapture and joy during a flood of desire; it is the stunning effect of self-concealed theatrical performance.

Shakespeare's dramatic engagement with Spenser's poetry of wonder is part of a larger, more complicated literary practice, which includes many authors and texts. I foreground Shakespeare's Spenserian extemporality, not simply because the topic has been neglected, but also because it provides a clear focusing lens for Shakespeare's evasive authorship, performed para-doxically before a national audience.

Shakespeare was not the first Elizabethan writer to counter the Spenserian laureate enterprise. Marlowe arrived first on the scene, with his radical politics, heterodox sexuality, and iconoclastic temperament, but he left the project incomplete at his death in 1593, yet not without bequeathing England's first substantive career combining poems and plays: from *Ovid's Elegies*, 'The Passionate Shepherd to His Love', *Lucan's First Book*, and *Hero and Leander* to *Tamburlaine*, *The Jew of Malta*, *Edward II*, and *Doctor*

---

[68] Cf. E. K, who notes that Spenser 'him selfe labor[ed] … to conceale' the 'general drift of his Aeglogues'. The sovereign-author analogy is worth exploring in connection with Shakespeare, an author well known to be fascinated with kingship, sovereignty, and crowns. The analogy derives from the myth of Apollo and its Roman tradition of crowning both poets and leaders with 'laurel boughs' (*Tit* 1.1.74). See, e.g., *3H6*, where Shakespeare refers to the sovereign crown of England as a 'laurel crown' (4.6.34), to be discussed in chapters 1 and 5.

[69] See Bishop, *Shakespeare and the Theatre of Wonder*.

Faustus.[70] At least for the Elizabethans, this fundamentally sixteenth-century model of authorship had an origin in Ovid, the counter-Virgilian Roman author who penned the tragedy *Medea* alongside the epic *Metamorphoses* and several elegies, including the *Amores*, which Marlowe was the first to translate into a European vernacular. Marlowe's translation reproduces Ovid's original fiction about the elegiac poet's inability to write epic and tragedy (1.1; 2.1; 2.18; 3.1) and then his final turn to tragedy in the concluding poem to the sequence (*Am* 3.15; *OE* 3.14). In 1601, Jonson put Marlowe's 'Ovid' on stage in *Poetaster*: the Ovidian author of elegy, represented in Jonson's translation of *Amores* 1.15 (remarkably appropriated from Marlowe); of tragedy, mentioned by Ovid Senior, who ridicules his son's penning of *Medea* for staging by the common players; and of counter-national epic, rehearsed in the metamorphic masque of the gods at the Roman banquet.[71] Shakespeare understood Marlowe's opposition to Spenser, and he himself became the first English author to structure the fiction of his works on this mighty literary opposition. Marlowe, then, naturally infiltrates a discussion of Shakespeare's engagement with Spenser because, for Shakespeare, Marlowe had begun the project of counter-laureate authorship that Shakespeare would complete, albeit in ways that the Canterbury youth could not imagine.

In the course of the following chapters, I examine particular passages from a wide range of Shakespeare's plays – on occasion, his poems – spread over his professional career, that exhibit Spenserian – and to a lesser extent Marlovian – extemporal intertextuality. Furthermore, I suggest that Shakespeare's freestanding poems, rather than being simply an interlude in his career,[72] form a keystone to his authorial corpus. The poems tell us not only that Shakespeare followed Marlowe – and preceded Jonson and Milton – in pioneering the English invention of modern authorship, the combination of poems and plays within a single career, but also that Shakespearean theatre stages an invaluable *literary poetics*. The defining feature of Shakespeare's career model, the presence of poems as an interleaf to his plays, reveals that his dramatic works, like his poetic ones, are intimately bound up with the notion of poetry, in ways we have yet to articulate.

It follows, then, that one of Shakespeare's major professional goals is to challenge and perhaps supplant the major print-poet of his day. Since he, not Spenser, is today the National Poet, with theatre and film, not poetry,

---

[70] On Marlowe as poet-playwright, see Cheney, 'Introduction', *Cambridge Companion to Christopher Marlowe* 1–23.
[71] See Cheney, 'Biographical Representations'.   [72] Wells, *Shakespeare* 115–31.

the world's premier entertainment art, and self-concealing rather than self-presenting literary consciousness the treasured-mode of modern identity, we might conclude that Shakespeare's counter-laureate authorship did not merely succeed; it did so at the expense of Spenser's laureate leadership.[73]

STRUCTURE OF THE BOOK

Since Shakespeare's dramatic canon is vast and intricate, I augment my earlier book on his poems (*Shakespeare, National Poet-Playwright*) through a two-part structure on the plays. In Part I, I introduce my model of Shakespearean authorship in order to suggest how we might rethink Shakespeare.[74] The first two chapters introduce a pentad of 'forms' for Shakespeare's counter-laureate authorship, highlighting Shakespeare's strategy of self-concealment. Chapter 1 uses the weird Achilles stanza in *The Rape of Lucrece* to introduce the first form, which is a displaced, mythological version of self-representation, to look further into both Shakespeare's self-concealing authorship and his relation to the defining laureate genre of Spenser's poetry, epic – a major topic in both *Hamlet* and *Troilus and Cressida*. Chapter 2 adds four other forms of counter-laureate authorship, which are all *refractional*, since they refract authorship obliquely, and do so through an array of gendered subject-positions. The next two chapters examine the more visible features of Shakespeare's counter-laureate authorship, concentrating on the tripartite contents of his literary authorship: books, poetry, and theatre. Specifically, chapter 3 examines the interconnections between theatre and poetry, while chapter 4 investigates the relation between theatre and books (including books of poetry). Throughout Part I, I select examples from Shakespeare's plays spread across the spectrum of genres and the phases of his career.

Then, in Part II, I specify the model of literary authorship by tracing Shakespeare's fiction of the counter-laureate author in the text of his plays, with its literary discourse intertwining books, poetry, and theatre, again in all four genres, early till late. Necessarily with such a large dramatic corpus,

---

[73] Helgerson, *Elizabethan Prodigals*, divides 'the great English writers into two Keatsian categories, on the one hand those possessed of "negative capability", and on the other those dominated by the "egotistical sublime"', with Sidney in 'the latter' (132). Helgerson does not mention Shakespeare here, but presumably he would place him where Keats did, in the former group.

[74] I take the concept from Belsey in her review of *SNPP*: 'The twenty-first century is witnessing a quiet revolution in Shakespeare studies ... [I]f they are right, it is time to think different about Shakespeare.'

the goal is to be suggestive rather than exhaustive, with one example standing for many. Indeed, readers may well be surprised or disappointed by some of the choices I make. I can only say that the choices have been hard ones, and that I've tried to write on plays, scenes, and topics for which I thought I could make a contribution to existing scholarship and criticism.

In particular, the two-part structure I've settled on lends access to three phases of authorial representation during Shakespeare's professional career. In the first or early phase, presented in the first historical tetralogy, in such comedies as *Two Gentlemen of Verona*, *The Taming of the Shrew*, and *Love's Labor's Lost*, and in the early tragedy *Titus Andronicus*, we can witness a *bookish* phase that critics often label 'lyrical', where Shakespeare seems thrilled with the collision between his education in classical, continental, and English culture and his new theatrical medium, so much so that he lets books and theatre become something like the intrusive topic of his work. The opening scene to the play that the editors of the *Oxford Shakespeare* print as the playwright's earliest production, *Two Gentlemen of Verona*, sets the pace:

VALENTINE.   And on a love-book pray for my success?
PROTEUS.   Upon some book I love I'll pray for thee.
VALENTINE.   That's on some shallow story of deep love,
           How young Leander cross'd the Hellespont.   (1.1.19–22)

As scholars recognize, here Shakespeare alludes to Marlowe's Ovidian epyllion, *Hero and Leander* (e.g., *Norton* 85). By doing so during the opening dialogue of what may be his first play, Shakespeare signals that his drama will come to terms with the Western canon of poetic books.

In the second or middle phase, presented in the second historical tetralogy, in such comedies as *Much Ado* and *Twelfth Night*, and in such tragedies as *Hamlet*, *Othello*, and *King Lear*, we witness not so much a bookish as a *conceptual* phase, where Shakespeare continues to include books and theatre, poetry and playing, in his fictions and discourse but moves philosophical and religious *thought* – his historic exploration of 'consciousness' (Bloom, *Genius* 20) – to the center of the stage. 'My tears begin to take his part so much, / They mar my counterfeiting', Edgar reports to the audience in disguise as Poor Tom, before the unfolding tragedy of the king (3.6.60–1). And when the exquisitely costumed Edgar lets out to Lear in a fit of feigned madness, 'The foul fiend haunts poor Tom in the voice of a nightingale' (3.6.29–30), Shakespeare shows just how extemporally invisible he can make his bookish intertextuality of poetry and playing, brilliantly submarining the myth of Philomela from Ovid (and, we shall see, Spenser), which he had made so visceral in such works from the early phase as *Titus*, where not merely 'the tragic tale of Philomel' (4.1.47) but the 'book' of 'Ovid's Metamorphosis' is brought on stage as a prop (41–2).

In the third or late phase, represented by the four romances, by *Henry VIII*, and by *Two Noble Kinsmen*, we can witness a *mythic* phase, where Shakespeare allows the discourse of books, poetry, and theatre to return to the surface of his work, not so much in a bookish as in an archetypal way.[75] Indeed, the late plays foreground Ovidian intertextuality, yet almost always through Spenserian (and Marlovian) inflection: not simply in *The Tempest* but also in *The Winter's Tale*, when Paulina performs the role of Pygmalion by animating Hermione's statue (5.3), and in *Cymbeline*, which returns the book of the *Metamorphoses* to the stage as a prop (2.2.45–6).

The boundaries among these three phases are anything but precise, as the presence of such bookish plays as *As You Like It* and *Hamlet* in the middle phase testifies, or as the presence of 'romance' in such early plays as *The Comedy of Errors* indicates. Yet this tripartite pattern might be useful here to see that even after his bookish phase Shakespeare continues to process his literary authorship, however much it alters over time.[76]

By 'finding Shakespeare' within the language of his own fictions, we may more accurately understand his authorship within its own historical moment, and thereby come to terms with our reception of that authorship today. He is the consummate man of the theatre who simultaneously manages a literary career committed to a profound national goal: the innovative use of both poems and plays – with their fictions of books, poetry, and theatre – to chart human consciousness for ends at once social, political, and religious. Finally, my book suggests that Shakespeare's literary authorship plays a central role in his enduring legacy.

---

[75] Cf. J. Bate, *Ovid*: 'In the last plays, as Shakespeare tried out a more mythic mode of composition, Ovid returned to the surface of the drama' (215).

[76] I have supplied an overview of Shakespeare's full dramatic career in the 'Play Scenes' and Epilogue to *SNPP*, and so do not repeat the connective tissue here.

PART I

Rethinking Shakespearean authorship

The epic spear of Achilles: Self-concealing authorship in The Rape of Lucrece, Troilus and Cressida, and Hamlet

In the Western literary tradition, Shakespeare's self-concealing authorship may indeed be unique. From Homer, Virgil, and Ovid, to Dante, Petrarch, and Chaucer, to Sidney, Spenser, and Marlowe, we can find nothing else like it. In varying degrees, all of these authors present themselves inside their fictions, whether through the personal voice (as with Homer) or through characters inside their fictions (as with the others).[1] Certainly, Homer, Virgil, and Chaucer are more reticent than Ovid, Dante, Petrarch, Sidney, and Spenser; yet the most reticent in the group, Chaucer, still presents himself recurrently in his fictions, and he manages to turn reticence, humility, and self-ironizing deprecation into an authorial signature.[2] Marlowe is something of a special case, in part because alone in this group he specializes in drama; but from Robert Greene to Stephen Greenblatt, readers have been quick to equate this author with his super-heroes.[3] In contrast, as we have seen, Shakespeare self-consciously conceals his authorship; he does so in response to the laureate tradition of authorial self-fashioning, producing a 'counter-laureate authorship'; and most importantly for Elizabethan England, he targets the art of one laureate poet in particular: Edmund Spenser.

In this opening chapter, I introduce the first of five forms of Shakespeare's self-concealing, counter-laureate authorship, which I call heraldic, by fore-grounding its literary dynamics: genre, especially epic; what we have called extemporal intertextuality, especially of authorship; and representation, espe-cially of an author-figure producing and produced by the epic form of

---

[1] A tradition coming out of antiquity identifies Homer with the blind bard Demodocus in the *Odyssey*. On biographical criticism and criticism on literary careers in antiquity, see Farrell, 'Greek Lives and Roman Careers'. According to Helgerson, *Elizabethan Prodigals*, Lodge differs from fellow prodigal poets Gascoigne, Lyly, Greene, and Sidney in that he 'deliberately removes himself from his work' (107).

[2] R. R. Edwards, 'Ricardian Dreamwork'. On Chaucer's penchant for disguising his political sympathies, see, e.g., Strohm, *Social Chaucer* 25; L. Patterson, *Chaucer and the Subject of History* 86.

[3] See Cheney, 'Biographical Representations'.

extemporal authorship. In the Shakespeare canon, as we shall see, epic extemporality becomes an important principle of authorship.

Specifically, we may find an initial model of Shakespeare's self-concealing authorship in the 1594 *Rape of Lucrece*, when the ravished Roman matron seeks consolation by viewing a painting of Troy hanging inside her home. During a 28-stanza ecphrasis, written in the Chaucerian rhyme royal stanzas of *Troilus and Criseyde*, the author re-frames the Virgilian Fall of Troy by combining two scenes from the *Aeneid*: in Book 1, when Aeneas views the frescoes of the Fall of Troy in Dido's Temple of Juno; and in Book 2, when Aeneas tells Dido the details of that story.[4] Effectively, Shakespeare maps the epic narrative of the second Virgilian scene on to the visual art of the first, creating a superimposed model of Virgilian epic within his printed minor epic.[5] Shakespeare's use of the native form from England's Old Poet, Chaucer, *Englishes* in miniature the central story of classical epic. Thereby, Shakespeare enters his 'graver labor' into the epic list, to compete with the New Poet himself, whose 1590 *Faerie Queene* had just presented London as 'Troynovant' in his Legend of Chastity (3.9.38).[6] In this typology, when Lucrece turns to the epic form of Troy to seek consolation for Tarquin's 'rifl[ing]' of her 'Chastity' (*RL* 692), not simply Virgil but the national project of Spenser is at stake.[7]

In remarkable detail, Shakespeare's ecphrasis narrates the action, locale, and principal characters of 'Priam's Troy, / Before the which is drawn the power of Greece, / For Helen's rape' (1367–9). Shakespeare includes portraits of such figures as 'Ajax and Ulysses' (1394), 'bold Hector' (1430), 'despairing Hecuba' (1447), 'Pyrrhus' standing on the corpse of Priam (1449), 'fond Paris' (1473), and most memorably 'perjur'd Sinon' (1521), who strolls through the pastoral fields to the epic city, 'To hide deceit, and give the harmless show / An humble gait' (1507–8). Here we are in the full company of epic.[8] Yet one figure remains absent, 'the self-totalizing … figure' of Achilles (Crewe 159).

---

[4] Shakespeare also draws on Ovid's story of *Met* 13; see Miola, *Shakespeare's Rome* 30.

[5] In *Metamorphic Verse*, Hulse places Shakespeare's two 'minor epics', *Venus* and *Lucrece*, along the famed 'Virgilian path': 'The minor epic was, in effect, the proving ground for … epic … . It was a genre for young poets ceasing to be young, a form somewhere above the pastoral or sonnet and below the epic, the transition between the two in the *gradus Vergilianus*' (*Verse* 12; see 175).

[6] In the dedicatory epistle to the 1593 *Venus and Adonis*, Shakespeare tells the Earl of Southampton that he will go on to write for him a work of 'graver labour' (*Riverside* 1799), which critics see fulfilled in *Lucrece*. 'Troynovaunt' derives from Geoffrey of Monmouth.

[7] On Shakespeare's response to Spenser's Legend of Chastity in the Troy painting, see *SNPP*, ch. 4. According to H. Smith, 'No poet writing in 1594 could fail to be influenced by the achievement of Spenser's publication four years earlier' (*Elizabethan Poetry* 117).

[8] Critics often situate *Lucrece* in the context of epic: Fineman, 'Shakespeare's Will' 59; Maus, 'Taking Tropes Seriously' 87; Crewe, *Trials of Authorship* 142.

It is in the stanza devoted to Achilles that I propose to locate the most formalized representation of self-concealing, counter-laureate authorship in the Shakespeare canon:

> For much imaginary work was there,
> Conceit deceitful, so compact, so kind,
> That for Achilles' image stood his spear,
> Grip'd in an armed hand, himself behind
> Was left unseen, save to the eye of mind:
>   A hand, a foot, a face, a leg, a head
>   Stood for the whole to be imagined.
>
>   (*Rape of Lucrece* 1422–8)

In 1990, Jonathan Crewe suggested that the 'hitherto unconsidered figure of Achilles … is conspicuously *not* pictured in the otherwise rather full Trojan tableau' (156; his emphasis): 'the 'whole' is a 'hole' in the text' (157). Valuably, Crewe detects the significance of this representation to the topic of authorship:

One reason why Lucrece cannot definitely locate the figure of the rapist [in the painting] is that he is to be found, if anywhere, in the authorial position, in keeping with the 'upward' displacement of violence in the poem. The compelling imaginative presence of Achilles is marked by the spear held in a mailed fist, but this figure is also the Shake-spearean signature in the poem. It is with the power of Achilles that 'Shakespeare' is thus identified, all the more so for its being an invisible but imaginative omnipotence, never compromised, as is that of Tarquin or Lucrece, by its own theatrical representation. Yet at the same time it is a power which is also an imagined power of sole authorship, never capable of being wholly embodied or possessed. (Crewe, *Trials of Authorship* 158–9)

For Crewe, the Achillean hand gripping the spear is a self-signed image that models a compound form of authorial agency; this agency resembles that of a laureate or national poet like Spenser in its self-presented fantasy of 'sole authorship', yet simultaneously it retreats through self-disembodiment.

Crewe's larger argument is complex, but, summarized briefly, he suggests that Achilles is 'the [real] fantasized hypermale warrior-rapist of the poem' (160), one who rapes women and men indiscriminately (155–6); that Shakespeare identifies himself, paradoxically, with both Achilles as rapist and with Lucrece as rape-victim, through a principle of 'cross-representation' (150; see 152–3), so that Shakespeare rehearses his own 'authorial position' as one of 'shame'; and finally that Shakespeare gets the latter strategy – the 'strategic incorporation by the male author of the woman's part' (162) – from the 'theater, in which there is a boy actor inside every represented woman' (160). For Crewe, in other words, the Achilles stanza reveals a self-presented fear about sexual identity in an author-figure he calls 'the male actor/poet/playwright' (162).

We might recall the historical innovation behind this authorial profile. Shakespeare became the leading member of his generation in what was fundamentally a sixteenth-century invention: the author as 'actor', 'poet', and 'playwright'. No other author of the English Renaissance would enact this professional profile more substantially than William Shakespeare. He became an actor and shareholder in a leading theatre company during the reigns of Elizabeth and James; he was the poet of five major printed poems in the genres of minor epic, philosophical hymn, sonnet sequence, and complaint, as well as many original lyrics embedded in his plays; and of course he was a playwright of some forty plays in the genres of comedy, history, tragedy, and romance.

The Achilles stanza is unusual because it specifies the precise character of authorship underwriting this corpus. It does so by unveiling a pentad of vectors: (1) the erotic or homoerotic; (2) the political; (3) the theological; (4) the affective, linking body to mind; and (5) the literary, which qualifies as the foundation of the other four, itself including figural and formal dimensions. In the Achilles stanza, published early in his career, Shakespeare (un) veils an authorship that counters the sexual, political, theological, affective, and literary dynamics organizing laureate authorship in the 1590s.

While localized in a single stanza, the Achilles representation turns out to have remarkable literary reach, tracing intertextually back to Ovid through a myth neglected in modern scholarship (that of Telephus), yet sustaining a powerful intratextual life in Shakespeare's plays, from *2 Henry VI* and *Edward III* to *Troilus* and *Hamlet*. By its very nature, the Achilles representation also speaks to a topic marginalized in studies of Shakespeare's authorship: his career-long fascination with the genre of epic. By using the exquisite details of the Achilles stanza as a kind of textual station for such heavy professional traffic, we can get an unusual glimpse of his inlaid authorial project at the height of his inventive prowess.

PENNING SHAKE-SPEAR: THE FAMILY COAT OF ARMS

Archival evidence suggests that Shakespeare thought of the spear as his own personal sign. Around 1576, John Shakespeare applied to the College of Arms for a coat of arms, probably supplying a sketch for the blazon, but no action was taken. Then in 1596 – two years after the publication of *Lucrece* – a grant of arms was made to the older Shakespeare, allowing him and his sons the right to sign their name 'Gentleman'. We do not know who

(a)   (b)

Figure 3. Coats of arms: (a) Shakespeare and (b) Drayton

made the final sketch of the 1596 coat of arms (Figure 3a), but quite possibly William designed the original and then had his theatre colleague Richard Burbage make the final version.[9] What has gone unnoticed is the connection between this chivalric coat of arms and the epic Achilles stanza.

According to Katherine Duncan-Jones, 'Shakespeare's notion for his family's coat of arms … sct off daringly bold chivalric associations' (93):

Not only does the Shakespeare crest show an aristocratic object, a golden tilting staff, held upright by a bird that has chivalric and aristocratic associations, the falcon itself exemplifies the bearer's exhibitionistic, swaggering pride in his inheritance. This gentleman, it is implied, is more than ready to take on all comers. The visual imagery seems to say 'we Shakespeares are courtly warriors, of gentle rank'. (Duncan-Jones, *Ungentle Shakespeare* 96)

---

[9] Duncan-Jones, *Ungentle Shakespeare* 91–2; on the coat of arms, see her ch. 4, 'Spear-Shaking Shakespeare', which contextualizes the arms within both *Lucrece* and Southampton's patronage (84, 87). See also Honan, *Shakespeare* 228–9; Greenblatt, *Will in the World* 78–86.

Duncan-Jones further notes 'the resemblance of the spear to a pen poised for writing' (94). Thus the Shakespeare coat of arms draws an equation between military prowess and authorship, the warrior and the writer. Usefully, Duncan-Jones reveals why a man named Shakespeare might (wittily) have signed his name to the figure of Achilles, the Western icon of the wrathful man: '"Shakespeare" … could be a nickname for a belligerent person' (94).

As Figure 3b further reveals, in the British Library's Harley MS 6140, the Shakespeare coat of arms appears next to one by Michael Drayton, a laureate author of Shakespeare's day and a disciple of Spenser.[10] As such, the juxtaposition affords an invaluable opportunity to compare Shakespeare's author-designed coat of arms alongside that of a self-avowed laureate.[11] Just as Shakespeare borrows his falcon from the Southampton family coat for patronage purposes, Drayton borrows the winged horse to express not merely his poetic aspirations but also his connection with the Inner Temple, on whom he depended for patronage. Yet Drayton adds the raindrops falling around Pegasus, and his crest is 'odd and distinctive, being a green "cap of Mercury" against a golden sun, alluding presumably to his own literary gifts, Mercury being the god of language' (Duncan-Jones 95).[12] Drayton's coat of arms, then, constitutes a heraldic form of laureate self-presentation: through the representation of Pegasus, traditional figure of poetic fame, surrounded by drops of poetic inspiration, and of Mercury, winged god of eloquence, Drayton marks his familial and social identity in terms of his laureate self-fashioning.[13]

In contrast, Shakespeare's coat is notably plainer, less ostentatious, and it does not clearly represent figures from classical mythology about the art of the poet. Instead, it presents the spear plainly as a writing implement, and it only gestures to the myth of poetic flight so prominent in the Drayton

---

[10] Helgerson, *Self-Crowned Laureates* 16. For two studies of Drayton indebted to Helgerson, see Brink, *Michael Drayton Revisited*; Hadfield, 'Michael Drayton's Brilliant Career'. On Drayton and Spenser, see Hardin, 'Drayton, Michael'.

[11] See the portrait of the laureate-crowned Drayton prefacing his 1619 *Poems*, reproduced in Hadfield (120), who discusses the portrait's laureate iconography and its Spenserian genealogy.

[12] See also Newdigate, *Michael Drayton and His Circle* 150–1. Shapiro, *1599*, notes that 'the pommel … on the Shakespeare coat of arms' resembles the one in Shakespeare's favorite 'image in Stratford's chapel': 'the painting of St. George fighting the dragon, plunging his spear into the monster's neck' (167–8).

[13] On the myth of poetic flight, including Spenser's selection of Pegasus as a self-representation, see Cheney, *Spenser's Famous Flight* 14–15, 72–4. Like Pegasus, Drayton's other mythological persona, Mercury, was vital to Spenser's self-presentation; cf. Brooks-Davies, *Mercurian Monarch*. In chapter 2, we shall return to the co-presence of Mercury and Pegasus in *1 Henry IV*.

coat.[14] Not merely the spear but the bird exemplifies the key verb in the author's name. Significantly, the Shakespearean author-bird appears grounded rather than soaring in flight (unlike Drayton's flying horse and hat), intimating an action not of transcendence but of contingency, a mooring in the material, with perhaps a promise of flight – whether modest or 'belligerent', it is hard to tell.[15] Moreover, Shakespeare's avoidance of mythological authorial figures, such as Pegasus and Mercury, for a disembodied metonymy equating militarism with authorship (spear as pen), itself suggests a version of Shakespearean self-concealment. Nonetheless, as in the Achilles stanza, agency remains fully paradoxical, since the coat simultaneously makes a 'belligerent' claim, not merely of 'chivalric and aristocratic associations' but of authorial ones. In Shakespeare's hands, authorship becomes theatrical, embedded in the 'exhibitionist' name but also in the shaking (or tilting) spear-pen and in the shaking-falcon. In sum, if Drayton presents his coat as that of a Spenserian laureate author, in the Shakespeare coat we see the arms of a *counter-laureate*.

We need to include this heraldic costume not only in our biographies but in our assessments of Shakespeare's authorship, because it is the only authorized self-representation in the Shakespeare archive. We can find nothing in Shakespeare's poems and plays resembling the fictionalized self-representation deployed by the laureates – most obviously, a poet-figure such as Colin Clout, whom Spenser uses to 'shadow ... himself, as sometime Virgil under the name of Tityrus'.[16]

READING SHAKE-SPEAR: THE ACHILLES STANZA

Shakespeare's counter-Spenserian heraldic self-representation looks conspicuously like his self-representation in the Achilles stanza. Oddly enough, critics neglect the stanza.[17] Similarly, editors annotate the stanza

---

[14] According to Duncan-Jones, 'While the four silver falcons on the Wriothesley coat are shown in profile, the silver falcon on the Shakespeare crest has "his wings displayed"', suggesting the moment in falconry called 'shaking', the action of a bird right before it lifts off for flight (95–6).

[15] On Shakespearean contingency rather than Platonic transcendence, see Engle, '"A float in Thick Deeps"' 186.

[16] Spenser, *Dedicatory Epistle* to *The Shepheardes Calender* 86. Of course, critics sometimes find Shakespearean self-portraits in various figures – e.g., in *As You Like It* both Touchstone (Duncan-Jones 26) and William of Arden (25, 123; see Bednarz, *Shakespeare and the Poets' War* 117–20); in *MW*, William (J. Bate, *Genius of Shakespeare* 7–8); and Williams in *Henry V*, whose name in the printed speech headings is spelled 'Will', forming an authorial 'signature' comparable to that of Will in the Sonnets (A. Patterson, *Shakespeare and the Popular Voice* 88–92).

[17] For brief discussion, see Maus 82; Fineman 57; Dubrow, *Captive Victors* 167.

only lightly. In addition to explaining words like 'compact' and 'kind' and phrases like 'imaginary work' and 'Conceit deceitful', editors tend to follow E. H. Gombrich in citing Philostratus' *Imagines* 1.4, where the artist paints soldiers at Thebes 'so that some are seen in full figure, others with the legs hidden, others from the waist up, then only the busts of some, heads only, helmets only, and finally just spear-points'.[18] Almost always, editors gloss the first line of the Achilles stanza – 'For much imaginary work was there' – with *Henry V* 1.0.17–18: 'let us ... / On your imaginary forces work'. This gloss is important for intimating the intriguing typological working of the Achilles stanza in Shakespeare's plays.[19] The syntactical conjunction between the two passages compels us to find a similar aesthetics in both a poem and a play, a tragic minor epic and a comedic stage history, but also both the theatrical working of the aesthetics in the poem and the poetic working of the aesthetics in the play. Furthermore, the conjunction establishes more concretely than heretofore the license we need for viewing *Henry V*, and indeed the entire Henriad: not simply an epic lifted on to the new London stage, it is a new kind of epic altogether; more than just a dramatic epic, the history play constitutes a kind of counter-laureate epic.

More surprisingly, editors turn up little information on the crucial image of Achilles' spear, and all neglect its authorial resonance.[20] Most editors do recall that Shakespeare had used the image of Achilles' spear at *2 Henry VI* 5.1.100,[21] when York chastises King Henry because 'That head of thine doth not become a crown' (5.1.96):

> Thy hand is made to grasp a palmer's staff
> And not to grace an aweful princely sceptre.
> That gold must round engirt these brows of mine,
> Whose smile and frown, like to Achilles' spear,
> Is able with the change to kill and cure.
> Here is a hand to hold a sceptre up.   (*2 Henry VI* 5.1.97–102)

York criticizes Henry's fitness to wear the royal crown of England, asserting that he is fit only to hold the staff of a palmer: to perform private monastic

---

[18] Quoted in C. Burrow, ed. 318. See also Roe, ed. 210; Duncan-Jones and Woudhuysen, eds. Thanks to Professors Duncan-Jones and Woudhuysen for allowing me to see their annotation in manuscript.

[19] Shapiro, *1599*, says that 'scholars have argued [that Shakespeare] ... played the part of the Chorus' in *Henry V*, quoting the line about 'imaginary forces at work' (99).

[20] Prince offers an enticing general statement: 'Achilles' spear was more famous in the Middle Ages than his shield, as described by Homer' (ed. 131). Roe glosses the image as 'A famous instance of metonymy: Achilles' spear was legendary and would stand as sufficient emblem for him' (ed. 210), while C. Burrow follows suit (ed. 318).

[21] Prince, ed. 131; Roe, ed. 210; C. Burrow, ed. 310; Duncan-Jones and Woudhuysen, eds. MS.

rites, not rule the country. Accordingly, York asserts his own ability to perform this national role, because only he has the necessary 'brow' – the head to perform the awful power of a true king, which, like the spear of Achilles, can both 'kill and cure'. In Shakespeare's imagination, York likens the Christian English crown to the pagan spear of Achilles, so that it is not too long a step to read the martial instrument as a displaced icon of sovereignty, nationalism, and even laureate self-fashioning. Thus, in *3 Henry VI* Shakespeare refers to this same sovereign crown as a 'laurel crown' (4.6.34; see Introduction and chapter 5). We might observe as well that Shakespeare offsets York's self-presentation, clearly modeled on that of the Marlovian overreacher, with a Henrician mode of quiet 'grace', and that the author comes very close to signing his own name to Henry's counter-laureate conduct: Henry's 'hand is made to grasp a palmer's staff'.[22] As with *Henry V*, the typological link between the epic part of *Lucrece* and *2 Henry VI* allows us to read the first tetralogy as also a new kind of epic.

We may add a *second* Shakespearean use of Achilles' spear as an instrument of both wounding and curing. In *Edward III*, in a scene that scholars now attribute to Shakespeare, the Earl of Warwick tries to convince the Countess of Salisbury to submit to the erotic desires of King Edward.[23] 'Apparell'd sin in virtuous sentences' (2.1.410), Warwick argues forcefully, 'He that hath power to take away thy life / Hath power to take thy honor' (385–6), for 'The king that would distain thee will advance thee' (391):

> The poets write, that great Achilles' spear
> Could heal the wound it made: the moral is,
> What mighty men misdo they can amend.
>
> (*Edward III* 2.1.392–4)

Presently, we shall consider who the 'poets' are who 'write' about the healing powers of 'great Achilles' spear'. For now, we may note that Shakespeare self-consciously advertises the intertextuality of his image, and thus reveals how he could transfer what other 'poets write' to what he himself writes when signing his name. Significantly, as in *2 Henry VI*, Shakespeare associates the

---

[22] In his memorial poem in the First Folio, Jonson twice puns on Shakespeare's name: 'And shake a stage' (37); 'shake a lance' (69). Duncan-Jones sees 'Falstaff as 'the flip side of "Shakespeare", denoting … a staff … that bends and falls in desertion or defeat' (106). Spenser had popularized the icon of the Palmer with a magic staff able both to harm (*FQ* 2.12.40–1) and to heal (2.12.86), although Spenser associates the staff with the caduceus of Mercury (2.12.40–1).

[23] In contrast to editors of *Lucrece*, editors of *Edward III* do note the link with the Achilles stanza (e.g., *Riverside* 1745). The likelihood of the Achilles-spear representation being by Shakespeare increases when we take the cue of the Chadwyk-Healy database to discover how rare the image of Achilles' spear, with its powers to wound and heal, is for Elizabethan poets and playwrights.

spear of Achilles with sovereignty and royal power, the power of the king both to heal and to wound, and specifically to 'heal the wound' that Achilles makes. Furthermore, Shakespeare presents a male character using the image as a rhetorical trope, with a poetic heritage, to persuade a female to bend her will to masculine desire.

In Warwick's speech, then, Shakespeare reveals how he understands the spear: as a literary metonymy of sovereign power, and in particular of ethical sovereignty within a gender dynamic: 'the moral is, / What mighty men misdo they can amend'. As in *2 Henry VI* and *Lucrece*, Shakespeare uses the Achilles-spear to sign his authorship – this time, to a scene that he pens so anonymously (in a collaborative production) that only recently have we begun to see it. Once we do, we discover a rare instance in which this author resists the material conditions of the collaborative theatre so prominently emphasized in recent Shakespearean criticism.

Among editors commenting on Achilles' spear in *Lucrece*, Katherine Duncan-Jones and Henry Woudhuysen take us where we need to go: 'The ability of Achilles' spear to wound and to heal became proverbial' (eds., MS); they cite R. W. Dent's *Shakespeare's Proverbial Language*, and leave it at that. We might wish to look further into the stanza, with its curious image of the great epic hero's magically curative spear, as well as into its origins, precisely because we can gather invaluable information regarding the nature of Shakespeare's authorship.

In the Achilles stanza, Shakespeare's signed image of the 'armed hand' gripping the spear turns out to have immediate political, religious, and affective significance. For instance, the severed hand holding a sword functions as an 'explicit icon of [political] power … distinguished by the … capacity to grasp' – an 'emblem of just rule' – as represented in George Wither's modification of it in Emblem 137 of his *Collection of Emblems*[24] (see Figure 4). The political icon 'draw[s] on the medieval convention of God's providential hand' (Rowe 62), but the image could be transposed to the arena of the affections, as represented in Wither's Emblem 230, which displays two clasping hands emerging from the clouds, and together holding a disembodied heart – an icon of mutuality in betrothal (Figure 5). Thus, in Shakespearean England the free-floating hand holding a military weapon is not isolated but a prominent icon of a religiously sanctioned political agency with potential affective significance.[25] The disembodied hand does not just

---

[24] Rowe, *Dead Hands* 62, 64.
[25] Rowe counters Freud, who privileges the 'acting person' as an individual with agency, in order to locate agency in objects, not persons – 'in the objects and instruments of an action' – in *objectivity*, not

To Kings, *both* Sword *and* Mace *pertaine ;*
And, thefe they doe not beare in *vaine.*

ILLVSTR. III.   *Book.* 3

Figure 4. Emblem of hands and weapons: George Wither's *Collection of Emblems*

problemetize agency; in the Achilles stanza (we might say), Shakespeare transposes the religio-political-affective power of the hand to the agency of his own authorship.

subjectivity: 'The severed hand' in Shakespeare 'exemplifies the supplemental and contingent nature of purposeful action' (59). In searching the emblems of Whitney, Paradin, Alciati, and Wither, I have not found a disembodied hand holding a spear; traditionally, the hand holds a sword.

Figure 5. Emblem of hands and heart: George Wither's *Collection of Emblems*

The first line of the stanza fuses the affective or subjective vector to the literary: 'For much imaginary work was there.' Using the key concept of Renaissance poetics, imagination, Shakespeare introduces the epistemological conundrum about the truth-value of 'poetry' at issue from Plato to Sidney.[26] Yet his specific formulation is rather impressive: how can

[26] For Plato, see Book 10 of the *Republic*; for Sidney, *Defence of Poesy*.

'imaginary work' be 'there'? The stanza about Shakespearean authorship may begin with an expression of the truth-value of poetry, but it assigns an active role to it: 'work'. Above all, the line marks out an oblique imaginative space for authorship: a space that is somehow 'there' yet 'unseen'.[27]

Line 2 identifies the concretion *in* the work, the imaginary 'Conceit'. The word *conceit* has both cognitive and literary meaning, referencing both thought and composition, and thus bridging the gap between them. Shakespeare assigns three characteristics to the conceit: 'deceitful', 'compact', and 'kind'. The final word, 'kind', means 'natural', again evoking the material truth of imaginary work. The second word, 'compact', merely *looks* uninteresting; the *OED*'s first definition reads, 'Compacted, knit, firmly put together' (Def. A1), and the first recorded usage, from Lydgate, uses the metaphor from knitting, suggesting a root in clothing. But the *OED*'s second definition reads, 'Made up by combination of parts; framed, composed *of*' (Def. A2).[28] More obviously, perhaps, Shakespeare depends on the *OED*'s Definition B2b, 'Of language or style: Condensed, terse, pithy, close; not diffuse'. Yet the metaphors of clothing and parts suggest precisely a *style* of theatrical identity, which the line renders most visibly in the first word describing the conceit: 'deceitful'.[29] The phrase 'Conceit deceitful' compactly expresses the epistemological conundrum of line 1, acknowledges Plato's charge that poets are liars and deserve to be booted out of the republic, yet goes beyond Sidney in playfully asserting the truthful operation of the theatrical conceit.

The authorial discourse of theatrical identity re-emerges in line 3 in the phrase 'Achilles' image': 'That for Achilles' image stood his spear'. Naturally, Achilles himself cannot appear, but surprisingly neither does his visual 'image'. At two removes from the real, Achilles appears only *as* his 'spear'; his military weapon is all that *stands* for the image of the real man. Line 4 puts the compacted conceit of Achilles' spear into staged action: 'Grip'd in an armed hand'. The word *grip* is the author's substitute term for 'shake' in his representational signature, and means to 'seize firmly' (*OED* Def. 1A).

The disturbing motion of the ethereal concretion – a disembodied hand grasping a spear – makes visible what line 5 declares to be 'left unseen', for Achilles hides 'himself behind': 'Was left unseen, save to the eye of mind'. Although Shakespeare's phrasing elides Achilles' motive for concealment, it

[27] According to faculty psychology, the imagination is 'there' in the form of perception. The imagination creates the images that convey knowledge by giving a perceptual shape to sense data. Though they are arbitrary, such 'imagines' are thus the trace of sense impressions formed by real objects. (Thanks to Robert R. Edwards for this formulation.)
[28] Citing *AYLI* 2.7.5 – 'If he compact of jars, grow musical'.
[29] Cf. Spenser, *FQ* 1.7.1.3: 'deceit doth maske in visour faire'.

precisely evokes Shakespeare's undeclared motive, bringing us into the familiar Shakespearean territory of motive hunting, especially in light of such figures as Hamlet and Iago, both notorious for the mystery of their motives, the first for delaying to revenge his father's murder, the second for targeting Othello. The remainder of line 5, 'save to the eye of mind', introduces the affective operation of the concealing art, its effect on the viewer, but it also registers Shakespeare's innovative achievement in his plays and poems: his profound plumbing of consciousness.[30] Since Achilles' spear was thought to have the power to wound and to heal, Shakespeare may use the self-image to acknowledge ambivalently the bifold powers of his own authorship, to hurt and to mend.[31]

The concluding couplet of the Achilles stanza sums up the preceding lines clearly and virtually defies comprehension. Since lines 3–5 insist that Achilles' 'hand' stands for the visual image, how can lines 6–7 report that several *unseen* body parts – 'a foot, a face, a leg, a head' – stand for the imagined whole? Perhaps the logical disconnect organizing the stanza is *our* cue to extend, typologically, the author's one-body-part representation to other body-parts in representations elsewhere – yet not before we've confronted the shadow of a figural ghost.[32]

If we follow this ghost, we learn that *figure* – image, metaphor, metonymy – plays something like an atomic role in the representation of Shakespearean art. Figure, not character, becomes Shakespeare's leading authorial actor.[33] If we then wish to 'see' *this* author, we may find him not only where we often look – in such famed characters as Hamlet – but more precisely in the character of the author's images, his figural representations, especially extemporal figures that operate intertextually.

EXTEMPORAL INTERTEXTUALITY IN THE ACHILLES STANZA:
OVID, DANTE, PETRARCH, CHAUCER, SPENSER

For instance, line 6 is noteworthy as a blazon; more precisely, line 6 explodes the concept of the blazon. In the Achilles stanza, Shakespeare

---

[30] See Duncan-Jones and Woudhuysen, eds.: the metaphor of the mind's eye 'can be traced back to Plato and is probably most familiar from *Ham* 1.2.185'.

[31] On the mending powers of theatre, see *RJ* Pr.13–14 (on tragedy); and *TS* Ind.2.129–36 and *MND* 5.1.423–38 (on comedy).

[32] Cf. Garber, *Shakespeare's Ghost Writers*: '"Shakespeare" is present as an absence – which is to say, as a ghost' (11).

[33] See Maus: 'An analysis that centers upon characterization, then, cannot fully explain how and why metaphor is so problematic in *The Rape of Lucrece* (76). On the centrality of figure to Shakespearean authorship, see Freinkel, *Reading Shakespeare's Will* xi–xxvii, 159–291.

combines 'two specific descriptive traditions', using the emblem of the spear from a family coat of arms to inscribe a poetic blazon of body parts.[34] Through this metonymic process, Shakespeare represents the heraldic family blazon of the hand-held spear.

In the Petrarchan tradition coming out of the *Rime sparse*, the male perceives his beloved by inventorying the beautiful parts of her body. Occasionally, Petrarch himself writes of Laura's 'eyes, and the arms and the hands and the feet and the face ... / the curling locks of pure shining gold'.[35] In his own Sonnet 106, Shakespeare counters this tradition when he transposes the blazon to the fair young man: 'the blazon of sweet beauty's best, / Of hand, of foot, of lip, of eye, of brow'. As in Sonnet 106, in the Achilles stanza Shakespeare homoeroticizes the blazon, but he goes even further, detaching the various limbs from the body's trunk.

Shakespeare does not overtly use the 'lopp'd ... branches' of the laurel-tree as he does in *Titus Andronicus* – that other Shakespearean work printed in 1594 – when Marcus performs his notorious blazon of the ravished body of Lavinia: 'Speak, gentle niece: what stern ungentle hands / Hath lopp'd and hew'd, and made thy body bare / Of her two branches ... ?' (2.4.16–18; see chapter 2).[36] But in the Achilles stanza Shakespeare may nonetheless allude to the laurel in Ovid's *Metamorphoses*, when Apollo inventories the body-parts of Daphne, but is left to imagine what he cannot see: 'He marvels at her fingers, hands, and wrists, and her arms, bare to the shoulder; and what is hid he deems still lovelier.'[37] The laurel-Daphne becomes Ovid's cross-dressed icon for his own illusionist aesthetic, which Shakespeare re-maps back on to the male epic hero Achilles.[38]

In contrast to Ovid, Shakespeare transposes the notion of aesthetic concealment from the artwork to the author himself. For all Ovid's resistance to Virgil, he does not simply share with his arch-rival the laureate strategy of self-crowning but turns this action into the concluding event of

---

[34] N. J. Vickers, '"The blazon of sweet beauty's best": Shakespeare's *Lucrece*' 95. Vickers adds that 'Shakespeare's encomium of Lucrece – his publication of *Lucrece* – stands as a shield, as an artfully constructed sign of identity, as a proof of excellence' (109).

[35] Petrarch, *RS*, Song 292:1–6; see also Song 157: 9–10.

[36] For the lopped branches as those of the Daphnean laurel tree, see James, *Shakespeare's Troy* 45.

[37] Ovid, *Met* 1.500–2: 'laudat digitosque manusque / bracchiaque et nudos media plus parte lacertos'. Thanks to Stephen Wheeler. In *Ovid's Poetics of Illusion*, Hardie calls the representation of Daphne here Ovid's 'illusionist aesthetic' (7) and connects it to theatre, including *The Winter's Tale* (193–206). Hardie notes the 'phallic fetish' in Daphne's metamorphosis into a laurel tree, and he further cites *Am* 1.5 (46).

[38] According to Hardie, 'Daphne is for ever on display, but for ever concealed', and she becomes a '"*tenuis liber*"' (*Met* 1.549), a '"thin bark" / "slender book"' (46).

his epic.[39] Shakespeare overgoes Ovid, metamorphosing his representation about the nature of art into a representation about the nature of authorship. Shakespeare may construct his shaking-spear of a concealed Achilles by remembering the intriguing conclusion to Ovid's version of the Daphne and Apollo myth, an etiology for poetry and poetic fame. ' "O laurel," ' says Apollo to the metamorphosed Daphne,

'With thee shall Roman generals wreathe their heads . . . Thou at Augustus' portals shalt stand a trusty guardian, and keep watch over the civic crown of oak ...' Paean was done. *The laurel waved her new-made branches, and seemed to move* [*adnuit* = *nod, shake*] *her head-like top in full consent.* (Ovid, *Metamorphoses* 1.560–7; emphasis added).

In this story of attempted rape ending with female consent – Daphne approves Apollo's masculine plan for her laurel bough to crown the brows of generals and the palaces of princes – Ovid uses the Latin verb '*adnuit*', from '*nutare*', meaning 'to sway back and forth' but also 'to shake' (Hardie, *Ovid's Poetics of Illusion* 48). Ovid's striking supernatural detail about authorship, haunting the natural world, might have fascinated Shakespeare's literary imagination.[40]

We have further evidence for thinking that Shakespeare's spear of Achilles is not simply proverbial but Ovidian.[41] First of all, Ovid thinks of Achilles as the antithesis-figure to his own elegiac art. In *Amores* 2.1, one of the five programmatic poems in his inaugural sequence, Ovid explains why he writes love elegy rather than epic, and asks, 'Of what avail will it be to me to have sung of swift Achilles?' (29). In another of the programmatic poems, *Amores* 2.18, Ovid further explains his refusal to write epic (*recusatio*): 'While you, Macer, are bringing your poem to the time of Achilles' wrath and clothing the conspiring chiefs with the war's first arms, I dally in the slothful shade of Venus, and tender Love is bringing to naught the lofty ventures I would make' (1–4).[42] From the outset of his career, Ovid presents himself as a counter-epicist, and he puts himself into competition not

---

[39] See Hardie on *Met* 12.612–19, about the funeral pyre of Achilles: 'The great Achilles has suffered death's transformation from invincible hero to a handful of dust . . . Achilles' full presence is merely the absent presence of *fama*, world-filling indelible *nomen* of Publius Ovidius Naso at the very end of the poem. In retrospect Ovid will turn out to have been the greatest and most expansive hero of this epic poem' (86).

[40] The passage is about authorship, not just because it is about Apollo and Daphne, but more particularly because it intimates that the poet 'keeps watch' over the state.

[41] Like editors and critics writing on *Lucrece*, those writing on Shakespeare and Ovid neglect this intertextuality. More surprisingly, K.C. King, *Achilles*, does not discuss the spear of Achilles, concentrating on the more famous shield.

[42] See Cheney, *Marlowe's Counterfeit Profession*, chs. 1 and 2.

merely with the great epic authors, Homer and Virgil, but also with the best of the Achaeans, whom Ovid imagines as a metonymic figure for the epic genre. Rather than freeing his verse from epic, Ovid interleaves epic into elegy through an authorial fiction about the two genres, and he uses the West's first epic hero as the figure for his interleaf.

Ovid can do so because Achilles is the consummate epic warrior as elegiac lover. The *Iliad* opens with Achilles' dispute with Agammenon over his coveted slave-girl Briseis – a dispute that turns out to have disastrous consequences for the Greeks, because it motivates Achilles to withdraw from the battle. When Agammenon sends Odysseus and Diomedes to retrieve the sullen warrior,

> they found Achilleus delighting his heart in a lyre clear-sounding, splendid and carefully wrought, with a bridge of silver upon it, which he won out of the spoils when he ruined Eëtion's city. With this he was pleasuring his heart, and singing of men's fame. (Homer, *Iliad* 9.186–9)

This original portrait of Achilles as an Apollonian poet-figure, 'delighting his heart' through lyre-playing and 'singing of men's fame', turns out to be significant to the tradition we are tracing.[43]

For instance, in the *Heroides* Ovid presents Briseis writing a letter to Achilles, and she imagines him just as Odysseus and Diomedes find him in the *Iliad*, albeit not in the company of Patroclus (as Homer narrates) but in an imagined embrace with another girl:

> you are wielding the plectrum, and a tender mistress holds you in her warm embrace! And does anyone ask wherefore do you refuse to fight? Because the fight brings danger; while the zither, and song, and Venus, bring delight. Safer it is to lie on the couch, to clasp a sweetheart in your arms, to tinkle with your fingers the Thracian lyre, than to take in hand the shield, and the spear with sharpened point . . . Ye gods forfend! and *may the spear of Pelion go quivering from your strong arm to pierce the side of Hector [validoque, precor, vibrata lacerto / transeat Hectoreum Pelias hasta latus!]* (Ovid, *Heroides* 3.113–26; emphasis added)

Ovid turns the solitary Homeric lyre-player into a lyre-playing lover, and presents Briseis trying to inspire Achilles to activate the military weapon that will perform the key action of the entire Trojan War: the killing of Hector, breaker of horses. For Ovid, the spear is a figure for action; his verb for that action, '*vibrata*', comes from the Latin *vibrare*, meaning to 'brandish'

---

[43] See Lateiner, 'The *Iliad*': 'The poem sings the achievements of men, so Homer is slyly metatextual, making Akhilleus here this poem's only character to sing of heroes' (15n11).

or 'shake'. As Homer primally narrates it in Book 22, 'Achilleus was shaking /
in his right hand' the 'pointed spear ... with evil intention toward brilliant
Hektor' (22.319–20), and when Achilles spies vulnerability in Hector's
armor, 'in this place / brilliant Achilleus drove the spear as he came on in
fury' (325–6).

Following Homer, Ovid imagines that Achilles inherits the spear, made
of an ash tree cut from Mount Pelion, from his father, Peleus, who in turn
was given it by the centaur Chiron (*Iliad* 16.140–4; 19.387–91; see 21.133).
Thus, Ovid joins Homer in imagining a military weapon functioning as an
instrument of paternal succession – a detail that a man named Shakespeare
might have taken to heart when designing his family coat of arms for his
own father. Yet Ovid elsewhere veers from Homer when he refers to the
story underwriting his reference to the Pelian spear: the post-Homeric myth
of Telephus (the name means 'dug' or 'doe').

Telephus is a son of Hercules by Auge who became king of Mysia, and
whom Achilles wounded in the thigh with his spear early in the Trojan War.
As the legend goes, when his wound did not heal, Telephus consulted the
Delphic oracle, which told him that only the person who inflicted the wound
could cure it. Telephus sought Achilles, who used rust from the tip of his spear
to salve the king's wound. It is this story that Shakespeare represents in the
passages from both *2 Henry VI* and *Edward III* discussed earlier. Reminiscent
of this author's representations of himself, the Achilles-Telephus story has
simply given us the slip; in this regard, the Telephus story may be a quintessential Shakespearean one.[44]

Shakespeare's favorite poet took a considerable interest in Achilles'
spear, putting it to specific use no fewer than eight additional times –
the last seven representing the spear's power to wound and heal. In *Amores*
2.9, Ovid first alludes to the myth when the poet tries to persuade Cupid
to relieve the pain from his bow-wound, which reads in Marlowe's
translation: 'Did not Pelides whom his spear did grieve, / Being required,
with speedy help relieve?' (*OE* 2.9.7–8). In the *Ars amatoria*, Ovid tells
the famous incident of Achilles' rape of the young princess of Skyros,
Deidamia – an episode that might have attracted the eye of an author who
produced such plays as *As You Like It* and *Hamlet*, since it is a counter-epic
event involving not merely draft-dodging but cross-dressing, disguise, and
thus theatricality, unfolding arguably antiquity's most famed narrative
of *delay*:

---

[44] Searches on both the World Shakespeare Bibliography and the MLA Bibliography, for instance,
come up empty.

Achilles had disguised his manhood in a woman's robe. What dost thou, Aeacides? wools are not thy business; by another art of Pallas do thou seek fame. What hast thou to do with baskets? thy arm is fitted to bear a shield. Why holdest thou a skein in the hand by which Hector shall die? Cast away the spindle girt about with toilsome windings! *That hand must shake the Pelian spear* [*Quassanda est ista Pelias hasta manu*] . . . It chanced that in the same chamber was the royal maid; by her rape she found him to be a man . . . Why with coaxing words, Deidamia, dost thou make to tarry the *author of thy rape*? [*Auctorem stupri*]? (Ovid, *Ars amatoria* 1.689–704; emphasis added)

Shake the Pelian spear / Author of thy rape: bolstered by the tradition of Achilles as the Apollonian player of the lyre, Shakespeare might have found here the license he needed to imagine the spear-shaking Achilles as an Ovidian 'author'-figure.

Not surprisingly, in the *Ars remedia* Ovid draws more directly on the Telephus story to assign a bifold power to the spear, to harm and to heal, and then associates the Achillean power with his own authorship: 'Learn healing from him through whom ye learnt to love [Ovid himself]: one hand alike will wound and succour ... [T]he Pelian spear which wounded once its Herculean foe, bore relief also of the wound' (43–8). In other words, Ovid's distinct strategy of counter-epic self-presentation consists of appropriating the Achillean power of the epic spear for the authority of his own elegiac authorship. This authorship is distinctly poetic, yet exhibits a clear penchant for self-theatricality.[45]

The next two representations of Achilles' spear come from Ovid's retelling of the Troy story in the *Metamorphoses*.[46] In the second, from Book 13, when Ajax and Ulysses argue over who has the right to bear the arms of the dead runner, the son of Laertes recalls the point of contact between the Telephus and Deidamia episodes:

Achilles' Nereid mother, foreseeing her son's destruction, had disguised him, and the trick of the clothing that he wore deceived them all, Ajax among the rest. But I placed among women's wares some arms such as would attract a man. The hero still wore girl's clothing when, as he laid hands on shield and spear, I said to him: 'O son of Thetis, Pergama, doomed to perish, is keeping herself for you! Why do you delay the fall of mighty Troy?' And I laid my hand on him and sent the brave fellow forth to do brave deeds. So then, all that he did is mine. *'Twas I who conquered the warring Telephus with my spear and healed him, vanquished and begging aid* [*ego Telephon hasta / pugnantem domui, victum orantemque refeci*]. (Ovid, *Metamorphoses* 13.162–72; emphasis added)

---

[45] Ovid's theatricality is well known, referred to in the title of Hardie's book; see also Cheney, *Marlowe's Counterfeit Profession*, esp. 31–98, including Ovid scholarship.

[46] For the first, see *Met* 12.112: 'Telephus twice felt the strength of my spear.'

Thus, Ovid brings the twin themes of Achillean disguise and healing, the
Deidamia and Telephus episodes, into clear narrative conjunction. These
post-Homeric episodes become in Ovid's hands counter-epic strategies for
confronting the genre of Homeric and Virgilian epic within love elegy.

Finally, in the *Tristia* Ovid uses the Telephus episode three times
to represent himself as a poet of exile.[47] In the second instance, from the
autobiographical poem that makes up Book 2, Ovid uses the Telephus-
Achilles myth to process his status as a poet of exile; he wants to write poetry
to Augustus to secure his return to Rome, yet Augustus relegated him in the
first place: 'Perchance, as once for him who ruled the Teuthrantian kingdom
[Telephus], the same object will both wound and cure me [*forsitan, ut
quondam Teuthrantia regna tenenti, sic mihi res eadem vulnus opemque
feret*], and the Muse who aroused the wrath will also soften it; song often
prevails on the mighty gods' (19–22). Ovid goes on to recall Augustus' public
use of poetry for moments of civic celebration (23–8), and once more he
subtly connects the Emperor's interest in poetry with his own art for the
purpose of securing a return home.

This important Ovidian authorial representation has an origin and
an afterlife. Both Sophocles in the lost play *The Assembly of the Achaeans*
and Euripides in the lost play *Telephus* retold the story, the latter satirized by
Aristophanes in *The Clouds*.[48] In the *Library* (2.7.4; 3.9.1) and its *Epitome*
(3.17–20), Apollodorus narrates the story in some detail, as does Ovid's friend
Hyginus in his *Fabulae* (99–101), while Propertius in his *Elegies* refers to it
(2.1.63). In the *Natural History*, Pliny twice describes a painting in which
Achilles scrapes the rust from his spear into the thigh wound of Telephus
(25.42; 34.152), and such a representation survives in the superb relief from the
Casa del Rilievo di Telefo in Ercolano, Italy [http://herculano.desdeinter.net/
ercoo100.htm].[49]

---

[47] For the first, see *Tr* 1.1.97–100: 'On a lucky day and with better fortune than your master may you
arrive there and lighten my misfortunes. For either nobody can remove them or, in the fashion of
Achilles, that man only who wounded me.' For the third, see *Tr* 5.2.9–18: 'The wounds that I thought
would close with passing time pain me no otherwise than if they had been freshly made. Yes, little
troubles are helped by the flight of years; with great ones time but increases the ruin they cause . . .
Telephus would have died, destroyed by his eternal disease, had not the hand that harmed him borne
him aid.'

[48] *Apollodorus: The Library* 2: 188–89n1. Research in this section benefited from conversations with and
work by Dustin Stegner and Tim Arner.

[49] For help with the Telephus relief, I am grateful to Sarah Court, Coordinatore Scientifico,
Herculaneum Conservation Project, The British School at Rome. After Ovid, Statius produces an
epic fragment, the *Achillead*, which opens with the Deidamia episode. Statius refers to Achilles' spear
a few times in passing (1.40–41; 1.879; 2.121–22), but he never mentions the spear's healing powers or
the Telephus myth.

Almost certainly, Ovid underlies Dante's pivotal reference to Achilles' spear in the *Inferno*. In canto 31, Dante writes,

> The very tongue [Virgil's in canto 30] that first wounded me,
> sending the color up in both my cheeks,
> was then to cure me with its medicine –
> as did Achilles' and his father's lance,
> even as I have heard, when it dispensed
> a sad stroke first and then a healing one.[50]

Dante's association of the Achillean spear with Virgil is curious, since Virgil himself never refers to the story, but the association is a natural one given Virgil's role as a guide on the pilgrimage to Paradise. Perhaps Dante uses Ovid to re-script Virgil as a physician whose 'tongue' – his words or epic poetry – can simultaneously wound and heal. If so, the intertextual moment is important, showing Dante to be retaking the icon from Ovidian erotic authorship and transplanting it to the civic authorship of Virgil.

As is to be expected, the great heir of both Dante and Ovid, Petrarch, frequently uses the wounding-curing trope from the Achilles-Telephus myth in the *Rime sparse*. Although never naming the principals or the spear, Petrarch deploys the trope in a fresh way: to describe the effect of Laura's beauty on his poetic imagination and the hope he has for a cure. Thus, in Song 75 he begins, 'The lovely eyes that struck me in such a way that they themselves could heal the wound' (1–2), while in Song 164 he laments, 'Thus from one clear living fountain alone spring the sweet and the bitter on which I feed; one hand alone heals me and pierces me' (9–11).[51] Petrarch may elide the masculine names in the myth because he transposes the homoerotic military myth of Achilles' wounding and curing Telephus' thigh into one of the erotic paradoxes of Petrarchism, the occult power of a lady's beauty to wound and cure her lover.

Perhaps, then, Chaucer has Petrarch, Dante, and/or Ovid in mind in 'The Squire's Tale', when the narrator inventories the magical instruments of King Cambyuskan, including the sword that can both heal and wound (156–67):

> That wolde percen thurghout every thyng,
> And fille in speche of Thelophus the kyng,
> And of Achilles with his queynte spere,
> For he koude with it bothe heele and dere,
> Right in swich wise as men may with the swerd

---

[50] Dante, *Inferno* 31.1–6; trans. Mandelbaum.
[51] See also Petrarch, *RS* 29.17; 159.12; 174.5–8; 221.12; 363.9. For details, see Santagata, ed., *Canzoniere*. Thanks to William J. Kennedy for directing me to this material.

Of which right now ye han youreselven herd

...

And how and whanne it shold yharded be,
Which is unknowe, algates unto me.

(Chaucer, 'The Squire's Tale' 237–46)

By 'Thelephus', Chaucer means Telephus; his phrase 'queynte spere' is especially intriguing, since the word *quaint* is 'one of the much debated Chaucerian terms, meaning artful (or artfully made)' but perhaps also having erotic resonance, since during the period the word could refer to the female genitals.[52] Be that as it may, Chaucer's use of the myth looks more Ovidian than Dantean, because of the erotic context of 'The Squire's Tale'; unlike Dante, Chaucer follows Ovid in presenting himself primarily as a poet of love (*House of Fame* 2.615–25; *Parlement of Foules* 1–12). Shakespeare almost certainly knew 'The Squire's Tale', and the last detail of the stanza above may have caught his eye: when Chaucer admits that he does not know how the spear could be hardened so magically, he exemplifies his famed poetics of indirection.[53]

In Book 4 of *The Faerie Queene*, Spenser announces that he will complete the unfinished 'Squire's Tale', in part because he considers Chaucer an epic poet.[54] Although Spenser does not refer to the spear of Achilles, he does include one magical spear in his national epic that Shakespeare might have remembered in *Lucrece*: Britomart's enchanted spear of chastity, which concentrates 'secret powre *unseene*' (*FQ* 3.1.7; emphasis added).[55] Shakespeare might have recalled this spear not simply because it 'secret[ly]' conceals an 'unseene' power, but also because, in this very stanza, Spenser uses a verse line containing the two halves of Shakespeare's own name: 'And shivering *speare* in bloodie field first *shooke*' (3.1.7; emphasis added; see 3.3.60).[56]

---

[52] Robert R. Edwards (personal communication).

[53] The definitive moment occurs in Book 3 of *The House of Fame*, where the god Aelous asks Chaucer his name, and the poet refuses to give it (1871–5); see also 3.1104–9, where Chaucer indirectly yet playfully claims laureate status. Thompson, *Shakespeare's Chaucer*, mentions the possibility of Shakespeare's use of 'The Squire's Tale' (60–1, 220).

[54] On Spenser's view of Chaucer as an epic poet, see J. A. Burrow, 'Chaucer, Geoffrey'; for details, see Cheney, ' "Novells of His Devise" '.

[55] See Cheney, ' "Secret Powre Unseene" '.

[56] Although Elizabethans rarely rely on the Achilles-Telephus myth, Shakespeare also could have found a brief version in Lodge's *Rosalynde*, perhaps in his *A Margarite of America*, but more enticingly in the Ovidian epyllion *Scylla's Metamorphosis*, when Cupid 'from his bow a furious dart ... sent / Into that wound [of Glaucus] which he had made before: / That like Achilles' sword became the taint / To cure the wound that it had carv'd before' (541–4, in Reese, ed., *Elizabethan Verse Romances*). But since the first two passages lack detail, and the third is inept in its scholarship about 'Achilles' sword', we may be confident that Lodge does not underlie Shakespeare's use of the myth.

SHAKESPEARE AND EPIC

If Shakespeare signs his name to Achilles in *Lucrece*, and in the process creates at once a wry joke and a heavily trafficked intertextual station, stretching from Homer to Spenser, we might find ourselves confronting a longstanding question important to the present argument: did Shakespeare write epic? The following response to this question bears directly on the topic of 'Shakespeare's literary authorship' because during the English Renaissance epic was the premier mark of a literary career. If we can connect Shakespeare with this genre in a way we have not yet imagined, we might be able to adjust our current lexicon, from his 'professional career' to a 'literary career'.[57]

Insofar as we know, Shakespeare did not write an epic poem. Although he displayed unusually eclectic generic skills, spread across several dramatic, lyric, and narrative genres, he did not pen an epic poem in the manner of Spenser, Daniel, Drayton, Chapman, or Milton. Nor did Shakespeare leave behind even a simple plan to write an epic, as Jonson did, when he told Drummond of Hawthornden, he 'had an intention to perfect an epic poem entitled *Herologia*, of the worthies of his country, roused by fame, and was to dedicate it to his country, it is all in couplets, for he detesteth all other rhymes'.[58] By contrast, in the Shakespearean canon epic looks conspicuous by its absence.

Not surprisingly, in our most important work on epic, comparative critics do not assign Shakespeare even a bit part.[59] Probably, we do not need to search too far for an explanation: since Shakespeare did not produce an epic poem of the order of the *Iliad*, the *Aeneid*, the *Orlando Furioso*, the *Gerusalemme Liberata*, *The Faerie Queene*, or *Paradise Lost*, we need not lend him a voice in the story. Yet we might wonder: what are the consequences for criticism on the epic tradition of not listening to Shakespeare's strange epic voice in *The Rape of Lucrece*, *Troilus and Cressida*, *Hamlet*, *Othello*, *Macbeth*, *Antony and Cleopatra*, or *Coriolanus*? And if we do listen, what do we hear? What would a study of epic look like if approached through works lying outside epic's formal boundaries? How might such a

---

[57] See esp. Thomson, *Shakespeare's Professional Career*; but also Bentley, *Profession of Dramatist in Shakespeare's Time*, which studies professional dramatists like Shakespeare because 'their productions have commonly been examined as literary phenomena rather than as working scripts for professional actors in a professional theatre. Most often the plays have been analyzed and evaluated as poetry' (7–8).

[58] Jonson, *Conversations*, in Parfitt, ed. 461.

[59] Important studies include T. M. Greene, *Descent from Heaven*; Durling, *Figure of the Poet in Renaissance Epic*; Giamatti, *Earthly Paradise and the Renaissance Epic*; Murrin, *History and Warfare in Renaissance Epic*; Fichter, *Poets Historical*; Bellamy, *Translations of Power*; C. Burrow, *Epic Romance*; Quint, *Epic and Empire*.

study modify our received story of the genre? In particular, what can we glean about epic through Shakespeare's sublimely *non-epic* contribution?[60]

In contrast to comparatist critics, Shakespeareans produce recurrent studies, usually of an individual work as a type of epic. Among the formulations, the most famous is perhaps the oldest, still very much in our lexicon: in the Henriad, Shakespeare brought epic to the English stage.[61] Curiously, the two conversations –comparatist epic and Shakespearean epic – do not enter into dialogue with each other.[62]

Even though Shakespeare did not write an epic, paradoxically he produced one of the most decisive engagements with the epic tradition on record – an engagement so prodigious that its composite form competes favorably with those by Spenser and Milton. In addition to his two 'minor epics', *Venus and Adonis* and *Lucrece*, Shakespeare produced three well-known installments to a concerted dramatic epic on the new London stage: first, during the early 1590s, in the *Henry VI* trilogy leading to Bosworth Field in *Richard III*; second, during the late 1590s, in the Henriad culminating at the Battle of Agincourt, but also in several plays from this period featuring military men, including in *Hamlet*, *Troilus and Cressida*, and, somewhat startlingly, *Much Ado about Nothing*; and third, between 1603–8, in several late tragedies, from *Othello* and *Macbeth* to *Antony and Cleopatra* and *Coriolanus*, which 'focus insistently on the unequaled feats of an individual male warrior'.[63] We have not yet mentioned an early portrait of the warrior in *Titus Andronicus* or late portraits in *Cymbeline*. Once we start counting, we see how recurrently Shakespeare foregrounds the theatrical military man as an epic figure of national leadership.

With the mention of *Cymbeline*, we may happily complicate the term 'epic' with that of 'romance', and remember that during the European Renaissance great poems by Ariosto, Tasso, and Spenser are in the form of epic romance. A poem like *The Faerie Queene* fuses medieval Arthurian romance with classical military epic, to create a new hybrid genre. Unlike

---

[60] In *Delirious Milton*, Teskey helps us understand why Shakespeare's self-concealing authorship would have made writing an epic impossible: 'none of the greatest epic poets, with the remote exception of the first, wrote more than one major epic. The epic is therefore a more radical expression of the self than even the lyric can be. If the lyric is a personal form, the lyric poet nevertheless wears a succession of masks, *personae*. The epic poet, by contrast, virtually becomes what he makes as a consequence of what he decides' (132).

[61] See Tillyard, *English Epic and Its Background*; Brower, *Hero and Saint*; Kernan, 'Henriad'; Bono, *Literary Transvaluation*; D. Hamilton, *Virgil and 'The Tempest'*; James, *Shakespeare's Troy*.

[62] The major exception is Suzuki, *Metamorphoses of Helen*, who records her debt to her Yale comparatist teachers, and who alerts us to Shakespeare's engagement of the epic tradition but also a genuine paradox: his *obsessive detachment* from epic.

[63] M. B. Rose, *Gender and Heroism in Early Modern English Literature* 19–20.

Spenser, Shakespeare not only does not write an epic, he does not write a romance. At the end of his career, nonetheless, he writes four plays that we now call 'romances' – *Pericles*, *Cymbeline*, *The Winter's Tale*, and *The Tempest* – to which we may add his collaboration with John Fletcher in the chivalric (Chaucerian) form, *Two Noble Kinsmen*.[64] The Shakespeare dramatic canon is notable for its sustained interest both in epic and in romance, with *Cymbeline* emerging not simply as Shakespeare's clearest British epic romance but also his weirdest (chapter 8).

Once we recall the three installments above, we may discriminate among them, and focus on the second, which looks to be the most surprising: in his great tragedies, Shakespeare engages Western epic. In criticism, it has become a commonplace to speak of 'the lyrical phase in Shakespeare's career', singling out *Love's Labor's Lost*, *A Midsummer Night's Dream*, *Richard II*, *Romeo and Juliet*, and *The Merchant of Venice*, and even to see a play like *Love's Labour's Lost* as 'very much about lyricism'.[65] To Shakespeare's lyric phase, we may profitably add an epic phase, and pursue its ramifications for reassessing Shakespearean authorship. Perhaps the First Folio's division of the dramatic works into comedy, history, and tragedy has blinded us to Shakespeare's obsession with epic throughout his career, but more particularly during the first decade of the seventeenth century, when he was so actively penning the twin Aristotelian genres.[66]

Although Shakespeare did not formally write an epic poem, then, he did *write* epic. That is to say, without penning the formal genre of epic, this author managed the mind-bending feat of erasing the form of epic from his canon, leaving in its absence something like the residue of epic, so magnetic we still cannot resist its pull. It is this challenging authorial space – the formal absence of epic that we can nonetheless see, a virtual Shakespearean epic black hole – that we might wish to enter.

Whereas Spenser went on to organize his literary career around writing the epic poem no one else in England had, Shakespeare appears to have set himself against this possibility, and instead produced a dramatic canon everywhere reminding us – if anything – of the tragedy of epic, as if his art were serving a powerful cultural swerve: the historic replacement of a Spenserian national epic with a Shakespearean national tragedy. In

---

[64] In *English Romance in Time*, Cooper builds on Frye to give Shakespearean romance a prominent part in her story, even if she not does connect Shakespeare's romance project with his epic one.

[65] Henderson, *Passion Made Public* 169.

[66] Following Bullman, 'Shakespeare's Georgic Histories,' Tudeau-Clayton assigns a tripartite Virgilian structure to the First Folio, with comedy performing the role of pastoral, history that of georgic, and tragedy that of epic (*Jonson, Shakespeare, and Early Modern Virgil* 4).

retrospect, such an event helps explain why all of Shakespeare's Greek and Roman plays, from *Titus* to *Troilus* to *Timon*, are tragedies – these three bizarre tragedies – but also why this author spent the energy of no fewer than eleven history plays, if not blackening dynastic comedy and romance as the somber tragedy of English history, then severely complicating Spenser's Tudor epic romance.[67]

Shakespeare's own contemporaries recognized his interest in epic, and often put him in the company of such national poets as Homer, Virgil, and Spenser. Perhaps less well known is Robert Chester's 1601 prefatory poem to *Love's Martyr*, which first printed 'The Phoenix and Turtle':

> Of bloudy warres, nor of the sacke of Troy,
> Of Pryams murdred sonnes, nor Didoes fall,
> Of Hellens rape, by Paris Troian boy,
> Of Caesars victories, nor Pompeys thrall,
> Of Lucrece rape, being ravisht by a King,
> Of none of these, of sweete Conceit I sing.
>
> (Chester, *Love's Martyr* 1–6, ed. Grosart 6)

In lines 1, 5, and 6, Chester 'alludes to the semi-epic status' of Shakespeare's *Lucrece* (Burrow, ed. 84n1). Moreover, line 4 on Caesar and Pompey may allude to Marlowe's translation of Lucan's *Pharsalia*, with the references to Homer and Virgil glancing at the recent epic projects of Chapman and Spenser. Although Chester places Shakespeare's *Lucrece* in the company of such great national epics as *The Faerie Queene*, we might record our discomfort. *The Rape of Lucrece* is not *The Faerie Queene*, even as the 1590s publication of both poems compels some to bring the two poems into the epic list together. What has proved difficult is marking the influence accurately. Unless we can discover a focusing lens illuminating the historic character of Shakespeare's engagement with epic, we may be fighting a losing battle. Yet we may find that lens in Shakespeare's most concentrated engagement with the epic tradition: the very work Chester singles out, *The Rape of Lucrece*, with its 28-stanza ecphrasis on the painting of Troy.

The Achilles stanza in *Lucrece* reveals that this author can formally sign Keatsian Negative Capability with his own name. Equally to the point, Shakespeare signs his name to the primary hero of the epic genre, and then refuses to show his authorial face. While this author's habitual indirection

---

[67] The eleventh history play is *Edward III*, included in the *Riverside*. Moreover, the First Folio speaks of *The Tragedie of Troylus and Cressida* (*Riverside* 526), originally placing the play amidst the tragedies but then moving it to a position between the histories and the tragedies (*Riverside* 478). The *Riverside* itself prints the play with the comedies, and today many continue to think of it as a 'problem comedy'.

may originate in his own personal reticence, or perhaps in a 'primal scene' of 'crossing the bridge' into London to view the piked heads of Catholic traitors,[68] a complementary origin may lie in his engaged Ovidian reading of Western laureate self-presentation. The counter-epic author enters the list of Western epic, confronts the iconic hero of epic, and then replaces epic character with the atomistic energy of his own concealed authorial image. Virgilian and Spenserian epic narrative appear as Shakespearean Ovidian metonymy. Instead of searching for the man in his works, to discover William Shakespeare in such characters as Hamlet, the self-signed Achilles stanza directs us to locate the terms of authorship within extemporal intertextual representations of a character's consciousness.

The author himself does not appear, but in the concretion of his figural intertextuality with Spenser, Petrarch, Ovid, and Virgil we can discern a portrait of a counter-laureate author of poems and plays – kind, compact, and always deceitful – that does not so much challenge the 'man of the theatre' model as *complete* it.

In 1594, Shakespeare constructs a clear lens for viewing the phenomenon that more than any other marks his counter-laureate authorship – his curious writing of the one genre he never formally attempts: epic. The Achilles stanza unfolds the paradox of this *recusatio*: in writing epic, he self-consciously refuses to write epic. Instead of using poetry to imitate the great tradition of epic, as Spenser had done, Shakespeare represents only a vacant epic 'hole'. Not the terrifying wrathful hero, but merely his mailed fist, becomes the visible metonymy standing for this author's 'unseen' epic. In the Achilles stanza, Shakespeare self-consciously makes epic the missing center – the targeted blank – of his counter-laureate authorship.[69]

'BEGINNING IN THE MIDDLE': *TROILUS AND CRESSIDA*

Once we glimpse Shakespeare's counter-epicist authorship, we might consider the Shakespeare canon a rather strange epicist universe. To take the most obvious case: *Troilus and Cressida* is so problematic a comedy that it may be dangerous to consider in brief, yet the preceding discussion suggests a surprisingly clear route: criticism on this play needs to begin by considering what 'author's pen or actor's voice' does with the genre

---

[68] Greenblatt, *Will in the World* 149–74.
[69] Cf. Maus: 'If *The Rape of Lucrece* seems to be narrative striving for a missing visual element, the painting described in the poem seems to yearn for the missing dimension of temporality, and to usurp the privileges of narrative by displaying successive episodes in a deceptive present' (81).

of epic (Pr.24).[70] For reasons of space, three points will have to suffice. The first is that the Prologue makes it clear that *Troilus and Cressida* is both *epic* and *not-epic*:

> In Troy, there lies the scene.
> …
>
> Now expectation, tickling skittish spirits,
> On one and other side, Troyan and Greek,
> Sets all on hazard – and hither am I come,
> A prologue arm'd, but not in confidence
> Of author's pen or actor's voice, but suited
> In like conditions as our argument,
> To tell you, fair beholders, that our play
> Leaps o'er the vaunt and firstlings of those broils.
> Beginning in the middle; starting thence away
> To what may be digested in a play.   (*Troilus and Cressida* Pr.1–29)

Troilus and Cressida is an epic in that it follows the start-up convention of epic: 'Beginning in the middle' – *in medias res*.[71] But a drama is not an epic, and can never be one, at least according to Plato (*Republic* 3.394c) and Aristotle (*Poetics* 1449b.9–11), who distinguish epic from comedy and tragedy. Shakespeare's phrase 'starting thence away' intimates the formal distinction between his comedy and epic: *Troilus and Cressida* follows epic by beginning in the middle but then *starts away* from it, 'digest[ing]' its action to that required by 'a play'.[72] In Shakespeare's formulation, we are to imagine *Troilus* as a comedy in epic form but simultaneously to distinguish it from epic. It is this subtle principle of similarity with difference that the Prologue represents syntactically. Yet the phrase 'Leaps o'er the vaunt' also suggests Shakespeare's peculiar *take* on epic; in *Troilus and Cressida*, we enter some of the strangest epic space on record.[73]

Second, no one is stranger than Shakespeare's Achilles. 'The great Achilles', Ulysses reports,

---

[70] On the quoted phrase, see Weimann, who uses it to probe the relation between authorship and acting, writing and performance (*Author's Pen and Actor's Voice*).

[71] Fineman observes that *Lucrece* also relies on this epic principle (32).

[72] See Hillman, 'Gastric Epic'.

[73] On Shakespeare's armed Prologue as a counter to Jonson's Prologue in *Poetaster*, see Bednarz: 'The principal cause of Jonson's ongoing debate with Shakespeare was the incompatibility of his own univocal vision of human perfectibility and confident self-assertion with the radical irony at the heart of his rival's poetics … [Shakespeare] would mimic Jonsonian neoclassicism – invoking Horace's famous literary dictum in *The Art of Poetry* that an epic should begin *in medias res* – to empty his drama of authority. He would cast his play in epic terms, but only to strip it of meaning' (260–1).

Lies mocking our designs. With him Patroclus
Upon a lazy bed the livelong day
Breaks scurril jests,
And with ridiculous and [awkward] action,
Which, slanderer, he imitation calls,
He pageants us ...
And like a strutting player, whose conceit
Lies in his hamstring, and doth think it rich
To hear the wooden dialogue and sound
'Twixt his stretch'd footing and the scaffolage.
(*Troilus and Cressida* 1.3.142–56)

In other words, Shakespeare's Achilles is a figure of theatrical epic: an epic hero who 'mock[s]' his own heroic drama. Rather than performing prodigious feats on the battlefield, he diminishes his epic stature through homoerotic lounging and scurrilous discourse, metamorphosing the severity of war into comedic play. Ulysses' speech picks up key words from Western poetics – 'imitation', 'conceit', the latter of which echoes the Achilles stanza in *Lucrece* – to present Achilles as a new type of (counter-)epic hero. Specifically, Ulysses locates Achilles' cognitive action in the vulnerability of his famed heel, adding that the warrior narcissistically delights in hearing his own theatrical voice. The word 'footing' is a particularly fine pun here, evoking both poetic meter and theatrical strutting, the language and action of the stage. Perhaps only Shakespeare could find consciousness in Achilles' heel.[74]

Third, we need to take Ulysses at his word, because his description of Achilles so accurately anticipates Achilles' weird behavior at the end of the play. Although Shakespeare does not here refer to Achilles' magical spear, able to wound or to heal, he does fully reduce the great warrior of the *Iliad* to an elegiac figure of Ovidian concealment, hiding from Hector when they finally meet, and then hiding behind his Myrmidons, who themselves perform 'the death of Hector' (5.6–8). The author's pen may not here formally sign the name of 'Shake-speare' to the figure of Achilles, but we can still hear the 'actor's voice' sounding between his stretched footing and the theatre's scaffolding. In this way, Shakespeare's grim comedy typologically fulfills the figure from *Lucrece*, presenting Achilles as a theatrical man who conceals his identity in martial costume. From the minor epic of 1594 to the 1609 printing of this problem comedy, Shakespeare presents Achilles as a personal figure for the nature of his self-concealing authorship.

---

[74] On *Troilus* and identity, see Charnes, *Notorious Identity* 70–102. On Achilles' theatrical self-concealment, see *TC* 2.3.126–9. On the Elizabethan political link between Achilles and the Earl of Essex, see James 113–18.

Back in *Lucrece*, Shakespeare inserts the Achilles stanza into a larger ecphrasis that fictionalizes the *failure* of epic to console the rifled victim for her loss: 'none it ever cured' (line 1581).[75] In this failure, a lot is at stake, especially in 1594. Without doubt, Shakespeare uses Ovid to counter Virgil, but simultaneously he counters Spenser, who had most famously presented a Virgilian epic to the British nation.

According to the narrative presented in this chapter, William Shakespeare is the consummate theatrical man whose original production of 'imaginary work', for both the page and the stage, quickly earns him a post-Spenserian counter-garland. In the 1640 frontispiece to John Benson's edition of Shakespeare's *Poems*, William Marshall re-engraves the famed Martin Droeshout portrait from the First Folio edition of Shakespeare's plays (Figure 6). In Marshall's portrait, the once handless playwright now metamorphoses into a theatrical poet whose gloved hand dramatically grips, Achilles-like, the branch of a cut laurel.[76]

Did Shakespeare write epic? Indeed, he did. Yet not as anyone before had written epic. Nor perhaps as anyone has since. By self-consciously combining a capacious array of dramatic forms – comedy, history, tragedy, romance – alongside a stunning panoply of poetic forms – lyric and narrative poetry – Shakespeare makes epic the black hole of his counter-laureate authorship.

HAMLET: 'OUT AT THE PORTAL'

Let us end this chapter, then, by turning briefly to what looks like Shakespeare's own metaphor for counter-laureate authorship, written probably soon after Spenser died in 1599 (Shapiro 67–83). Although we do not know that Shakespeare acted the part of Achilles in *Troilus and Cressida* (or planned to), we do think he performed the role of the Ghost in *Hamlet*. This figure functions, not simply as a religious, political, and familial icon, but also as 'the embodiment of lost epic and heroic values'.[77]

---

[75] See Fineman on the failure of the epic Troy painting to help Lucrece (58–60), including on 'the way Shakespeare's own authorial voice is called forth by what belies it' (68).

[76] On the iconography of the gloved hand, see Stallybrass and Jones, 'Fetishizing the Glove in Renaissance Europe'. Marshall's engraving encourages us to complement the social and political significance assembled by Stallybrass and Jones: the gloved hand is also a sign of the agency of authorship. For the image of the cut laurel branch, see the Epilogue to Marlowe's *Doctor Faustus*, itself an imitation of Petrarch's *Rime sparse* (Eriksen, 'Marlowe's Petrarch').

[77] Garber, *Shakespeare After All* 486. Garber notes how two different martial battles bookend the narrative (Old Hamlet versus Old Norway in their 'epic combat' (487), and Hamlet versus Laertes in their post-epic rapier duel); and she recalls how habitually the Prince remembers his father as a (dead) epic hero (1.2.139–40; 3.4.55–8).

This Shadowe is renowned Shakespear's Soule of th'age
The applause? delight? the wonder of the Stage.
Nature her selfe, was proud of his designes
And joy'd to weare the dressing of his lines,
The learned will Confess, his works are such,
As neither man, nor Muse, can prayse to much.
For ever live thy fame, the world to tell,
Thy like, no age, shall ever paralell.
W.M. sculpsit.

Figure 6. Frontispiece to *Poems: Written By Wil. Shake-speare. Gent.*,
ed. John Benson (London, 1640)

Perhaps, then, we should view *Hamlet* as a play about *the death of epic as a Western literary form* – nay, its 'murther' (1.5.25) – perhaps by a mercenary post-epic culture bent on eliminating heroic values, with Claudius and Fortinbras its competing icons.[78] If indeed the 'Ghost is

---

[78] In the *October* eclogue, Spenser complained that Elizabethan culture was in danger of enacting just this elimination: 'woundlesse armour rusts, / And helmes unbruzed wexen dayly browne' (41–42).

Shakespeare',[79] we may *remember* the Ghost not simply as another figure for William Shakespeare, but as this author's most memorable icon for an epic figure that is not there. In this sullen warrior, armed head to foot, stalking off the stage, and calling for revenge, Shakespeare conjures up the epic figural ghost of Achilles.

At the outset of the tragedy, Hamlet may mourn the death of this ghostly warrior out of Homeric epic, yet even after his audience with the Ghost – perhaps because of it – the Prince longs to hear a Virgilian epic speech about the faith of Hecuba for the fallen Priam. But in the Bedroom Scene of 3.4, when the Prince is alone with his mother the queen, Shakespeare stages the most haunting moment of solitude in the play, but also perhaps a fable for the form and fate of Shakespearean epic:

HAMLET.	Do you see nothing there?
QUEEN.	Nothing at all, yet all that is I see.
HAMLET.	Nor did you nothing hear?
QUEEN.	No, nothing but ourselves.
HAMLET.	Why, look you there, look how it steals away!
	My father, in his habit as he lived!
	Look where he goes, even now, out at the portal.
	Exit Ghost.

(*Hamlet* 3.4.131–6)

In this evaporation of the ghostly father of Western epic, stealing 'out at the portal' in the costume of the living, and bearing with him the invisible consciousness of guilt, we might witness the haunting figural 'nothing' that gives birth to the counter-laureate conundrum of Shakespearean authorship.

Shakespeare echoes this passage at *RL* 101–4, *R3* 1.1.6, *Henry V* 5.Ch.16–19, suggesting not that he joined Spenser in trying to fill the void but precisely that he did not. The instance from *Henry V* suggests that we may be off the scent if we even dare to see this history play as Shakespeare's national epic.
[79] Garber, *Shakespeare's Ghost Writers* 176.

CHAPTER 2

The forms of 'counter-laureate authorship': Titus Andronicus, A Midsummer Night's Dream, 1 Henry IV, The Tempest

> ['Tis] wisdom to conceal our meaning.
>
> *3 Henry VI* 4.7.60

Building on the last chapter, this one looks further into the topic of Shakespeare's strange authorship. Shakespeare's authorship is strange, we have seen, because it deftly conceals the author. As Edward IV says in the epigraph to this chapter, addressing his brother Gloucester (later, Richard III), ''tis wisdom to conceal our meaning'. Shakespeare's concealment of his own 'meaning' is so complete, successful, and consummate that generations of critics have denied the status of 'author' to William Shakespeare. Classifying him as a 'man of the theatre', most critics today continue to see Shakespeare set apart from the 'laureate' standard of literary authorship consolidated by Edmund Spenser and carried forward by Ben Jonson. Rather than present himself as an author with a literary career in search of fame, Shakespeare disappears quietly into the dramaturgy of his works, exchanging one historic invention, the author, with another, character. Such an exchange, we are told, well serves the commercial demands of the collaborative London theatre.

During the past few years, however, the critical climate appears to have cleared sufficiently for a project that aims to disrupt the binary thinking organizing this fundamentally twentieth-century myth. Today, it may be less irrational to view Shakespeare's obvious commitment to the theatre as compatible with his underlying fascination with the literary career of the author. As we have also seen, for any number of personal or professional reasons Shakespeare forges theatrical self-concealment in response to the laureate self-presentation of Spenser and indeed most authors of the 1590s, from Marlowe to Jonson, including Sidney, Daniel, Drayton, and Chapman.

Furthermore, during the Elizabethan and Jacobean eras Shakespeare's self-concealment, we have finally seen, is so unusual that it might be best to think in terms of *counter-authorship*, a form of authorship that exists not in isolation as the stroke of 'genius' but also in reaction to the dominant 1590s model of authorship. Because this model was 'laureate', defined by self-presentation and national leadership in Virgilian genres like pastoral and epic, we can profitably speak of Shakespeare's *counter-laureate authorship*; and, because the leading laureate of the day was Spenser, of Shakespeare's counter-Spenserian authorship. Through this authorial strategy, Shakespeare engages Spenserian texts, including on the topic of authorship itself, by deploying an extemporal principle of intertextuality. In Shakespeare's hands, Spenserian intertextuality appears extemporal because it often lacks the precise lexical repetition or echo we find in such authors as Spenser himself, well-versed in the classical art of imitation.[1] No wonder we have bypassed this titanic literary relationship.

Whereas in the last chapter we looked at a single form of Shakespeare's counter-laureate authorship – the *heraldic*, as represented in the epic Achilles stanza from *Lucrece* as it unfolds in *Troilus and Cressida* and *Hamlet* – in this chapter we shall explore four additional forms, all of which operate through a principle of *refraction*. In each of these forms, Shakespeare does not *reflect* authorship so much as *refract* it, as through a prism.[2] That is to say, instead of introducing a character who represents the author, like Colin Clout in *Faerie Queene* 6 or Horace in *Poetaster*, Shakespeare refracts authorship onto a character or group of characters who seems to have little to do with authorship. To make matters worse (that is to say, more intriguing), Shakespeare's refraction tends to lack laureate triumphalism, disappearing into mockery and tragic loss.

Of the four forms to be discussed here, only the second, from Theseus' speech on imagination in *A Midsummer Night's Dream*, can be said to be formally about the 'poet', but it is so overtly critical that only a lunatic or a lover would deduce a form of Shakespearean authorship from it.[3] The fourth form, from Prospero's farewell to magic in *The Tempest*, has long been regarded as Shakespeare's farewell to the theatre, but characteristically the speech is about the abandonment of theatre, and it follows hard on a

---

[1] Cf. Hieatt, 'Shakespeare, William': 'the understanding that ought to arise from thinking about them together is still confused and rudimentary. Spenser's undoubted influence on Shakespeare is hard to particularize, and there is no evidence to show what feeling – anxiety or any other – Shakespeare entertained about it' (641).

[2] The *OED* records that the words *refract* and *prism* first occur in the late sixteenth and early seventeenth centuries. Under Def. 1a for *refract*, the *OED* cites Sir Thomas Browne's 1646 *Pseudo Epidemica*, which usefully distinguishes between *refraction* and *reflection*. Shakespeare's reliance on prismatic refraction disrupts the cardinal principle of early modern poetics, imitation or reflection, as discussed recently by Lees-Jeffries, *England's Helicon*, ch. 4, who emphasizes Sidney's and Spenser's use of mirror imagery to represent their authorial projects. See, e.g., *FQ* 3.Proem.5. Hamlet articulates this specular poetics when defining 'the purpose of playing' as 'hold[ing] ... the mirror up to nature' (3.1.20–2; see chapter 7).

[3] On Shakespeare's 'uniformly disparaging' portrait of the poet in his works, see Muir, *Shakespeare the Professional* 22–40: 40.

speech about artistic failure ('Our revels now are ended' [4.1.148]). Both the first and the third forms are nominally about something else, with one about the brutality of lost virginity and the other about the grandeur of successful horsemanship: in *Titus Andronicus*, Marcus describes his ravished niece, Lavinia; and in *1 Henry IV* the English rebel Vernon describes Prince Hal mounting his horse at Shrewsbury. While each of these forms differs, I shall argue that all cohere in their reliance on the principles of Shakespearean counter-authorship, counter-laureate authorship, and counter-Spenserian authorship. I have chosen these four in particular because they include instances of Spenserian extemporal intertextuality, but also because they are all sufficiently detailed, and refer or allude to well-known classical myths of the poet (rather than, say, the more obscure myth of Telephus examined in chapter 1).

Through this practice, we may witness Shakespeare refracting his counter-laureate authorship in dialogue with the national art of Spenser. By staging *refraction* dramatically, Shakespeare deflects attention from what Keats calls the 'egotistical sublime', displacing the terms of authorship on to a character in the fiction detached from Shakespeare's professional work.[4] By examining Shakespeare's practice, we can learn a good deal about this author's literary ambitions, and come to appreciate his theatrical genius more fully within his own historical moment.

By no means are the four forms of counter-laureate authorship examined in this chapter the only ones in the Shakespeare corpus. Yet the examples we shall examine do spread over the four dramatic genres of Shakespeare's career, from early till late, and allow us to glimpse a range of counter-laureate principles: what I call *heterosocial refraction* in *Titus Andronicus*; *homosocial refraction* in *1 Henry IV*; *refracted social critique* in *A Midsummer Night's Dream*; and *bi-social refraction* in *The Tempest*.

HETEROSOCIAL REFRACTION IN *TITUS ANDRONICUS*

The first form of counter-laureate authorship, *heterosocial refraction*, appears in Marcus' notorious description of Lavinia in the early or 'bookish' tragedy *Titus Andronicus* and subsequently in Lavinia's unusual performance of literary agency. In Marcus' speech, Shakespeare uses his masculine voice to

---

[4] Keats, Letter to Richard Woodhouse, 27 October 1818, in E. Cook, ed., *John Keats* 418. Keats speaks of 'the wordsworthian or egotistical sublime; which is a thing per se and stands alone', and differs from 'the poetical Character' of himself, which 'is not itself – it has no self – it is every thing and nothing – It has no character – it enjoys light and shade; it lives in gusto, be it foul or fair, high or low, rich or poor, mean or elevated – It has as much delight in conceiving an Iago as an Imogen'.

project the terms of male authorship – evident in discourse about the authorial myths of Philomela, Orpheus, and Daphne and Apollo – on to the screen of a female body and feminine consciousness. This extemporal intertextual technique *displaces* authorship on to a much more visible gender dynamic, where questions about the masculine perception of the female, rape, mutilation, and even murder emerge viscerally, almost always within a nationalist setting (Rome is a site for England and so forth). Yet this displacement suggests that *heterosocial refraction* enfolds a rather durable model of cultural experience. Here, we might say, the author pens a gender-based form of consciousness, about sexuality, within the political context of the nation, in order to serve a religious or philosophical telos, literary immortality.

In this process, on display from *Titus* forward, Shakespeare deploys *a characterological* discourse of displaced authorship, a specifically literary technique perhaps best described as a *palimpsest*, especially as theorized by Gerard Genette in *Palimpsests: Literature in the Second Degree*: 'on the same parchment, one text can become superimposed upon another, which it does not quite conceal but allows to show through'.[5] Three passages from Shakespeare's first tragedy, published in 1594, direct us to what Genette calls 'a *palimpsestuous* reading' (399; his emphasis), produced from the text's self-conscious 'literarity' (9).

In *Titus*, Shakespeare stages classical Rome in the Senecan mode of blood-revenge, complete with Latin quotations from Seneca (2.1.135: *Hippolytus* 1180; 4.1.81–2: *Hippolytus* 671–2), a direct reference to 'Horace' complete with quotation (4.1.20–1: *Odes* 1.22.1–2), allusions to Virgil's *Aeneid* (2.3.21–4; 3.2.27–8; 5.3.80–7), quotations from Ovid (4.3.4: *Met* 1.150), along with many references to Ovidian myths (e.g., Diana and Actaeon at 2.3.61–5, or Pyramus and Thisbe at 2.3.231–2), and much more. Especially visible are Ovid's myths of Philomela (2.3.43; 2.4.26, 41–3; 4.1.47–8, 52; 5.2.194–5) and Orpheus (2.4.51), but also Ovid's story of Lucrece from the *Fasti* (2.1.108–9; 3.1.298; 4.1.64, 91). This overt textualizing of classicism does not so much betray the young, bookish Shakespeare as make visible the intertextual strategy the mature Shakespeare comes to finesse.

Under directions from Aaron, Chiron and Demetrius rape Titus' daughter, named Lavinia after Aeneas' destined bride. Then, to silence her, they cut out her tongue and cut off her hands. Aaron invents this brutal act of violation from Ovid's myth of Philomela, as he informs Tamora: 'Philomel must lose her tongue to-day, / Thy sons make pillage of her chastity' (2.2.43–4). As critics observe, in this play characters routinely *pattern* their behavior on classical texts.

---

[5] Genette, *Palimpsests* 398–9.

Thus, when Titus realizes that his daughter has been raped by someone who has read the *Metamorphoses*, he remarks on the underlying literary strategy: 'Pattern'd by that the poet [Ovid] here describes' (4.1.57).

Earlier, in Act 2, scene 4, Titus' brother Marcus discovers his ravished niece:

> Speak, gentle niece: what stern ungentle hands
> Hath lopp'd and hew'd, and made thy body bare
> Of her two branches, those sweet ornaments
> Whose circling shadows kings have sought to sleep in,
> And might not gain so great a happiness
> As half thy love? Why dost not speak to me?
> Alas, a crimson river of warm blood,
> Like to a bubbling fountain stirr'd with wind,
> Doth rise and fall between thy rosed lips,
> Coming and going with thy honey breath.
> But sure some Tereus hath deflow'red thee,
> And lest thou shouldst detect [him], cut thy tongue.
> Ah, now thou turn'st away thy face for shame!
> …
> Fair Philomela, why, she but lost her tongue,
> And in a tedious sampler sew'd her mind;
> But, lovely niece, that mean is cut from thee.
> A craftier Tereus, cousin, hast thou met,
> And he hath cut those pretty fingers off
> That could have better sew'd than Philomel.
> O, had the monster seen those lily hands
> Tremble like aspen leaves upon a lute,
> And make the silken strings delight to kiss them,
> He would not then have touch'd them for his life!
> Or had he heard the heavenly harmony
> Which that sweet tongue hath made,
> He would have dropp'd his knife, and fell asleep,
> As Cerberus at the Thracian poet's feet.   (*Titus Andronicus* 2.4.16–51)

Even though recent performances demonstrate the stage-worthiness of this speech, we still cannot explain its details simply through performativity, or sexuality and psychology.[6] Strikingly, Marcus voices the trauma of female

---

[6] According to Kermode, Marcus' speech has become 'something of an embarrassment' to the 'modern director' (*Shakespeare's Language* 8). Kermode draws on Bate's inventory of this matter in his Arden 3 edition, which recalls that in 1955 Peter Brook cut the speech entirely, that in 1972 Trevor Nunn cut twenty-nine lines, and that only in 1998 did Debora Warner perform the complete speech. Yet Kermode takes issue with Bate's defense of the speech as 'acceptable modern psychology' (9), arguing that the immature Shakespeare here 'is making poetry about the extraordinary appearance of Lavinia … exactly as he would if he were in a non-dramatic poem' (8). Cf. J. Bate, ed. 55–69.

rape through discourse from the male tradition of Ovidian authorship. Appearing to violate the psychological realism we expect of this author, Shakespeare divides our attention from the dramatic trauma we witness on the stage, compelling us to fix simultaneously on the intertextual fabric making up the theatrical spectacle. By taking this discourse to heart, we may see a precise model of extemporal intertextual authorship.

The speech shows Marcus filtering the situation through 'human consciousness'.[7] Marcus, then, does not just describe Lavinia's body; he records the very birth of tragic recognition – and a specific kind of tragic consciousness: a literary consciousness.[8] As Aaron patterns the rape on Ovid's Philomela myth, so Marcus patterns his *comprehension* of her rape on the same Ovidian narrative: 'sure some Tereus hath deflow'red thee'. At once the origin of artistic invention and readerly recognition, the Ovidian book forms the complex center of a theatrical hermeneutic process. Then, as Marcus looks more closely, he realizes that the rapist bests Tereus: 'A craftier Tereus ... hast thou met.' Finally, discovering the extent of the crime, Marcus expresses the compassion that the rapist lacked, likening Lavinia's once 'sweet tongue' to the music of Orpheus, demarcating a poetics of loss. As critics observe, Shakespeare self-consciously overgoes Ovid. The absolute literariness of the representation requires an extreme version of palimpsestuous reading in the second degree. For Ovid (as later for Spenser), Philomela and Orpheus are both arch-myths of the poet.[9]

To see the extremity of the palimpsest here, consider alone line 45: 'Tremble like aspen leaves upon a lute.' Marcus describes Lavinia's trembling hands, yet his author clearly eyes other *English* poets, engaging in a complex intertextual genealogy that includes Chaucer's *Troilus and Criseyde*, Golding's translation of the *Metamorphoses*, Spenser's *Faerie Queene*, and Marlowe's *Tamburlaine*. The genealogy is so complex we might best view it in tabular form (Figure 7).

An *Englishing* of Ovid if ever there was one, Shakespeare alone adds to the longstanding arboreal metaphor the image of the 'lute'. The lute is the instrument of Apollo, god of poetry and inventor of the self-crowned laureate poet himself. As Spenser puts it in *The Ruines of Rome* (1591), 'Nath'les my Lute, whom Phoebus deignd to give'

---

[7] Alan Dessen, quoted in J. Bate, ed. 62.
[8] Jonathan Bate calls Marcus' speech 'possibly the most literary moment in the whole of Shakespeare' (ed. 90).
[9] See Segal, *Orpheus*; Hardie, *Ovid's Poetics of Illusion*, esp. 259–72 on Philomela. On Ovid's Philomela as a poet-figure in the Renaissance, see Enterline, *Rhetoric of the Body* 1–5, 88–90, 139–40, esp. 152–7 (on *Lucrece*); Keilen, *Vulgar Eloquence* 99–123.

1. Ovid, *Metamorphoses* 3.46–8: said of the Phoenicians confronting Cadmus:
   nec mora, Phoenicas, sive illi tela parabant / sive fugam, sive ipse timor prohibebat utrumque, / occupat. (He makes no tarrying, but seizes on the Phoenicians, whether they are preparing for fighting or for flight or whether very fear holds both in check.)

2. Chaucer, *Troilus and Crisyede* 3.1200: said of Crisyede holding Troilus in her arms:
   Right as an aspes leef she gan to quake.

3. Golding, trans. of Ovid's *Metamorphoses* 3.46: said of the Phoenicians confronting Cadmus:
   Stoode trembling like an Aspen leafe.

4. Spenser, *The Faerie Queene* 1.9.51: said of the Redcrosse Knight confronting Despayre:
   And trembled like a leafe of Aspin greene.

5. Marlowe, *Tamburlaine, Part 1* 2.4.4: said of the weak king Mycetes confronting Tamburlaine:
   Stand staggering like a quivering aspen leaf.

6. Shakespeare, *Titus Andronicus* 2.4.45: said of the ravished Lavina seen by her uncle Marcus:
   Tremble like aspen leaves upon a lute.[a]

Figure 7. Intertextual genealogy in the 'aspen leaf' simile from *Titus Andronicus*, Ovid to Shakespeare

Note   [a] Critics find the origin of Shakespeare's line in both Marlowe and Golding, but they neglect Spenser; see Cheney, *Marlowe's Counterfeit Profession* 125–6. For Chaucer, see Maxwell, ed. 57. Maxwell also cites Spenser's *Amoretti* 1.1–4: 'Happy ye leaves when as those lilly hands, / which hold my life in their dead doing might, / shall handle you and hold in loves soft bands, / lyke captives trembling at the victors sight.' But, he adds, 'It is probably a coincidence; if not, Spenser must presumably have seen the printed text of *Titus*. *Amoretti* was entered on the Stationers' Register on 19 November 1594, and published in 1594' (ed. 57).

(32.6 [line 443]).[10] Shakespeare makes the 'aspen leaves' line into a form of national auto-reflexivity beyond the second degree.

Most visibly, then, Marcus reads the body of Lavinia as an Ovidian text and discovers how her ravished body records a revision to the *Metamorphoses*. Initially a pensive reader of a disturbing post-Ovidian text, Marcus uses creative

---

[10] On this line for supporting commentary, see Lyne, *Ovid's Changing Worlds* 90. While we cannot assign intentionality to the deep intertextuality here, we can at least discern self-consciousness in Shakespeare's insertion of the authorial lute, and, because of this instrument, we may infer that he likely had his eye on Spenser, not just Marlowe.

speech to morph into a new Ovidian author-figure. In this complex process of Ovidian intertextuality, Marcus crosses the divide of agency, between passivity and action, for he is at once subject to the Ovidian work of Aaron and in opposition to him through sympathetic language toward Lavinia. It is this dynamic – Marcus' articulation of Lavinia's traumatized subjectivity across the divide of agency – that captures paradigmatically this form of Shakespeare's counter-laureate authorship.

Marcus' reference to Lavinia's 'two [lopped] branches' alludes to Ovid's central myth in the *Metamorphoses*, Daphne's change into the laurel tree when escaping from Apollo – a project that Petrarch appropriates for his own in the *Rime sparse*.[11] The significance of Shakespeare's laurel image is not just political; it is also literary. Earlier, for instance, Titus appears as an icon of Virgilian poetics, as presented by Titus himself (James 51–2):

> Hail, Rome, victorious in thy mourning weeds!
> Lo, as the bark that hath dischar'd his fraught
> Returns with precious lading to the bay
> From whence at first she weigh'd her anchorage,
> Cometh Andronicus, bound with laurel boughs,
> To re-salute his country with his tears.   (*Titus Andronicus* 1.1.70–5)

The details suggest that here the author uses Ovid to counter not only Virgil but more particularly the Virgilian Spenser and his model of laureate self-crowning.[12] The two *laurel* speeches – Titus presenting himself as a Virgilian hero self-crowned with laurel, and Marcus presenting Lavinia as a ravished Ovidian lady lopped of her laurel – model laureate and counter-laureate authorship, respectively. If George Peele wrote Titus' laureate speech (and indeed the whole of Act 1), as now seems likely, an argument about Shakespeare's counter-laureate authorship may acquire even more technical force.[13]

---

[11] James, *Shakespeare's Troy* 45, 47, 62, who emphasizes the political significance of the image: 'Following the examples of Ovid's Apollo and of Petrarch, Shakespeare appropriates the laurel tree as his image for his poetic project: his practice of disjoining icons from their normative political significance' (45). Cf. Keilen 132–3.

[12] Hence perhaps the term 'weeds' from the Proem to *FQ* 1, where the Virgilian poet 'maske[s]' in 'lowly Shepheards weeds', as well as the vocational image of the bark, derived from Ovid and others, and becoming Spenser's vehicle for concluding his Legend of Holiness (1.12.42). James sees Shakespeare here extending his critique to 'Elizabethan petrarchism' (64). According to Paglia, *Titus* is 'a devastating parody of Spenser': 'This play is Shakespeare's taunting farewell to Spenser. He is about to launch his own original explorations of love and gender. In *Titus Andronicus* Shakespeare tries to fix and reduce Spenser, in order to pin him down and get past him. Lavinia's endlessly stressed amputated tongue and hands are Atalanta's balls, blood red-herrings tossed along the racetrack of the Muses' (*Sexual Personae* 194–5).

[13] For he himself would not be the composer of the play's most overt instance of laureateship, but only its counter-form. On Peele's authorship in *Titus*, see B. Vickers, *Shakespeare as Co-Author* 148–243. Vickers has largely persuaded the Shakespeare community that Peele wrote Act 1, including Jonathan

We can extend Shakespearean authorship here to the topic of literary careers because Marcus' speech relies on generic indicators, especial[ly the striking link between tragedy and lyric poetry.[14] We might brood about Shakespeare's use of a lyric monologue to stage the core of a tragedy. Effectively, he disrupts our received binary, which separates drama from poetry: he inserts lyric into tragedy; further, he uses lyric to *voice* tragedy. Marcus' speech, I suggest, signals the birth moment not merely for Shakespearean tragedy but for a counter-laureate authorship underwriting it.

Marcus' speech sets up Act 4, scene 1, where Shakespeare brings the book of Ovid on to the stage as a prop.[15] The scene opens when the ravished Lavinia chases the young son of Lucius, because the boy bears a book she needs: "'tis Ovid's Metamorphosis' (42). Lavinia leaves through to 'the tragic tale of Philomel', which, in Titus' words, 'treats of Tereus' treason and his rape – / And rape, I fear, was root of thy annoy' (47–9). Lavinia pursues Ovid's Philomela story to communicate to her male family members the 'Pattern' (57) or origin of her ravishment. Then Marcus invokes 'Apollo, Pallas, Jove, or Mercury' to 'Inspire' him, that he 'may this treason find' (66–7), and in the stage direction after line 68 he goes on to demonstrate a curious form of literary invention: '*He writes his name with his staff, and guides it with feet and mouth*'. Subsequently, Marcus says to his niece, 'Heaven guide thy pen to print thy sorrows plain, / That we may know the traitors and the truth!' (75–6), and Lavinia dramatically imitates her uncle's action in the stage direction after line 76: '*She takes the staff in her mouth, and guides it with her stumps, and writes*' the Latin word for rape and names the rapists: '*Stuprum* – Chiron – Demetrius' (78). In this conversation, Shakespeare's language is acute, relying on terms from print culture to perform the authorship of theatre: Marcus prays that the gods will guide Lavinia's 'pen' to 'print' her concealed, emotional condition, so that they may see the outward 'truth'.

Here Shakespeare appears to dramatize an event that (at least in retrospect) looks historic: a conjunction and transfer in literary media, from the printed book of Ovid's poetry to the very Senecan-styled tragedic theatre

---

Bate; see Bate's review in *Times Literary Supplement*. However, Bate is not persuaded that Peele wrote the next scene I discuss, 4.1. Similarly, in his review from *Review of English Studies* R. Berry accepts Act 1 as Peele's but not 4.1.

[14] Jonathan Bate classifies the speech as a 'lyric monologue' (ed. 117) yet sees 'Marcus ... figure[ing] ... forth the process that is at the very core of tragedy': the process of empathy for someone else's suffering and the concomitant understanding of tragic causality (ed. 117; see also 63, 112).

[15] In ascribing 4.1 to Shakespeare, I would note that the overt classicism does not appear until Act 2; that the references to both Philomela and Orpheus, which also start appearing after Act 1, show up in the 1594 *Lucrece*; and that Marcus' speech concluding 4.1 (123–9) looks distinctly 'Shakespearean'.

that Shakespeare scripts.[16] Hence, Marcus refers to 'the lustful sons of Tamora' as '*Performers* of this heinous, bloody deed' and Titus' own Latin quotation from Seneca's *Hippolytus* (79–82). In other words, Shakespeare uses the printed poem of Ovid to stage what becomes a central achievement of Shakespeare's counter-laureate career: the transposition of a culture of printed poetry to a culture of staged theatre.

Lavinia's action represents a stunning counter-laureate moment, in which the *literary* distribution of the signs of *authorship* is worked out.[17] Rather than present himself, Shakespeare transfers authorship to the female, a character within his fiction who is subject to a literary sensibility, at once generic and intertextual. Lavinia becomes Shakespeare's poignant counter-laurel icon. Initially, she exhibits not self-presentation but the *loss* of self-presentation, masculine literary authorship mapped on to the traumatized body of the female. Yet, when she takes up the staff to *perform* the Ovidian book, she becomes Shakespeare's figure for a counter-laureate career transposing page to stage.

Instead of depending on Spenser's overt strategies of self-crowning in the writing of nationhood, then, this early and tragic form of counter-laureate authorship does four things in particular. First, it transfers the image of laurel self-crowning to the other – a character in the fiction, whom many think of as a political, religious, or erotic figure, not a literary one. Second, this form presents the laurel-crowned character as having *lost* the authority of self-presentation. Third, such authorship uses a clear discourse of extemporal intertextuality about authorship itself to present the laurel-crowned character undergoing radical loss. Finally, this form of counter-laureate authorship loads authorial discourse not on to the male author but on to a female character who has been ravished, raped, or otherwise traumatized.

Marcus' blazon of Lavinia as a site for the heterosexual refraction of authorship is not an isolated phenomenon in the Shakespeare canon. Another early

---

[16] Barkan, *Gods Made Flesh*, is on the verge of articulating this idea when he speaks of 'a myth about the competition amongst media of communication' (245). Cf. Keilen: Shakespeare presents Lavinia 'as a relay between the Latin eloquence of Ovid's poem and the new kind of eloquence that arises from the plot of *Titus Andronicus*' (130).

[17] This idea responds to Rowe, who has written most insightfully on agency: 'Lavinia seems to undergo a more radical loss of the signs and instruments of agency. In losing her hands, Lavinia appears to lose the ability to *do* for herself ... Loss of ... means represents a contingent loss of self-representation, of the capacity to "bewray" her own meaning ... Lavinia's stumps seem continually to point elsewhere: indices to the powerful ability of someone else's hand' (*Dead Hands* 70–1). Like other critics, Rowe understands agency in Shakespeare as 'political' (75), but she well articulates the paradox at the heart of Shakespeare's representation: 'Lavinia functions ... as a space where the political distribution of the signs of agency is worked out ... Lavinia converts herself from a figure of dismemberment into a figure of agency' (73, 80).

version appears in *Love's Labor's Lost* during Berowne's comedic representation of 'woman's face' as 'the true Promethean fire' (4.3.297, 300), the tragic fulfillment of which emerges in the late tragedy *Othello*, when the Moor prepares to kill his sleeping wife Desdemona, curiously resurrecting the myth of Prometheus: 'but once put out thy light, / Thou cunning'st pattern of excelling nature, / I know not where is that Promethean heat / That can thy light relume' (5.2.10–13).[18] In chapter 4, we will return to the Prometheus myth from *Love's Labor's Lost*, while in chapter 6 we will look at Friar Francis' description of the fallen Hero's face in terms of 'the story ... printed in her blood' (4.1.122). Then in chapter 8 we will look at Iachimo's description of the sleeping Imogen relying on terms from the story of 'Philomele' (2.2.46). Repeatedly, Shakespeare relies on the discourse of masculine authorship to portray a male character describing the sleeping, unconscious, or traumatized body of the female. Such heterosocial refraction may be Shakespeare's most innovative form of counter-laureate authorship.

HOMOSOCIAL REFRACTION IN *I HENRY IV*

The second form of counter-laureate authorship is a *homosocial* version of *heterosocial refraction*, which we may see represented in Vernon's magnificent description of Hal mounting his horse in *1 Henry IV*, as communicated to Hotspur and others in the rebel camp. Here Shakespeare depicts a masculine voice projecting the terms of male authorship – especially visible in the myths of Pegasus and Mercury – on to the screen of a *male* body and identity.

At the onset of the Battle of Shrewsbury, in Act 4, scene 1, Hotspur has just inquired about the whereabouts of the king's son, and he graphically sets up – and offsets – Vernon's subsequent description by speaking of 'The nimble-footed madcap Prince of Wales, / And his comrades, that daff'd the world aside / And bid it pass' (95–7). In Hotspur's wishful thinking, Hal is athletic ('nimble-footed') but uses agility to escape from the masculine business of warfare. The word 'mad-cap' means 'wildly impulsive or extravagant; bizarre, zany' (*OED*, Def. 1B), and thus playful and theatrical, a sovereign's fool, not heir to the English throne.

In contrast, Vernon offers a quite different picture of Hal:

---

[18] Cf. *Tit* 2.1.16–17, where Aaron likens Tamora under the spell of his own 'charming eyes' to 'Prometheus tied to Caucasus'. In all three cases, Shakespeare associates the female with a classical myth of masculine creativity.

> All furnish'd, all in arms;
> All plum'd like estridges, that with the wind
> Bated like eagles having lately bath'd,
> Glittering in golden coats like images,
> As full of spirit as the month of May,
> And gorgeous as the sun at midsummer;
> Wanton as youthful goats, wild as young bulls.
> I saw young Harry with his beaver on,
> His cushes on his thighs, gallantly arm'd,
> Rise from the ground like feathered Mercury,
> And vaulted with such ease into his seat
> As if an angel [dropp'd] down from the clouds
> To turn and wind a fiery Pegasus,
> And witch the world with noble horsemanship.
>
> (*1 Henry IV* 4.1.97–110)

The speech is pivotal in the action of the play because it is our first verification that Hal is in the process of reforming from tavern wastrel to national hero.[19] Earlier, in the Reconciliation Scene of 3.2, the Prince has responded to his father's judgment that he is 'degenerate' (128) by promising to change: 'I will redeem all this on Percy's head' (132).

Even earlier, however, in Hal's 'I know you all' soliloquy in Act 1, scene 2 (195–217), we learn that the Prince works from a plan: it begins in self-concealment, proceeds to self-presentation, and blossoms in national wonder. He will 'imitate the sun', which disappears behind 'base contagious clouds', so that 'when he pleases again to be himself, / Being wanted, he may be more wond'red at' (197–201). By disguising himself in the costume of a madcap prince daffing the world aside, Hal can prepare to step out of his costume and reveal his true nature as Prince of Wales, producing wonder in his subjects. This process can work because of the special character of wonder. Hal wants his subjects in a state of wonder because it puts them in a condition of admiration: by admiring him, they will be attracted to him; if attracted, they will be pliable, ready for civic duty, service to the nation. We may infer, then, that Hal understands wonder as the magical center of a patriotic process that binds the subject to the sovereign. Through wonder, Hal can carry out his political program of national leadership.

To his credit, the Prince recognizes the theatricality that underwrites his politics of wonder: 'So when this loose behavior I throw off / And pay the debt I never promised ... / By so much shall I falsify men's hopes ... / My reformation glitt'ring o'er my fault, / Shall show more goodly and attract

---

[19] See Gillett, 'Vernon and the Metamorphosis of Hal' 351; see also Weill and Weill, eds. 163.

more eyes' (208–14). For Hal, identity is a form of attire that he can put on and 'throw off', the way an actor does his costume, to 'show' 'more goodly' and 'attract more eyes'. National leadership depends on a theatrical theory of subjective perception controlled by a politics of wonder.

Hal's strategy appears brilliant, but, as we have seen in the Introduction, it runs in the family. As King Henry confides during the Reconciliation Scene, he succeeded Richard II by trumping Richard's unguarded strategy of (laureate) self-presentation through one of self-concealment. Whereas Richard 'had occasion to be seen, / He was but as the cuckoo is in June, / Heard, not regarded; seen, but with such eyes / As, sick and blunted with community', he 'Afford[ed] no extraordinary gaze' (3.2.74–8). In contrast, Henry was 'seldom seen', so that he 'could not stir / But like a comet' he 'was wond'red at': 'I did pluck allegiance from men's hearts' (46–52). Anticipating his son, Henry deploys wonder as a self-conscious strategy of theatre: 'My presence, like a robe pontifical, / Ne'er seen but wond'red at, and so my state, / Seldom but sumptuous, show'd like a feast' (56–8). In this way, both son and father rely on self-concealment leading to self-presentation to create wonder in their subjects. Yet the two strategies also differ: whereas Henry conceals himself from view to appear in a state of royal wonder, Hal conceals himself through disguise visible to the public, only to throw it off and create the effect of wonder.[20]

Yet for Shakespeare, Hal's theatrical strategy also has an intertextual origin. As we have seen, Spenser had begun *The Faerie Queene* by throwing off the 'maske' of 'lowly Shephards weeds' that the 'Muse' has 'taught' him to disguise himself with (1.Proem.1) so that he can write epic. Marlowe had then appropriated this Spenserian strategy of self-presentation for the stage in *Tamburlaine*, when the 'Scythian Shepherd' becomes a 'mighty monarch' (1590 title page), deconstructing Spenser's national authority. Marlowe transfers Spenserian theatricality from the author-figure to a title-character, but Robert Greene was not fooled, and ever since commentators have wanted to equate Tamburlaine with Marlowe himself.[21] Given the national arena in which this curious case of authorship played out – on page and on stage – we likely need to read into Hal's theatrical strategy of national wonder both Spenserian and Marlovian resonance. Once we do, we see Hal emerging as a refracted figure of authorship.[22]

---

[20] In *Henry V*, we learn just how successful Hal's strategy has been (1.1.24–67; 1.2.274–8; 2.4.133–7). For the idea that Hal derives his strategy from his father, see *H5* 3.2.47, 57.

[21] On Greene's Marlowe and its critical afterlife, see Cheney, 'Biographical Representations' 184.

[22] On Marlowe and Hotspur in *Henry IV Part 1*, see Garber, 'Marlovian Vision / Shakespearean Revision'.

Specifically, Vernon's description encourages us to view Prince Hal through a Spenserian lens. Hence, editors routinely gloss the description with Book 1, canto 11 of *The Faerie Queene*.[23] We can build on editorial tradition by looking further at the details of this intriguing moment of extemporal intertextuality – in particular, at the contours of Vernon's speech in the action of the play itself. Shakespeare intimates the presence of authorship by having Vernon's speech perform a 'choric' function (Weill and Weill, eds. 163). Accordingly, the details are 'exceptionally vivid in its imagery, its symbolism of royalty (eagles, gold, sun, heavenly messengers), rich display (plumes, golden coats, spring and summer splendour, gallant arms), and vital energy (beating wings, eagles, spirited warrior, youthful goats, young bulls, horses and their riders)' (Humphreys, ed. 124). We can also see what the royalty, richness, and energy serve: 'Vernon's speech expresses his wonder at the appearance of Hal and the assembled forces, and the disjunctive syntax may therefore voice his own breathless effort to find the appropriate terms for what he has seen, one simile tumbling over the next' (Kastan, ed. 286).

In these terms, Vernon becomes Shakespeare's figure for the national subject in the state of wonder, who, even against his political sympathies, is stunned into a super-rational state of wonder by the sudden transformation he witnesses in the heir to the throne. Through Vernon, the audience understands how successfully Hal's theatre of wonder operates. Hotspur is so outraged he can only cry, 'No more, no more!' (111). Evidently, Shakespeare deploys Vernon's choric speech to get the voice of the author on to the stage. As the details reveal, Shakespeare presents Hal as a chivalric hero out of epic romance, mounting his horse with such 'uncommon strength' that he vaults fully armed into the saddle (Humphreys, ed. 125; see Bevington, ed. 247). As such, this moment of authorship lines up with the epic dynamic discussed in chapter 1: like Achilles, Prince Hal is a military man of superior prowess. Unlike the Greek warrior, however, the English one does not conceal himself behind others in battle, but performs a heroic feat to inspire combat. Such inspiration is animated by a budding form of consciousness – he is 'as full of spirit as the month of May' – rendered consistent with the divine: 'As if an angel [dropp'd] down from the clouds'.

Yet Shakespeare goes further than representing character, when Vernon invests Prince Hal with myths of authorship from antiquity. This exuberant warrior possesses the miraculous ability to 'Rise from the ground like feathered Mercury', and then, once in the saddle, 'To turn and wind a fiery Pegasus', like the gorgon-slaying Perseus. Mercury and Pegasus are the myths that Michael Drayton uses in his 1596 heraldic coat of arms, which

---

[23] See Kastan, ed., *King Henry IV, Part 1* 286; Bevington, ed. 246; Weil and Weil, eds. 163.

shows up next to Shakespeare's coat in the British Library's Harley MS 6140 (chapter 1; see Figure 3a and b).[24] To present his authorial identity as a laureate poet, Drayton uses Pegasus as a figure of poetic fame, surrounded by raindrops of poetic inspiration, and Mercury as a figure of authorial eloquence.

We need not insist that Shakespeare knew the Drayton coat of arms, or that he remembered it; nor need we see Shakespeare alluding to Drayton in Prince Hal. Rather, we may locate in Shakespeare's portrait a familiar iconography of laureate self-fashioning, which authors like Drayton were drawing on at this time. 'Mercury' is especially complex, for traditionally he performs a number of different roles: 'Messenger of the gods, psychopomp or guide of the souls of the dead, god of language, interpretation, silence, and reason; also peacemaker, musician, shepherd god, leader of the dance, god of spring and of thieves'.[25] Among his roles, Mercury is also a poet, especially in his medicinal role as intermediary, figured through his caduceus.[26] Pegasus is less complex; traditionally, this high-flying horse is a figure for the poet's fame, in Drayton's coat of arms and more directly in Spenser's 1591 *The Ruines of Time*: 'fame with golden wings aloft doth flie … / Then who so will vertuous deeds assay / To mount to heaven, on Pegasus must ride, / And with sweete Poets verse be glorifide' (421–7).[27]

While Spenser precedes Drayton in using both Pegasus and Mercury as a recurrent part of his laureate self-fashioning, at the end of *The Ruines of Time* England's national poet presents himself as the witness to Sir Philip Sidney's apotheosis. Significantly, Spenser sees Sidney in terms that anticipate those of Vernon on Prince Hal:

> Still as I gazed, I beheld where stood
> A Knight all arm'd, upon a winged steed,
> The same that was bred of Medusaes blood,
> On which Dan Perseus borne of heavenly seed,
> …
> At last me seem'd wing footed Mercurie,
> From heaven descending to appease their strife,
> The Arke did beare with him above the skie,
> And to those ashes gave a second life.
>
> (Spenser, *Ruines of Time* 645–69)

---

[24] Editors have long noted Vernon's imagery from the heraldic coat of arms in line 100: 'Glittering in golden coats like images'; see Humphreys, ed. 125; Kastan, ed. 286.

[25] Brooks-Davies, 'Mercury' 469.

[26] Brooks-Davies, 'Mercury' 469, citing Bryan, 'Poets, Poetry, and Mercury in Spenser's *Prosopopia*'. In *The Mecurian Monarch*, Brooks-Davies sees Spenser using Mercury to invent an occult myth that represents Elizabeth as a mystical monarch (11–84).

[27] On the symbolism of Pegasus, see Cheney, *Flight*, esp. 252n17.

In this homosocial vision, Spenser uses the classical images of Pegasus and Mercury to represent the Christian knight's chivalric resurrection. Most often, critics link Hal, especially as Henry V, with the Earl of Essex, because the text licenses us to do so (*H5* 5.Ch.29–36). Since Essex had inherited both Sidney's sword and his wife, we should not be surprised to discover that in Vernon's portrait of the chivalric warrior Essex eulogizes Sidney.[28] As Spenser makes clear in his 1596 betrothal poem, *Prothalamion*, after the deaths of Sidney in 1586 and his uncle, the Earl of Leicester, in 1588, the New Poet presents himself as the champion of Essex before a national audience.[29]

Not surprisingly, then, in Vernon's speech Shakespeare glances at still another resonant moment in Spenser, highlighting God's providential care for England's patron saint during his climactic military battle. Toward the end of the Legend of Holiness, Una sees the Redcrosse Knight knocked unconscious by the Dragon during the first day of their fight, and it happens that the knight falls into '*The well of life*' (29). In the morning,

> she saw, where he upstarted brave
> Out of the well, wherein he drenched lay;
> As Eagle fresh out of the Ocean wave,
> Where he hath left his plumes all hoary gray,
> And deckt himselfe with feathers youthly gay,
> Like Eyas hauke up mounts unto the skies,
> His newly budded pineons to assay,
> And merveiles at himselfe, still as he flies:
> So new this new-borne knight to battell new did rise.
>
> (Spenser, *Faerie Queene* 1.11.34)

In this feminized version of heterosexual refraction, Una sees Redcrosse miraculously arise from the well, which the poet presents through a Christian-ized image of resurrection representing baptism (A. C. Hamilton, ed. 143). Spenser likens the ascending knight first to the 'Eagle fresh' rising out of an 'Ocean wave'; this king of fowls has remarkable agency, leaving his old 'plumes all hoary gray' and decking 'himselfe' anew with 'youthful gay' feathers. Next, in another striking image of agency, Spenser likens Redcrosse to the 'Eyas hauke', a young untamed bird who mounts the skies to 'assay' or test his 'newly budded pineons', and in the process to 'merveil … at himselfe', even as he flies. The powerful agency of both the young hawk and the fresh eagle represents the

---

[28] Ogilvy, 'Arcadianism in *1 Henry IV*', discusses a parallel between Hal's speech at the Boarshead Tavern at 2.4.490–505 and Sidney's *Arcadia*; Davidson, 'Falstaff's Catechism on Honor', finds a potential source for Falstaff's famous speech in Sidney and Arthur Golding's translation of Philippe de Mornay's *On the Trueness of the Christian Religion*.

[29] Cheney, *Flight* 225–45.

knight's youthful zest during a moment of spiritual regeneration. While the terms of Una's perception emphasize her lover's agency, the allegory of Christian baptism subtly reminds us of God's grace.[30]

By deploying the images of both Mercury and Pegasus, Shakespeare does not so much present Prince Hal as an author-figure as superimpose on to his portrait the terms of authorship. The effect is double: it portrays Hal as a national hero, yet it leaves traces of the author's construction of the portrait. It is not Vernon within the fiction but the audience witnessing it who gleans the laureateship creating England's national hero.

How, then, does Shakespeare's extemporal intertextual competition with Spenser (and perhaps Drayton) form a moment of counter-laureateship? On the surface, Shakespeare appears to follow Spenser. Yet the representation qualifies as 'counter-laureate' for two reasons. First, Shakespeare presents Vernon representing Hal, rather than having Hal present himself; and second, Shakespeare writes the monarchical icon of national leadership through with the terms of laureate authorship *opaquely*. In Shakespeare's mid-career history play, Prince Hal remains the once and future king of England, yet his text records signs of the author's making of this inspiring national icon.

Although perhaps not as recurrent as heterosocial refraction, homosocial refraction does appear elsewhere in the Shakespeare canon. Hamlet's soliloquy 'O, what a rogue and peasant slave am I' (2.2.550), which reacts to 'this player here', limits the form to theatre. But Philo's opening description of Antony, 'O'erflow[ing] … the measure', 'transform'd / Into a strumpet's fool' (1.1.2, 12–13), presents a more formal metamorphosis from Virgilian epic hero to Ovidian elegiac 'fool'. Coriolanus' ironic description of himself – 'My throat of war be turn'd, / Which quier'd with my drum, into a pipe / Small as an eunuch, or the virgin voice / That babies lull asleep' (3.2.112–15) – introduces a wry parody of homosocial refraction (*SNPP* 204). Perhaps the most famous example occurs in *The Winter's Tale*, when Polixenes describes his youthful friendship with Leontes in terms of a Marlovian discourse of 'boy eternal' (1.2.64).[31] Like heterosocial refraction, homosocial refraction provides a glimpse of Shakespearean authorship in places we might not expect.

---

[30] Helgerson emphasizes the similarity between the Redcrosse Knight and the laureate poet who narrates his legend (*Self-Crowned Laureates* 98–9). Shakespeare borrows Spenser's double-avian image and repeats the action of miraculous ascent. The eagle appears in both descriptions, but whereas Spenser includes a hawk Shakespeare includes the 'estridge'. As editors note, an estridge could be either an ostrich or a goshawk. In the 1596 *Fowre Hymnes*, Spenser uses both hawk and eagle to represent himself in his role as divine poet (Cheney, *Flight* 195–224).

[31] See Cheney, *Profession* 82.

REFRACTED SOCIAL CRITIQUE IN *A MIDSUMMER NIGHT'S DREAM*

The third form of counter-laureate authorship, *refracted social critique*, emerges in a much more obvious place: Theseus' speech on 'the lunatic, the lover, and the poet' in the mid-1590s romantic comedy *A Midsummer Night's Dream* (5.1.7). This time, Shakespeare uses the masculine voice to comment derisively on a community of male and female lovers, who have become subject to the theatrical songs of Puck and Oberon.

We need a concept like counter-authorship to account for why 'the greatest playwright not of his age alone but of all time' so recurrently mocks the figure of the poet,[32] even as we register what splendid theatre Shakespeare makes out of the ignominy of such figures as the Poet in *Timon*, Cinna the Poet in *Julius Caesar*, or, even more compellingly in this last tragedy, the 'cynic' Poet who rudely tries to become Sidney's 'companion' of camps (4.3.123–38), only to be humiliated by Brutus and sent off by Cassius.

Theseus' set speech has long been understood to be of genuine importance, but rarely for what light it might shed on Shakespeare's strange authorship. The speech differs from Marcus' speech on Lavinia or Vernon's on Hal in that Theseus does not portray an individual; nor does he use the convention of the blazon either to sympathize with a traumatized female or to praise a resplendent male. Rather, in a communication to his wife, the Amazonian queen Hippolyta, Theseus reacts to a story told by two sets of lovers, Hermia and Lysander and Helena and Demetrius, who have all undergone a fantastic experience in the woods outside Athens. In this way, the gender dynamic of paired lovers underwriting Theseus' speech coincides exactly with the marital goals of romantic comedy. Unlike Marcus and Vernon, Theseus refers directly to the art of the poet; but rather than celebrate this artist-figure, Theseus ridicules him for his falsehood, and places him in the company of madmen and lovers. Again, the speech does two things simultaneously: nominally, it presents a male sovereign mocking the poet and his grand delusion before his bride; yet paradoxically, the speech relies on some of Shakespeare's most *poetic* language to authorize the very artist being ridiculed. The distinction between the character mocking the poet and the author celebrating him identifies this speech as one of Shakespeare's supreme moments of authorship.[33]

---

[32] Greenblatt, *Will in the World* 11.
[33] Cf. Muir: 'What Theseus intends as a gibe against poetry is a precise account of Shakespeare's method in this play' (*Professional* 27). See also Bloom, *Shakespeare: The Invention of the Human* 169.

We have even more technical grounds for viewing Theseus' speech as a moment of authorship. For textual scholarship establishes that Shakespeare revised the speech, inserting the discourse about the 'poet' as company for the 'lunatic' and the 'lover'.[34] Shakespeare's self-reflexive revision turns a speech about the madness of love into one about the poet's role in forming an eternizing state of consciousness. The principal auditor of Theseus' speech, Hippolyta, serves as a guide to this interpretation. Let us listen in on the famed premarital dialogue.

HIPPOLYTA.   'Tis strange, my Theseus, that these lovers speak of.
THESEUS.   More strange than true. I never may believe
             These antic fables, nor these fairy toys.
             Lovers and madmen have such seething brains,
             Such shaping fantasies, that apprehend
             More than cool reason ever comprehends.
             The lunatic, the lover, and the poet
             Are of imagination all compact.
             One sees more devils than vast hell can hold;
             That is the madman. The lover, all as frantic,
             Sees Helen's beauty in a brow of Egypt.
             The poet's eye, in a fine frenzy rolling,
             Doth glance from heaven to earth, from earth to heaven;
             And as imagination bodies forth
             The forms of things unknown, the poet's pen
             Turns them to shapes, and gives to aery nothing
             A local habitation and a name.
             Such tricks hath strong imagination,
             That if it would but apprehend some joy,
             It comprehends some bringer of that joy;
             Or in the night, imagining some fear,
             How easy is a bush suppos'd a bear!
HIPPOLYTA.   But all the story of the night told over,
             And all their minds transfigur'd so together,
             More witnesseth than fancy's images,
             And grows to something of great constancy;
             But howsoever, strange and admirable.
                          (*A Midsummer Night's Dream* 5.1.1–27)

Significantly, it is Hippolyta who begins and ends the conversation – as if to mark the play's much-discussed rebuke to patriarchal authority, including on

---

[34] For details, see H. F. Brooks, ed. xl-xliii and Appendix III; P. Holland, ed. 257–68; Foakes, ed. 144–6, who observes: 'The additions to the speech of Theseus … are … especially interesting, because they add the figure of the poet to those of the lunatic and lover, and so complicate the argument of the speech by incorporating, as it were, the dramatist reflecting on his art' (146).

the topic of the lovers' 'dream'. In between Hippolyta's authoritative remarks, Theseus delivers a stinging critique of lovers as fit company for madmen and poets. Indeed, from Act I forward, this imperial figure has been the spokesman for a civic world of daytime reason, law, and order, featured in his initial enforcement of the play's most pressing institution, arranged marriage. When Egeus informs the Duke that his daughter, Hermia, refuses to abide by his will and marry Demetrius, choosing Lysander instead, Shakespeare opens up the play's primary cultural problem. Hermia and Lysander's resistance to enforced marriage leads them to escape to the woods, with Demetrius and Helen following. In the play's opening lines, Theseus participates in the institution he tries to enforce when reminding his Amazonian bride, 'I wooed thee with my sword, / And won thy love doing thee injuries' (1.1.16–17).[35] From the opening scene to the closing one, Shakespeare undercuts the Duke's cultural authority, allowing him to reign on stage with conviction, yet humourously subjected to powers he cannot see.

The contents of Theseus' speech are so well known that we need not belabor them here. Suffice it to say that this rational monarch manages to evoke the primary idea in Renaissance poetics, voiced eloquently by Sidney in *The Defence of Poesy*: in contradistinction to Plato's banishment of poets from the republic for lying, poets use their imagination to create a golden world higher than nature, performing society's most civilizing work. In Theseus' eloquent words: 'And as imagination bodies forth / The forms of things unknown, the poet's pen / Turns them to shapes, and gives to aery nothing / A local habitation and a name'. Like Plato, Theseus criticizes the poet, reducing imagination to a theatrical 'trick' that deceives the rational mind into mistaking a 'bush' for a 'bear'.[36] Yet Shakespeare's revision to the speech, in the very terms of Western poetics, reveals a particularly self-conscious moment of authorial representation.

We can multiply the presence of authorship through attention to intertextuality, which undermines Theseus' critique of the poet and lays bare a dialogue on the art of poetry right within the stage production. Editors find not merely Sidney and Plato but Chaucer, Sackville, Lyly, and Golding's Ovid.[37] In line II, Shakespeare also likely evokes Marlowe's *Doctor Faustus* – 'Sees Helen's beauty in a brow of Egypt' – perhaps to critique Marlowe for his Faustian hyperbole about erotic 'beauty'. Most important for the present argument, Theseus' scorn for 'These antic

---

[35] See Montrose, '*A Midsummer Night's Dream* and the Shaping Fantasies of Elizabethan Culture' 82.
[36] See H. F. Brooks, ed. 104; P. Holland, ed. 231; Foakes, ed. 124.
[37] See H. F. Brooks, ed. 103–5; P. Holland, ed. 230–2.

fables' and 'fairy toys' evokes and formally *parodies* the national epic of Spenser's *Faerie Queene*.[38]

By transporting Spenser's romantic epic faeryland to the comedic woods outside Athens, Shakespeare crafts a new theatrical space for his poetic authority. He does so finally through Hippolyta's concluding response to her husband's mockery, revealing that Shakespeare follows Spenser in presenting the fairies as more than 'fancy's images', or simple products of the mind. By emphasizing the way in which the lovers 'grow ... to something of great constancy ... / ... howsoever, strange and admirable', Shakespeare uses the Spenserian world of fairy to advocate the utility of the poet and his metaphysical art within the civic sphere. Yet Shakespeare also 'counters' Spenser, by concealing the authority of his art within a monarch's critique; by transporting the scene from printed poetry to stage theatre; and by rehearsing the epic romance's civic project on behalf of companionate marriage in the genre of comedy.

If looked at closely, then, Hippolyta's concluding speech performs what may be English literature's first commentary on the most precious detail of Spenser's fairy poetics, memorably revealed in another famous dream, that of Prince Arthur, once upon a midsummer's day, about the Faerie Queene herself:

> When I awoke, and found her place devoyd,
> And nought but pressed gras, where she had lyen,
> I sorrowed all so much, as earst I joyed,
> And washed all her place with watry eyen.
> From that day forth I lov'd that face divine.
> From that day forth I cast in careful mind,
> To seeke her out with labour, and long tyne.
>
> (Spenser, *Faerie Queene* 1.9.15)

Through the detail of the 'pressed gras', Spenser represents the material presence of the dream spirit, revealing consciousness to originate in a divine or 'fairy' world, and lending to the Prince the evidence he needs to set out on his quest to find the personal embodiment of 'that face divine'.[39]

---

[38] For persuasive detail, see Bednarz, 'Imitation of Spenser in *A Midsummer Night's Dream*': Shakespeare appears 'both deeply impressed by Spenser's achievement and critical of it' (97–8).

[39] Frye often recalls Keats on Adam's dream in Milton's *Paradise Lost*, in which 'a mental image ... becomes reality' (*Return of Eden* 74), but to my knowledge Frye does not connect the Miltonic moment of 'revelation' with either Spenser's 'pressed gras' or Hippolyta's speech, including in *A Natural Perspective*. In chapter 8, on *Cymbeline*, we shall find more technical evidence for Shakespeare's interest in Spenser's dream image of the 'pressed gras'.

In *A Midsummer Night's Dream*, Shakespeare counters Spenser one final way. While Arthur's dream of Gloriana forms part of the larger narrative of epic romance controlled by the first-person narrator, the collective dream of the young Athenian lovers emerges independently of any authorial presence. Although this may be the product of dramatic convention, which substitutes the authorial 'I' for third-person character, Shakespeare's insertion of 'the poet' into the speech about the truth content of the fairy 'dream' highlights the central paradox we are exploring: in the fiction of the *Dream*, Theseus is mistaken, because no 'poet' ever appears as the creator of the lovers' fantastic experience. The woods outside Athens are peopled not by poets but by fairies, especially Oberon and Puck, who direct the performance of enchantment, while other figures of the theatre merely visit (those rude mechanicals who rehearse an Ovidian play). What Theseus' speech finally communicates, then, is wonder indeed. By not being able to see the 'poet' who performs the illusion, the audience comes to read into the script the *author invisible*. Shakespeare nowhere appears, yet all signs point to him, howsoever strange and admirable.

BI-SOCIAL REFRACTION IN *THE TEMPEST*

The fourth and final form of counter-laureate authorship, *bi-social refraction*, combines the first and third forms, as represented in Prospero's farewell to his art in *The Tempest*. Here Shakespeare uses a fictional masculine voice to ventriloquize a feminine myth of art, as revealed initially through the well-known intertextuality with Ovid's Medea, and subsequently through intertextuality with Spenser.

In contrast to the other three forms, Prospero's farewell to magic has long been regarded as a moment of theatrical authorship. As 'one of the most sustained passages of close imitation of any author' in the Shakespeare canon, critics have unsurprisingly privileged Shakespeare's imitation of Ovid.[40] For, as we have seen, Prospero bids farewell to his art by paraphrasing Medea's famous speech on her magic in Book 7 of the *Metamorphoses* (196–209), especially as Arthur Golding Englished it in his 1567 translation.[41]

Immediately after Ariel convinces Prospero that 'The rarer action is / In virtue than in vengeance' (5.1.27–8), the mage, alone on stage, draws '*a*

---

[40] Lyne, 'Ovid, Golding' 150.

[41] Shakespeare also likely evokes Faustus' final Ovidian monologue in Marlowe's tragedy, 'I'll burn my books' (A text 5.2.122), with Prospero's 'I'll drown my book' (57). See J. Bate, *Genius of Shakespeare* 129.

magic circle with his staff (SD after line 32), and utters his valedictory incantation:

> Ye elves of hills, brooks, standing lakes, and groves,
> And ye that on the sands with printless foot
> Do chase the ebbing Neptune, and do fly him
> When he comes back; you demi-puppets that
> By moonshine do the green sour ringlets make,
> Whereof the ewe not bites; and you whose pastime
> Is to make midnight mushrumps, that rejoice
> To hear the solemn curfew: by whose aid
> (Weak masters though ye be) I have bedimm'd
> The noontide sun, call'd forth the mutinous winds,
> And 'twixt the green sea and the azur'd vault
> Set roaring war; to the dread rattling thunder
> Have I given fire, and rifted Jove's stout oak
> With his own bolt; the strong-bas'd promontory
> Have I made shake, and by the spurs pluck'd up
> The pine and cedar. Graves at my command
> Have wak'd their sleepers, op'd, and let 'em forth
> By my so potent art. But this rough magic
> I here abjure; and when I have requir'd
> Some heavenly music (which even now I do)
> To work mine end upon their senses that
> This airy charm is for, I'll break my staff,
> Bury it certain fadoms in the earth,
> And deeper than did ever plummet sound
> I'll drown my book.   (*The Tempest* 5.1.33–57)

Instead of looking at Prospero's speech simply as 'a form of intertextuality' (Lyne, 'Orid, Golding' 150), we might consider it also as a form of authorship. Along this avenue, intertextuality operates as a principal mode of authorship, and what is at stake is not simply an artistic technique but the terms of an author's literary career.

The author of Prospero's speech is a poet-playwright working at the end of his career, invested both in the theatre and in the printing house. We need to read Prospero's speech in terms of both 'stage and page', drama and poetry, in part because Shakespeare relies on overt theatrical intertextuality with the printed book of Ovid's poetry; but also because the speech includes a discourse of books ('I'll burn my book'), theatre ('demi-puppets' [36]), and most ingeniously, printed poetry: 'printless foot' (34; see Introduction). Prospero's speech is as fine a theatrical representation of invisible poetic authorship as Shakespeare produced.

The other major intertextual trace in Prospero's Ovidian art is the print-poetry of Spenser – in particular, a passage in *The Faerie Queene* that shares with the Ovidian one an artistic discourse of magic. In Book 3, canto 3, Spenser describes the magic art of his most important figure of magic, Merlin, who 'had in Magick more insight, / Than ever him before or after living wight' (11):

> For he by words could call out of the sky
> > Both Sunne and Moone, and make them him obay:
> > The land to sea, and sea to maineland dry,
> > And darkesome night he eke could turne to day:
> > Huge hostes of men he could alone dismay,
> > And hostes of men of meanest things could frame,
> > When so him list his enimies to fray:
> > That to this day for terror of his fame,
> The feends do quake, when any him to them does name.
>
> (Spenser, *Faerie Queene* 3.3.12)

Here Spenser presents his arch-magician able to control the sun and moon, the land and sea, even warring armies, but also the 'feends' themselves – in short, the spirit world, the world of astral bodies, and the human sphere. As with Prospero's speech, Spenser's portrait of Merlin is almost certainly indebted to Ovid's portrait of Medea.[42]

In Golding's translation, Medea addresses Hecate and other demons of the night in terms that anticipate not just Prospero's magic but Merlin's:

> Ye Ayres and windes: ye Elves of Hilles, of Brookes, of Woods alone,
> Of standing Lakes, and of the Night approche ye everychone.
> Through helpe of whom (the crooked bankes much wondring at the thing)
> I have compelled streames to run cleane backward to their spring.
> By charmes I make the calme Seas rough, and make ye rough Seas plaine
> And cover all the Skie with Cloudes, and chase them thence againe.
> By charmes I rayse and lay the windes, and burst the Vipers jaw,
> And from the bowels of the Earth both stones and trees doe drawe.
> Whole Woods and Forestes I remove: I make the Mountaines shake
> And even the Earth it selfe to grone and fearfully to quake.
> I call up dead men from their graves: and thee O lightsome Moone
> I darken oft, though beaten brasse abate thy perill soone
> Our Sorcerie dimmes the Morning faire, and darkes ye Sun at Noone.
>
> (Ovid, *Metamorphoses* 7.265–77; trans. Golding)

---

[42] A. C. Hamilton cites only Virgil, Eclogue 8.69 (ed. 313), while other modern editions remain silent (e.g., Maclean and Prescott, eds.). The *Variorum Spenser* cites Horace, Epode 5.45; Virgil, Eclogue 8.69; Lucan, *Pharsalia* 6.499–504 (2: 225–6).

This is not the place to make a full case for the need to add Ovid and Golding to the annotation of Spenser's Merlin. As one of the most detailed – and famous – descriptions of magic in antiquity, the case would not be hard to make.[43]

Instead, let us look at Figure 8, which inventories the *objects of magic control* performed by the three magicians, with Xs indicating shared features.

Of the twelve objects of control identified, Ovid's Medea, Spenser's Merlin, and Shakespeare's Prospero share five: they all command nature spirits; move the land; blow the wind; dim the sun; and dabble in demons. Of the twelve objects of control, Ovid's Medea and Shakespeare's Prospero share six, while Ovid's Medea and Spenser's Merlin also share six. Finally, Spenser's Merlin and Shakespeare's Prospero share five objects of control. Not simply, then, do we need to consider Ovid's Medea as a model for Spenser's Merlin. We also need to include Spenser's Merlin as a model for Shakespeare's Prospero.[44]

Relying on Renaissance convention, Spenser uses Merlin's magic to represent his own magical poetics.[45] Thus, Spenser says of the magic mirror that Merlin has made for Britomart's father, King Ryence, 'It was a famous Present for a Prince, / And worthy worke of infinite reward, / That treasons could bewray, and foes convince; / Happie this Realme, had it remained ever since' (3.2.21.6–9). Like Spenser, Shakespeare uses magic as a metaphor for poesy, but transposes the literary art from epic romance to stage romance. The poet-playwright may gesture to Spenser's fairyland in the opening lines of Prospero's speech, when the mage invokes the aid of the fairy world of 'elves', who 'By moonshine do the green sour ringlets make' – a feature not present in Ovid or Golding. But Shakespeare also intimates a particular stance toward the politicized genre of epic, when Prospero refers to the traditional tree of epic, the oak, in lines 45–6: 'and rifted Jove's stout oak / With his own bolt'.[46] The word 'rifted' means 'Split, cleft, cloven; broken by a rift or rifts' (*OED*), perhaps drawing attention to the violence inherent in Shakespeare's counter-epic art. Prospero's use of Jove's own thunderbolt to cleave open Jove's tree suggests a form of political subversion, for which Ovid is famous, even though the image does not appear in

---

[43] In *Spenser and Ovid*, Syrithe Pugh observes that Spenser imitates features of Ovid's Medea at *FQ* 3.1.60.1 (126–7).

[44] Only Kermode glosses Prospero's speech with Spenser (ed. 114). But curiously, he glosses Prospero's 'Weak masters' in line 41 with *FQ* 3.7.4, about the old witch making the False Florimell.

[45] See Cheney, '"Secret Powre Unseene"'.

[46] On the oak as the tree of epic in Virgil, Lucan, and Spenser, see Cheney, '"Novells of His Devise"'. In Prospero's 'multitudinous winds', Vaughan and Vaughan see a 'possible reference to an episode in the *Odyssey*' (ed. 265).

	nature spirits	land	sea	trees	clouds	wind	moon	sun	vipers	thunder	enemies	spirits of dead/ creates men
Ovid's Medea	X	X	X	X	X	X	X	X	X			X
Spenser's Merlin	X	X	X			X	X	X		X	X	X
Shakespeare's Prospero	X	X		X		X		X				X

Figure 8. Intertextual magic: Ovid's Medea, Spenser's Merlin, Shakespeare's Prospero

Medea's speech. Unlike Golding, Ovid does refer to the 'oak', but he does not name Jove, presumably because the god was connected with Augustus Caesar. Shakespeare is bolder, although he retains Ovid's symbolic language, suggesting a literary art that uses the sovereign's political power against him, even as he himself appropriates that power for dramatic use.

Prospero's Medean speech on magic technically qualifies as a counter-laureate act, not simply for its ghostly hair-raising violence but also for its turn away from politics. Prospero evokes magic power to 'abjure' the art, while Shakespeare dilates on the power of a magician's art in order to bid it farewell. Moreover, when Prospero vows, 'I'll break my staff', Shakespeare may glance at the most famous instrument-breaking act in Elizabethan literature. At the close of the *Januarye* eclogue of *The Shepheardes Calender*, Colin Clout ends his complaint to Pan with a climactic valediction: 'Both pype and Muse, shall sore the while abye' (71). Spenser then offers his own narration: 'So broke his oaten pype, and downe dyd lye' (72). In *December*, Spenser brings closure to this authorial act, when Colin announces, 'Here will I hang my pype upon this tree, / Was never pype of reede did better sounde' (141–2). Years later, in Book 6, canto 10, of *The Faerie Queene*, Spenser returns to the topos of the broken poetic instrument. On Mount Acidale, after Calidore causes Colin's magical Dance of the Graces to vanish, the shepherd 'for fell despight / Of that displeasure, broke his bag-pipe quight' (18.4–5). From early till late, Spenser presents his persona breaking his poetic instrument, again and again. By contrast, in *The Tempest* Prospero renounces his art, once and for all.

In this regard, Shakespeare's late portrait of the author as an old man differs from that of the old laureate Spenser, who ends his national self-presentation in disillusionment with his laureate enterprise.[47] In contrast, at the end of *The Tempest*, Prospero does not appear disillusioned but *resigned*. He gives up his art not because he is pessimistic about its potency, but because he is *satisfied*. He has completed his 'project' (5.1.1) of bringing Alonso, Sebastian, and Antonio to justice, and forgiven them, along with their comical counterparts, Caliban, Stephano, and Trinculo; he has also secured the dynastic marriage of his daughter to Ferdinand, prince of Naples. With 'Every third thought' toward the 'grave' (5.1.312), Prospero does not lose faith, either in life or in art; he becomes resigned to the end of art as the end to life. In his final action, voiced in the play's Epilogue, he subordinates himself to the servant-role of Ariel, asking the audience to 'set' him 'free' (20). Rather than abandon authorship, Prospero disappears powerfully into it.

---

[47] On Spenser's final disillusionment with his laureate career, see Helgerson, *Self-Crowned Laureates*, esp. 82–100.

CHAPTER 3

Lyric poetry in Shakespearean theatre: As You Like It, 1 Henry IV, Henry V, The Tempest

> The truest poetry is the most feigning.
> *As You Like It* 3.3.19–20

Shakespeare's counter-laureate authorship does not always proceed through the authorial strategy of self-concealment or operate through the artistic principle of refraction. To complement his self-conscious staging of theatrical art, Shakespeare recurrently puts the art of poetry on the stage. Most obviously, he writes much of his dramatic corpus in poetic verse, whether in blank verse or in rhyme. But he also includes over 130 lyrics in his plays, as poems or songs, with over 100 of them original compositions.[1] Not simply, then, are his plays made largely of poetry but set-lyrics appear in them. Most often, Shakespeare clarifies the poet-figures who write, sing, or perform these lyrics, such as the courtier Orlando in *As You Like It*, who fondly hangs his love poems to Rosalind on trees in the Forest of Arden. In Shakespeare's plays, the performance of poetry becomes a recurrent stage action, and the presence of active poet-figures means that characters habitually carry on a conversation about poetry.

The epigraph to this chapter registers one such conversation, when the court clown Touchstone in *As You Like It*, also visiting the Forest of Arden, tries to woo the country girl Audrey:

TOUCHSTONE.　Truly, I would the gods had made thee poetical.
AUDREY.　　　I do not know what 'poetical' is. Is it honest in deed and word? Is it a true thing?
TOUCHSTONE.　No, truly; for the truest poetry is the most feigning.
　　　　　　　　　　　　　　　　　　　　　　　　(*As You Like It* 3.3.15–20)

If the tone of this conversation is playful, the terms are aesthetically serious, confirming that Shakespeare imagines poetry as both a language and an action ('word' and 'deed'), and showing the author to enter a historical debate about the nature of poetry and the new medium it serves, theatre, as

---

[1] Collected conveniently in Hubler, ed., *Shakespeare's Songs and Poems*.

90

the climactic word 'feigning' hints.[2] In Shakespearean drama, the conversation the audience hears turns out to exist in detailed, compelling form from the beginning of his dramatic career to the end – from *The Two Gentlemen of Verona* to *The Tempest* – and constitutes a sustained fiction about the art of poetry within the plays.

While we have had several valuable studies of Shakespeare's fictions of the poet and the art of poetry, none situates the topic within the context of Shakespeare's counter-laureate authorship, or his status as a sixteenth-century poet-playwright, or seems to have become a part of the critical conversation today.[3] Collectively, these studies draw two major conclusions that may have worked to cancel each other out. On the one hand, Shakespeare recurrently represents his knowledge of Renaissance poetics, with its humanist theories of mimesis and didacticism, divine inspiration and Platonic furor, as presented in classical, medieval, and Elizabethan treatises, and especially illustrated in Sidney's *Defence of Poesy* and practiced in Spenser's *Faerie Queene*. On the other hand, Shakespeare habitually mocks the poet and his civilizing achievement, as Theseus does famously in *A Midsummer Night's Dream* and Touchstone wryly in *As You Like It*. Consequently, we are told, Shakespeare came to London to be a poet, but then abandoned a literary career for the profession of the theatre: sometime during the 1590s, 'he stopped being a poet'.[4]

To reach an alternative conclusion, we might look further into the presence of 'poetry' in Shakespeare's dramatic corpus. As we shall see, Shakespeare never stops being a poet. Writing poetry throughout his career, including freestanding poems, he exhibits a fascination with the multifaceted art of the poet from early till late, in plays as in poems. While some of his most vibrant theatre mocks the poet and his art, such mockery constitutes a second major strategy of counter-laureate authorship, joining that of self-concealed refraction. Not simply does Shakespearean mockery almost always work paradoxically, to mark off the achievement of the author, as it does in the case of Touchstone, or, as we shall see, Hotspur and the French Dolphin from the

---

[2] In *Shakespeare, the Invention of the Human*, Bloom singles out this line as 'Shakespeare's own credo' (220).

[3] For the steady trickle of studies, from 1950 to 2003, all very helpful, see Pettet, 'Shakespeare's Conception of Poetry'; E. R. Hunter, *Shakespeare and the Common Sense* 89–133; Muir, *Shakespeare the Professional* 22–40; Schmidgall, *Shakespeare and the Poet's Life* 123–60; Faas, *Shakespeare's Poetics*, esp. vii–xxiv; Hyland, *Introduction to Shakespeare's Poems* 35–41. For an excellent allied study focusing more on metatheatre, see Kernan, 'Shakespeare's Essays on Dramatic Poesy'.

[4] Schmidgall 2. This is Schmidgall's book-length thesis: 'Shakespeare ... appears to have left the arena of fashionable poets for that of "quick comedians", thinking ... that his professional pleasure and profit might lie in the [theatre]' (202).

Henriad. At times, Shakespeare releases his authorship more affirmatively into the spirit of poetry, as he does in the case of Ariel.

FEIGNING POETRY

To begin, we might recall Shakespeare's own vocabulary of poetry. For instance, as the dialogue from *As You Like It* indicates, he uses the word 'poetry' itself, along with the related terms 'poesy', 'poetical', 'poem', and 'poet' or 'poets' – a total of about fifty times.[5] Thus, in *Two Gentlemen* Proteus remarks to the Duke of Milan, 'Orpheus' lute was strung with poets' sinews' (3.2.77) – Orpheus being a legendary founder of poetry in Greek and Roman mythology and understood in the Renaissance to be a figure for the civilizing power of the poet.[6] Similarly, Shakespeare uses 'rhyme' and its cognates, and 'verse' and its cognates (over 100 times); these are the more usual terms by which Shakespeare designates a poem or poetry. Thus, in *As You Like It* Orlando says, 'Hang there, my verse, in witness of my love' (3.2.1).[7]

Shakespeare also refers to the traditional sources of poetic inspiration, the Muse or Nine Muses, another twenty times, as when Iago, trying to invent a poem before Desdemona, remarks, 'my Muse labors, / And thus she is deliver'd' (2.1.127–8). As the earlier quotation about Orpheus indicates, Shakespeare often links poets with such musical instruments as the lute (20 times) or harp (5) and the pastoral pipe (20). He does not often use generic terms for poetry, but he uses 'pastoral' and related terms 3 times, 'sonnet' 14, 'epitaph' 18, 'satire' 5, 'elegies' 2, 'epigram' 1, 'ballad' 24, and 'song' 77. In *Love's Labour's Lost*, for instance, the country schoolmaster Holofernes asks Sir Nathaniel, the curate, 'will you hear an extemporal epitaph on the death of the deer?' (4.2.50–1), and produces a six-line memorial poem on said beast in a sixain stanza rhyming *ababcc* (56–61), beginning, 'The preyful Princess pierc'd and prick'd a pretty pleasing pricket' (56). The word 'ditty' occurs nine times, as in *A Midsummer Night's Dream* when Oberon says to the fairies attending him, 'And this ditty, after me, / Sing, and dance it trippingly' (5.1.395–6). Sometimes, Shakespeare uses even more unfamiliar

---

[5] All statistics come from Spevack, *Complete and Systematic Concordance to the Works of Shakespeare*.

[6] See Cain, 'Spenser and the Renaissance Orpheus'; Armitage, 'Dismemberment of Orpheus'.

[7] By 'poet', Shakespeare sometimes means 'playwright' (*Ham* 2.2.328); and on the one occasion he uses the word 'poem' he means 'play' (*Ham* 2.2.366). The absence of a modern distinction between a poem and a play, a poet and a playwright, speaks to the early modern fusion of poetry and theatre that is the subject of this book. Cf. Maguire, who relies on Webster's preface to *The Duchess of Malfi* to distinguish between poem and play within drama itself (*Shakespearean Suspect Texts* 155).

terms, as when Holofernes calls a poem a 'canzonet' (4.2.120), or Viola in *Twelfth Night* says she will 'write loyal cantons of contemned love' (1.5.270).[8]

As the mention of songs, pipes, lutes, and harps reveals, in Shakespearean drama as in Renaissance culture, the vocabulary of poetry is deeply connected to the vocabulary of music. Sometimes, Shakespeare means music (*R2* 5.5.41–3, *WT* 5.3.98), but often he depends on the Elizabethan convention that metaphorizes music as poetry, song as lyric poetry, the musician as a poet.[9] For the Elizabethans, Orpheus is more precisely the archetype of the singer-musician as civilizing poet, and Shakespeare's fellow writer Edmund Spenser had put this convention at the center of his national art – his self-presentation as 'the Virgil of England'[10] – by depicting his Orphic persona, Colin Clout, as a musician-singer, in both his inaugural pastoral poem, *The Shepheardes Calender*, and his national epic, *The Faerie Queene* (Book 6, canto 10).[11] Shakespeare often follows suit, so that the original 100-plus dramatic lyrics firmly embed the figure of the poet, as well as the topic of poetry, in his plays, more so than perhaps is often realized. In *The Taming of the Shrew*, he reveals how closely he imagines the two arts, when the trickster Tranio says to Lucentio, 'Music and poesy use to quicken you' (1.1.36), or when Baptista says that Kate delights 'In music, instruments, and poetry' (93).

In *Measure for Measure*, a remarkable performative moment linking poetry with music occurs. Shakespeare concludes Act 3, scene 2, with a poem, and then, without verbal transition, he opens Act 4, scene 1, with a song, followed by a statement about the Orphic art of music. Specifically, in concluding 3.2, Duke Vincentio performs a soliloquized poem of rhymed couplets (22 lines) – his only soliloquy in the play – to communicate his plan to the audience: 'So disguise shall by th' disguised / Pay with falsehood false exacting, / And perform an old contracting' (280–2). As the word 'perform' and the doubly iterated 'disguise' indicates, the Duke announces a theatrical plan to sift his counselor, Angelo, who has sentenced Juliet and Claudio to death for pre-marital intercourse. Shakespeare likely portrays the Duke performing poetry to mark off a stable ground for truth, detachable from the corrupt theatricality

---

[8] On 'cantons', see *SNPP* 33.

[9] See esp. Lindley, *Shakespeare and Music*, who tends to treat the songs in Shakespeare's plays under the rubric of performance, neglecting their composition for both page and stage. Nonetheless, what Lindley says about musical figures such as Orpheus often applies to Shakespeare's figures of the poet.

[10] Thomas Nashe, *Pierce Pennilesse*, in McKerrow, *Works of Thomas Nashe* 1: 299.

[11] Spenser's glossarist E. K. goes so far as to equate music with poetry, citing classical precedent: 'Musick,) that is Poetry, saith Terence, *Qui artem tractant musicam*, speking of Poetes' (*Dec* 165–6). Hence, Spenser calls his national epic a 'song': 'Fierce warres and faithfull loves shall moralize my song' (1.Proem.1). On Spenser and Colin Clout as Orphic poets, see Cheney, *Spenser's Famous Flight*. On Orpheus's songs and writing, see Keilen, *Vulgar Eloquence* 32–88.

plaguing Venice. Accordingly, to open Act 4, Mariana enters, accompanied by a Boy *'singing'* (SD) a 'Song': 'Take, O, take those lips away, / That sweetly were forsworn' (1–2). When the Duke enters *'disguised as a friar'* (SD after line 6), Mariana hastily commands the Boy, 'Break off thy song' (7). The embarrassed Mariana apologizes to the reverent man for catching her 'so musical' during her time of sadness, and tries to explain: 'My mirth it much displeas'd, but pleas'd my woe' (11–13). Yet the Duke will have none of it, and he supports her practice by producing a poetic couplet on the ethical power of Orphic art: "Tis good; though music oft hath such a charm / To make bad good, and good provoke to harm' (14–15).

The Duke's sudden movement into rhymed couplets concluding Act 3 and the Boy's song opening Act 4 have seemed so peculiar that scholars have long questioned whether Shakespeare wrote either. Most scholars now believe that he wrote the Duke's poem, while they remain divided over whether he wrote the song.[12] Given the inconclusiveness of the debate, it is not unreasonable to assign the shift from the Duke's poem to the Boy's song to Shakespeare. Yet it might be safer to suggest that we are witnessing here a classic fable of modern Shakespearean scholarship: we have fixated on the one moment in this metadramatic play infiltrated by the *poetical*, in both its stylized Shakespearean lyric forms, performed poem and performed song. It is, we might add, the juxtaposition of both lyric forms as a device of interruption that makes the structural hinge between two Acts near the center of this play so striking, and problematic, as if the text were doing everything it could to draw attention to itself.

An alternative approach might find a signature moment here, in which Shakespeare as a new English poet-playwright imprints his lyric seal on the dramatic scene. Such an approach helps explain the shift from intense interior tragedy without resolution in the Duke's soliloquized poem, to controlled social comedy with resolution in the Boy's Song and its follow-up conversation between the Duke and Mariana.[13] The use of lyric to mark the shift is all the more striking because *Measure for Measure* is the first play since *The Comedy of Errors* to be relatively free of *poetical* discourse and representation. In disguise, the Duke is himself a man of the theatre, the governor figure who controls the action, yet it is he who also inserts poetry into the play and then gives voice to the value of Orphic song.

[12] For a recent review, see *Riverside* 619, which reports that the *Oxford Shakespeare* assign the song to Middleton, but that Gibbons disagrees and assigns the song to Shakespeare. Lever was first to propose that two lines in the Duke's poem are missing (ed. 95).
[13] Noted by Bawcutt (ed. 50).

In addition to Orpheus, whom Shakespeare elsewhere mentions five times and alludes to several others, Shakespeare mentions a whole host of mythological figures conventionally representative of poetry. He mentions Arion, another legendary founder of poetry (once), but alludes to him elsewhere (*MND* 2.1.148–54; *AC* 5.2.87–9); Pegasus, the flying horse who used his hoof to open the Muses' fountain on Mount Helicon (3 times); Actaeon, the voyeur of Diana who was turned into a stag and became for Shakespeare's favorite poet, Ovid, a figure for the author in political exile (3 times); and Prometheus, who stole fire from heaven and was punished for his crime, becoming a figure for the political danger of the poet's integrity (4 times). In *Two Gentlemen*, Shakespeare takes the shape-changing poet-figure Proteus from classical mythology (cf. *3H6* 3.2.192) and makes him a lead character in the plot. As Proteus' earlier reference to Orpheus indicates, this character takes a considerable interest in the art of poetry.

If we look into these mythological references, we discover a detailed network of discourse on the poet and his art. The network expands considerably when we consider Philomela (mentioned 14 times), the Athenian princess raped by her brother-in-law Tereus and metamorphosed into the nightingale (another 14), the Western icon of the poet who produces powerful music out of tragic suffering – in Ovid and Virgil as in Spenser.[14] As noted in earlier chapters, during two memorable moments of his career, one early and one late, Shakespeare brings the most important version of the Philomela myth on to the stage as a prop, through the 'book' of 'Ovid's Metamorphosis' (*Tit* 4.1.41–2): in *Titus Andronicus*, Marcus says, 'This is the tragic tale of Philomel' (4.1.47); and in *Cymbeline*, Iacomo discovers that Imogen 'hath been reading late / The tale of Tereus: here the leaf's turn'd down / Where Philomele gave up' (2.2.44–6).[15]

Unlike his rival Ben Jonson, Shakespeare is notoriously reticent about naming historical figures other than those he fictionalizes in his English history plays or Roman tragedies, but as the case of *Titus* indicates he does occasionally name historical poets: in addition to Ovid (4 times), he mentions Horace (3), Juvenal (4), Petrarch (1), and Mantuan (3). In *Romeo and Juliet*, for instance, Mercutio says of Romeo, 'Now is he for the numbers that Petrarch flow'd in' (2.4.38–9), while in *Shrew* Tranio tells Lucentio that they should not 'As Ovid be an outcast quite abjur'd' (1.1.33). Among Ovid's poems, Shakespeare certainly mentions his favorite book, the *Metamorphoses*, but he also refers to the *Ars amatoria* (*Art of Love*)

---

[14] See Cheney, *Flight* 81–6, *SNPP* 130–4, 234–6.
[15] See Thompson, 'Philomel in *Titus Andronicus* and *Cymbeline*'.

(*TS* 4.2.8) and the *Heroides* (*Heroical Epistles*), the latter quoted in Latin (*TS* 3.1.28–9; *3H6* 1.3.48).

In addition to classical and continental poets, Shakespeare brings English poets on to his stage. Most visibly, he presents John Gower, author of the medieval poem *Confessio Amantis*, as the Prologue and Chorus to *Pericles*, written probably in collaboration with George Wilkins: 'To sing a song that old was sung, / From ashes ancient Gower is come' (Pr.1–2). Similarly, in *Two Noble Kinsmen*, also written late, this time in collaboration with John Fletcher, the playwright(s) stage(s) Chaucer's 'The Knight's Tale', the opening chivalric poem of *The Canterbury Tales*, understood during the period (including by Spenser) as Chaucer's epic: 'A learned, and a poet never went / More famous yet 'twixt Po and silver Trent. / Chaucer (of all admir'd) the story gives' (Pr.11–13).[16]

Shakespeare can also use the stage to name contemporary English poets and books of poetry. In *The Merry Wives of Windsor*, for instance, Abraham Slender refers to his 'Book of Songs and Sonets' (1.1.199), also known as *Tottel's Miscellany* (1557), which first published poems by the Henrician court poets Sir Thomas Wyatt and Henry Howard, Earl of Surrey. In *Twelfth Night*, the clown Feste sings a line from one of Wyatt's lyrics, 'Hey, Robin, jolly Robin' (4.2.72). In *Merry Wives* as well, Falstaff courts Mrs Ford by quoting a line from Sir Philip Sidney's *Astrophil and Stella*, 'Have I caught thee, my heavenly jewel?' (3.3.43; *AS*, Second Song, line 1). While Shakespeare can certainly see poetry as a private, manuscript, or oral art, he tends to imagine poetry most often as a product of print culture. In *Shrew*, for instance, Gremio tells Hortensio that he is enquiring after a schoolmaster for Bianca, one 'well read in poetry / And other books' (1.2.169–70). In *Love's Labour's Lost*, the fantastical Spaniard, Don Adriano de Armado, voices many of the contours we have mentioned, when he declaims, 'Assist me, some extemporal god of rhyme, for I am sure I shall turn sonnet. Devise, wit, write, pen, for I am for whole volumes in folio' (1.2.183–5). Indeed, the intimate link between poetry and books runs throughout the Shakespearean dramatic corpus (chapter 4).

Although Shakespeare never names such important Greek, Roman, and English national poets as Homer, Virgil, and Spenser, he finds ways to get their massive poetic projects on to his stage: Homer, most directly in *Troilus and Cressida*, where we visit Troy; Virgil, throughout the dramatic canon,

---

[16] On Chaucer as an epic poet for the Renaissance and for Spenser, see J. A. Burrow, 'Chaucer, Geoffrey'.

including numerous references to Aeneas and his tragic beloved, Dido, from the beginning (*2H6* 3.2.116–18; 5.2.62–6) to the end (*Temp* 2.1.77–83); and Spenser, most visibly in two appearances by the Faerie Queene: Titania in *A Midsummer Night's Dream*; and Mistress Quickly, who performs the lead role in the playlet directed at Falstaff in the final scene of *Merry Wives* (5.5). A vast amount of criticism exists on Shakespeare's engagement with Ovid and Virgil, to a lesser extent with Homer, Chaucer, and Spenser, but most of it directs us to a salient point: this author uses the new theatre to engage the major Roman and English national poets and thus the art of the national poet himself.[17]

Nor does Shakespeare name his most famous rival, Christopher Marlowe, but in *As You Like It* he alludes to Marlowe as the 'dead shepherd' (3.5.81), quotes a line from Marlowe's poem *Hero and Leander*, 'Who ever lov'd that lov'd not at first sight?' (3.5.82; *HL* 176), and perhaps alludes to Marlowe's death as 'a great reckoning in a little room' (3.3.15) – if so, an echo of Marlowe's much-quoted line from *The Jew of Malta*, 'infinite riches in a little room' (1.1.37). Additionally, in *Merry Wives* the Welsh parson Sir Hugh Evans garbles Marlowe's great lyric, 'The Passionate Shepherd to His Love' (3.1.13–25); this play also refers to Marlowe's *Doctor Faustus* (1.1.130, 4.5.69–70). Moreover, Shakespeare recurrently puts Marlovian super-heroes on to his stage, from York and Gloucester in the *Henry VI* plays, to Richard III in his historical tragedy and Hotspur in *1 Henry IV*, to Edmund in *King Lear* and Coriolanus.[18]

Shakespeare's dramatic and historical vocabulary for poetry is merely the tip of a theatrical iceberg. So many characters qualify as poet-figures that it would be hard to count them. In addition to such courtiers as Orlando, Shakespeare stages professional lyricists like the Fool in *King Lear*, who does not simply recite poems and sing songs to indict his sovereign for banishing Cordelia and handing Britain over to Goneril and Regan, but, according to Lear himself, turns to lyric precisely because this occasion emerges. 'When were you wont to be so full of songs, sirrah?', Lear asks the Fool, who replies, 'I have us'd it, nuncle, e'er since thou mad'st thy daughters thy mothers' (1.4.170–2). We also meet tricksters like Autolycus in *The Winter's Tale*,

---

[17] Other national or laureate poets who have been found important to Shakespeare include Daniel, Drayton, and Chapman. On Shakespeare and Chapman's Homer, see Brower, *Hero and Saint*; Ide, *Possessed with Greatness* For criticism on the other authors, see (e.g.) Introduction, note 51.

[18] Critics also find Shakespeare processing his literary relationship with other University Wits, especially Greene, but also Lyly, Nashe, Peele, and Lodge. On Marlowe and Shakespeares see Shapiro, *Rival Playwrights*; Cartelli, *Marlowe, Shakespeare*; and, most recently, Logan, *Shakespeare's Marlowe*.

who sings songs in the pastoral countryside of Bohemia, sometimes just for amusement, often his own: 'The lark, that tirra-lyra chaunts … / Are summer songs for me and my aunts, / While we lie tumbling in the hay' (4.3.8–12). Occasionally, Shakespeare uses lyric to invent the voice and inwardness of madness, as he does powerfully in the scattered rhymes of Ophelia: 'He is dead and gone, lady, / He is dead and gone' (*Ham* 4.5.29–30). At other times, Shakespeare presents lyricists as supernatural songsters, like Puck in *A Midsummer Night's Dream*, the Witches in *Macbeth*, or Ariel in *The Tempest*, the last of whom voices some of the most profound lyrics in the English language: 'Full fadom five thy father lies, / Of his bones are coral made: / Those are pearls that were his eyes' (1.2.397–9).

Sometimes, too, we encounter professional poets. In *Timon of Athens*, for instance, a figure named the Poet turns out to be a print poet (1.1.26), complete with a voiced poetics, which we overhear him reciting: 'When we for recompense have prais'd the vild, / It stains the glory in that happy verse / Which aptly sings the good' (15–17). In *Julius Caesar*, Cinna the poet does not recite any of his own verse on stage but instead is killed by the angry Roman mob when it mistakes him for Cinna the conspirator: 'Tear him for his bad verses' (3.3.30). Everyone remembers Cinna, but what about the unnamed poet at the court of Leontes in *The Winter's Tale*, who reverses Cinna's tragic fate, and thus his political failure? In Act 5, scene 1, this 'servant' enters to announce to Leontes and Paulina the arrival of a mysterious beauty the audience knows as Perdita. When the servant relies on blank verse to describe the princess of Bohemia – 'the most peerless piece of earth, I think, / That e'er the sun shone bright on' (94–5) – Paulina rebukes him for betraying his career-long celebration of Sicilia's deceased queen, Hermione:

> Sir, you yourself
> Have said and writ so, but your writing now
> Is colder than that theme, 'She had not been,
> Nor was not to be equall'd' – thus your verse
> Flow'd with her beauty once. 'Tis shrewdly ebb'd
> To say you have seen a better.   (*Winter's Tale* 5.1.98–103)

Courteously, the servant begs pardon, but remains true to what appears as a new poetic form of religious faith: 'This is a creature, / Would she begin a sect, might quench the zeal / Of all professors else, make proselytes / Of who she but did follow' (106–9). Neither torn to pieces nor mocked, this gentle poet, intimate with king and counselor, appears precisely to announce the play's momentous event: the return of Perdita to her home and parents, a stunning prophecy of the apocalyptic resurrection of Hermione through visionary perception of the lost one.[19]

Yet Shakespeare's most detailed portrait of the poet working harmoniously with his sovereign is even more neglected, because it appears in *Edward III*. As scholars have determined, Shakespeare likely wrote Act 2, scene 1, in which the king turns to his confidant, Lodwick, to request a poem to help court the Countess of Salisbury. As Edward says to himself, Lodwick is

> well read in poetry,
> And hath a lusty and persuasive spirit:
> I will acquaint him with my passion,
> Which he shall shadow with a veil of lawn,
> Through which the queen of beauty's queen shall see
> Herself the ground of my infirmity.   (*Edward III* 2.1.53–8)

In keeping with this author's counter-laureate strategy, the political figure of the king turns out to have more to say about the art of poetry than the poet himself. Line 56 even constitutes a Shakespearean signature, relying on a term from the theatre, 'shadow', meaning *actor*, to describe the action of the court poet, as the clothing term 'veil of lawn' confirms: like an actor wearing his costume, the poet will shadow (conceal, represent) his passion in metaphorical, allegorical language.[20] Perhaps not surprisingly, the king goes on to gesture to the great allegorical poet, Spenser, including a remarkable reference to the politics of Spenserian pastoral poetry. 'Then in the summer arbor sit by me', the king says to his poet, 'Make it our council house, or cabinet: / Since green our thoughts, green be the conventicle, / Where we will ease us by disburd'ning them' (61–4). Here Shakespeare refers to the central locus of Western pastoral poetry, the 'green cabinet', of which Spenser had advertised himself the keeper in the *December* eclogue of *The Shepheardes Calender*, when Colin sings to 'soveraigne Pan thou God of shepheards all' (7): 'Hearken awhile from thy greene cabinet, / The rurall song of carefull Colinet' (17–18).[21]

---

[19] E. R. Hunter discusses Leontes' court poet as one of only two 'Persons who Draw Favorable Comment for Poetizing' in Shakespeare, the other being the Second Citizen in the opening act of *Coriolanus* (126–31). Leontes' poet resembles the 'laureate' in that he 'belongs at the court' and creates 'an ideal community' at 'the side of the monarch' (Helgerson, *Self-Crowned Laureates* 239). For details, see Cheney, 'Perdita, Pastorella, and the Romance of Literary Form'.

[20] On 'shadow' as a noun for *actor*, see *MND* 5.1.423–4.

[21] On the 'green cabinet' as 'the *locus amoenus* of Greek pastoral poetry', see Rosenmeyer, *Green Cabinet* vii. On Spenser's use of the 'green cabinet' to 're-vert' to the 'paradise principle', see Berger, *Revisionary Play* 378–415. On Spenser's imitation of the 'green cabinet' in Marot as 'a rustic summerhouse or bower', a 'private chamber of the privileged, for reading, writing, or keeping one's treasures', and as a locus for the union of art and politics, see A. Patterson, *Pastoral and Ideology* 107–8, 128–30. For further detail, see Cheney, *Flight* 137. Significantly, in the 1586 quarto of the *Calender*, someone (we do not think Spenser) changed Colin's 'rurall song' to 'laurell song', and the phrase gets reprinted in the 1591 and 1597 editions, as

Accordingly, Edward goes on to encourage Lodwick to perform his Orphic art: 'For if the touch of sweet concordant strings / Could force attendance in the ears of hell, / How much more shall the strains of poet's wit / [Beguile] and ravish soft and humane minds?' (76–9). Telling Lodwick to 'Write on' by comparing the Countess's 'voice to music or the nightingale' (105–6), he suddenly realizes that he has conjured up the specter of Philomela: 'The nightingale sings of adulterate wrong' (110). When Lodwick finally produces his first line of poetry, he compares her initially to Proserpina (141), but when the king objects, the poet adds a scriptural comparison: ' "More fair and chaste than is the [queen] of shades, / More bold in constancy ... than Judith was' (167–9). This scene, rich and intricate, goes on, but its counter-laureate strategy subtly presents the poet as a critic of a king trying to commit adultery, even as it offers a rare glimpse into the process of poet-making for both erotic and political purposes.[22]

Other professional singers like Balthasar in *Much Ado about Nothing* or Amiens in *As You Like It* also perform their lyric songs in detail, and in the process produce some extraordinary lyrics that often get overlooked: Balthasar's 'Sigh no more, ladies' (2.3.62–74) or Amiens' 'Under the green-wood tree' (2.5.1–57). According to Hallett Smith, 'quite possibly the most resonant lyric lines Shakespeare ever composed' are sung not by a professional poet-figure at all but by the lost princes of Britain, Arviragus and Guiderius:[23]

> Fear no more the heat o' th' sun,
> ...
> Golden lads and girls all must,
> As chimney-sweepers, come to dust.   (*Cymbeline* 4.2.258–81)

As we have observed, Shakespeare, unlike Spenser (or Jonson), does not clearly mark out figures in his dramatic works that 'secretly shadoweth himself, as sometime did Virgil under the name of Tityrus', to quote Spenser's glossarist, E. K. (*Jan* 85–6). Shakespeare's reticence in self-identification, like his habitual staging of such critics of poetry as Theseus, goes some way toward explaining why we might have relegated the topic of poetry in his plays.

If poet-figures produce lyrics, they do so in specific geographical locales, and Shakespeare tends to associate them with particular poetic genres: most

---

in the 1611/17 folio (Smith and de Sélincourt, eds. 1: 115). On the green cabinet at *TN* 1.5.268–74, see *SNPP* 32–4. For the connection between the green cabinet and Shakespeare's life as a Catholic, see R. Wilson, *Secret Shakespeare* 25.

[22] For support, see Muir, *Shakespeare the Professional* 28–30, who adds (not quite accurately) that Lodwick 'is the only one of [Shakespeare's] ... poets who emerges with much credit' (30).

[23] Smith, intro. to *Cymbeline, Riverside* 1568.

memorably the countryside with pastoral, as in *As You Like It*; and the city with epic and romance, as in *Antony and Cleopatra*.²⁴ The country-court dynamic is arguably the most recognizable topography of Shakespearean drama; perhaps less often recognized, this topography has deep generic resonance,²⁵ placing the major Virgilian and Spenserian forms of pastoral and epic right at the center of Shakespeare's stage, from *Two Gentlemen* through *The Winter's Tale*. Shakespeare uses the stage to associate theatrical space with other poetic genres as well – the court or private chamber with lyric and sonnet.²⁶ Thus, in the final comedic scene from *Much Ado*, set in Leonato's house, Claudio pulls out of Benedick's 'pocket' a 'halting sonnet of his own pure brain, / Fashion'd to Beatrice', and Hero pulls 'another' from the pocket of Beatrice, 'Containing her affection unto Benedick' (5.4.87–90; see chapter 6).

Shakespeare imagines poetry as a playful art of entertainment, but he also understands the potency of poetry to perform cultural work, not always as admirable as Duke Vincentio imagines. In *Two Gentlemen*, Proteus educates Thurio in the art of winning Silvia:

> You must lay lime to tangle her desires
> By wailful sonnets, whose composed rhymes
> Should be full-fraught with serviceable vows.
> (*Two Gentlemen of Verona* 3.2.68–70)

'Ay', the Duke replies, 'much is the force of heaven-bred poesy' (71), to which Proteus adds, 'Write till your ink be dry … / … and frame some feeling line / That may discover such integrity: / For Orpheus' lute was strung with poets' sinews' (74–7). Just as Hamlet will use the play-within-the-play, *The Mousetrap*, to 'catch the conscience of the King' (2.2.605), so Proteus advises Thurio to use the divine nature of poetry, with its Orphic power to affect an audience emotionally, to trap the desire of Silvia.

Sometimes, the conversation about poetry seems secreted in the dramatic discourse, as if we were hearing the voice of the author himself. As we have seen in the last chapter, in *Titus Andronicus*, when Marcus comes across the ravished Lavinia, he compares her rather surprisingly with Orpheus and with Philomela: 'Fair Philomela, why, she but lost her tongue … / O, had the monster [who raped you] seen those lily hands … / He would have

---

²⁴ On pastoral in *As You Like It*, see Alpers, *What is Pastoral?* 71–8, 123–34, 197–203. On romance and epic in *AC*, see Sullivan, 'Sleep, Epic, and Romance in *Antony and Cleopatra*'.
²⁵ See Sullivan, 'Shakespeare's Comic Geographies'.
²⁶ The locus classicus is Donne's 'The Canonization': 'We'll build in sonnets pretty rooms' (32) (in Clements, ed., *John Donne's Poetry*). See also Marlowe, *Ovid's Elegies*, when Dame Elegy says to Dame Tragedy, 'Thy lofty style with mine I not compare, / Small doors unfitting for large houses are' (3.1.39–40).

dropp'd his knife, and fell asleep, / As Cerberus at the Thracian poet's feet' (2.4.38–51). Even though recent productions have demonstrated the stage worthiness of this speech, we cannot account for its weirdness until we recognize Shakespeare's concern to lay bare his own literariness, his extemporal intertextual authorship, especially with Ovid (and Spenser). Marcus expresses horror at the tragedy he witnesses, while Shakespeare reveals how he himself makes such tragedy.

In such intertextual moments, we become privy to something like the playwright's own poetic workshop. Thus, Shakespeare's conversation about poetry does not occur in a historical vacuum but responds to a larger conversation about poetry coming out of classical Greece and Rome, migrating to the Middle Ages, and entering Renaissance Europe and England. Some plays make this 'meta-poetics' explicit, as Holofernes does when he quotes the first pastoral eclogue of Mantuan (Baptiste Spagnuoli) before the country wench Jaquenta: 'Old Mantuan, old Mantuan! who understandeth thee not, loves thee not. *Ut, re, sol, la, mi, fa.* Under pardon, sir, what are the contents? or rather, as Horace says in his – What, my soul, verses?' (4.2.99–102). In such a *meta-conversation*, Shakespeare's text enters into (comic) dialogue with several important European poets, cut along generic lines.

To complement this more 'literary' use of poetry, Shakespeare includes a more formally 'theatrical' one. For instance, he presents characters breaking out of their blank verse line into rhymed couplets in order to create a certain dramatic mood or effect. We have already seen an instance in the soliloquy of Duke Vincentio. Another occurs in the opening scene of *A Midsummer Night's Dream*, when Hermia engages in detailed conversation with her lover Lysander in the blank verse used in the earlier part of the play, but then, inexplicably and amid speech, she moves into rhyme: 'By the simplicity of Venus' doves, / And that which knitteth souls and prospers loves' (171–2). Only when her friend Helena enters can we make sense of the change, for Helena is the first character to speak fully in couplets. Thus, her first spoken line completes a couplet begun by Hermia in the preceding line:

HERMIA.   God speed fair Helena! whither away?
HELENA.   Call you me fair? That fair again unsay.
           Demetrius loves your fair, O happy fair!
           Your eyes are lodestars, and your tongue's sweet air
           More tunable than lark to shepherd's ear
           When wheat is green, when hawthorn buds appear.
                                    (*A Midsummer Night's Dream* 1.1.180–5)

In context, Helena's rhymed pastoral speech sounds stylized, at once artful and artificial, distinct yet perhaps comical. During the next fifty lines, she joins Hermia and even Lysander in maintaining the rhyme, but after these friends leave the stage, Helena anticipates Duke Vincentio by delivering a 26-line soliloquy in rhymed couplets, concluding, 'But herein mean I to enrich my pain, / To have his sight thither and back again' (250–1). Such poetical dramaturgy opens up rather than closes down the actor's oppor-tunities to reveal character and create dramatic effect – in the case of Helena, most likely a charming mockery of lovely character.

Some plays seem more concerned with the art of poetry than others. The list includes *Two Gentlemen*, *Shrew*, *Love's Labour's Lost*, *Merry Wives*, *Much Ado*, *As You Like It*, *Twelfth Night*, *All's Well that Ends Well*, *Cymbeline*, *The Winter's Tale*, and *The Tempest*. This list suggests that Shakespeare pre-dominantly uses the genres of comedy and romance to transact his poetic fiction. Each of these plays could easily sustain an individual essay, and some, like *Love's Labour's Lost* and *As You Like It*, seem to be virtually about the relation between poetry and its twin Shakespearean art, theatre.

Yet several tragedies make important contributions to the conversation, especially *Titus*, *Romeo*, *Hamlet*, *Othello*, *Lear*, *Antony*, *Timon*, and (perhaps surprisingly) *Coriolanus*. The presence of Ovid's tale of Philomela in *Titus*; the renowned Petrarchan lyricism of *Romeo and Juliet*, which includes three and a quarter sonnets (Pr; 1.5.93–110; 2.Ch); Iago's poem on Desdemona (2.1.129–60) and her own famed willow song (4.3.40–57); the haunting lyrics of the Fool (1.4; 2.4; 3.2) and of Edgar in disguise as Poor Tom (3.4; 3.6); and Coriolanus' difficulty in 'turn[ing]' his 'voice' to the applause of the people (2.3.85–6): these show the tragedian's all-abiding concern with the role of poetry on the new London stage. As Edgar powerfully puts it, 'The foul fiend haunts poor Tom in the voice of a nightingale' (3.6.29–30).[27]

Among the history plays, the first tetralogy is especially important, because it features Henry VI as a Spenserian author-figure, the shepherd-king: 'O God! methinks it were a happy life / To be no better than a homely swain, / To sit upon a hill, as I do now, / To carve out dials quaintly, point by point' (*3H6* 2.5.21–4).[28] But *Richard II* warrants close attention as well; the King's commitment to tragic lyricism is well known: 'Let's talk of graves, of worms, and epitaphs, / Make dust our paper, and with rainy eyes / Write sorrow on the bosom of the earth' (3.2.145–7). Yet the archly theatrical Richard III's fear of poetry is often overlooked: 'a bard of Ireland

---

[27] In the 'Play Scenes' of *SNPP*, I discuss some of these figures (and others in the following paragraph).
[28] On the Spenserian shepherd-king figure, see *SNPP* 43, 63, 77, 245, 272.

told me once / I should not live long after I saw Richmond' (4.2.106–7; see 4.4.507; 5.3.306; and chapter 4).

The preceding inventory suggests how deep-seated the presence of poetry – especially lyric poetry – is in all four genres of Shakespeare's dramatic career, from its inception in the late 1580s till its close during the second decade of the seventeenth century. He puts on the stage a *vocabulary* of poetry, the *character* of the poet, the *prop* of the poem or poetic book, the *action* of poetry, the landscape or *scene* of poetry, and both a *conversation* and a *fiction* about poetry.

CAPRICIOUS POETRY IN *AS YOU LIKE IT*

The epigraph from *As You Like It* shows how deftly Shakespeare can use a comic conversation between characters to represent an engaging aesthetics of counter-laureate poetry pertaining to the interlock between poetry and theatre. When Touchstone tells Audrey that he wishes 'the gods had made [her] … poetical', he means 'Having the character of a poet' (*OED*, Def. 2b, citing *AYLI* 3.3.16). When viewed in context, this line, overheard by the melancholic courtier Jaques, identifies not simply the lustful wit of Touchstone but also the learned art of his author:

TOUCHSTONE.   I am here with thee and thy goats as the most capricious poet, honest Ovid, was among the Goths.
JAQUES.   [*Aside.*] O knowledge ill-inhabited, worse than Jove in a thatch'd house!
TOUCHSTONE.   When a man's verses cannot be understood, nor a man's good wit seconded with the forward child, understanding, it strikes a man more dead than a great reckoning in a little room. Truly, I would the gods had made thee poetical.
                                              (*As You Like It* 3.3.7–16)

In its historical context, 'poetical' means something like 'learned in the Elizabethan art of literary imitation' – learned about Shakespeare's own rivalry with Ovid, but also with the Elizabethan Ovidian poet par excellence, Marlowe, as perhaps the rewriting of the famous line from *The Jew of Malta* indicates; and with Jonson, whom Jaques embodies as Horatian satirist.[29]

In the first speech, Touchstone, marooned from court in the Forest of Arden, compares himself to Ovid, who was exiled from Rome by the

---

[29] For a recent statement about Marlowe and Ovid in *As You Like It*, see M. P. Jackson, 'Frances Meres and the Cultural Contexts of Shakespeare's Rival Poet Sonnets': 'the Marlowe-Ovid-Chapman nexus seems to have haunted Shakespeare as he wrote *As You Like It*' (233). On Jaques, Jonson, and Horatian satire, see *SNPP* 145–8; Bednarz, *Shakespeare and the Poets' War* 108–11.

Emperor Augustus because (Elizabethans believed) he was caught in a sexual embrace with Julia, the Emperor's daughter, and sent to Tomis, a barbaric land that Touchstone identifies with the Goths. The clown's wit naturally cascades, for he delights in his pun on 'goats' (beast of *lust*) and 'Goths' as a way to condemn the land he visits, and he wittily praises Ovid for being paradoxically 'capricious' and 'honest': the most honest poet is the most capricious – or inventive. Thus, Shakespeare suggests both a form of ethics and a mode of aesthetics, as he weaves language together to present Touchstone as an Ovidian poet of lustful desire who excels at verse because of his ingenious wit.

It is the scholarship underwriting this wit that Jaques maligns during his aside. His own wit cascading, he uses the image of the house to compare Touchstone's 'knowledge' with the 'thatch'd house' once visited by Jove. Here, Shakespeare combines two myths from Ovid's *Metamorphoses*: when Jove disguises himself as a shepherd before Mnemosyne, god of memory (6.114); and when Mercury and Bacchus disguise themselves as mortals in the pastoral cottage of Baucis and Philemon (8.611–724).[30] Jaques criticizes Touchstone's knowledge of Ovid, while Shakespeare alludes both to Marlowe's Ovidian scholarship and to Jonson's.

In his second speech, Touchstone nominally complains about Audrey's inability to understand his learned Ovidian art, equating such ignorant reception with death or oblivion, the loss of poetic fame. But Shakespeare's rewriting of Marlowe's line, and evocation of his death in the small room in Deptford over who would pay the 'reckoning' or bill, precisely *remember* his dead colleague, contradicting Touchstone's point. As such, Shakespeare fictionalizes the loss of poetic fame in order to memorialize Marlowe's Ovidian renown, and to clear an original space for his own achievement.

Touchstone's complaint leads him to wish the gods had made Audrey more 'poetical'. When she expresses ignorance about the meaning of 'poetical', she raises a major question about the art of poetry, from Plato to Sidney: is poetry 'a true thing'? In the *Republic*, Plato had answered in the negative, yet in *The Defence of Poesy* Sidney rehearsed Plato's banishment of poets from his ideal state because they are liars – capricious or fanciful inventors – in order to defend them: poets are crucial to the ideal state because they invent fictions above nature.[31] For Sidney, poets can use

---

[30] Shakespeare also probably glances at Marlowe, *1 Tamb* 1.2.198 and 5.1.184–7; see *SNPP* 146.

[31] Plato, *Republic*, Book 10; Sidney, *Defence of Poesy*, in *Sir Philip Sidney*, ed. Kimbrough. See *Tim* 1.1.214–27, where Shakespeare alludes to this tradition by representing the philosopher Apemantus accusing the Poet of being a liar and forger.

delightful instruction to move readers to virtuous behavior on behalf of the commonwealth. Wittily, Shakespeare shows the unlearned female able to articulate the question at the heart of classical, medieval, and Renaissance poetics.

When Touchstone replies, 'No, truly; for the truest poetry is the most feigning', his repetition of the concept of *truth* militates against his word 'feigning', wrapping a paradox around the 'poetical' that we might unravel. The word 'feigning' can mean both *imaginative* and *deceptive*; Touchstone means the former, that the truest poetry is the most imaginative; but his author also evokes the latter.[32] Shakespeare does so not to agree with Plato, but to draw attention to the *theatricality* of poetry: the truest poetry is the most theatrical. In this way, Shakespeare acknowledges the theatricality of Ovid's poetry and of Marlowe's, even as he produces a statement defining the achievement of his own counter-laureate art. Significantly, this statement fuses the arts of poetry and theatre, suggesting not merely that poetry is theatrical but that theatre is made up of poetry, is substantively about poetry, and is often in service of poetry.

'MINCING POETRY' IN I HENRY IV

While critics often discuss poetry in such comedies as *As You Like It*, we might be more hard pressed to find similar discussion of poetry in the Henriad.[33] The reason is perhaps not hard to find. For Shakespeare, the history play is primarily a genre designed to probe the political dynamics of the English nation, and it focuses on the relation between the sovereign and the subject, and thus the topics of patriotism and rebellion. Nonetheless, as we shall see in more detail in chapter 5, when Shakespeare turns from comedy and tragedy to the history play he does not forsake the art of poetry as a key feature of his fiction, but discovers how to accommodate it to the political topic of nationhood.

For instance, in Act 3, scene 1, of *I Henry IV*, during the electrifying dialogue between the Welshman Owen Glendower and the Englishman Hotspur, Shakespeare uses poetry to dramatize a boundary between British nations:

[32] The *OED* cites this line under Def. 1, 'Given to inventing; imaginative', but goes on to cite *MND* 1.1.31 under Def. 2, 'dissembling, deceitful'.
[33] For brief discussion, see E.R. Hunter (108–10), who puts Hotspur in the company of such 'Anti-poets' as Theseus, Mercutio, Falconbridge, Benedick, and Jaques (101–112): 'a fine array of brave, hearty, even brilliant chaps, . . each ... skeptical about poetry' (111).

GLENDOWER.   I can speak English, lord, as well as you,
                For I was train'd up in the English court,
                Where being but young I framed to the harp
                Many an English ditty lovely well,
                And gave the tongue a helpful ornament,
                A virtue that was never seen in you.
HOTSPUR.   Marry,
                And I am glad of it with all my heart.
                I had rather be a kitten and cry mew
                Than one of these same metre ballat-mongers.
                I had rather hear a brazen canstick turn'd,
                Or a dry wheel grate on the axle-tree,
                And that would set my teeth nothing on edge,
                Nothing so much as mincing poetry.
                'Tis like the forc'd gait of a shuffling nag.   (*1 Henry IV* 3.1.119–33)

Characteristically, Glendower uses his pompous Welsh speech to claim 'virtue' as an 'English' poet of the 'court', capable of creating 'lovely' lyrics and their 'ornament'. Effectively, he presents himself as an English Orpheus, powerful through his Apollonian 'harp'. Also characteristically, Hotspur uses some of the finest blank verse in the play to dismantle Glendower's claims to poetic authority, buttressed by no fewer than three inventive similes. Hotspur reduces the affective force of Glendower's courtly lyric to the 'metre' of 'ballat-mongers' – street poets who cry their songs amid the rude public. For his part, Hotspur prefers to hear kittens cry, 'brazen' candlesticks turned on a lathe, or the grating of a 'dry wheel' against its 'axle' – noises that for him mark poetry off as trivial, shameful, and harsh. But, he adds, nothing sets his teeth 'on edge' like 'poetry' itself, which he classifies as 'mincing' and compares derisively with the 'forced gait' of an old hobbled horse.[34] In contrast to *Romeo and Juliet* earlier in Shakespeare's career, when the lovers form a sonnet together to mark the civic fragility of companionate love (1.5.93–106), here poetry frames the inner division between rebellious forces disloyal to England. Shakespeare maps this division precisely on to the merits of poetry for military conduct, with Glendower claiming poetry to be consistent with the life of a soldier and Hotspur rejecting the claim as pure affectation.

    Yet for someone so critical of poetry, Hotspur sure knows a lot about it. The irony further underscores the limitation of this glorious rebel to the

---

[34] Kastan, ed., *King Henry IV, Part 1*, remarks that 'Hotspur is delighted that he has no skill in poetry, which he views as a courtly affectation unbecoming to a true soldier' (248).

crown. For instance, the word 'mincing' is loaded. According to the *OED*, it means 'affectedly dainty, elegant, or mannered. In later (usu. derogatory) use often associated with an effeminate or effete manner or behaviour in a man, esp. a homosexual' (Def. 1a). For Hotspur, poetry is a feminine art, and it takes manly identity away; behind his critique of Glendower lies a veiled assault on the Welshman's manhood. But the word 'mincing' may have a second meaning: 'minimizes, extenuates, or diminishes; palliative' (Def. 2). This definition pertains not just to identity but to language, and suggests that poetry 'gloss[es] ... over a matter; the suppression of part of a fact or statement' (Def. 1 under noun). According to this meaning, Hotspur criticizes poetry and its Welsh practitioner for the art of concealment, disguise, falsehood, and thus theatricality.

Yet Hotspur's final line on the forced gait of a shuffling nag constitutes a *tour de force*. He uses blank verse to imitate the very contents of the action he criticizes. His use of the metaphor of poetic 'feet' to describe poetic meter transposes a technical term to one of prosody's traditional representations, horsemanship.[35] Thus, Shakespeare presents Hotspur as one of the poet-haters Sidney mentions in his *Defence of Poesy*. Yet Hotspur invents exciting poetry *as if against his will*. His uncle, the Earl of Worcester, listening to another of Hotspur's poetic tirades, exclaims, 'He apprehends a world of figures here, / But not the form of what he should attend' (1.3.209–10) – a description that pinpoints Hotspur as the very high-flying poet of imagination whom Theseus mocks as fit company for madmen and lovers. In this way, Shakespeare invents Hotspur's famed histrionic identity largely by making him a naturally poetic man who despises poetry. By attending to this scene, we can catch a glimpse of the author's self-conscious making of theatrical character itself.

While the dialogue between Hotspur and Glendower about poetry might seem off-center in this history play, Shakespeare's discourse makes it clear that he addresses the grandest national project for English Renaissance poets: what Spenser calls the 'labour ... to restore, as to theyr rightfull heritage, such good and naturall English words ... to our Mother tonge'.[36] If Spenser struggles to restore English to its native luster after the decline of Middle English in the fifteenth and sixteenth centuries, Shakespeare interposes a sensitive topic, in which an Englishman criticizes a Welshman for his

---

[35] Kastan suggests that Hotspur voices the opposite view to that of Spenser's friend Gabriel Harvey, who defines good verse as being like a 'good horse, that trippeth not once in a iourney' (Harvey, in G. G. Smith, ed., *Elizabethan Critical Essays* I: 96; quoted in Kastan, ed. 248).
[36] Spenser, *Shepheardes Calender, Dedicatory Epistle* 84–8.

claim to have given the 'English … tongue a helpful ornament'. For Hotspur, the Welshman's education at the English court is not sufficient.[37] The scene shows Glendower citing his own English poetry as evidence of his authority to speak the language, and Hotspur seizing on this claim as grounds for ridicule.

One suspects that for most readers or viewers of *1 Henry IV*, Shakespeare selects another professional dialogue for center-stage: not that between Glendower and Hotspur about the art of poetry but that between Hal and Falstaff about the art of theatre. Memorably, in Act 2, scene 4, at the Boarshead Tavern, Falstaff says jovially, 'What, shall we be merry, shall we have a play extempore?' (279–80). Then Falstaff proceeds to 'play out the play' (484) at considerable and comedic length, as he performs the role of Hal's father, King Henry IV, who speaks on behalf of 'sweet Jack Falstaff, kind Jack Falstaff, true Jack Falstaff, valiant Jack Falstaff' (475–6), only to be usurped by Hal, who appropriates his father's role to indict Falstaff. 'O Jesu,' says the Hostess of Falstaff's performance, 'he doth it as like one of these harlotry players as ever I see' (395–6).

While Shakespeare presents the Boarshead Tavern largely as a place of the stage, and thus more directly representative of the art the audience watches, he presents Glendower's castle in Wales as largely a place of poetry, as Mortimer reports of his Welsh wife, Glendower's sweet daughter, who does not speak a word of English: 'I will never be a truant, love, / Till I have learn'd thy language, for thy tongue / Makes Welsh as sweet as ditties highly penn'd, / Sung by a fair queen in a summer's bow'r, / With ravishing division, to her lute' (3.1.204–8). As the Spenserian language here intimates, Shakespeare presents Mortimer, who never does show up at the Battle of Shrewsbury, as enthralled to an Acrasia-like figure who uses lyric song to lure her warrior to sleep.[38] In this history play, poetry becomes largely the art of the politically rebellious and the defeated; theatre, the art of the patriotic victors. Shakespeare divides his dramatic plot between them.

---

[37] On 'race' in the plays, see Floyd-Wilson, *English Ethnicity and Race in Early Modern Drama*; although she does not discuss Glendower or *1 Henry IV*, she suggests that Sidney's characterization of the ancient Britons in Wales as bards who maintained their poetic powers, despite repeated conquests and invasions, has a racialist tinge (106). On the dynamic of Welsh and English in *Henry V*, see Baker, *Between Nations* 17–65. In '*1 Henry IV*: Metatheatrical Britain', Greenfield emphasizes the 'literary forms' of the play (72) – in particular, the way 'location' figures 'genre' (74), including the 'generic environment' of 'Glendower's house' as a site for 'epic and romance' (74–5).

[38] Cf. Greenfield: 'Glendower presides over a seduction like those of Spenser's Bower of Bliss or Armida's Island in Tasso's *Gerusalemme Liberata*. His daughter's weeping, her music, and her sexuality, all represented as a kind of overflowing or incontinence, work to feminize her husband and rob him of an Englishness that is gendered male' ('*1 Henry IV*: Metatheatrical Britain' 74).

MOCKING THE SONNET IN *HENRY V*

In *Henry V*, Shakespeare follows up on his use of poetry as a dramatic marker of political rebellion against the English nation when he delivers a send-up of the Petrarchan sonnet form tragically romanticized in *Romeo and Juliet*. While in Act 5 of *I Henry IV* Hotspur dies at the hands of Prince Hal, in *Henry V*, after Hal becomes king, the French Dolphin replaces Hotspur as Henry's arch-antagonist. In Act 3, scene 7, the Dolphin arms himself for battle in the camp near Agincourt by exercising a bantering poetic wit – voiced wittily by the play's author in prose – during a conversation with the Constable of France and the Duke of Orleance:

I will not change my horse with any that treads but on four [pasterns] ... he bounds from the earth, as if his entrails were hairs; *le cheval volant*, the Pegasus, *chez les narines de feu!* When I bestride him, I soar, I am a hawk; he trots the air; the earth sings when he touches it; the basest horn of his hoof is more musical than the pipe of Hermes ... It is a beast for Perseus. He is pure air and fire; and the dull elements of earth and water never appear in him, but only in patient stillness while his rider mounts him. (*Henry V* 3.7.11–23)[39]

When the Dolphin claims that his horse is thus 'the prince of palfreys' (27), he finds occasion to extend his 'vary deserv'd praise'(32):

It is a theme as fluent as the sea; turn the sands into eloquent tongues, and my horse is argument for them all. 'Tis a subject for a sovereign to reason on, and for a sovereign's sovereign to ride on; and for the world, familiar to us and unknown, to lay apart their particular functions and wonder at him. I once writ a sonnet in his praise and began thus: 'Wonder of nature' –. (*Henry V* 3.7.33–40)

Orleance quips, 'I have heard a sonnet begin so to one's mistress', to which the Dolphin retorts, 'Then did they imitate that which I compos'd to my courser, for my horse is my mistress' (41–4). Orleance ends, 'Your mistress bears well' (45).

Even in a history play, Shakespeare stages sonneteering. By placing this homosocial conversation on the battlefield, in the violence of the wide-open air, he rehearses a witty reversal of the sonnet tradition erotically locked in a pretty room. Most obviously, he inserts the conversation for comic relief on the eve of the play's climactic battle. The scene is funny, or designed to be, with its central (French) joke, told by an English author to an English audience: a poet-figure humorously delivers a Petrarchan sonnet on his

---

[39] The *Riverside* vigorously rejects the textual substitution in this scene of the Dolphin's speeches for those of Bourbon (1016), as argued for by some previous editors and critics. Those who see the quoted speech as delivered by Bourbon will need to adjust the following commentary accordingly.

beloved horse. Yet the French misogyny prizing a horse over a mistress
also undermines French heroism. Shakespeare inserts a scene of mock-
sonneteering to enact international critique.[40]

Yet Shakespeare also stages a critique of authorship. For the Dolphin
associates his royal steed with Pegasus, the flying horse, whose nostrils
breathe fire. For Spenser, as we have seen in chapter 2, Pegasus is a figure
for the sublime exaltation of the poet's fame, as he is in *The Ruines of Time*
(1591): 'Then who so will with vertuous deeds assay / To mount to heaven,
on Pegasus must ride, / And with sweete Poets verse be glorifide' (425–7). As
the words 'heaven' and 'glorifide' reveal, Spenser uses the classical figure of
poetic inspiration to trope the Christian poet's power to participate in
salvation.[41] Early in his career, Spenser even selected Pegasus as his personal
myth; in a letter printed in 1580, Gabriel Harvey remarks that 'gentle
Mistresse Rosalinde [Spenser's first wife] once … christened [Spenser] her
Segnior pegaso'.[42] For Spenser, as for Christian poets like du Bartas and
later Milton, Pegasus is fundamentally a myth about the divine origin and
goal of poetic art.[43] Also in *The Ruines of Time*, Spenser presents a recently
deceased 'Knight', Sir Philip Sidney, riding 'a winged steed' to 'heaven'
(646–57), 'The same that was bred of Medusaes blood, / On which Dan
Perseus borne of heavenly seed, / The faire Andromeda from perill freed'
(647–9). Here Spenser uses the Pegasus-Perseus myth to represent the
apotheosis of the Christian poet Sidney. No doubt it is the myth of the
warrior riding the winged horse that leads the Dolphin (ludicrously) to
adopt it as his own personal myth.

By the time Shakespeare wrote *Henry V* (around 1598–9), Sidney and
Spenser were England's most famous Petrarchan sonneteers. While we
cannot determine with certainty that Shakespeare gibes at the sonneteering
of either colleague (Sidney died in 1586, Spenser in 1599), the Sidney
passage in Spenser's poem reveals what may lie behind the Dolphin's wit:
a heady reading of the Pegasus-Perseus myth as a sublime model for poetic
exaltation, here transposed to the martial field as a source of military
inspiration.[44] The Dolphin alludes to the notion of poetic inspiration
when saying that 'the earth sings when he touches it', and he evokes a

---

[40] Cf. *E3* 2.1.95–8, when the king responds to Lodwick's question, '[Write] I to a woman?', with 'What,
thinkest thou I did bid thee praise a horse?'
[41] Cheney, *Flight* 14–15.   [42] Harvey, *Three Letters*, in G. G. Smith, ed. i: 106.
[43] Cheney, *Flight* 72–4.
[44] For the importance of Spenser's death to Shakespeare, see Shapiro, *1599*, who devotes a chapter to the
topic (67–83). Shapiro associates *Henry V* with Spenser; 'Like Spenser, Henry V … had not lived to
fulfil his great promise. Shakespeare also knew that not even the most celebrated of English kings, let
alone a great poet, could be assured that posterity would be kind … *Henry the Fifth*, like Spenser's

specific myth important to England's leading laureate poet: 'when Pegasus struck Mount Helicon with his hoof, the fountain of the Muses sprang forth'.[45] The Dolphin's championing of his Pegasus-steed's 'basest hoof' as 'more musical than the pipe of Hermes' is indeed striking, alluding to the originary moment of poetic inspiration in classical mythology, but also introducing Pegasus as a competitor to the messenger god, who, as 'Ovid tells [in the *Metamorphoses*] ... with the music of his pipe ... lulled to sleep Argus, a monster with a hundred eyes'.[46]

If the scene tries to make the Dolphin a worthy foe to Henry himself, it does so only to reveal the Frenchman's worth to be an illusion: the Dolphin is a glib and flippant poet who loves his horse more than his mistress and shouts heedlessly for English blood. Although the Dolphin cannot hold a candle(stick) to the electrifying Hotspur, Shakespeare's mockery of the royal French sonneteer remains characteristic of this author when staging a fiction about the art of poetry. Yet within the mockery lies a careful artistic strategy; this author understands poetry on the stage to operate as a counter-laureate principle of nationhood.

'SOUNDS, AND SWEET AIRS': ARIEL'S SONGS
IN *THE TEMPEST*

While in the Henriad Shakespeare mocks the Dolphin, along with Hotspur and Glendower, as poet-figures, at the very end of his career, in *The Tempest*, he presents Ariel more affirmatively as the theatrical spirit of poetry itself.[47] As we have seen in the preceding chapter, Ariel's master functions as this late romance's bookish man of the theatre, performing a magic art out of Ovid's *Metamorphoses* that alludes to Spenser's *Faerie Queene*. As a poet-playwright figure, however, Prospero never writes a poem or sings a lyric song – unlike, say, that other famed theatrical man of book and poem, the Prince of Denmark (chapter 7). Instead, Prospero directs Ariel to perform his magic art for him, when purging the 'three men of sin' (3.3.53) – Alonso, Antonio,

---

death, was turning into drama that marked the end of an era for Shakespeare. Like the relics of Henry's military campaigns hanging in Westminster, the chivalric world celebrated in Spenser's epic and his own early histories had become increasingly tarnished' (81–3).

[45] *Norton* 1488.

[46] *Riverside* 997. As we saw in chapters 1 and 2, Mercury is also important to Spenser's self-presentation, while both Mercury and Pegasus show up in the Drayton coat of arms.

[47] Those who read *The Tempest* as a colonialist play might see Ariel as the theatrical spirit of *colonialist* poetry. For recent criticism turning away from colonialism to a staging of the professional circumstances of the theatre, see Bruster, *Quoting Shakespeare* 117–42.

and Sebastian – of their corruption or uniting Miranda with Ferdinand in dynastic marriage.

If Prospero's art represents the author's poetic book of theatre, Ariel puts such a compound art into practice. The spirit, not the magus, performs such theatrical spectacles as the banquet of the harpies before the marooned royals (3.3) and the wedding masque for Ferdinand and Miranda (4.1). As Sebastian says of the banquet, 'A living drollery' (3.3.21); and as Prospero says of the 'Spirits' who have 'enact[ed]' his 'present fancies' in the masque (4.1.120–2), 'These our actors … were all spirits' (148–9), meaning also that his spirits are all actors. Equally important here, Ariel performs four original lyrics, some among the most priceless poems in English. To them, we could add two descriptions of Arielian songs, by Caliban (3.2.135–43) and by Ariel himself (4.1.175–84), as well as the patronage poem performed by Ariel to Prospero (4.1.44–8).[48]

The *literary* relationship between magus and spirit remains difficult to decipher, but Shakespeare appears to represent – or perhaps to suggest – the occult relation between a poet-playwright figure and his metaphysical spirit of imagination, especially as it operates on the natural, social, and political world. By distinguishing between the author and the imaginative spirit of art, he innovatively opens up a dramatic gap of agency between wish and fulfillment, command and enactment, the desires of the author and his professional practice. Yet Shakespeare goes further, investing each of the principals with individual character, allowing the audience to glimpse both intermittently as figures of the author. Prospero may use his art to fulfill his own dynastic ambitions, but Ariel simply wants to be 'free' (5.1.241). As the action unfolds, the dynamic of freedom and servitude takes on religious, political, marital, psychological, and finally literary significance. In foregrounding the literary as the foundation of this expansive cultural dynamic, we see how Ariel formally bears the theatrical burden of poetry.[49]

Shakespeare presents the songs of Ariel as a multifaceted theatrical poetics, the climactic performance of lyric as a form of literary power in society.[50] Through the lyric art of Ariel, Shakespeare locates truth-value firmly inside human subjectivity – in the imaginative power of the emotions, the social bond that aligns the self with the other, the individual

---

[48] A fuller analysis would include all seven. On the musical basis of Ariel's songs, see Lindley, *Music* 218–33, and '*Tempest*' 85–110, 216–35.

[49] Of course, Caliban, Stephano, and Trinculo invert Ariel's poetics. On this opposition with respect to 'music', see Lindley, *Music* 219–23.

[50] Dubrow's forthcoming book on lyric and narrative especially attends to the topic of power for the singers in Shakespeare's fictions. I am grateful to Professor Dubrow for sharing her work with me.

with those around him or her. In this romance, the emotions are primarily love and compassion, bonds not simply of desire and control but fellow feeling and attachment. When tempered through reciprocity, such emotions help nurture a civilized society, glimpsed wondrously by Miranda as a 'brave new world' (5.1.183), however we might ironize it. When Ariel first appears, he tells Prospero, 'I flam'd amazement' (1.2.198), referring to the effect the magically induced 'tempest' has had on the individuals sailing by the island on the ship. As in the myth of Orpheus, Shakespeare's spiritual figure of performative lyric functions as a civilizing force.[51] Here, we can merely intimate that Shakespeare uses the lyric complexities of Ariel's songs to crystallize a theatrical poetics of spiritual immanence.[52]

In Act 1, scene 2, Ariel sings his first two songs to affect the emotions of Ferdinand, who has become separated from his father, Alonso, and other members of the royal party. In both songs, Shakespeare stages a process of art: Ariel sings a song, and then Ferdinand expresses his emotional reaction to it. The first song, 'Come unto these yellow sands' (375–87), is a twelve-line lyric in rhymed couplets, and it works to arouse the immediate wonder of the lost youth, for Ferdinand hears the lyric voice but cannot see the lyric singer. The stage direction describes Ariel as '*invisible, playing and singing*' (SD after line 374). Since the audience can see the sprite, the scene represents a complex artistic figure who is both there and not there. Reminiscent of the 'unseene' Achilles in the Troy painting of *Lucrece* (chapter 1), Ariel gestures to the self-concealing author, performing an art without visible agency, wondrous in effect.

In Ferdinand's words,

> Where should this music be? I' th' air, or th'earth?
> It sounds no more; and sure it waits upon
> Some god o' th' island. Sitting on a bank,
> Weeping again the King my father's wrack,
> This music crept by me upon the waters,
> Allaying both their fury and my passion
> With its sweet air; thence I have follow'd it,
> Or it hath drawn me rather. But 'tis gone. (*The Tempest* 1.2.388–95)

If in *The Defence* Sidney argues that the poet aims to delight, instruct, and move the reader to virtuous action, Shakespeare redeploys the Sidneian aims

---

[51] On Prospero as an Orpheus figure, see Vaughan and Vaughan, eds. 18.
[52] On Shakespeare's 'art as having the broadly "spiritual function" of materializing another world', see Fernie, 'Introduction' to *Spiritual Shakespeares*, referring specifically to Theseus' speech on poets, madmen, and lovers in *A Midsummer Night's Dream*, including a stunning insight: 'Poetry and spirituality are kin in that both traffic beyond the known world … Poetry and spirituality both promise no less than another world' (ed. 4).

in an innovative way. Ariel's 'air' delights Ferdinand, as the word 'sweet' intimates; the lyric also motivates the young man to action: 'I have follow'd it.' Yet in no way does Ariel's song instruct Ferdinand – that is, rationally alter the structure of his mind – for he remains ignorant about what he hears. Instead of dramatizing the success of the Sidneian poetics, Shakespeare renders it oblique, concentrating on the affective power of lyric to 'Allay' the competing emotions of anger and sadness ('fury' and 'passion'). For Ferdinand, Ariel's lyric song performs simply a wondrous power, tempering his interior life and rescuing him from a dangerous emotional paralysis. Shakespeare's most innovative counter-Sidneian rehearsal, however, pertains to authorial agency: while Ferdinand can only express the effect of Ariel's self-concealing lyric, the audience witnesses this author actually producing his lyric.

No sooner does Ferdinand proclaim the music 'gone' than 'it begins again' (395–6), leading Ariel to perform his second song, the most famous:

> Full fadom five thy father lies,
> Of his bones are coral made:
> Those are pearls that were his eyes:
> Nothing of him that doth fade,
> But doth suffer a sea-change
> Into something rich and strange.
> Sea-nymphs hourly ring his knell:
>   *Burthen [within].* Ding-dong.
> Hark how I hear them – ding-dong bell.
>   (*The Tempest* 1.2.397–405)

If in the first song Ariel uses the simplicity of the nursery rhyme to create the comedic effect of interior order, in this one he probes the depth of tragic loss, even as he intimates a romance of paternal immortality. As Ferdinand puts it, 'The ditty does remember my drown'd father. / This is no mortal business, nor no sound / That the earth owes. I hear it now above me' (406–8). For the son, Ariel's song is uncanny, because it 'remember[s]' the death of the drowned father, but also because the memorial art appears divine, a 'business' beyond mortality, able to resurrect the ghostly presence of the 'drown'd' patriarch. In particular, Ariel's lyric song gives voice to a 'sea-change', in which the body of the dead father metamorphoses into the living nature of art – his bones, coral; his eyes, pearl – so 'rich and strange' that 'Sea-nymphs hourly ring his knell'. Yet perhaps more rich and strange is the author himself, who turns a grim narrative about petrifaction into the haunting beauty of lyric care: 'Hark how I hear them – ding-dong bell.' Again, Shakespeare depicts the sprite singing the song, and then expresses its mysterious power to affect the emotional life of the hearer; as Ferdinand says, 'I hear it now above me' (408).[53]

Ariel's third song is quite different from the first two, because it *politicizes* the affective power of an occult lyric. In Act 2, scene 1, Ariel '*Sings in Gonzalo's ear*' (SD after line 299), once the sprite has put the old man and Alonso to sleep:

> While you here do snoring lie,
> Open-ey'd conspiracy
> His time doth take.
> If of life you keep a care,
> Shake off slumber, and beware.
> Awake, awake!   (*The Tempest* 2.1.300–5)

A kind of politicized aubade, this song of awakening works to discover 'conspiracy', the assassination of a king by his brother and a dark confederate. Instead of allaying the passions, this lyric infiltrates Gonzalo's sleeping consciousness in the paradoxical form of a benign nightmare, warning him to 'keep a care' of 'life'.

Yet Shakespeare also invests the scene with religious significance. As Antonio and Sebastian step forward to assassinate Alonso, Gonzalo awakes, exclaiming, 'Now, good angels / Preserve the King!' (306–7). The terms compel us to compare the event Shakespeare stages with the one Gonzalo voices – that is to say, the old man's Christian prayer for God's grace within the fiction to the poet-playwright's performance of poetic grace in the theatre. If we discern a gap between Christian grace and an actor's art, between the promise of redemption and the business of the stage, we prepare ourselves to grasp this author's theatrical poetics of spiritual immanence.

In Ariel's fourth and final song, 'Where the bee sucks', we experience perhaps the summation of Shakespeare's art of theatrical poetry, his faith in the artful beauty of nature to reinvigorate the human spirit:

> Where the bee sucks, there suck I,
> In a cowslip's bell I lie;
> There I couch when owls do cry.
> On the bat's back I do fly
> After summer merrily.
> Merrily, merrily shall I live now,
> Under the blossom that hangs on the bough.
>   (*The Tempest* 5.1.88–94)

---

[53] Cf. Frye, *A Natural Perspective*: 'The kernel of the Jonsonian tradition is something abstract and sophisticated; the kernel of the Shakespearean tradition is something childlike and concrete' (33).

This song differs from the preceding three: 'it is the single example of Ariel using the first-person pronoun in song', and thus 'the only one of his performances which asks the audience to identify directly with him as singer'.[54] No longer invisible, Ariel foregrounds authorial agency. Moreover, unlike his previous songs, this one has no overt social goal, whether to affect the hearer emotionally or to awaken him politically; it seems designed purely for pleasure. In Act 5, scene 1, Ariel sings the song while he '*helps to attire* [Prospero]' (SD after line 87), and after it, the magus comments appreciatively, 'Why, that's my dainty Ariel!' (95). Yet the carefree, leisurely performance of the song is exquisitely belied by its deep philosophical content.[55]

Ariel's image of the bee derives from Plato's *Ion*, representing 'the poet's divinely inspired wisdom and eloquence'.[56] Thomas Nashe had expressed the idea that 'profitable knowledge may be "sucked" from Virgil's poetry' (Tudeau-Clayton 106n74), which Shakespeare echoes in the image of the bee sucking nectar from the cowslip. We can add that the locus of Ariel's lyric performance, couched '*In*' a flower, '*Under* the blossom that hangs on the bough', is not merely lovely but philosophically precise. A metaphysical spirit of song takes up residence in the material beauty of nature's floral design: 'Merrily, merrily shall I live now.' Arguably, no other song in the English language better expresses the spiritual state of 'freedom' within the natural world (5.1.96), which Ariel cheerfully secures from his master through the successful performance of lyric art.[57]

POET OF THE THEATRE

In such plays as *The Tempest*, *Henry V*, *1 Henry IV*, and *As You Like It*, Shakespeare stages a counter-laureate authorship, fusing the form of poetry with the form of theatre, and making the art of the poet integral with the art of the playwright, not simply in the lyrical phase of his career but in both its middle phase and its closing one. Often, Shakespeare stages scenes of poetry with engaging mockery – represented through Touchstone with Audrey, Hotspur with Glendower, and the Dolphin with his horse – as if their

---

[54] Lindley, *Music* 230.
[55] The following paragraph responds to Lindley, *Music*, who sees the song 'test[ing]' the 'period's debates about music': whether its 'harmonies' can 'reflect … celestial order' for a 'curative function' or whether its 'self-indulgence … opens up the possibility that music itself is morally neutral, that its effects ultimately depend upon the uses to which it is put' (231–2).
[56] Tudeau-Clayton, *Jonson, Shakespeare, and the Early Modern Virgil* 106n74.
[57] On political freedom here, see A. Patterson, *Shakespeare and the Popular Voice* 154–62. Lindley is more guarded about the song's 'celebration of a freedom' (232), but he usefully recalls the antithesis in Caliban's 'song of freedom in 2.2', with both songs 'celebrat[ing] … the possibility of release' (230–1).

author were deflecting attention from his own literary practice, privileging theatre over poetry and abandoning a literary career. Yet Shakespeare also stages scenes of poetry that more clearly affirm the cultural value of the poet in his civilizing authority, as represented in Lodwick in *Edward III*, Leontes' court poet in *The Winter's Tale*, and Ariel in *The Tempest*. In particular, the last two suggest that late in his practice the author continues to process a literary career within the place of the stage. In all cases, however, the audience is left to confront the representation pretty much on its own. While some may find occasion to move beyond the category of the author, we have acknowledged this urge, and sought a different route.

Throughout his career, Shakespeare is a theatrical man who wrote enduring poems that he himself published (or saw published through the agency of others); who engaged vigorously the Western poetic tradition; and who made the art of the poet an abiding figure on the new London stage. In the end, the counter-laureate author transformed both media in which he worked, poems as well as plays, and made this his principal legacy to future English and European authors. In all his works, the English poet-playwright succeeds in making the truest poetry the most theatrical, the truest theatre poetical.

CHAPTER 4

Books and theatre in Shakespeare's plays: Richard III, Love's Labour's Lost, Romeo and Juliet, Othello

> Lechery, by this hand; an index and obscure prologue to the history of lust and foul thoughts.
>
> Iago, *Othello* 2.1.257–8

While Shakespeare often stages lyric poetry in his plays, he augments this visible rehearsal of counter-laureate authorship by creating a fiction about the theatre of the book. In particular, the epigraph to this chapter, taken from a speech by Iago on the companionate marriage of Othello and Desdemona, speaks to the way that Shakespearean authorship often inter-laces the language of books and the language of theatre. It voices subjective vectors – here 'lust' and 'thought', or desire and consciousness; it includes their social dynamics, since Iago objects to the marriage of a Moor with a racially white woman; and it gestures to larger questions of 'history' that in this tragedy turn out to have deep religious significance. In Iago's com-pound of 'index' and 'prologue', Shakespeare linguistically registers the historic conjunction of Elizabethan England's two professional institutions as the premier sites of a counter-laureate authorship: the theatre and the printing shop.

For Shakespeare, Iago's word 'index' is rare, occurring only four other times in his canon – and only in his plays (*R3* 2.2.149; 4.4.85; *Ham* 3.4.52; *TC* 1.3.343). According to the *Oxford English Dictionary*, Shakespeare uses the term in *Othello* under Definition 5a: 'A table of contents prefixed to a book, a brief list or summary of the matters treated in it'. All of Shakespeare's other uses subscribe to this textual definition; for instance, in *Troilus and Cressida*, Nestor remarks to Ulysses, 'And in such indexes (although small pricks / To their subsequent volumes) there is seen / The baby figure of the giant mass / Of things to come at large' (1.3.343–6). When Iago uses the term, he also does so metaphorically, to mean that Desdemona's public display of affection for her husband is a summary of her unruly desire.

More often than 'index', Shakespeare uses the word 'prologue' – twenty-five times, again only in his plays. Not surprisingly, he almost always connects the term to theatre, as appears in the *OED*'s Definition 2: 'One who speaks or recites the prologue to a play on the stage'. In his plays, Shakespeare does not simply use the word 'prologue', or occasionally preface his drama with formal prologues (as in *Henry V* and *Troilus and Cressida*); he also stages meta-prologues, fictions rehearsing a formal prologue (as in *Love's Labour's Lost*, *A Midsummer Night's Dream*, and *Hamlet*), often with characters commenting on them. 'Is this a prologue, or the posy of a ring?', Hamlet inquires of Ophelia before *The Mousetrap* (3.2.152). For his part, Iago again uses the term metaphorically, to express Desdemona's physical affection as a predictor of her interior corruption.

As a conjunction, however, Iago's 'index and ... prologue' yokes a bibliographical with a theatrical term in order to get, not at Desdemona's literary consciousness, but inadvertently at his own. This ambitious military man purports to rely on a combined discourse of books and theatre to interpret the physical action of a beautiful young woman in relation with her husband, when in fact he unwittingly conveys the terms of his own agency. Within the fiction, this agency acquires a literary valence, depicting an underlying tragic utility to both books and theatre.

It is true that the *OED* does indicate slippage for both terms in Iago's conjunction. An *index* can mean 'a preface, prologue' (Def. 5a), while a *prologue* can mean 'The preface or introduction to a discourse or performance; a preliminary discourse, proem, preface, preamble; esp. a discourse or poem spoken as the introduction to a dramatic performance' (Def. 1). During the period, then, each term could have both a bibliographical and a theatrical resonance. At one point in his canon, in the first quarto of *Romeo and Juliet*, Shakespeare appears to elide the distinction between *book* and *prologue*, when Benvolio turns up the curious phrase 'without-book prologue' (1.4.7) – referring to a prologue delivered without a promptbook. In fact, then, Benvolio's book is not printed but a tool of the playhouse. Acknowledging this instance of potential slippage, we can conclude that Shakespeare tends to select out the bibliographical meaning of *index* and the theatrical meaning of *prologue*.[1]

If we look further into the Shakespeare canon, we see that very often 'books' turn out to be books of poetry, more so than past criticism avers. In *The Taming of the Shrew*, Tranio makes the identification explicit: 'well read

---

[1] In his recent Cambridge edition, N. Sanders glosses Iago's 'index' as 'indicator of; lit. "table of contents prefacing"', and he leaves 'prologue' unglossed, presumably because its theatrical meaning is clear (ed. 105). In his Arden 3 edition, Honigman glosses 'index' as 'table of contents prefixed to a book; preface; prologue', and similarly leaves 'prologue' unglossed (179).

in poetry / And other books, good ones' (1.2.169–70). As we shall see, Iago is more than a dark model for the Shakespearean man of both books and theatre; he is also a shrewd practitioner of the art of poetry. In his deployment of poetry and books, as in his staged theatre, Iago joins a whole host of other figures in the Shakespeare canon.[2]

During the past decade, critics have increasingly attended to Shakespeare's interest in putting 'reading and writing' on to the stage, but we still lack a detailed study of his theatre of the book, especially his theatrical book of poetry.[3] As we shall see, sometimes Shakespeare rehearses a discourse of the book detached from theatre, offering fresh insights into such literary topics as consciousness, fame, and authorship. At other times, he conjoins book and theatre in a single utterance, opening up further insights into these topics and others, including the art of poetry. While a large number of examples appear in the Shakespearean dramatic canon, *Richard III* and *Love's Labour's Lost* offer especially intriguing windows into his counter-laureate authorship, both from the mid-1590s, across the genres of history and comedy. The rhetorical figure called *hendiadys* offers a sturdy frame for bringing the tragedy of Iago's dark literary authorship into perspective later in Shakespeare's career.

'FIND DELIGHT WRIT THERE WITH BEAUTY'S PEN': BOOKS OR THEATRE

Shakespeare's discourse of the theatre is so well known that it has become virtually equated with the name 'William Shakespeare', and not surprisingly a small industry on 'metadrama' was a major form of twentieth-century criticism.[4] Recurrently, Shakespeare makes the theatre an integral part of his fiction, as when he stages a play-within-a-play in *The Taming of the Shrew*, *Love Labour's Lost*, A *Midsummer Night's Dream*, *1 Henry IV*, and *Hamlet*, or

---

[2] Krier, *Birth Passages*, sees Shakespeare's 'career' as 'creat[ing] … for himself' a 'place' between 'a specific poetic history and the radically developing institution of the theater' (162). Bednarz, *Shakespeare and the Poets' War*, reminds us how Renaissance treatises tended to see the relation between poetry and theatre: 'Sidney's *Apology for Poetry* and Heywood's *Apology for Actors* are linked by the proposition that drama is a subset of "poetry" that deploys a wide range of fictional constructs to move an audience to moral action' (253).

[3] In *Shakespeare and the Idea of the Book*, Scott identifies her study as the first to examine fully Shakespeare's use of the book in his plays. Related studies include R. S. Knapp, *Shakespeare: The Theater and the Book*; F. Kiefer, *Writing on the Renaissance Stage*, which often refers to Shakespeare, among others; but also Bergeron, ed., *Reading and Writing in Shakespeare*; Hackel, 'The "Great Variety" of Readers and Early Modern Reading Practices', and *Reading Material in Early Modern England*.

[4] In addition to Righter (later Barton), *Shakespeare and the Idea of the Play*, see, e.g., Calderwood, *Metadrama in Shakespeare's Henriad* and *To Be and Not To Be*; Kernan, 'Shakespeare's Essays on Dramatic Poesy'. Metadrama continues to inform important criticism today, as it does Greenblatt's *Will and the World* and Garber's *Shakespeare After All*.

such masques as that of Hymen in *Much Ado*, the Fairy Queen in *Merry Wives*, Ceres and Juno in *The Tempest*, or the shepherds in *Henry VIII*. Most dramatically, he inserts the fiction of the strolling players into *Hamlet*, leading the Prince to produce his famous instructions on 'the purpose of playing' (3.2.20). More often, Shakespeare presents characters who turn to the theatre as a metaphor, as when Jacques reports humourously in *As You Like It*, 'All the world's a stage, / And all the men and women merely players' (2.7.139–40); or Macbeth laments hauntingly, 'Life's but a walking shadow, a poor player, / That struts and frets his hour upon the stage, / And then is heard no more' (5.5.24–6). The effect is to render character *theatrical* – lending to us one of this author's most historic accomplishments. Indeed, the Shakespearean discourse of the theatre is so rich and famous we hardly need to remind ourselves of it.

While not as much has been written on Shakespeare's discourse of the book, readers probably recognize it as a familiar feature of his theatre. For instance, the word *book* and its cognates occur over 130 times in the Shakespeare canon, spread over nearly all of his works, from early to late.[5] Allied words and cognates include *volume* (15 times); *text* (13); and *library* (3), this last revealing the author's occasional reference to the architectural place of the book, as in Prospero's recollection of his 'library', which contains 'books' and 'volumes' that once he 'prize[d] above … [his] dukedom' (1.2.166–8). More rarely, Shakespeare uses such words as *folio* (once) and *edition* (once), while other terms from print culture pepper his plays: *character*, *binding*, *copy*, *press*, *print*, and of course *publish*.[6]

From the plays, we hear about a lot of different types of books. These include such historical books as the Bible, called 'God's book' (*2H6* 2.3.4), or even specific books of Scripture such as the 'book of Numbers' (*H5* 1.2.98). Other historical books include a 'book of prayer' (*R3* 3.7.98), perhaps the *Book of Common Prayer*; the 'Book of Riddles' (*MW* 1.1.201–2); and the 'Absey book' (*KJ* 1.1.196), a book of ABCs or primer. Still other types of books include a 'note-book' (*MW* 1.1.145), a 'table-book' (*WT* 4.4.598), a 'copy-book' (*LLL* 5.2.42), and 'lenders' books' (*KL* 3.4.97). Shakespeare even manages to come up with a single phrase to circumscribe them all: 'all the books in England' (*1H4* 2.4.49–50).

---

[5] All statistics again come from Spevack, *Complete and Systematic Concordance to the Works of Shakespeare*.

[6] On such terms, see *SNPP*, esp. chs. 1, 4, and 8. On Shakespeare worrying about print publication, see, e.g., C. Burrow, 'Life and Work in Shakespeare's Poems'. Thus, Kastan is misleading: 'Shakespeare was, for the most part, uninterested in print' (*Shakespeare and the Book* 136).

Yet many of the 'books' turn out to be figures of speech, of every imaginable type: a 'book of memory' (*1H6* 2.4.101); a 'book of life' (*R2* 1.3.202); a 'book of heaven' (*R2* 4.1.236); a 'book of beauty' (*KJ* 2.1.485); a 'lawless bloody book / Of forg'd rebellion with a seal divine' (*2H4* 4.1.91–2); a 'beggar's book' (*H8* 1.1.122); a 'book [of] … love' (*TGV* 1.1.20); a 'book of words' (*MA* 1.1.307); a 'book … for good manners' (*AYLI* 5.4.91); a 'book of sport' (*TC* 4.5.239); a 'book of all that monarchs do' (*Per* 1.1.94); a 'book of virtue' (*WT* 4.3.122); a 'book of arithmetic' (*RJ* 3.1.102); 'sour misfortune's book' (*RJ* 5.3.82); a 'saw … of books' (*Ham* 1.5.100); a 'bloody book of law' (*Oth* 1.3.67); 'nature's infinite book of secrecy' (*AC* 1.2.10); a 'book of … good acts' (*Cor* 5.2.15); and 'Jove's own book' (*Cor* 3.1.291) – this last being the book of fame, which arguably names the telos of the Shakespearean book itself.[7]

Occasionally in his plays, Shakespeare appears to eye specific early modern printed books. In *As You Like* It, for instance, Touchstone can quip, 'we quarrel in print, by the book – as you have books for good manners' (5.4.90–1). According to the *Riverside Shakespeare*, 'There were, in fact, such books, hardly less fantastic than Touchstone's … One which may be glanced at here is Vincent Saviolo's *Practice of the Rapier and Dagger* (1594–5)' (433).[8] At least twice, Shakespeare intimates that the printed books he has in mind would be quartos. In *2 Henry 4*, near the middle of his career, the Earl of Northumberland says of his retainer Morton,

> Yea, this man's brow, like to a title-leaf,
> Foretells the nature of a tragic volume.   (*2 Henry 4* 1.1.60–1)

The Earl likens the face of his retainer – literally, his forehead – to a book, as the technical words 'title-leaf' and 'volume' indicate, but he particularizes the printed book as a tragedy in his phrase 'tragic volume'. Indeed, at this time it was conventional for tragedies to be printed in quartos, as was Shakespeare's first printed tragedy, *Titus Andronicus*, in 1594.

---

[7] The claim that Shakespeare 'never admitted' to 'literary ambition' (Kastan 135) is belied everywhere in the Shakespearean text – including in the Sonnets, where the poet, as Leishman long ago observed, 'has written both more copiously and more memorably [on the idea of poetic immortality] than any other sonneteer' (*Themes and Variations in Shakespeare's Sonnets* 22). See also Duncan-Jones, *Ungentle Shakespeare*, for the Shakespearean commitment to fame in the Sonnets as coming from 'the printed book' (177); and *SNPP*, for index entries under the following: 'eternity', 'fame', 'glory, Christian', 'immortality', and 'oblivion'.

[8] Other editions cite other books printed at the time, including specific 'books of good manners'.

Similarly, late in his career in *Pericles*, the King of Pentapolis, Simonides, addresses the knights who have just come to a banquet from a tilting tournament:

> To say you're welcome were superfluous.
> [To] place upon the volume of your deeds,
> As in a title-page, your worth in arms,
> Were more than you expect, or more than's fit,
> Since every worth in show commends itself. (*Pericles* 2.3.2–6)

Rather than a tragedy, the chivalric discourse suggests a book of epic romance, fitting the genre being staged.[9] Here Simonides refers to the early modern printing convention of detailing the contents of a book on its 'title-page', which he declares 'superfluous', and then he adds a rationale based on a metaphor from the theatre: 'Since every worth in show commends itself'.[10]

Just as Shakespeare often stages plays-within-plays, so he recurrently brings books on to the stage as a prop. Hamlet is not merely a theatrical man but also a bookish man; this literary compound may form his final signature. Another theatrical man from the mid-point of Shakespeare's career is similarly prone to reading books on stage. In Act 4, scene 3, of *Julius Caesar*, Brutus tells his page, young Lucius, 'here's the book I sought for so; I put it in the pocket of my gown' (252–3), and after the boy plays his harp, Brutus picks the book back up: 'Let me see, let me see; is not the leaf turn'd down / Where I left reading? Here it is, I think' (273–4), prompting the Ghost of Caesar to appear.

This sort of fiction also emerges early in Shakespeare's career. In *The Taming of the Shrew*, Shakespeare quotes Ovid's *Heroides* (3.1.28–9; see *3H6* 1.3.48), while the trickster Tranio pulls out a 'small packet of Greek and Latin books' (2.1.100) in a play that seems to be as much about the erotic theatre of books as it is about eros. In *Love's Labour's Lost*, Shakespeare constructs a plot that is more formally about book-learning, as the four 'book-men' (2.1.227, 4.2.34) retire from public life to form an academy organized around scholarship: 'Our court shall be a little academe, / Still and contemplative in living art' (1.1.13–14). Among Shakespeare's kings, Henry VI is particularly prone to scholarship: his 'bookish rule hath pull'd fair England down' (*2H6* 1.1.259). As we have seen previously, in Act 4,

---

[9] Some editors now believe that George Wilkins wrote Acts 1–2 of *Pericles* and that Shakespeare wrote Acts 3–5 (B. Vickers, *Shakespeare as Co-Author* 292–332). Nonetheless, Shakespeare may have added 'touches' to the opening acts (*Riverside* 1528), and this passage may be one of them, as its similarity with that in *2 Henry IV* suggests. For recent skepticism about collaboration in *Pericles*, see Kastan 64–6.

[10] On Shakespeare's use of 'show' as his habitual term for theatre, see *SNPP* 108–13, 240–2, citing esp. *Hamlet* 3.2.140–6.

scene 1, of *Titus Andronicus* Shakespeare brings the 'book' (41) of 'Ovid's Metamorphosis' (42) on stage as a prop – a feat he will reprise in *Cymbeline* at the end of his career. Also in *Cymbeline*, Posthumus awakens from his dream of the Leonati in Act 5, scene 4, to discover a 'book' lying on his chest (5.4.133), the detailed contents of which he then reads out loud on stage (138–50).

In *The Tempest*, the books of the magician Prospero become an important feature in the plot. Like Henry VI, Brutus, and Hamlet, Prospero is a bookish man. Initially, he locates the origin of his fall in his obsession with 'the liberal arts', as he recalls to Miranda: 'those being all my study, / The government I cast upon my brother, / ... being transported / And rapt in secret studies' (1.2.73–7). Yet Prospero also tells his daughter of the good services of his counselor Gonzalo: 'Knowing I lov'd my books, he furnish'd me / From mine own library with [prized] volumes' (166–7). Accordingly, in the subplot Caliban fixates on getting hold of Prospero's books as the key to revolt: 'first [seize] ... his books ... First ... possess his books ... Burn but his books' (3.2.89–95). Finally, at the end of the play Prospero decides to abandon his bookish art as a prelude to his return home to Milan: 'I'll drown my book' (5.1.57).

From Henry VI to Hamlet to Prospero, the Shakespearean dramatic canon can be said to be about the book of scholarship. For an author routinely considered, since Jonson, to be a poet of nature (not a poet of learning, like Jonson himself), this might appear surprising. Yet the evidence of the plays bears it out.[11] Thus, in *As You Like It*, after Orlando declaims, 'Hang there, my verse', he adds, 'O Rosalind, these trees shall be my books, / And in their barks my thoughts I'll character' (3.2.1–6). The audience may hear an echo of Duke Senior's remark earlier, when he praises the 'life' he leads in the Forest of Arden for its magical power to 'Find ... tongues in trees, books in the running brooks, / Sermons in stones, and good in every thing' (2.1.15–17). Such lines merely look like they support Shakespeare's standing as a poet of nature; in fact, they do the opposite, *textualizing* the very authorship of nature.

One of the most intriguing sites for viewing Shakespeare's authorial discourse of scholarship emerges in his recurrent representation of the *body* as a *text* – or more precisely, the seemingly gratuitous conceit of *the human face as a book*. In *Macbeth*, for instance, Lady Macbeth says to her husband, 'Your face ... is as a book, where men / May read strange matters'

---

[11] For recent discussion, with special attention to the scholar Hamlet, see Trevor, *Poetics of Melancholy* 63–86.

(1.5.62–3).[12] Othello deploys the conceit when confronting his wife; touching Desdemona's beautiful face, he says, longingly, 'Was this fair paper, this most goodly book, / Made to write "whore" upon?' (4.2.71–2; see Honigman, ed. 277). Although the conceit may be conventional, we might wonder whether the following lines from the opening scene of *Pericles* were written by the author of such passages: 'Her face the book of praises, where is read / Nothing but curious pleasures' (1.1.15–16). Underlying the equation may be a term from the culture of books, and perhaps the printing house, for, according to the *OED*, a *face* could also be 'a leaf in a book' (III.11b), citing Fulke Greville in 1575 as the first example.[13]

Following from Shakespeare's body-as-face conceit is his conceit of identity – inwardness, subjectivity, consciousness – as a book. In *Twelfth Night*, for instance, Duke Orsino tells Viola (disguised as Cesario), 'I have unclasp'd / To thee the book even of my secret soul' (1.4.13–14). The equation here between a material object, the 'book', and consciousness, the 'secret soul', speaks to a rather precise relation between 'subject and object in Renaissance culture' and more particularly in Shakespeare.[14] In Shakespeare's lexicon, the 'soul' has a bibliographical and thus a literary character, composed of books, made up from books, and expressive of books. Occasionally, Shakespeare puts together an articulation that operates along the border of subject and object. In *Richard II*, for instance, the king defends himself against accusation: 'I'll read enough, / When I do see the very book indeed / Where all my sins are writ, and that's myself' (4.1.273–5). Similarly, in *1 Henry IV* the Earl of Worcester tells his rebel relatives, 'now I will unclasp a secret book, / And to your quick-conceiving discontents / I'll read you matter deep and dangerous' (1.3.188–90).

Yet Shakespeare's most detailed figural representation of the book comes from *Romeo and Juliet*, deploying the face-as-book conceit and gathering in several of the conceptual leaves we have perused. In Act 1, scene 3, Lady Capulet tries to persuade her daughter to marry the County Paris:

> Read o'er the volume of young Paris' face,
> And find delight writ there with beauty's pen;

---

[12] In his poems, Shakespeare deploys the conceit several times. See, e.g., *RL* 99–105, 615–6, 806–12, 1183, 1195; *Son* 77.1–4. On the Tudor 'aesthetics of the body', see Hulse, 'Tudor Aesthetics' 30. For the conceit in Shakespeare, see Thompson and Thompson, *Shakespeare, Meaning, and Metaphor* 165–70. For the conceit during the period, see F. Kiefer 89–107.

[13] The word *face* also refers to the surface of a piece of type (= typeface), but the *OED* does not record the first example until 1683. The *OED*'s Def. III.13c reads 'Of a document: The inscribed side,' tracing to 1632. As Jonson reveals through the name of a lead character in *The Alchemist*, *face* also has a theatrical meaning.

[14] For a different model, see de Grazia, 'Introduction' to *Subject and Object in Renaissance Culture*, ed. de Grazia, Quilligan, and Stallybrass, who emphasizes the primacy of 'object' over 'subject'.

> Examine every married lineament,
> And see how one another lends content;
> And what obscur'd in this fair volume lies
> Find written in the margent of his eyes.
> This precious book of love, this unbound lover,
> To beautify him, only lacks a cover.
> …
> That book in many's eyes doth share the glory,
> That in gold clasps locks in the golden story.
>
> (*Romeo and Juliet* 1.3.81–92)

Shakespeare brings considerable ingenuity to the conceit – too much, thought Alexander Pope, who omitted the 'ridiculous speech' in his 1725 edition, with modern directors and critics following suit.[15] Similarly, in his recent Cambridge edition G. Blakemore Evans calls Lady Capulet's praise of Paris 'precious and nonsensical' and its results 'unhappy' (ed. 87) – without recognizing that this mode is characteristic of the *self-effacing Shakespearean literary*. If we deride or omit the speech, we miss not only a textbook example of the Shakespearean 'conceit' but also an unusual model of Shakespearean counter-laureate authorship.

Juliet, her mother advises, is to read Paris as a book – in particular, the physical beauty of his face as the book's 'content[s]'. But the young girl is also to look into Paris' eyes to find a marginal gloss on the 'obscure' terms of his outward appearance, the inner truth to his beauty and heart. Perhaps referring to the early modern book trade, Lady Capulet identifies Paris as an 'unbound' book, in need of the 'cover' that Juliet can supply by becoming his wife. Juliet can 'share the glory' through this 'married' act, just as a book acquires beauty and fame when the act of binding completes the process of printing.

The book in question may be the 'book of love', but Shakespeare goes further: it is also a book of poetry. Thus, in the third line Lady Capulet moves into rhymed couplets to describe the 'content' of the book, and editors have even detected an allusion to a particular book: Ovid's *Ars amatoria* (Evans, ed. 87). Not simply a conceit, Lady Capulet's trope may function as a moment of intertextuality, linking Shakespeare's Renaissance stage play with a famous book of classical love poetry. Indeed, book-learning goes into the conceit, for line 90, 'For fair without the fair within

---

[15] Pope, quoted in Levenson, ed. 177. The following analysis is indebted to Levenson's detailed annotation; as well as to Gibbons, ed. 104; Evans, ed. 87–8. Levenson points out that Shakespeare's main source for the play, Arthur Brooke's poem *Romeus and Juliet* (1562), 'mentions only that Capulet's wife "paints" an impression of Paris "with curious words" (1893–6)' (ed. 176).

to hide', refers to the 'Neoplatonic concept of *fair* outside reflecting *fair* inside' (Levenson, ed. 177). Underlying Lady Capulet's 'ridiculous' conceit, then, is a rather ingenious gloss on the philosophical Shakespearean book of consciousness.

Yet most striking is what remains unseen: the very author of the book. Shakespeare may attend to the book's material make-up – its 'writ[ing]', its 'content[s]', and even the 'pen' that 'writ' it – but nowhere does he identify the author behind the book: 'find delight writ there with beauty's pen'. The disembodied action of a pen writing a book with delight rather *conceals* the author, much as we have seen in chapter 1 with respect to the Shakespeare coat of arms.[16]

In sum, from the beginning to the end of his professional career Shakespeare seeks innovative ways to bring both books (including poetic books) and plays on to the stage as part of the historic making of the London theatre. Yet even more historic are moments that conjoin a discourse of the book with a discourse of the theatre.

'HE READS MUCH ... HE LOVES NO PLAYS': BOOKS AND THEATRE

The divided literary man in question is 'spare Cassius' (1.2.201), as reported by Julius Caesar to Marc Antony near the beginning of their tragedy:

> He reads much,
> He is a great observer, and he looks
> Quite through the deeds of men. He loves no plays,
> As thou dost, Antony; he hears no music.   (*Julius Caesar* 1.2.201–4)

Here Shakespeare uses the discourse of books and theatre to portray Cassius as private, introspective, and socially penetrating. In contrast to his love of reading, Cassius' lack of love for the theatre marks him out as a distinct (patently flawed) breed of literary man – different, say, from Hamlet, or even from his own best friend, Brutus, or from his future arch-enemy, Antony, and presumably from Caesar himself.[17] However we interpret the Cassius portrait, through it Shakespeare voices one of his primary inventions for dramatic character, cut from the discourse of his professional career.

---

[16] Evans anticipates this idea when he identifies the speech as 'an ornamental set-piece calculated to display the writer's wit rather than a character's feeling' (ed. 17).

[17] Daniell, in his Arden 3 edition, remarks that Caesar's criticism of Cassius 'puts positively what Brutus ... dismissed as superficial in Antony' earlier in the scene, when Brutus told Cassius that he was not interested in running in the race that Caesar sponsors: 'I am not gamesome. I do lack some part / Of that quick spirit that is in Antony' (ed. 176). The characterization does not come from Plutarch.

As to be expected from the preceding discussion, often the books con-joined with theatre turn out to be books of poetry. In chapter 3, we quoted Don Adriano de Armado from *Love's Labor's Lost*, who rhapsodizes, 'Assist me, some extemporal god of rhyme, for I am sure I shall turn sonnet. Devise, wit, write, pen, for I am for whole volumes in folio' (1.2.183–5). Here Armado captures the entire process of early modern print-poetry author-ship, from invention ('Devise, wit'), to composition ('write, pen'), to pub-lication itself ('volumes in folio'). Yet, as his word 'extemporal' indicates, Armado also understands his utterance as a form of theatre.

We can find Shakespeare's poetic theatre of books in the most unusual places – such as Juliet's confused indictment of Romeo after she learns that he has killed her cousin Tybalt:

> O serpent heart, hid with a flow'ring face!
> Did ever dragon keep so fair a cave?
> Beautiful tyrant! fiend angelical!
> Dove-feather'd raven! wolvish ravening lamb!
> Despised substance of divinest show!
> Just opposite to what thou justly seem'st,
> …
> Was ever book containing such vile matter
> So fairly bound? O that deceit should dwell
> In such a gorgeous palace!   (*Romeo and Juliet* 3.2.73–85)

If Romeo had earlier 'kiss[ed] by th' book' (1.5.110), here Juliet *storms* by the book – the book of Petrarch, as the heavy articulation of erotic oxymoron reveals.[18] On the surface, Juliet's conceit of the beloved as a book looks merely conventional, but it is more engaging than its appearance shows.

For one thing, the conceit turns the convention on its head, exchanging Petrarchan praise for Shakespearean dispraise (on display, for instance, in the dark lady sonnets); for another, it deploys Shakespeare's famed theatri-cal trope of *inner* and *outer*, contrasting Romeo's physical beauty and his 'gorgeous' person with the ugly character of his inward identity. As a book, Romeo is 'fairly bound', but inside the attractive cover he is 'vile matter'. Yet what is especially notable is the surge of theatrical terms surrounding the discourse of the book: not simply 'seem'st' and 'deceit' but more formally 'divinest show'. In her anger, Juliet jumbles book and theatre, accusing Romeo of falsely staging a religious play of affection and writing a deceitful

---

[18] Cf. Romeo at 1.1.175–81. On the Petrarchan idiom, see Whittier, 'Sonnet's Body and the Body Sonnetized in *Romeo and Juliet*'; Dubrow, *Echoes of Desire* 262–7; Henderson, *Passion Made Public* 1–7; Levenson, ed. 52–61.

book of companionate love. In attacking his agency as a lover, she inadvertently casts up the literary terms of her creator's own authorship.

That Shakespeare is thinking of his own authorship emerges through the likelihood of a self-allusion in the passage's opening line: 'O serpent heart, hid with a flowering face!' This is as fine a rendering as any of a line then infamous: 'O tiger's heart wrapp'd in a woman's hide' (*3H6* 1.4.137). As readers will recall, the line had been rewritten before – in 1592 by Robert Greene (or more likely Henry Chettle), when criticizing Shakespeare as 'an upstart Crow, beautified with our feathers, that with his *Tygers hart wrapt in a Players hyde*, supposes he is as well able to bombast out a blanke verse as the best of you: and beeing an absolute *Iohannes fac totum*, is in his owne conceit the onely Shake-scene in a countrey'.[19] Importantly, Greene reads the Shakespearean author *into* the 'blank verse' of a dramatic text, turning York's savage indictment of Queen Margaret into an attack against a fellow writer, a misogynistic cut at the cruel hypocrisy of a woman into a homosocial jab at a colleague's professional impersonation (whether Shakespeare's skill at literary plagiarism, his role as an actor, or more likely both).

Shakespeare's terms of indictment in both speeches are eerily similar, including when York calls Margaret 'She-wolf of France, but worse than wolves of France' (111), but more notably when he uses the metaphor of the theatrical face – twice iterated: 'thy face is vizard-like, unchanging ... / And yet be seen to wear a woman's face?' (116, 140). Let us put the two lines together:

> O tiger's heart wrapp'd in a woman's hide!
>
> (*3 Henry VI* 1.4.137).
>
> O serpent heart, hid with a flow'ring face!
>
> (*Romeo and Juliet* 3.2.73)

Not simply do both lines put a powerful exclamation in a single blank-verse line, and share a trochaic inversion in what is otherwise an iambic pentameter line, but both begin with the exclamatory 'O', use the word 'heart' as a noun modified by an adjectival beast, and include cognates of the theatrically ringing word *hide*, in order to get at an individual's false concealment of an ugly identity. The phrase at the end of Juliet's line, 'flow'ring face', merely looks innocuous.[20] While it might be too much to see a reference to printer's flowers ornamenting title pages of early modern books, 'flowers'

---

[19] *Greenes Groats-worth of witte*, repr. *Riverside* 1959.
[20] Levenson's gloss reads, 'face serving as a floral cover' (ed. 268).

was a conventional metaphor for poetry during the period, and 'face (we have seen) is a theatrical word, making 'flow'ring face' a rather fine metonymy for the poetry-theatre conjunction. If this self-reference has not made it into annotation on *Romeo and Juliet*, perhaps it is because we have neglected the signature terms of Shakespearean counter-laureate authorship.[21]

Yet perhaps the most direct – and bizarre – representation of Shakespeare's poetic theatre of the book occurs in *Two Gentlemen of Verona*. In Act 2, scene 1, the witty servant Speed attempts to explain to his master Valentine the subtle wooing strategy of Silvia: 'That my master being scribe, to himself should write the letter … / [S]he woos you by a figure' (140, 148). That is to say, Silvia has had Valentine write a love letter to a man he thinks is her lover when in fact he is the lover himself. Speed tries to convince Valentine that he is reporting the strategy accurately by devising an unusual performance of truth; he breaks into the quotation of a four-lined verse in fourteeners, followed by a summarizing one-line statement in prose on the topic of print culture:

> 'For often have you writ to her; and she in modesty,
> Or else for want of idle time, could not again reply;
> Or fearing else some messenger, that might her mind discover,
> Herself hath taught her love himself to write unto her lover'.
> All this I speak in print, for in print I found it.[22]
>
> (*Two Gentlemen of Verona* 2.1.165–9)

To 'speak in print' is a contradiction of terms, but early in his career it seems to be Shakespeare's witty formulation for the conjoining economy of books and theatre along with poetry. While Speed's utterance remains gnomic, he intimates that the dramatic lines he 'speak[s]' in a play on the new London stage originate 'in print', and that his theatrical utterance therefore has a published derivation, which the details of the comedy trace to such poetry as Marlowe's *Hero and Leander* (e.g., 1.1.19–26; 3.1.119; *Norton* 85) and Ovid's *Metamorphoses* (e.g., 1.1.66; 2.1.30–1; J. Bate, *Ovid* 43).

That Shakespeare is still rehearsing a theatre of the printed book at the end of his career is evident in *The Winter's Tale*, where we find one of his most innovative and witty representations during the sheep-shearing festival of Act 4, scene 4:

AUTOLYCUS.   … I have about me many parcels of charge.
CLOWN.   What hast here? Ballads?

---

[21] The annotated editions of Levenson, Evans, and Gibbons pass the self-reference by.

[22] In his Arden 2 edition, Leech glosses 'in print' in the last line as '(1) with exactness … (2) in a printed book, etc. The second meaning could suggest that the preceding lines were a quotation' (ed. 30). Indeed, the *Riverside* prints the lines as such.

MOPSA.   Pray now buy some. I love a ballad in print, a-life, for then we are
                sure they are true.
AUTOLYCUS.   Here's one to a very doleful tune, how a usurer's wife was brought
                to bed of twenty money-bags at a burthen, and how she long'd to
                eat adders' heads, and toads carbonado'd.
MOPSA.   Is it true, think you?
AUTOLYCUS.   Very true, and but a month old.

                                                    (*The Winter's Tale* 4.4.257–67)

A remarkable poet-playwright figure, Autolycus here uses theatrical disguise
to dupe the gullible Clown and Mopsa, pretending to sell them ballads pulled
out of his coat lining when in fact he's there to pick their pockets.[23] Too often,
critics want to see Autolycus as a man of the theatre, or alternatively as a figure
from popular culture, connected simply to the performance of balladeering.[24]
Yet two features of this dialogue suggest that Shakespeare uses a fiction of
theatrical balladeering to dramatize the print-poet.[25]

   The first feature is the formal discourse of print culture, evident in Mopsa's
memorable line, "I love a ballad in print.' The second consists of references to
the long debate about the truth-value of high-culture print poetry, derived
from Plato's *Republic* and eloquently addressed in Sidney's *Defence of Poesie*
(chapter 3). For her part, Mopsa is convinced that if Autolycus' ballad is 'in
print', it is 'true'. Then, when he pulls out another ballad with a flurry of
violent detail, she wants to know whether it is 'true', leading the trickster to
mock the entire Western tradition of poetry, 'Very true, and but a month
old.' A bit later, Autolycus himself gestures to the topic when he says in self-
defense, 'Why should I carry lies abroad?' (4.4.271), and he goes on to
mention 'another ballad', 'sung ... against the hard hearts of maids ... The
ballad is very pitiful, and as true' (275–81). While the scene is one of playful
mockery, it reveals Shakespeare's career-long commitment to creating memorable theatre out of poetry and books.[26]

---

[23] On Autolycus as a poet-playwright, see *SNPP* 273–4.

[24] On Autolycus as an actor, see Mowat, 'Rogues, Shepherds, and the Counterfeit Distressed'; Lamb,
    'Ovid and *The Winter's Tale*'; Palfrey, *Late Shakespeare* 117–26, 231–43. On Autolycus and popular
    culture, see Fabiszak, 'Portrait of the Artist as a Shakespearean Character in *The Winter's Tale*' 154.

[25] In 'Popular Culture in Print', Sullivan and Woodbridge prepare us to see Shakespeare's extraordinary
    move here. Initially, they distinguish between ' "great" and "little" traditions' (267), but then they
    emphasize how the little became implicated in the great: 'The Renaissance posited a popular culture
    against which to define – and usually to exalt – high culture' (283).

[26] According to Garber, here 'the playwright allows himself to mock both the emergent print culture of
    print and the claim for poetic truth' (*Shakespeare After All* 846). She concludes: 'Just as the
    shepherdesses who listened to (and bought from) Autolycus loved a ballad in print, "for then we
    know they are true", the statue of Hermione is the extraordinary emblem of Shakespearean crafts-
    manship – a blend of nature and art, awakened by the faith of the Shakespearean audience' (851).

In the following two sections, we shall see in greater detail how Shakespeare relies on a combined discourse of poetic books and staged theatre in an early history play and another mid-1590s comedy, before returning to the later tragedy of *Othello*.

'THE FLATTERING INDEX OF A DIREFUL PAGEANT': *RICHARD III*

Shakespeare's phrase from *Othello* conjoining 'index and … prologue' recalls a phrase earlier in his career, when he experimented with the history play. In *Richard III*, old Queen Margaret, widow of Henry VI, tells the younger Queen Elizabeth, wife of Edward IV,

> I call'd thee then vain flourish of my fortune;
> I call'd thee then poor shadow, painted queen,
> The presentation of but what I was;
> The flattering index of a direful pageant.　　*(Richard III* 4.4.82–5)

Nestled amid Margaret's use of theatrical terms ('shadow', 'painted', 'pageant') is the complicating bibliographical term, 'index'.[27] Margaret rails at Elizabeth and the Duchess of York for their complicity in the death of the young princes in the Tower, yet simultaneously she forms a chorus of sisterly grief with them.

As is well known, Shakespeare presents old Queen Margaret as a ghostly figure of prophecy – a 'mortal-living ghost' (26) – haunting the margins of the stage. Often relying on ghostly asides that visibly perform a choral function, she alone penetrates the hypocrisy of Richard's theatre of deception, and often her appearance works to offset his falsehood with harsh curses of truth.

As a chorus figure, Margaret is a tragic spirit of historical theatre itself, voicing not simply the hypocrisy of Richard but his (predestined) fall, and her soliloquy opening this scene draws attention to her metadramatic role: 'A dire induction am I witness to, / And will to France, hoping the consequence / Will prove as bitter, black, and tragical' (5–7).[28] Yet what is especially unusual in this scene is Margaret's reliance on, and association with, a discourse of the book. When she calls Elizabeth 'The flattering index of a direful pageant', she

---

[27] Thus, Lull in her recent Cambridge edition glosses the word 'index' as 'preface', and 'pageant' as 'spectacle, drama' (168).

[28] Cf. Greenblatt, introduction to *Richard III* in *Norton*: 'This ritual process – the inexorable working out of retributive justice or nemesis through the agency of Richard – is best conveyed perhaps by the chorus of grief-crazed women, above all by old Queen Margaret' (ed. 510). For detail on 'Women and Determinism', see Lull, ed. 9–12. See also W. C. Carroll, '"The Form of Law"'.

means that Elizabeth is a preface to her own dramatic tragedy. Not simply does Margaret's utterance seamlessly evoke the performed and the printed, but a few lines earlier the Duchess calls Margaret 'Woe's scene ... / Brief abstract and record of tedious days' (27–8), once more linking theatre with print. In such a lexicon, the choral figure of ghostly Margaret functions as the embodiment of both the tragic scene and the printed historical document. Effectively, Shakespeare uses the discourse of books and theatre to render syntactically the literary economy driving his play.

Perhaps the twinned discourse characterizing Margaret's role points to the two primary sources of the play: the printed chronicles of Edward Hall, Raphael Holinshead, and others, and the dramatic Machiavellian tragedies of Marlowe.[29] Most important to recall, however, is the absence in the chronicles of a formal discourse of print. For instance, in his *Union ... of York and Lancaster* Hall can anticipate Shakespeare's focus on Richard's theatricality by calling him 'close and secrete, a depe dissimuler, lowly of countenaunce, arrogante of herte, outwardely familier where he inwardely hated', yet nowhere associate this arch theatrical man with book culture.[30]

The example of Margaret's 'flattering index of a direful pageant' intimates that *Richard III* might be in part a history play about the literary relation between books and theatre.[31] In a soliloquy from Act I, scene 3, Richard himself (when still Duke of Gloucester) communicates that his early historical tragedy might be about the collision between theatre and a particular book, when he considers how 'To be reveng'd on Rivers, Dorset, Grey' (332):

> I sigh, and, with a piece of scripture,
> Tell them that God bids us do good for evil:
> And thus I clothe my naked villainy
> With odd old ends stol'n forth of holy writ,
> And seem a saint, when most I play the devil.
> (*Richard III* 1.3.333–7)

Nominally, *Richard III* is a history play about the providential triumph of a Christian king, Richmond or Henry VII, over a Machiavellian king, Richard. And without question Shakespeare makes England a Christian

---

[29] Both sets of sources are commonplace in *Richard III* criticism; see, e.g., *Riverside* 748, 750; *Norton* 507–8. For recent detail, see Jowett, ed., esp. 12–21 on the chronicles, and 27–32 on 'Barabas and the Vice'.

[30] Repr. in Hammond, ed. 343.

[31] Cf. Garber, 'Descanting on Deformity', in *Shakespeare's Ghost Writers*, on 'the play's preoccupation with writing and the preemptive – indeed pre*scrip*tive – nature of its political design', singling out the fascinating scene with the scrivener (3.6) 'as a model of history as a kind of ghost writing, since it encodes and "engross[es]" the fashioning of a rival text' (38; her emphasis).

country and its political leaders concerned about their Christian identity as subjects of the 'King of kings' (2.1.13), the 'Redeemer' Christ (2.1.4), who depends on the 'worm of conscience' (1.3.221), the inward soul that links the subject with the deity.[32] Yet Richard is notable for his manipulation of this Christian system, and, as he communicates above, he uses that system to great advantage, performing the role of Christian king to gain political power. In his Machiavellian model, religion provides a costume for power politics, and he is successful in grabbing power because he is a consummate man of the theatre.

While his theatrical prowess is a commonplace of criticism, Richard's deployment of the book is not.[33] In the soliloquy above, Richard reveals how he will steal the 'holy writ' of 'scripture' from its textual mooring, and put it to performance. He will present himself as a godly man in order to 'clothe' his 'naked villainy'. He will use the book to conceal his theatre. In doing so, he will not simply vilify the book; he will perform a process that converts the book into theatre.

In Act 3, scene 5, Richard voices this hypocritical literary economy publicly when he sees the head of the recently executed Hastings:

> I took him for the plainest harmless creature
> That breath'd upon the earth a Christian;
> Made him my book, wherein my soul recorded
> The history of all her secret thoughts,
> So smooth he daub'd his vice with show of virtue.
>
> (*Richard III* 3.5.25–9)

To borrow Buckingham's phrase a few lines earlier (for what he mistakenly thinks is his own agency in the historical action), Richard here 'counterfeit[s] the deep tragedian' (5), charging Hastings with deceiving him as a true Christian when in fact he has merely played a part – daubed his vice with 'show' of virtue. Yet Richard's exquisite lines about making Hastings his 'book' are important, and anticipate Iago's formulation: Richard has made Hastings a book in that he recorded the 'history' of his 'secret thoughts' – expressed the truth of his inward 'soul'. As clearly as any passage in the Shakespeare canon, this one reveals how Shakespeare understands the 'book': not simply a material object, it is also a site of theatrical consciousness.

---

[32] On conscience in *Richard III*, see Wilkes, *Idea of Conscience* 78–99. On Christianity more broadly, see R. G. Hunter, *Shakespeare and the Mystery of God's Judgments* 67–100; Hassel, 'Last Words and Last Things'.

[33] On Richard's theatricality, see Rossiter, *Angel with Horns* 17–20. In his introduction to the play in *Norton*, Greenblatt is incisive on the 'theatrical force of Richard': 'Shakespeare himself in *Richard III* seems to play with the seductive power of theatrical performance' (ed. 511). Indebted to the medieval stage figure of the Vice (ed. 510), 'Richard's manifest theatricality' is on display in '[v]irtually all of [his] … speeches … cast as self-conscious performances'. Greenblatt concludes by suggesting that theatre scripts the divine power of Tudor ideology, and that the divine power of Tudor ideology scripts theatre (ed. 512).

In Act 3, scene 7, Richard enacts this literary economy before the mayor and citizens of London in order to secure his kingship. Thus, he likely does not need Buckingham's advice, which is

> And look you get a prayer-book in your hand,
> And stand between two churchmen, good my lord –
> For on that ground I'll make a holy descant –
> And be not easily won to our requests:
> Play the maid's part, still answer nay, and take it.
>
> (*Richard III* 3.7.47–51)

At the core of Buckingham's advice, and Richard's own Machiavellian politics, we find a dark devotion to Christianity as merely a form of theatre. When Richard assumes the position his friend advises, Buckingham publicly declares Richard a Christian man of the book, devoid of theatre:

> Two props of virtue for a Christian prince,
> To stay him from the fall of vanity;
> And see, a book of prayer in his hand –
> True ornaments to know a holy man.   (*Richard III* 3.7.96–9)

Perhaps only through cognizance of this literary economy can we come to terms with the play's most haunting tragedy, in Act 4, scene 3, the death of the princes in the Tower: 'The most arch deed of piteous massacre / That ever yet this land was guilty of' (2–3). Tyrell's soliloquy describing 'The tyrannous and bloody act' (1) by the hit men Dighton and Forrest seems purposely devoid of theatre, except for one trace, in that last word, 'act', which reminds us that we are watching a play, Shakespeare's own and Richard's, too. Tyrell's poignant portrait of the 'gentle' princes sleeping together 'Within their alabaster innocent arms' (9–11) is among the most renowned in the Shakespeare canon, complexly mediated to the audience through the dialogic voices of Dighton and Forrest, hard on the tragic scene: the Princes'

> 'lips were four red roses on a stalk,
> [Which] in their summer beauty kiss'd each other.
> A book of prayers on their pillow lay,
> Which [once],' quoth Forrest, 'almost chang'd my mind;
> But O! the devil' – there the villain stopp'd;
> When Dighton thus told on, 'We smothered
> The most replenished sweet work of Nature
> That from the prime creation e'er she framed.'   (*Richard III* 4.3.12–19)

In this self-consciously told 'story' (8), rendered in exquisite poetry belying the character telling it, the dying princes emerge as literal 'babes' (9) of the 'book', vulnerable to Richard's theatrical 'piece of [ruthless] butchery' (5).

With the prayer-book protecting them on their pillow, the boys become immortalized as the Christian princes that Richard savagely pretends to be.

To glean the high stakes imagined for this scene, we might return to one of the most unusual conversations in Shakespeare, especially if we consider him a man of the theatre who eschews literary fame. Back in Act 3, scene 1, young Prince Edward questions his uncle Gloucester and Buckingham about a particular edifice:

PRINCE [EDWARD].   I do not like the Tower, of any place.
                        Did Julius Caesar build that place, my lord?
BUCKINGHAM.   He did, my gracious lord, begin that place,
                        Which, since, succeeding ages have re-edified.
PRINCE.   Is it upon record, or else reported
                        Successively from age to age, he built it?
BUCKINGHAM.   Upon record, my gracious lord.
PRINCE.   But say, my lord, it were not regist'red,
                        Methinks the truth should live from age to age,
                        As 'twere retail'd to all posterity,
                        Even to the general all-ending day.
GLOUCESTER.   [*Aside.*] So wise so young, they say do never live long.
PRINCE.   What say you, uncle?
GLOUCESTER.   I say, without characters fame lives long.
                        [*Aside.*] Thus, like the formal Vice, Iniquity,
                        I moralize two meanings in one word.
PRINCE.   That Julius Caesar was a famous man;
                        With what his valor did enrich his wit,
                        His wit set down to make his valure live.
                        Death makes no conquest of this conqueror,
                        For now he lives in fame though not in life.
                                    (*Richard III* 3.1.68–88)

Appropriate for the Christian prince he is, young Edward expresses suspicion about the truth of books originating in Roman culture. In his conversation with Buckingham and Richard, Edward wants to know the 'truth' about the builder of the Tower: did Julius Caesar build it 'upon record' or only by 'report'? When Buckingham assures him, 'Upon record', the prince imagines a higher form of 'truth' than that recorded in books, one 'retail'd to all posterity, / Even to the general all-ending day' – the Day of Judgment. In other words, the prince voices a form of truth above books of pagan history, one originating in a divine realm, yet presumably textualized in Scripture on earth. The word 'retail'd' means 'told over again' or *retold*.[34] In this model, the

---

[34] Jowett, ed. 236. Jowett adds the possible meaning of 'irrevocably bestow' (236).

originary classical story of Julius Caesar building the Tower in England gets retold 'to all posterity' on earth, but lasts only 'to' the Day of Judgment. For his part, Richard vocalizes a version of truth that secures 'fame' independently of 'characters' in a text, but his subsequent aside expresses the only truth he serves: that of theatre, 'the formal Vice, Iniquity'.

The scene, in other words, appears to rehearse three colliding models of truth and immortality, the first two of which are bibliographically based: (1) the classical model of earthly fame grounded in written books; (2) the Christian model of eternal glory grounded in the Book of Scripture but originating in heaven; and a new Ricardian model of earthly fame grounded in theatre, which opposes classical and Christian books. In this historical tragedy early in Shakespeare's career, the author inventories different models of literary fame.[35] When Shakespeare relies on literary discourse to situate classical literary fame in terms of the Christian Last Judgment, we confront an unusual phenomenon that we will meet in each of the chapters in Part II, to be discussed in most detail in chapter 7 on *Hamlet*: the concept of the *literary eternal*.

'THE RIGHT PROMETHEAN FIRE': *LOVE'S LABOUR'S LOST*

A couple of years later, Shakespeare writes a comedy that probes the erotic process by which such literary fame comes into production. In *Love's Labor's Lost*, he *mocks* a particular version of the economy of poetic books and staged theatre as the reason that 'love's labour' becomes 'lost'.[36] In this version of the literary economy, both Petrarchan poetic books and popular staged theatre depend on a single disenabling action: the male perceives the female as an object of desire, subject to the will of the male.[37] In Act 4, scene 3, Shakespeare rehearses the problem of this economy in acute detail.

[35] Richard's theatrical antagonism to the book goes some way toward explaining his fear of poetry, mentioned on three occasions late in the play (4.2.106–7; 4.4.507; 5.3.306). In his opening soliloquy ('Now is the winter of our discontent'), Richard inaugurates his and the play's opposition between theatre and poetry, when he rejects 'caper[ing] ... nimbly in a lady's chamber / To the lascivious pleasing of a lute', in favor of 'Plots ... inductions dangerous' (12–13, 32).

[36] According to Archer, '*Love's Labour's Lost*', the play has moved into a third phase of criticism during the past thirty years: from an emphasis on 'language' during the 1970s and 1980s, to an emphasis on 'gender' during the 1990s, to a recent emphasis on the ways in which language and gender play out in the context of 'print' and 'nationality' (esp. 320–1). This evolution prepares for a discussion of literary authorship in *Love's Labour's Lost*, where the word *mock* and its cognates occur seventeen times, tying it with *Henry V* for the most appearances in the Shakespeare canon.

[37] According to Breitenberg, 'Anatomy of Desire in *Love's Labour's Lost*', 'Petrarchan poetry' is 'a form of male empowerment' that 'constructs and confirms men as looking and writing subjects' at 'the expense of women' (437): 'the Petrarchan sonnet represents the beloved as a "dispersed" (and in a sense, dismembered) Other against which the male poet can measure and retain his own "coherent", unified identity' (437).

The courtier Berowne relies on a discourse of 'book', 'poet', and 'show' to articulate the folly he and his three courtly friends, Navarre, Longaville, and Dumaine, have committed, when they vowed to forsake 'affection' and 'desire' (1.1.9, 10) for 'scholar[ship]' and 'philosophy' (17, 32) – effectively, 'woman' (37) for 'book' (74) – in order to become 'heirs of all eternity' (7). Having caught his friends breaking their vows by authoring 'sonnets' to their respective ladies (4.3.15), Berowne breaks into a 78-line verse-speech with a new argument: women are the real object of study, and thus the authors of masculine immortality. The 'ground of study's excellence', Berowne asserts, lies in 'the beauty of a woman's face' (296–7):

> From women's eyes this doctrine I derive:
> They are the ground, the books, the academes
> From whence doth spring the true Promethean fire.
> ….
> For where is any author in the world
> Teaches such beauty as a woman's eye.
>
> (*Love's Labour's Lost* 4.3.298–309)

The word 'author' in the penultimate line is ambiguous, referring both to male authors 'in the world' who fail to teach the immortalizing beauty of the feminine eye and to beautiful women as immortalizing authors.

Yet Berowne's most striking phrase, 'true Promethean fire', intimates that he identifies the beautiful eyes animating a woman's face as the primal inspiration for the male's immortalizing art. The 'Love' that such beauty creates, he goes on to observe extravagantly, is

> as sweet and musical
> As bright Apollo's lute, strung with his hair.
> And when Love speaks, the voice of all the gods
> Make heaven drowsy with the harmony.
> Never durst poet touch a pen to write
> Until his ink were temp'red with Love's sighs:
> O then his lines would ravish savage ears
> And plant in tyrants mild humility.
>
> (*Love's Labour's Lost* 4.3.339–46)

Complexly, Berowne charts a collaborative model of individuated authorship, in which women author male 'poets' to make such authors divine (the force of the splendid conceit of the love-laden gods becoming 'drowsy with the harmony'). The model is doubly collaborative, however, because in the last two lines Berowne refers to the powers of the Orphic poet, who tames wild beasts (in particular, tyrannical monarchs) by planting mild humility in them – in the mid-1590s, likely a counter to England's self-avowed

Orphic poet, Spenser (see chapter 3). The male author, inspired by female beauty, can produce an art that affects the emotions, the political state, and even the 'heaven' of the 'gods'.

As if Berowne fears that he has not made his point clear, he repeats the terms of his primary theory for the feminine origin of masculine authorship, yet shuffles lines and introduces new terms:

> From women's eyes this doctrine I derive:
> They sparkle still the right Promethean fire;
> They are the books, the arts, the academes,
> That show, contain, and nourish all the world.
> (*Love's Labour's Lost* 4.3.347–50)

Typically, editors identify the repetition here as a textual crux, owing to Shakespeare's revision.[38] No doubt the lines do constitute a revision, yet in context they also seem explainable as part of Berowne's academic character, and texts like the *Riverside* follow early editions in presenting them as if they were. During the play's most ornate moment of authorial representation, the text appears to *stutter*, repeating the representation of literary authorship, in a way we find problematic. Not once but twice we witness the self-conscious author deploying a classical myth of literary creation in the dramatic performance of poetic authorship.

Significantly, the repetition features the classical myth of Prometheus, who functions for the Elizabethans as a type of poet. In the 1594 *Shadow of Night*, for instance, George Chapman identifies the poet with Prometheus, the mortal who stole fire from heaven: 'Therefore Promethean poets with the coals Of their most genial, more than human souls, In living verse created men like these.'[39] Yet in Book 2, canto 10, of *The Faerie Queene*, Spenser presents Prometheus as the creator of Elf, the eponymous ancestor of the Elfin race. To open the *Elfin chronicles*, Spenser records how this 'book'

> ... told, how first Prometheus did create
> A man, of many partes from beasts derived,
> And then stole fire from heven, to animate
> His worke.   (Spenser, *Faerie Queene* 2.10.70)

As a creator who animates his 'worke', Prometheus recalls Spenser himself, who invents this particular version of the myth.[40] Perhaps because of Spenser, Marlowe was likely influenced by the Prometheus myth in *Doctor Faustus*,

---

[38] See, e.g., David, ed. III.   [39] Chapman, *Shadow of Night*, quoted in David, ed. III.
[40] For an overview of Prometheus in Spenser and the tradition informing his use of the myth, see Gallagher, 'Prometheus'. For further detail on the myth, see Wutrich, *Prometheus and Faust* 14–94.

but he also probably drew upon the Roman view of the Titan as 'a symbol of conspiracy to overthrow the government, treason, and even the threat of arson'.[41]

If we look further at Berowne's speech, we see something strange and perhaps shocking: a male gazes at a female, but does not simply stir in his desire for her; as with Marcus viewing Lavinia in *Titus Andronicus* (chapter 2), Berowne throws up on to the screen of her body the terms of masculine authorship, represented by the myth of Prometheus. More overtly than elsewhere, this passage indicates why Shakespeare's literary ambition has been difficult to track. Rather than present Berowne as an author figure, Shakespeare shows the conceptual process by which the male becomes an author. Depicting what seems like a conventional process of poetic inspiration, he gestures to a cardinal principle of theatre, the theatrical cross-dressing of the female.[42] Shakespeare's intertextual engagement with the Prometheus myth compels us to identify the cross-dressing author not simply as the character in the fiction but as the individual who wrote it.

As we have seen, the word 'show' in the last line of Berowne's second Prometheus passage is a term from Shakespeare's vocabulary of theatre. As such, the word connects Berowne's discourse of Petrarchan poetry with the book, art, and academy of drama: female beauty shows all the world, reflects it, performs it, and does so with a nourishing power. Accordingly, after Navarre suggests that the men 'devise / Some entertainment' for the ladies 'in their tents' (369–70), Berowne articulates the role of theatre in this economy of Elizabethan authorship: 'revels, dances, masks' will 'solace' the ladies, and thus become the 'Forerun[ner]' to 'fair Love, strewing her way with flowers' (374–7). Theatre will create the masculine scene, venue, and occasion for union with the female, because it delivers the female into the state of 'solace'.

Right before delivering his Prometheus speech, Berowne refers to the Christian Last Judgment (the only such reference in the play), saying of his beloved, 'I'll prove her fair, or talk till doomsday here' (4.3.270). The emphasis on the performance of verbal action ('talk') on earth ('here') leading up 'till' the Day of Judgment ('doomsday') is one we will meet again and again in the Shakespearean canon. Although in this early comedy from his 'bookish' and 'lyric' phase the author clearly subjects the literary eternal to considerable mockery, in the mature tragedy *Othello* from the height of his conceptual phase he renders it absolutely haunting. After killing the 'divine Desdemona'

---

[41] Wutrich 57; on Marlowe and the Roman Prometheus, see 37–94.
[42] As Crewe reminds us, 'there is a boy actor inside every represented woman' (*Trials of Authorship* 160).

(2.1.73), Othello graphically imagines his resurrected wife's apocalyptic agency at the Day of Judgment:

> O ill-starred wench,
> Pale as thy smock! When we shall meet at compt
> This look of thine will hurl my soul from heaven,
> And fiends will snatch at it.   (*Othello* 5.2.272–5)

INDIVIDUATION AND/OR COLLABORATION: SHAKESPEARE'S HENDIADYS-AUTHORSHIP IN *OTHELLO*

In the tragedy of *Othello*, Iago constitutes a dark homosocial underside of this eternizing literary process. The ensign is arguably the grimmest version of the poet-playwright in the Shakespeare canon, as if the author were imagining or perhaps processing his fear of what his art could perform civically. Most often, Iago is remembered as a man of the theatre. Near the beginning, he informs Roderigo that he has a theatrical 'soul' (1.1.54), a performed consciousness: 'trimm'd in forms and visages of duty', he keeps his 'heart' attending on himself, 'throwing but shows of service' on his lord, does 'well' by him, and when he has 'lin'd' his 'coat', does himself 'homage' (50–4). Later, in soliloquy, he tells the audience, 'I play the villain': 'When devils will the blackest sins put on, / They do suggest at first with heavenly shows, / As I do now' (2.3.336, 351–3).[43]

Yet Iago is also the author of poetry. In Act 2, scene 1, he insinuates himself into the consciousness of Desdemona by performing the role of a Petrarchan poet, after she asks him, coyly, 'What wouldst write of me, if thou shouldst praise me?' '[M]y invention', he replies (117, 125),

> Comes from my pate as birdlime does from frieze,
> It plucks out brains and all. But my Muse labors,
> And thus she is deliver'd.   (*Othello* 2.1.126–8)

Iago then lapses into a fourteen-line extemporal verse in rhymed couplets, the opening lines of which read, 'If she be fair and wise, fairness and wit, / The one's for use, the other useth it' (29–30). Iago redeploys Sidney's metaphor of invention from Sonnet 1 of *Astrophil and Stella* – that of pregnancy and childbirth – showing that for early modern writers invention was not merely a technique but a topic, a dramatic representation in a fiction about authorship.

---

[43] Critics have long seen Iago as a shadow figure for the Shakespearean theatrical author. See, e.g., M. Rose, 'Othello's Occupation': 'Iago, the cunning artist of tragedy, is at least in part a representation of Shakespeare himself' (310).

What is noteworthy in *Othello* is Shakespeare's transposition of Petrarchan invention from printed poetry to the place of the stage.[44]

In short, Shakespeare presents Iago not merely as a malicious villain but as a literary man practiced in the compound art of his own creator, yet removed to the very edge of evil, that fathomless cult of the self, organized powerfully to 'plume up ... [the] will' (1.3.393): ''tis in ourselves that we are thus or thus' (319–20). Perhaps authorship is evil here because Iago so powerfully locates agency in the hands of the self, detached from the feminine other at the heart of Berowne's comedic model.

Consequently, when Iago charges Desdemona with 'Lechery' – an 'index and obscure prologue to the history of lust and foul thoughts' – he expresses the terms of his own dark consciousness, and locates the literary as its primary 'content'. Indeed, half of Iago's key vocabulary here – 'obscure', 'lust', 'thoughts' – indicates that he gives verbal rather than 'ocular proof' (3.3.360) to the hidden nature of female consciousness. The word 'obscure' means 'unclearly expressed, hidden' (Honigman, ed. 179), underscoring perhaps the sense that in the depths of Iago's authorship consciousness is merely a form of concealment, secrecy, disguise, theatricality.

Yet we cannot come to terms with the most perplexing part of Iago's vocabulary, the conjunction of 'index and ... prologue', until we identify it as one of Shakespeare's most striking uses of hendiadys. George Wright, and more recently Frank Kermode and James Shapiro, have all written invaluably on this rhetorical figure, which 'means, literally, "one through two"'.[45] In particular, Wright marks the development of Shakespeare's language by tracking the presence of hendiadys: at the beginning of his career, Shakespeare employs the device sparingly, but 'in the great plays of his middle career' he uses it 'with some frequency', in two plays centrally: *Hamlet* (66 times) and *Othello* (28 times) (168, 173).

Although Wright's essay is on *Hamlet*, he discusses *Othello* briefly (175–6), and although he does not cite 'index and obscure prologue' as an example of hendiadys he creates a frame by which we might do so. Tracing the origins of the figure to Servius' commentary on Virgil's *Aeneid* (168) – an epic poem – he emphasizes that 'the device is appropriate to the '"high style"', since it appears in 'passages of a certain elevation, dignity, or remoteness from ordinary experience' (173). Moreover, Wright shows how Shakespeare suits the device to

---

[44] On the metaphor during the period, see Maus, 'A Womb of His Own: Male Renaissance Poets in the Female Body', *Inwardness and Theater in the English Renaissance* 182–209. On Iago as a satirical poet, see Muir, *Shakespeare the Professional* 35–6.

[45] Wright, 'Hendiadys and *Hamlet*' 168; Kermode, *Shakespeare's Language*, esp. 101–2 and 167–9 (on *Othello*); Shapiro, *1599* 321–2.

'character', to 'theme', to 'story', to 'setting' (176), and even to 'the problematic depths of thought and feeling' (173): 'The device is always somewhat mysterious and elusive, and its general appropriateness to ... *Hamlet* is obvious' (176). Wright does not identify hendiadys as Shakespeare's premier figure for theatre, but he comes close: 'hendiadys is a stylistic means of underlining the play's themes of anxiety, bafflement, disjunction, and the falsity of appearances ... A miniature stylistic play within the play, hendiadys holds its mirror up to *Hamlet*' (178, 181).

According to Shapiro, in Hamlet

> Shakespeare clearly wanted audiences to work hard and one of the ways he made them do so was by employing an odd verbal trick called hendiadys ... a single idea conveyed through a pairing of nouns linked by 'and'. When conjoined in this way, the nouns begin to oscillate, seeming to qualify each other as much as the term each individually modifies. (Shapiro, *1599* 321)

Shapiro adds, 'The more you think about examples of hendiadys, the more they induce a kind of mental vertigo', and, like Wright, he finds the superabundance of the figure in *Hamlet* 'suit[ing] the mood of the play perfectly': 'an acknowledgement of how necessary and impossible it is to suture things together' (321–2). Kermode, who discusses *Othello* in the most detail, notes the examples of hendiadys in such phrases as 'loving his own pride and purposes', 'trimm'd in forms and visages of duty', and 'flag and sign of love', but does not mention 'index and obscure prologue'. Well we may, because it is in this hendiadys alone that we can locate an accurate model of Shakespearean literary authorship. The vertigo is not only mental but professional; the necessary and impossible suture, authorial. In other words, because hendiadys is such a self-conscious, stylized rhetorical device, we can view its use as a sublime concentrate of Shakespearean counter-laureate authorship.

Indeed, hendiadys offers a clear frame for bridging the gap between criticism on Shakespeare's literary authorship and criticism on Shakespearean bibliography, theatre, and page to stage (see introduction). Above all, hendiadys is a principle that asserts conjunction and *thwarts* it (Wright 169, 181). We need such a principle to explain the conjoined presence of books and theatre in Shakespeare's career *and* their 'opposition, disequilibrium' (181). According to David Scott Kastan, through the 1623 printing of the First Folio,

> if Shakespeare cannot with any precision be called the creator of the book that bears his name, that book might be said to be the creator of Shakespeare. Ben Jonson, driven by a powerful literary ambition, actively sought his role as an author. Shakespeare ... was largely indifferent to such individuation, comfortably working in the collaborative ethos of the theater. (Kastan, *Shakespeare and the Book* 78)

Here Kastan slots 'Shakespeare' into the received story about the invention of early modern authorship – yet minus Jonson's predecessor, Spenser. According to this narrative, Spenser and Jonson, not Shakespeare, transact the large-scale cultural shift from the older notion of authorship to the one held widely today: the author as a self-shaping agent in the production of his own literary oeuvre and fame. Kastan's formulation helps us understand why Shakespeare has been excised from the story: indifferent to the 'individuated authorship' (16) of Jonson and Spenser, Shakespeare took comfort in the collaborative authorship that has been the hallmark of criticism about the materiality of the book.

Individuation and/or *collaboration*: these are the terms of the battle early in the twenty-first century. Neither party seems quite willing to imagine a Shakespeare who was at once comfortable with the 'collaborative ethos of the theater' *and* troubled by the 'individuated authorship' of the literary print-house. Yet Shakespeare's use of hendiadys helps us to imagine a 'Shakespeare' who prints precisely this strange authorial costume.

Accordingly, the 'Shakespeare' presented in Part I of this book has been that of a *hendiadys-author*, for whom the boundary between conjunction and disjunction virtually disappears. This author is a poet and a playwright, yet always seeming to evade easy classification; he is interested in page and stage, yet famous for expressing the stigma of both; he is intent to represent books and theatre, in his staged plays as in his printed poetry, yet forever resisting the singular authorship of either. In the end, it is Shakespeare's unsettling counter-laureate authorship that serves as a profound index and clear prologue to the history not of lust and foul thoughts but of English literature.

PART II

Fictions of authorship

CHAPTER 5

'Show of love ... bookish rule': Books, theatre, and literary history in 2 Henry VI

In Part I of this book, we have touched on the major contours of Shakespeare's literary authorship, from early in his career till late: his invention of a self-concealing authorship in response to the laureate self-presentation of Edmund Spenser (and to a lesser extent, Christopher Marlowe); his extemporal inter-textuality with the major authors of the Western tradition, from Homer, Virgil, and Ovid to Petrarch, Chaucer, and Sidney; his literary discourse combining the terms of book and theatre, including poetic books and staged theatre; his recurrent staging of both epic and lyric forms as instrumental to the dramatic genres of the new London theatre; his search for a historic version of immortality, cut along the divide between Reformation Christianity and secular modernity; and thus his rehearsal of a fiction of authorship to form a new kind of literary career: that of an English and European poet-playwright.

In Part II, we shall look at four plays in particular, to see in more detail how Shakespeare's literary authorship develops from beginning to end in the major dramatic genres. The goal will be to see how individual plays composed and performed at different times represent distinct 'fictions of authorship', which foreground the interplay among books, poetry, and theatre. Despite intriguing points of contact, the four plays selected do not stage their literary fictions in precisely the same ways. *2 Henry VI* is a very different play from *Much Ado about Nothing*, and *Hamlet* differs from both and from *Cymbeline*. And not just because of genre. For instance, a Spenserian and a Marlovian discourse are right at the surface of *2 Henry VI*, but not, it seems, of *Much Ado*, despite the presence of both authors in the comedy. Similarly, a discourse of books appears in *Much Ado*, but not as visibly as it does in *Hamlet* – or, for that matter, *2 Henry VI* and *Cymbeline*. Yet among the four plays *Much Ado* alone makes sonneteering central to its story. In the history, the tragedy, and the romance here examined, Petrarchism may play a part, but no character produces a sonnet the way Benedick and Beatrice do. Thus, while each of the four following chapters advances the general argument about Shakespeare's literary authorship, each does so in its own idiosyncratic way, subject to genre, plot-line, the linguistic nexus of cultural ideas, and finally the time of authorial composition and theatrical performance.

2 Henry VI is especially important to a study of Shakespeare's literary authorship because it may well exhibit an embryo form. In the soliloquy concluding the opening scene, for instance, Richard, Duke of York, inserts a professional literary dynamic into Shakespeare's version of fifteenth-century English history:

> And therefore I will take the Nevils' parts,
> And make a show of love to proud Duke Humphrey,
> And, when I spy advantage, claim the crown,
> …
> Till Henry, surfeiting in joys of love
> With his new bride and England's dear-bought queen,
> And Humphrey with the peers be fall'n at jars:
> …
> And force perforce I'll make him yield the crown,
> Whose bookish rule hath pull'd fair England down.
>
> (*2 Henry VI* 1.1.240–59)

York communicates a plan to the audience. Like an actor who 'takes' a 'part', he will rely on a mere 'show of truth' to 'claim the crown' and pull King Henry's 'bookish rule' down. Targeting male and female weakness for sex and violence, he will use theatrical hypocrisy against Queen Margaret, Humphrey (Duke of Gloucester), and the barons to subvert their sovereign's textual authority. Put simply in terms of the present argument, he will use theatre to supplant the book.

Readers have long recognized York's theatricality, just as they have Henry's bookishness, because Shakespeare makes these features patently visible in his historical plot.[1] To date, however, no one has used York's bifold formulation as a lens for viewing the conjunction of book and theatre as constituting an early version of Shakespearean authorship.[2] Initially, the

---

[1] On theatricality in *2 Henry VI*, see Hattaway, ed., *Second Part of King Henry VI* 1; Garber, *Shakespeare After All* 104. On books, see Mazzaro, 'Shakespeare's "Books of Memory"'; M. R. Smith, 'Henry VI, Part 2'. In his 2001 overview of criticism, Pendleton limits critical 'insistence on a remarkably self-reflexive Shakespeare' to metadrama, citing Calderwood, *Metadrama in Shakespeare's Henriad*, and Blanpied, *Time and the Artist in Shakespeare's English Histories* ('Introduction' to *Henry VI: Critical Essays* 18).

[2] For the only study of 'authorship' in *2 Henry VI*, see Kuskin, 'Recursive Origins'. Kuskin argues that the play 'is engaged with the production of literary authority through constructing the English past' (MS 7), that '*2 Henry VI* represents books as material vehicles for authority and thus open to manipulation' (MS 16), and finally that Shakespeare remains 'skeptic[al]' about 'textual representation' (MS 17). Kuskin neglects theatre, and he does not discuss Shakespeare as an author, but he helps

lens is important because it helps identify the most important conflict structuring Shakespeare's plot: the conflict between York's reliance on theatricality to 'claim the crown', and Henry's reliance on books to retain it. As the action unfolds, not just York but several major characters jockey for political power and their own divine destiny with reference to this literary economy. Among the aristocrats, Gloucester and his duchess, Eleanor, get caught in the cross-fire, as do subsequently the Duke of Suffolk and Queen Margaret. Jack Cade only thinks he is free of such an aristocratic standard, but here Shakespeare rehearses Cade's rebellion in terms of a glaring anachronism: the Elizabethan opposition between a populist theatricality and an elitist print culture.[3]

Accordingly, in this chapter I suggest the following general argument: Shakespeare structures his fiction of authorship in *2 Henry VI* on a literary economy relating theatre and book, derived from a symbiosis between these media in late sixteenth-century English literary culture, in order to stage a conflict at the heart of his own literary authorship as a poet-playwright. Rather than simply retell the chronicle narrative of fifteenth-century English political history for the stage, Shakespeare includes a second narrative about sixteenth-century English literary history.[4]

'Authorship' is not simply a topic in *2 Henry VI* but its most vexing problem. Indeed, three interrelated sets of authorial problems plague scholarship and criticism. First, we possess two different versions: the 1594 quarto, titled *The First Part of the Contention Betwixt the Two Famous Houses of Yorke and Lancaster*, which is a shorter version of the play, and which was reprinted in 1600 with a version of *3 Henry VI*, and again in 1619; and the longer 1623 folio version, which is preceded by *The First Part of King Henry the Sixth* and followed by *The Third Part*. Second, we do not know the precise chronology of authorial composition: whereas the First Folio prints the three *Henry VI* plays in their historical order as *1*, *2*, and *3 Henry VI*, most scholars today believe that *2 Henry VI* and *3 Henry VI* came before *1 Henry VI*. Third, we do not know whether Shakespeare authored *2 Henry VI* by himself

---

us understand why: the Shakespearean text does not represent authorship so much as refract it. Cf. Cartelli, 'Suffolk and the Pirates': 'the citizen consciousness … serves as something like the author-function in this play' (336). Blanpied sees a symmetry between Henry's wish to be 'absent' (46), York's to 'escape' (50), Gloucester's to be 'misplaced' (52), and Shakespeare's to relinquish 'artistic control' (63).

[3] On anachronism, see esp. Rackin, *Stages of History* 1–2, 8–10, 86–104. For reasons of space, I have limited analysis of Gloucester and Eleanor, Margaret and Suffolk.

[4] Shakespeare's superimposition of sixteenth-century *political* culture on to the chronicles is a commonplace of criticism; see, e.g., Riggs, *Shakespeare's Heroical Histories* 114.

or worked in collaboration with others; recent authoritative arguments exist for both positions.[5]

The three textual problems pose a challenge to any discussion of 'authorship' in *2 Henry VI*. The challenge, however, forms only an extreme version of the problem discussed in Part I: we always have difficulty 'finding Shakespeare' in his texts. As an alternative to locating the man from Stratford in *2 Henry VI*, we may concentrate on his representations of the author in his historical fiction. To determine which parts of the fiction to examine, we may follow textual scholarship in accepting the authority of the folio version, although when pertinent refer to the quarto version; and we may concentrate on those parts of the play wherein Shakespeare's authorship is not in dispute (York's soliloquies are a good example, as are the scenes with Jack Cade). The risk of this project is worth taking, because in this play we indeed encounter what may be the earliest form of Shakespearean authorship extant.

We can highlight the emergence of the form that this authorship takes by recalling that Shakespeare's bifold discourse of book and theatre has no equivalent in the primary source-texts for *2 Henry VI*: the chronicles of Edward Hall and Raphael Holinshed. Thus, in his *Union of the Two Noble and Illustre Families of Lancaster and York* (1548) Hall does not describe Henry VI in terms of book or print culture; rather, he writes of the king's contemplative studiousness: he 'was a man of a meke spirite, and of a simple witte, preferryng peace before warre, rest before businesse, honestie before profite, and quietnesse before laboure … [He] studied onely for the health of his soule' (repr. in Cairncross, ed. 162–3). Similarly, Hall does not associate York with theatricality, relying instead on a broader discourse of secrecy and deception: 'Rychard duke of Yorke, perceivyng the Kyng to be a ruler not Ruling, & the whole burden of the Realme, to depend in the ordinaunces of the Quene & the duke of Suffolke, began secretly to allure to his frendes of

---

[5] Each of these three problems has spawned an industry of scholarship, best summarized in Hattaway, ed. 56–68; Knowles, ed. 111–41; Warren, ed. 60–100. For the first problem, the two versions, recent critics contest the view that the quarto *Contention* is a memorial reconstruction, suggesting that it is an early version that Shakespeare revised as *2 Henry VI*. On the second problem, chronology, the 'prevailing modern view' is that *2 and 3 Henry VI* came before *1 Henry VI* (Warren, ed. 67). On the third problem, authorship, where we lack consensus, neither Knowles nor Warren is comfortable with Hattaway's 'premise': 'that Shakespeare wrote the whole of the trilogy, and in the order of the events it portrays' (ed. 61). Knowles mentions 'Greene and others' (ed. 121, 141), while Warren opts for 'agnosticism', the 'focus best placed on the play itself rather than on its authorship' (ed. 68n). Curiously, however, most literary critics writing on *2 Henry VI* today assume that Shakespeare wrote the play. Kreps, 'Bad Memories of Margaret', relies on textual scholarship to argue that Shakespeare revised the *Contention* when creating *2 Henry VI*. Manley, 'From Strange's Men to Pembroke's Men', relies on performance history to argue that 'the origins of *2 Henry VI* lie in a script first written for Strange's Men and then adapted for Pembroke's Men' (273).

the nobilitie, and privatly declared to them, his title and right to the Crowne' (repr. in Cairncross, ed. 165).[6] Presumably, however, Shakespeare took cues like these when grounding Henry's studious contemplation within a late sixteenth-century discourse of printed books, and York's secretive manipulation within a late sixteenth-century discourse of staged theatre. Both are glaring anachronisms; but precisely because they are such, they lay bare the terms of Shakespearean authorship at the outset of his career.

MARLOVIAN THEATRE, SPENSERIAN BOOK

By looking further into this topic, we discover that Shakespeare processes a specific literary conflict affecting his own authorship during the early 1590s, one mounted between 'two mighty opposites, poised in antagonism': Marlowe, the major theatrical author of the day, with his notorious combination of Ovidian erotic poetry and Machiavellian political theatre, which contests the authority of the English monarchy; and Spenser, the major print-author, with his Virgilian nationalism announcing its service to monarchy, even as it pays homage to an aristocratic nobility. In York's theatrical plot to overthrow the bookish Henry, Shakespeare replays the era's most intense literary competition.[7]

York's deployment of Marlowe's Machiavellian theatre is a commonplace of criticism on *2 Henry VI*, as is the general presence of Ovid, so we need not belabor either here.[8] Alternatively, we may concentrate on a neglected

---

[6] On Hall as 'the major source for all three [Henry VI] plays', see Baker, introduction, *Riverside* 624.

[7] For the 'mighty opposition' between Marlowe and Spenser, see Greenblatt, *Renaissance Self-Fashioning* 222; Cheney, *Marlowe's Counterfeit Profession*. For Shakespeare's processing of the opposition, see *SNPP*. On Spenser's service to the Tudor monarchy, see Montrose, 'Subject of Elizabeth'. In contrast, Helgerson, *Forms of Nationhood*, argues that Spenser supports a nationhood based on aristocratic power (25–62); Hadfield, 'Was Spenser a Republican?', argues that Spenser's works display republican leanings. In identifying Spenser as a Virgilian national poet, I assimilate his acute Ovidianism to his Virgilian career; see Cheney, *Spenser's Famous Flight*, ch. 4; Pugh, *Spenser and Ovid*. For Marlowe's Machiavellian contestation of monarchy with a 'counter-nationhood' organized around the Ovidian author, see Cheney, *Marlowe's Counterfeit Profession*; for a definition of counter-nationhood, see 9–25; for Marlowe's contribution to late Elizabethan republican writing, see Cheney, 'Marlowe's Republican Authorship'. If Spenser wrote a nationhood of either aristocratic or republican power, I can find no evidence that Marlowe or Shakespeare knew it.

[8] Marlowe and Ovid show up more often in modern annotated editions of *2 Henry VI* than any other source, except perhaps Scripture. Curiously, however, critics neglect Ovid in the play. For brief discussion of Marlowe, see Ribner, 'Marlowe and Shakespeare' 41–3; N. Brooke, 'Marlowe as Provocative Agent in Shakespeare's Early Plays' 70–3; Shapiro, *Rival Playwrights* 90–4; Cartelli, *Marlowe, Shakespeare* 86–8; Caldwell, *Breach of Time* 202–22; Bloom, *Shakespeare: The Invention of the Human* 46–50. Similarly, critics often refer to Machiavelli; see, e.g., Riggs 117; E. I. Berry, *Patterns of Decay* 40–1; Kastan, *Shakespeare and the Shapes of Time* 16; the most recent study, Roe, *Shakespeare and Machiavelli*, neglects *2 Henry VI* but does link Marlowe with the Machiavellian York in *1 Henry VI* (5–6). Rackin sees Machiavelli as a new early modern model of 'historical causation' challenging the providentialism of Scripture with 'secondary causes – the effects of political situations and the impact of human will and capabilities' (6–7, 27–8, 54–5: 6).

feature of this history play: Shakespeare associates York's Machiavellian theatre with the counter-national poetry of Ovid. Ovid's poetry is counter-national in the sense that it writes not a collective form of nationhood, whether imperial or republican, but rather an individual form of nationhood foregrounding the authority of the poet.[9] By translating Ovid's inaugural poem of counter-nationalism, the *Amores*, Marlowe assumed the role of Elizabethan counter-national author, a project he continued throughout his corpus, both in subsequent poems and in plays.[10]

Despite the monarchical-sounding title of *2 Henry VI*, Shakespeare disperses dramatic agency among 'five characters' who each speak 'between 10 and 12 percent' of the lines. Even so, York emerges as 'the single figure of significant internalization, delivering forty-eight percent of the soliloquies and asides'.[11] Like Marlowe's Ovidian author, York takes little interest in the collectivity of England as a nation; throughout, he makes it clear that he seeks the material sign of kingship, the crown: 'From Ireland thus comes York to claim his right, / And pluck the crown from feeble Henry's head' (5.1.1–2).[12] Thus, in his soliloquy concluding the opening scene York formulates his theatrical plan not simply to acquire the crown at the expense of the king, the queen, and the barons, but more precisely to circumvent the powerless, tragic destiny imposed on the Calydonian hero Maleager by the Three Fates working through his mother, Althaea (1.1.233–5), which York has read about in Ovid's counter-Virgilian epic, the *Metamorphoses* (8.451–525).[13] Thus, from the outset Shakespeare presents York as an aggressive reader of an Ovidian book of poetry who turns to a Machiavellian theatre to supplant the divine book of his sovereign and wear England's crown.[14]

In contrast to criticism on Marlowe, Ovid, and Machiavelli, criticism on Spenser in *2 Henry VI* remains sparse and intermittent, even though modern editions identify Spenser as a recurrent presence.[15] Moroever, major books on

---

[9] See Braudy, *Frenzy of Renown*: in Ovid, 'the poet begins to assert himself as the true nation' (135).

[10] The major studies of Marlowe in *2 Henry VI* have little to say about the Ovidian Marlowe. On Marlowe's fusion of Ovidianism and Machiavellianism, see Cheney, *Profession*, chs. 6–8.

[11] Champion, *Perspective in Shakespeare's English Histories* 24, 34.

[12] York's obsession with the crown evokes Tamburlaine (*1 Tamb* 2.7.28–9). In *Henry VI Part 3*, York's son, Richard, Duke of Gloucester, will imitate Tamburlaine's discourse (1.2.29–31). See Ribner 41–2: 'Instead of Marlowe's celebration of victory in self-sufficient human power …, in the early Shakespeare there is an awareness of human limitation and frailty' (43).

[13] On the *Metamorphoses* as Ovid's anti-Virgilian epic, see Hardie, 'Ovid's Theban History'.

[14] At the end of *Henry VI Part 1*, York accuses the French Alanson of being a 'notorious Machevile' (5.4.74) – effectively communicating the model for his own theatrical cunning.

[15] Cairncross glosses five passages with Spenser (ed. 25, 38, 71, 87, 98, 149); Hattaway, two passages (ed. 81, 139); Knowles, six passages (ed. 151, 244, 247, 279, 284, 336). Curiously, Warren does not include Spenser as a gloss.

Shakespeare's history plays have little to say about Spenser, who emerges typically as part of a general literary background for Shakespeare's project.[16] Yet the critical consensus, that Shakespeare in this play, as in the first tetralogy generally, critiques the Elizabethan Protestant ideal of heroic poetry within its providential framework (Knowles, ed. 51–65), may profitably be grounded in Shakespeare's acute engagement with Spenser from both *The Shepheardes Calender* (1579) and *The Faerie Queene* (1590).[17]

For instance, in the *October* eclogue Spenser had presented himself as the New Poet criticizing his countrymen for failing to produce a heroic or Virgilian epic in service of the Tudor state. Thus the wise old shepherd Piers advises the younger Cuddie, 'the perfecte paerne of a Poete' (Argument), to abandon his lowly calling as a pastoral poet and turn to the higher genre of epic:

> Abandon then the base and viler clowne,
> Lyft up thy selfe out of the lowly dust:
> And sing of bloody Mars, of wars, of giusts,
> Turne thee to those, that weld the awful crowne,
> To doubted Knights, whose woundlesse armour rusts,
> And helmes unbruzed wexen dayly browne.   (Spenser, *October* 37–42)

Then, in the opening stanza to the 1590 *Faerie Queene* Spenser presents himself as the Virgilian poet who turns from pastoral to epic (as we have seen in Part I). While Spenser scholars see the 1596 installment of the epic, Books 4–6, darkening the heroical project, they largely agree that Books 1–3 perform a robust championing of the English Protestant nation.[18] In the *Henry VI* plays, Shakespeare joins Marlowe in being among the first to

---

[16] Riggs's 1971 title speaks to a Spenserian matrix, *Shakespeare's Heroical Histories*, yet he mentions Spenser only twice in passing (56, 107); for Riggs, the 'literary tradition' is largely 'Heroical-Historical Drama' (ch. 1). Little changes by Goy-Blanquet's 2003 monograph, *Shakespeare's Early History Plays*, except that Spenser disappears altogether. In the 2002 *Cambridge Companion to Shakespeare's History Plays*, Spenser shows up twice, with one of them substantive. In 'Shakespearean History Play', Hattaway remarks, 'There is so much questioning of glory in Shakespeare that we might even claim that the histories are a rejoinder to Elizabethan projects for a revival of heroic poetry. In the October eclogue in *The Shepheardes Calender* Piers had sounded a clarion call for poets [to abandon pastoral for epic, quoting lines 36–42] ... Shakespeare implicitly asserts that if a poet is to address the ancient topics of heroism and return to the depiction of knights fighting for fame and honour, it is necessary to eschew the pieties of romance epic that emerge in *The Faerie Queene*' (Hattaway 10). Finally, in the 2003 *Histories* volume in *Companion to Shakespeare's Works*, ed. Dutton and Howard, Spenser appears incidentally only five times (8, 66, 113, 199, 251).

[17] Long ago, A. C. Hamilton saw the *Henry VI* plays responding to Spenser's 'Poet historical' in the *Letter to Ralegh* (*Early Shakespeare* 30, 33). See also Rackin 18–19. Caldwell briefly locates *2 Henry VI* in the context of Spenser's national epic (3, 13–14).

[18] See, e.g., McCabe, *Spenser's Monstrous Regiment* 101–20, 213–31.

anticipate – and perhaps even to influence – Spenser's darkening of his Virgilian project. In *2 Henry VI*, Shakespeare uses particular features of Spenser's poetic corpus to mark his theatrical characters' optimistic vulnerability in the face of York's Machiavellian and Ovidian Marloweism.

More specifically, then, I shall argue that in *2 Henry VI* Shakespeare rehearses a collision between two major forms of late Elizabethan authorship. By emphasizing the tragic nature of this collision within a larger providential narrative, he refracts a version of his own literary authorship. In the early history play, Shakespeare uses the new London theatre to present himself as an authority on a newly traumatized literary culture: he reads the major literary conflict of the day, Marlowe's aggressive targeting of Spenser; he contains it within his art; and in the process he moves beyond it, offering his own work as a distinct form of authorship.[19]

At stake for Shakespeare in this literary collision is a major question of the day: just where is the individual (and the author) to locate 'godlike pre-eminence'?[20] Henry locates godlike preeminence in Christian terms, in the individual's faith in Christ, sanctioned by the books of Scripture (and of Spenser), lodging agency outside the self. Conversely, York locates godlike preeminence in the books of Ovid and Machiavelli (and of Marlowe), lodging agency within the self. Both national leaders participate in a literary economy of immortality to tragic effect, for themselves as for England. In *2 Henry VI*, Shakespeare clears the stage for arguably a momentous invention: his reconception of immortality as a literary phenomenon, situated on the border between Ovidian, Machiavellian, and Marlovian earthly fame, and Augustinian and Spenserian Christian glory.[21]

---

[19] Cf. Hadfield, *Shakespeare and Republicanism*, who sees the four works published in 1593–94 – *The Contention, Titus, Venus, Lucrece* – as works of 'a published author' (99) with a Spenserian literary 'career': 'These four texts could be seen to announce the start of Shakespeare's career in print, in the same way that Edmund Spenser had proclaimed the start of his literary career by asserting that he was going to revolutionize English literature in *The Shepheardes Calender*' (100). Kuskin's work allows us to extend the genealogy back to Caxton, Lydgate, and Chaucer.

[20] Riggs: '[T]he import of the entire cycle [the *Henry VI* plays] is that the original drive towards a godlike pre-eminence cannot, finally, be contained within any human society that would be recognizable to an Elizabethan audience' (100).

[21] Cf. Kastan, *Shapes of Time*, who responds to Tillyard's and Ribner's older providentialist theory by identifying 'two models of historical time' in Renaissance England and in Shakespeare's *Henry VI* plays, one classical and the other Christian (18): 'just as the providential view of human time is held up for examination in the *Henry VI* plays, so too is this humanistic, exemplary conception of history' (21). The most important discussion of fame remains Riggs's chapter on *Richard III* and *1 Henry IV*, to which we shall return.

POETRY IN *2 HENRY VI*

As the preceding discussion anticipates, the opposition between York's Marlovian theatricality and Henry's Spenserian bookishness is complicated by the presence of a third medium in Shakespeare's literary economy: poetry. For Shakespeare associates Henry's bookishness with the print poetry of Spenser, and York's Marlovian theatricality with the poetry of Ovid. Finally, then, I shall argue that Shakespeare selects a poetically informed discourse of Marlovian theatre to stage an outward mode of deceptive thought and action dangerous to the English nation, and a competing discourse of the book, informed by Spenserian printed poetry, to stage a vulnerable mode of inward truth haplessly protective of the nation. By using the chronicle of York's triumph over Henry VI at the Battle of St Albans (the play's concluding event and the inaugural event of the War of the Roses), *2 Henry VI* bequeaths an early 1590s model of Shakespearean authorship.[22]

In this early version of authorship, poetry seems to occupy an unusually subordinate place with respect to the theatre–book dyad. While York is clearly a man of the theatre, and Henry a man of the book, inside the fiction neither figure functions as a poet. Nor does anyone else. Unlike most later plays, *2 Henry VI* does not record a substantive conversation about the role of the poet or the art of poetry. No one sings a song or writes a lyric. Nor does anyone present himself or herself as a poet, or present someone else as a poet.[23] For the most part, the author himself deploys poetry silently, when the Machiavellian York speaks in the idiom of Marlowe or Ovid, or the Christian king Henry speaks in the idiom of Spenser. In this early history, poetry forms an extemporal intertextual register for the poetic make-up of theatre and book.

We might attribute the subordinate role of poetry in *2 Henry VI* to generic constraints: the history play is simply less suitable for a literary discourse than comedy or romance and even tragedy. While no doubt true, this view is misleading, for, as we saw in chapter 3, such later history plays as *Richard III*, *1 Henry IV*, and *Henry V* rehearse a formal conversation about the art of poetry. For instance, in the last play of the first tetralogy, Richard, Duke of Gloucester (the later Richard III), will open with a famous speech, 'Now is the winter of our discontent' (I.I.I), and he will do so by communicating a *literary* plan, like his father York before him: Richard will invent his famed theatricality out of a scathing critique of King Edward IV's peacetime culture of courtly poetry. Near the beginning of his soliloquy,

---

[22] On poetry and history, see Rackin 18–19.   [23] The closest is Suffolk; see I.3.88–90.

he criticizes the personified figure of 'Grim-visag'd War' because 'He capers nimbly in a lady's chamber / To the lascivious pleasing of a lute' (9–13) – the lute being for Shakespeare not simply a musical instrument of the court but also a metaphor for Apollonian or 'laureate' poetry (as in Marcus' speech on Lavinia in *Titus Andronicus* [chapter 2]). As noted parenthetically in the last chapter, later in his soliloquy Richard reports that he will take advantage of 'this weak piping time of peace' to lay his 'Plots ... inductions dangerous' (24–32). His discourse deploys the formal terms of tragic theatre to target a pastoral of retirement. From the outset, then, Richard defines his secretive theatrical 'dissembling' (19) against the outward display of courtly erotic poetry.

In *2 Henry VI*, which lacks the precision of this discourse, we might conclude that Shakespeare had not yet fully realized the importance of poetry to his historic art. While also no doubt true, it does not follow that Shakespeare came to London to be a playwright, only subsequently to discover poetry when the theatres closed in 1592–3.[24] After all, poetry is a vital topic of conversation in *Two Gentlemen of Verona*, another contender for the title of Shakespeare's first play (see *Oxford*; *Norton*). Nonetheless, while Shakespeare could have come to London to be a playwright as well as a poet, the subordinate role of poetry in *2 Henry VI* might confirm this play's standing as the author's inaugural work.

THE OPENING SCENE: YORK'S MARLOVIAN THEATRE

As a display of authorship, the opening scene of *2 Henry VI* is remarkable; it keeps peeling back layers of political loyalty that turn out to be political cunning, until the once cluttered stage empties for the Duke of York, who reveals in soliloquy the Ovidian origin of his Machiavellian theatricality. It is as if we are watching the very invention of Shakespearean theatre itself, or at least an early Marlovian form of what becomes, by *Hamlet*, its most revolutionary feature: a character steps forth from the populated stage of social intrigue to communicate his inner thoughts to the audience.[25]

The opening scene ends with York's theatricality but begins with its inversion: Suffolk publicly announces the royal marriage between King Henry and the French Margaret of Anjou. The First Folio invites the reader

---

[24] To the contrary, critics from Schmidgall to Kermode believe that Shakespeare came to London to be a poet, only subsequently to discover the theatre. Both arguments seem misleading; see *SNPP* 23–4.

[25] On Shakespeare's revolutionary 'inwardness', see Greenblatt, *Will in the World* 298–305, which begins with York's heir, Richard III, and proceeds to Richard II, Brutus, and the breakout figure, Hamlet. Probably, we need to push the history of Shakespearean inwardness back to York in *Henry VI Part 2*.

to view this marriage through the lens that Suffolk provides in the concluding speech to *1 Henry VI* – the dynastic lens of Homeric and Virgilian epic:

> Thus Suffolk hath prevail'd, and thus he goes,
> As did the youthful Paris once to Greece,
> With hope to find the like event in love,
> But prosper better than the Troyan did.
> Margaret shall now be Queen, and rule the King;
> But I will rule both her, the King, and realm. (*1 Henry VI* 5.5.103–8)

Whether this speech was written before or after the opening scene of *2
Henry VI*, scholars agree that it was written as a transition between the two
plays (Warren, ed. 68–9).

Back in Act 5, scene 3, of *1 Henry VI*, Suffolk functions as a poet more
formally than perhaps any character in the first tetralogy, when he uses the
idiom of Petrachism to woo Margaret, nominally on Henry's behalf but in
fact for himself: 'So seems this gorgeous beauty to mine eyes. / Fain would I
woo her, yet I dare not speak: / I'll call for pen and ink, and write my mind'
(64–6).[26] Here Shakespeare deftly represents a complex aesthetic process,
one that will preoccupy him or was preoccupying him in the Sonnets. First,
Suffolk expresses his Petrarchan perception of Margaret's physical 'beauty',
then his desire to woo her; suddenly, however, he fears to speak, so he relies
on writing to communicate to his beloved the truth of his 'mind'. Timidity
of sexual performance leads to written erotic discourse.

When alone, Suffolk is prone to rely on Ovidian myth to imagine himself,
including as the inventor Daedalus finding his way out of the labyrinth
(5.3.187–96), but he conceals his Machivellian strategy of ambition by relying
on the terms of book culture. When Henry goes on to praise him for his
'wondrous rare description' of Margaret (5.5.1), the duke disappears behind a
modesty topos based on the book, which Shakespeare redeploys in his later
plays: 'this superficial tale / Is but a preface of her worthy praise. / The chief
perfections of that lovely dame … / Would make a volume of enticing lines'
(10–14). Suffolk asserts that his brief praise of Margaret forms merely
a 'preface' to her larger 'volume of enticing lines', the distinction between
the two parts of a book, preface and contents, metaphorically embroidering
the depth of Margaret's beauty.

In the speech that concludes *1 Henry VI*, then, Suffolk turns from
public Petrarchan lyric to private epic theatre. For both literary forms,
this is a striking reversal of literary convention, and helps to mark this

---

[26] As Kuskin reports, William de la Pole was a poet, esp. a Chaucerian poet (MS 8). On Suffolk's
Petrarchism in Shakespeare, see Ornstein, *Kingdom for a Stage* 44; Riggs 112.

play's conclusion as open-ended and problematic.[27] In particular, Suffolk recalls Marlowe's Doctor Faustus in imagining himself as a Paris figure, overgoing his 'Troyan' original in the seizure of a beautiful woman. Whereas Faustus thinks of himself as a new Paris wounding Achilles to unite with the conjured phantom Helen of Troy (A text 5.1.98–103), Suffolk plans to unite with a historical woman who remains bewitching. Appearing to conclude the play on a hopeful note of fulfilled Petrarchan desire within the context of dynastic epic, Suffolk's epic simile appears ominous, if not outright predictive, of his failure to marry the new queen and become king of England.

Most important for our purposes, Shakespeare picks the Homeric and Virgilian story back up in *2 Henry VI* as a mythic backdrop for what many consider to be his broad professional project: the transposition of epic to the new London stage (1.4.17), complete with quotations from and references to Virgil's *Aeneid* (2.1.24; 3.2.114–21; 5.2.61–5), as well as references to important events and myths circulating around the Troy story.[28] Yet the weirdness of Suffolk's concluding heroic simile – it is not simply ominous but indecorous, especially for a play titled *Henry VI* – reminds us that Shakespeare prepares for one of his most significant literary projects: the counter-laureate staging of an epic that is not there (chapter 1).

As the opening scene to *2 Henry VI* unfolds, Shakespeare's counter-epic theatre acquires Spenserian resonance. Once Suffolk announces to the court that he has 'perform'd' his 'task' (1.1.9) of bringing to England 'The fairest queen that ever king receiv'd' (16), Henry thanks the duke for 'espous[ing]' (9) him to 'this beauteous face / A world of earthly blessings to my soul, / If sympathy of love unite our thoughts' (21–3). Yet perhaps not until Margaret reciprocates Henry's hope of sympathetic marriage with her own avowal of 'mutual conference' (25) can we discern Shakespeare's attempt to bring Spenserian companionate marriage to the stage. For Henry moves into a discourse recognizable as Spenserian:

> Her sight did ravish, but her grace in speech,
> Her words yclad with wisdom's majesty,
> Makes me from wond'ring fall to weeping joys.
> *(2 Henry VI 1.1.32–4)*

---

[27] Cf. Hodgdon: 'In yet another interrupted, truncated ceremony, *1 Henry VI* concludes by disrupting and subverting the genealogical bases of monarchy' (*End Crowns All* 58).

[28] Cf. Hattaway, 'Shakespearean History Play': 'Shakespeare's histories ... seem to make a statement about a destiny for England. In other words, although Homer and Virgil are never primary sources, magnitude of action, grandiloquence of style, the invocation of deity, and what are taken as signs of divine intervention have suggested to critics since Coleridge relationships not only to tragedy but to epic' (10).

Ravish, grace, wisdom, majesty, wondering: these are among the major words organizing *The Faerie Queene*, especially its epic romance deployment of Petrarchan verse for the purpose of royal encomium. Henry expresses wonder and joy created by his sensual perception of a queen's beauty, majesty, and graceful speech. As modern editors determine, however, the giveaway Spenserian word is 'yclad'.[29] By presenting his English king as a figure of Spenserian discourse and vision, Shakespeare does not merely signal Henry's naïvete as a character; he also intimates the vulnerability of Spenser's affirmative authorship on behalf of the nation.

Thus, when the king exits the stage with his new queen 'To see her coronation be perform'd' (74), an initial scene of harmonious Spenserian marriage gives way to a jarring (Marlovian-sounding) tirade by the Duke of Gloucester. Gloucester is furious not simply because Margaret has arrived 'without having any dowry' (61–2) but also because England has given up the French regions of Anjou and Maine, hard won by Henry V. The barons are angry because they have lost blood fighting to win these very regions. And everyone is unsettled because, as Gloucester puts it, 'Suffolk, the new-made duke ... rules the roast' (109). It is Gloucester's address to the 'peers of England' (98) that acquires particular literary resonance:

> Fatal this marriage, cancelling your fame,
> Blotting your names from books of memory,
> Rasing the characters of your renown,
> Defacing monuments of conquer'd France,
> Undoing all, as all had never been!   (*2 Henry VI* 1.1.99–103)

This speech constitutes one of Shakespeare's most detailed formulations of the frenzy of renown. For a playwright popularly known to eschew literary fame, such a speech must appear anomalous.[30] Yet, as we shall see, Shakespeare also ends *2 Henry VI* with a formal expression of fame, suggesting that his history play is deeply concerned with the question of immortality, and thus perhaps the telos of a literary career.[31] Gloucester's vocabulary of renown is so intense as to betray a personal –and perhaps a family – obsession: *fame, names, memory, renown, monuments*. This is also the obsession of Shakespeare's Sonnets, especially Sonnet 55, where the vocabulary memorably

---

[29] Cairncross glosses 'yclad' as 'possibly due to Spenser's influence' (ed. 5), while Hattaway is more precise: "Spenser had revived this archaic form of the past participle' (ed. 81).

[30] Garber, *Shakespeare After All*, sees Gloucester here expressing 'dismay in terms of writing, print, and reputation' (103).

[31] Gloucester's use of 'monuments' connects to Margaret's later use of the word during her farewell to Suffolk at 3.2.339 (Mazzaro 403–4), thereby locating fame at the mid-point of the play.

recurs – forming perhaps a unique back-bridge from the printed 1609 sonnet sequence to the early 1590s play.

The details of Gloucester's speech open up an unusual moment of Shakespearean authorship. Inside the fiction, Gloucester accuses the peers of compromising their chances for historical renown; he sees their subjection as a national disgrace threatening their role in history. Yet outside the fiction (so to speak), Shakespeare communicates with his audience about the very process of historical making that he is staging. How else can we understand the mind-bending feat voiced in lines 99–100: the peers blot their names from a history book that has already written them in; they erase the 'characters' of a fame already printed on their behalf?[32] Not simply does Gloucester use a bibliographical term, 'books of memory', but by it he means 'history books, chronicles' (Warren, ed. 117). The theatrical discourse gestures to the way in which a chronicle book like Hall's or Holinshed's remembers the heroic deeds of historic individuals. But because Shakespeare performs the role of national chronicler, he, too, performs the act of authorial remembrance. Inside an English history play, a character refers to his own reading of books about English history, while the author of the fiction draws attention to his own reading of and making of a national chronicle. We need to read the speech of fame doubly, as at once Gloucester's expression of anxiety about the loss of English baronial fame and Shakespeare's artistic hope for his own literary fame.

Not surprisingly, in Gloucester's speech we may detect a specific moment of Spenserian extemporal intertextuality. In Book 2 of *The Faerie Queene*, canto 12, the hero of temperance, Sir Guyon, and his guide, the Palmer, sneak up on the enchantress Acrasia, who has enticed the youthful knight Verdant into her Bower of Bliss:

> His warlike armes, the idle instruments
> Of sleeping praise, were hong upon a tree,
> And his brave shield, full of old moniments,
> Was fowly ra'st, that none the signes might see;
> Ne for them, ne for honour cared hee,
> Ne ought, that did to his advauncement tend.
> (Spenser, *Faerie Queene* 2.12.80)

Spenser's metaphor of ruined renown may differ outwardly from Shakespeare's, since it locates 'old moniments' on a chivalric shield hung

---

[32] See Mazzaro: 'Printer's terms "cancelling", "blotting", "erasing", and "character" surround [Gloucester's books of memory]' (403).

on a tree within a romance fiction.[33] Yet the repetition of the Spenserian words *monuments* and *raise* reveals a similar idea: that noble knights of Gloriana have performed a shameful action erasing their heroic conduct for the nation. Shakespeare can be seen to overgo the author of England's national epic by transposing the fiction of the aristocratic erasure of national fame under the spell of an enchanting beauty, from printed romance epic to historical drama.

Gloucester's speech makes clear where the good duke Humphrey locates truth: in the 'books of memory' – printed books that record the past: a textual version of fame. He becomes incensed because he believes that the marriage between Henry and Margaret secures not simply a 'shameful … league' between England and France but more particularly fame's haunting inversion, 'Undoing all, as all had never been!': oblivion. Although Gloucester is not explicit, the full discourse of the opening movement in which he appears contrasts the public theatre of a dangerous international marriage 'perform'd' between male and female with a homosocial 'book of memory' printing national renown.

It is this opening dynamic of book and theatre that York's opening soliloquy brings to center stage. But only after Shakespeare peels back two other layers of theatrical scheming. First, once Gloucester exits, the barons plot to oust the good duke; and second, after Cardinal Beaufort, Bishop of Winchester, departs, Buckingham and Somerset plot to oust him. Yet it is only after Warwick and Salisbury depart that York announces his plan to use the Nevilles in his 'show of love' to pull Henry's 'bookish rule' down. As the opening of York's soliloquy makes plain, he derives his theatrical plan in response to the poetic book of Ovid:

> So York must sit, and fret, and bite his tongue,
> While his own lands are bargain'd for and sold.
> Methinks the realms of England, France, and Ireland
> Bear that proportion to my flesh and blood
> As did the fatal brand Althaea burnt
> Unto the Prince's heart of Calydon.   (*2 Henry VI* 1.1.230–5)

As editors report, Ovid tells the story of Meleager and his protective mother Althaea in Book 8 of the *Metamorphoses* (451–525).[34] Yet Shakespeare's

---

[33] Mazzaro sees the corresponding passage on the 'book of memory' in *1 Henry VI* (2.4.95) as indebted to Spenser's description of Phantastes' chamber in *FQ* 2.9 (400). Anticipating Hamlet's 'book and volume of my brain' (1.5.103) as an 'internal' model, the passage in *Henry VI Part 1* differs from the *Henry VI Part 2* use, which 'images actual books' (Mazzaro 399, 403).

[34] In Hattaway's version, 'Ovid tells in *Metamorphoses* VIII, 593ff. how Meleager, Prince of Calydon, was destined to live only as long as a brand burning in the fire at the time of his birth. His mother Althaea

reference to the story is curious, in part because it is his only reference to this myth in his corpus; in part because the myth does not make it into the standard stories of 'Shakespeare and Ovid'.[35]

Ovid's version of the myth supplies a few details not mentioned in editorial annotation. First, in the *Metamorphoses* Ovid narrates how the three Fates visit Althaea during her childbirth, 'and sang: "An equal span of life we give to thee and to this wood, O babe new-born"' (8.453–5). From the outset, the myth is about childbirth, creativity, and invention, and thus its afterlife, destiny, and renown. Indeed, the log becomes the talisman for the complete 'span of life' mapped on to a political career that comes to signify a literary career. Second, after Meleager kills Althaea's two brothers, she throws the log into the fire in anger at her son, bringing about his death; thereafter, Meleager's sisters build a funeral pyre for his body and bury his ashes in a funeral monument, 'on which his name has been carved' (540–1). Both of these details – the deadly song of the Fates and the sisters' inscription of their brother's name on his monument – lead Ovid to present the myth as one about his own poetic authorship. As Philip Hardie explains,

the poet's name is as potent a magic talisman as is the log with which the life of Meleager's body is coterminous ... The equivalence of log and life is itself the product of a *carmen*, the song of the Fates as they spun at Meleager's birth ... The common use of spinning, and of the spinning of the Fates in particular, as an image of poetry suggests an analogy between the magic worked by the song of the Fates and the magic worked by Ovid's poetry ... In the story of Meleager there is a symmetry between the log and the *nomina* of the epitaph ... The link between bodies and words in the Meleager episode made it attractive for Ovid as a way of figuring his own relationship to the words of his poem in *Tristia* 1.7.[36]

In particular, in *Tristia* 1.7 Ovid compares Althaea's burning of the log with his own attempt to burn the *Metamorphoses*: 'Just as Thestius' daughter burned her own son, they say, in burning the branch ... so I placed the innocent books consigned with me to death, my very vitals, upon the devouring pyre, because I had come to hate the Muses as my accusers, or because the poem itself was as yet half grown and rough' (18–22). As Hardie puts it, 'the mythical narrative now comes to stand in allusively for Ovid's

snatched it out, but years later, after he had killed her brothers, cast it back into the flames' (ed. 89). See also Cairncross, ed. 15; Knowles, ed. 164; Warren, ed. 123. A. C. Hamilton calls York Shakespeare's 'first *political* character' and York's soliloquy probably 'Shakespeare's first effort to create character', a 'major breakthrough in the imitation of history', quoting the lines on the Maleager myth but not discussing them (*Early Shakespeare* 36–7; his emphasis).
[35] Barkan mentions the myth only once in passing as one of several Ovidian stories about 'the secret intimacies of different things' (*Gods Made Flesh* 91). See also Lyne, *Ovid's Changing Worlds* 231.
[36] Hardie, *Ovid's Poetics of Illusion* 242, 244–5.

lived experience. Ovid's essence resides in the scrolls of his poems, as Meleager's essence resided in the log' (245).

To this account, we may add that Ovid goes on to interrupt his telling of the Meleager story by inserting his authorial voice in a striking manner: 'Not if some god had given me a hundred mouths each with its tongue, a master's genius, and all Helicon's inspiration, could I describe the piteous plight of those poor sisters' (8.533–5). Yet Ovid next describes the sisters' piteous plight, further underscoring the Heliconian inspiration for his metamorphic art. In *Tristia* 1.7, we might say, Ovid takes self-reflexivity one step further than he does in the *Metamorphoses*, comparing his role as poet directly to figures in the Meleager-Althaea story.

We know that Shakespeare wove the *Metamorphoses* into the fabric of *2 Henry VI*, but editors also provide evidence that he was working with the *Tristia*.[37] When York resurrects the story, he does so to imagine the way in which 'England, France, and Ireland' seal his burning fate. Like Ovid in *Tristia* 1.7, York turns to the myth as a personal story about his 'essence'. In other words, York uses Ovid to achieve a realization about his destiny, and then, in that Ovidian state, he announces his turn to theatre to rewrite the fate that he feels thrust upon him, as if he were bringing the funereal name of Meleager back to life.

For his part, Shakespeare presents York putting the 'book' of 'Ovid's Metamorphosis' on to the stage, just as we have seen him doing in *Titus Andronicus* (4.1.41–2). Rather than simply use the Machiavellian Marlowe's Ovidian theatre to oppose the 'bookish rule' of King Henry, York performs a more complex dynamic that relates book and theatre. He originates this authorial economy from the poetic book of Ovid, especially as Marlowe had brought that book on to the London stage with the figure of the Machevile in *The Jew of Malta*, and then York deploys his own bookish rule against the book of his sovereign.

MARGARET, SUFFOLK, AND HENRY'S SPENSERIAN BOOK

If *2 Henry VI* specifies York's 'part' as a poetic man of the theatre, the play also delineates the particular poetic contents of Henry's 'bookish rule'. The king himself makes it clear which book he has been reading: 'God's book', which Henry uses to 'adjudg' Eleanor 'to death' (2.3.4) for witchcraft and treason. Henry's book is a Christian book, the Bible itself, and he

---

[37] Hattaway, for instance, glosses 3.2.339–42 with *Tr* 1.3 (ed. 159); 3.2.388–402 with *Tr* 3.43–4, 61–2 (ed. 161); and 5.2.59 with *Tr* 3.9.25–8 (ed. 211).

operates his monarchical rule according to the codes of miracle that he reads in Scripture and such ancillary texts as prayer books: meekness, quietness, peacefulness, and contemplation. Following Holinshed's more critical portrait of Henry, Shakespeare presents the king as the arch-bookish man whose study impedes his sovereignty. In Henry's hands, the Christian book interferes with English kingship: reading sabotages rule; contemplative study undermines political justice: textuality becomes a threat to national leadership. It is as if Shakespeare were dramatizing how the Reformation, with its commitment to print culture, recoils on itself.[38]

Yet in Act 1, scene 3, Shakespeare enriches his portrait of the Christian king of books when Queen Margaret, in rapt conversation with her chivalric lover, Suffolk, expresses disillusionment with her new husband:

> I tell thee, Pole, when in the city Tours
> Thou ran'st a-tilt in honor of my love
> And stol'st away the ladies' hearts of France,
> I thought King Henry had resembled thee
> In courage, courtship, and proportion;
> But all his mind is bent to holiness,
> To number Ave-Maries on his beads;
> His champions are the prophets and apostles,
> His weapons holy saws of sacred writ,
> His study is his tilt-yard, and his loves
> Are brazen images of canonized saints.
> I would the college of the Cardinals
> Would choose him Pope and carry him to Rome,
> And set the triple crown upon his head –
> That were a state fit for his holiness.   (*2 Henry VI* 1.3.50–64)

As modern editors point out, Shakespeare borrows the chivalric event to which Margaret refers from Hall's chronicle: in 'the citee of Toures in Tourayne', after Suffolk stood in for Henry during the marriage ceremony with Margaret, 'There wer triumphaunt Iusts, costly feastes, and delicate banquettes'.[39] Yet Shakespeare does not simply embroider the historical detail; he particularizes it in terms of the Reformation poetics of Spenser's epic romance.

Just as Spenser had titled the first book of *The Faerie Queene* the 'Legende of Holinesse', so Margaret twice uses the word 'holiness', as if to provide a

[38] On print and the Reformation, see, most recently, Lander, *Inventing Polemic*.
[39] Repr. in Cairncross, ed. 161; see 23–4. Kreps discusses the differences between the folio and quarto versions of this speech (165–8), revealing that most of the detail discussed below shows Shakespeare's hand at revision.

signpost for a staging of the Spenserian chivalric project. While Hall emphasizes Henry's holiness, Shakespeare's lexicon evokes the chivalric matrix of Spenser's Protestant Legend. For instance, Shakespeare builds Spenser's anti-Catholic polemic into Margaret's speech, when she portrays her husband not simply as a Christian king but as a Catholic one, as demonstrated by his 'Ave-Maries', 'beads', 'brazen images', 'canonized saints', 'College of the Cardinals, the 'Pope', and 'Rome'.[40] In Margaret's eyes, Henry is a Catholic king of contemplation deserving ridicule because he inverts Suffolk's chivalric heroism. As she recalls, through Suffolk's prowess as a jousting knight in the tilt-yard, her lover becomes the beloved hero of French ladies, including herself, for earlier she made the mental error of thinking that her future husband 'resembled' Suffolk in his military bravery, courtly manners, and physical beauty.

Yet by expressing disillusionment with Henry for not being Suffolk, Margaret performs the artful maneuver of superimposing Suffolk's chivalric heroism on to and against Henry's Catholic contemplation. In her speech, Henry does not simply enact his Catholic faith; he substitutes the admirable values of courtly chivalry for the contemptible values of Catholic faith. Instead of praising 'champions', Henry worships 'prophets and apostles', the heroes of Scripture rather than those of epic romance; he exchanges 'weapons' for the 'holy laws of sacred writ', the chivalric instruments of war for the teachings of the Bible. He replaces the 'tilt-yard' with the 'study', the site of jousting with that of scholarship, making his 'loves' not 'ladies' but 'brazen images and canonized saints'. Evidently, Margaret can criticize her new husband for his Spenserian bookishness because (as we have seen) during their first conversation he had addressed her in precisely the terms of Spenserian companionate marriage.[41]

Shakespeare's strategy of characterization, which describes Henry's choice to perform Catholic worship *at the expense of* chivalric heroism, reveals a divide that Spenser himself was at pains to bridge. In Book I, canto 10, after the hermit Heavenly Contemplation shows Redcrosse the vision of the New Jerusalem, the knight asks to remain in the holy city forever, but the old man refuses the request, reminding Redcrosse that he

[40] Cf. Spenser's portrait of Archimago, the black magician in disguise as a (hypocritical) Catholic priest: 'He told of Saintes and Popes, and evermore / He strowd an Ave-Mary after and before' (*FQ* I.1.35). In his edition of *The Faerie Queene*, A. C. Hamilton glosses this passage as follows: 'This Protestant scorn is nicely rendered in Shakespeare, 2 *Henry VI* I.3.55–56' (ed. 39).

[41] In their glosses on Margaret's speech, editors encourage us to refer to Spenser by glossing lines 57–8 with Ephesians 6 (Hattaway, ed. 97; Knowles, ed. 177; Warren, ed. 133). The most famous 1590s literary representation of Paul's Christian warrior appears in Spenser's Legend of Holiness, in the Redcrosse Knight (A. C. Hamilton, ed. 717).

owes service to Gloriana (58–63). Whereas the Spenserian hero learns to enact Christian faith through courtly chivalry, Henry fails to bridge the gap. Shakespeare's strategy is acute, compelling us to see Henry not simply as a weak Catholic king but as a failed Spenserian hero. In this portrait of the national sovereign, Shakespeare's discourse of the book includes more than 'God's book'. It includes the book of Spenser.[42]

CADE'S REBELLION: POPULIST THEATRE, ELITIST PRINT

Given the presence of Shakespeare's literary economy in the rivalry between Henry and York in the early acts of the play, we should not be surprised to find a discourse of books and theatre infiltrating the scenes of Cade's rebellion. As York reveals in his soliloquy in Act 3, scene 1, he has 'seduc'd' the 'headstrong' Cade as a 'minister' of his own 'intent' (355–6). Like York, Cade wants to be king of England, differing mainly in the outrageousness of his claim: 'I hope to reign, / For I am rightful heir unto the crown' (4.2.130–1). Critics justly admire the scenes of Cade's rebellion, and during the past few decades they have attended especially to his subversion of Elizabethan political norms through his championing of populist or egalitarian freedom.[43] We may build on this criticism by locating Cade within the literary economy of Shakespearean authorship.

What York admires about Cade is not simply his athletic prowess but his robust theatricality. One time in Ireland, York saw Cade sustain so many 'darts' in his 'thighs' that he resembled 'a sharp-quill'd porpentine', yet Cade could still 'caper upright like a wild Morisco, / Shaking the bloody darts as he his bells' (362–6). Thus, Cade himself can tell his followers: 'And you that love the commons, follow me. / Now show yourselves men, 'tis for liberty': 'take your parts' (4.2.182–7). Like identity in Shakespeare, political position is not stable but notoriously in motion – theatrical motion. Hence, George Bevis, one of Cade's rebels, instructs John Holland, 'get thee a sword,

---

[42] In contrast to many, Goddard finds Henry 'a remarkable piece of characterization', serene in his commitment to retirement, anticipating Duke Senior, Duke Vincentio, and Prospero, as well as Desdemona (*Meaning of Shakespeare* 1: 30, 32).

[43] Bloom finds Cade 'all that is memorable' in *2 Henry VI*: 'everyone else blends into a harmony of Marlovian rant' (48). On the politics of Cade, see, e.g., Hobday, 'Clouted Shoon and Leather Aprons'; Greenblatt, 'Murdering Peasants'; A. Patterson, *Shakespeare and the Popular Voice* 32–51; Knowles, 'Force of History'; Pugliatti, '"More Than History Can Pattern"'; Sullivan, *Drama of Landscape* 223–9; Cartelli, 'Jack Cade in the Garden' and 'Disordered Relations'. In *Shakespeare and Republicanism*, Hadfield sees the first tetralogy as 'Shakespeare's *Pharsalia*' (ch. 3 title), but he refers to Cade only in passing (109, 120–1). In *Forms of Nationhood* (207–15), Helgerson sees Shakespeare raising the specter of '[P]opular power' (206) in order to 'exorcise' (212) it in favor of 'royal power' (234).

though made of a lath' (1–2), referring to the instrument used by the morality play figure of the Vice (Warren, ed. 236), for 'Jack Cade the clothier means to dress the commonwealth, and turn it, and set new a nap upon it' (4–6).[44] Cade's rebellion is not simply performed in the popular theatre of London but wittily representative of its populist roots (Rackin 22–3). Accordingly, Cade's masculine theatre aims to perform egalitarianism at the expense of the monarch, as Cade himself announces: 'our enemies shall [fall] before us, inspir'd with the spirit of putting down kings and princes ... All the realm shall be in common' (35–6, 68).

In addition to performing the spirit of inspiration to put kings and princes down, Cade spends much of his energy using theatre to erase print culture. Thus his first victim is a clerk, who has been taken 'setting of boys' copies' (88) – making copies for penmanship (Knowles, ed. 305): 'H'as a book in his pocket with red letters in't' (90–1), either a school primer or an almanac (Knowles, ed. 305). After Cade mocks the juridical system by examining the clerk, and the proceedings turn up the young man's 'confess [ion]' (for he can 'write' his 'name'), Cade delivers the sentence: 'Hang him with his pen and inkhorn about his neck' (106–10). When the brother of Sir Humphrey Stafford declares, 'Jack Cade, the Duke of York hath taught you this' (153–4), we realize the extent to which Cade functions as York's common heir in rebellion against King Henry. Like York, Cade uses theatre to supplant the book.

Nowhere is Cade's anti-literary project more pronounced than in his arrest of Lord Say, the Treasurer of England, who has 'sold the towns in France' (4.7.21). In Cade's estimation, Say has used the nation's money to build the institution of English education, with its literacy and scholarship dependent on print and book culture:

Thou hast most traitorously corrupted the youth of the realm in erecting a grammar school; and whereas, before, our forefathers had no other books but the score and the tally, thou hast caus'd printing to be us'd, and, contrary to the King, his crown, and dignity, thou hast built a paper-mill. (*2 Henry VI* 4.7.32–7)

Reminiscent of the death of the scholar Ramus in Marlowe's *Massacre at Paris*, this scene does not simply rely on the much-noted anachronism of Say's building of the 'paper-mill' to promote 'printing'. The anachronism illuminates an unusual moment of Shakespearean authorship. Shakespeare both outwardly ridicules Cade for his political corruption and inwardly

---

[44] Cf. R. Wilson, 'Shakespeare and the Cloth Workers'. My student Steele Nowlin points out that Cade is a terrible actor, often changing his part, rewriting the political script, and never consulting his acting company (personal communication).

exults in his theatricality. He also creates this memorable character out of the page-and-stage dynamic organizing his own career.[45]

While Cade's standing as a Marlovian overreacher is well documented, his connection with Spenser is more tenuous.[46] As soon as Cade sends Lord Say off to execution, the rebel announces his attack on yet another set of victims:

> There shall not a maid be married, but she shall pay to me her maidenhead ere they have it. Men shall hold of me *in capite*; and we charge and command that their wives be as free as heart can wish or tongue can tell. (*2 Henry VI* 4.7.121–5)

In Shakespeare's hands, this comical Marlovian overreacher dangerously targets the heart of Spenser's *Faerie Queene*, with its twin prizing of virginity and chaste marriage. Yet Cade's final phrase, 'none can tell', has specific literary associations. Andrew S. Cairncross cites Kyd's *Spanish Tragedy* 1.1.57–8: 'I saw more sights then thousand tongues can tell, / Or pennes can write, or mortall harts can think' (ed. 128). Yet, in print Spenser most famously is obsessed with this inability topos, so much so that he uses the phrase 'none can tell' on multiple occasions, making Cade's phrase a technical Spenserian repetition.[47] In opposition to Spenser, Cade presents himself as a bold figure of language who uses a free heart to devirginate maids and rape chaste married women.

Accordingly, in Act 4, scene 10, when Cade finds his last respite in the garden of Richard Iden, the rebel speaks in soliloquy to the audience by using mock-heroic discourse:

> And I think this word 'sallet' was born to do me good; for many a time, but for a sallet, my brain-pan had been cleft with a brown bill; and many a time, when I have been dry and bravely marching, it hath serv'd me instead of a quart pot to drink in; and now the word 'sallet' must serve me to feed on. (*2 Henry VI* 4.10.10–15)

According to Ronald Knowles, 'If Cade removes his helmet here, this would create a mock-heroic touch in the disarming of the hero at a point of danger', and he cites not merely Hector at *Troilus and Cressida* 5.9 but also 'the Redcrosse Knight in Spenser, 1.vii.2–3' (ed. 336). While we need not insist that Shakespeare consciously echoes the moment Redcrosse takes off his helmet to rest beside the Enfeebling Fountain – another garden setting – we

---

[45] Cf. Greenblatt, *Will in the World*, who reads the Cade scenes in terms of 'Shakespeare' himself (167–72) – 'the sources of his own consciousness' (171).

[46] Cairncross (ed. 115), Warren (ed. 243), and Knowles (ed. 309) all gloss Cade's reference to 'Fellow kings' at 4.2.164 as a verbal repetition of Marlowe at *2 Tamb* 1.6.24.

[47] *FQ* 2.1.11; 2.1.49; *Astrophel* 171; see also 'Ne toung did tell' (*FQ* 2.7.19), as well as *Teares of the Muses* 600; *Daphnaida* 74; *FQ* 1.10.55. Versions of the phrase appear in Spenser's later poetry: *FQ* 4.11.9; 4.11.44; *Hymne of Love* 264; *Hymne of Heavenlie Beautie* 204.

may nonetheless recall the importance of this topos to *The Faerie Queene* as a whole: the hero pausing in a *locus amoenus* to take off his armor signals impending disaster.[48] Although Cade is primarily a Marlovian overreacher who uses theatre to target print culture, he also functions as a parody of the Spenserian chivalric knight who protects 'maidenhead'.

Shakespeare's parody of the Spenserian hero emerges finally in Cade's attitude toward the monuments and records of national fame. If in Book 2, canto 9, of *The Faerie Queene* Spenser had advertised his role as the national preserver of 'Briton monuments', in *2 Henry VI* Shakespeare presents Cade destroying the monuments of Britain. Thus, in Act 4, scene 6, Cade orders his men to 'set London Bridge on fire, and if you can, burn down the Tower too' (14–15), while in scene 7 he commands, 'burn all the records of the realm, my mouth shall be the parliament of England' (4.7.14–15).[49] As if a shadow of the Ovidian author in Marlowe, Cade would turn his own voice – his 'mouth' – into the official government of Spenser's England, reducing the outwardly proclaiming egalitarian to a nation of one.

No wonder, then, that Shakespeare presents Iden's garden victory over the rebel in heroic terms:

> Sword, I will hallow thee for this thy deed,
> And hang thee o'er my tomb when I am dead.
> Ne'er shall this blood be wiped from thy point,
> But thou shalt wear it as a herald's coat,
> To emblaze the honor that thy master got. (*2 Henry VI* 4.10.67–71)

Although 'a man of property' in Kent (Greenblatt, 'Murdering Peasants' 126), Iden imagines himself as a chivalric knight victorious in battle. Yet Shakespeare does not allow Iden's epic self-presentation to emerge untarnished. In his dying breath, Cade insists that the self-proclaimed man of chivalry is deceived: Cade says he dies 'vanquish'd by famine, not by valor' (75).[50] As such, Shakespeare complicates his inset chivalric epic with the dire constraints of material reality (Rackin 212). By presenting Cade's populist rebellion in literary terms, the poet-playwright turns this much-admired figure into a virtual icon of Shakespearean authorship itself. By taking

[48] See Guillory, *Poetic Authority* 28.

[49] Cf. Rackin: 'Cade's command to burn the historical records and tear down the historical monuments not only specifies the literal objects he wishes to destroy; it also specifies the present political significance of his antihistorical project and recognizes the function of historical writing in the world of the Tudors as a basis for an oppressive present authority' (209).

[50] Glossing 4.10.60–4, Knowles remarks that 'Cade's close echoes the words of Marlowe's Tamburlaine (2, 5.3.249)' (ed. 374).

Marlowe's cue to call the Spenserian chivalric epic into question, Shakespeare makes his greatest theatre to date.

THE BATTLE OF ST ALBANS: YORK'S LITERARY TRIUMPH

In Act 5, scene 1, Shakespeare presents 'York as Cade's apotheosis' (Hodgdon 66), when the Duke echoes Iden's plan to 'cut off' Cade's 'most ungracious head, / Which I will bear in triumph to the King' (4.10.82–3): 'From Ireland thus comes York to claim his right, / And pluck the crown from feeble Henry's head' (5.1.1–2; Garber, *Shakespeare After All* 114). In this late speech, York reprises his Ovidian frame of mind:

> Ring bells, aloud, burn bonfires clear and bright
> To entertain great England's lawful king!
> Ah, *sancta majestas!* who would not buy thee dear?
> Let them obey that know not how to rule;
> This hand was made to handle nought but gold.
> I cannot give due action to my words,
> Except a sword or sceptre balance it.
> A sceptre shall it have, have I a soul,
> On which I'll toss the flow're-de-luce of France.
>
> (*2 Henry VI* 5.1.3–11)

It is hard to tell whether York addresses his army in public or the audience in private. When Buckingham enters, York clearly moves into private utterance – the utterance of self-concealed theatricality: 'Whom have we here? Buckingham to disturb me? The King hath sent him sure; I must dissemble' (12–13). While the opening eleven lines of the soliloquy leave room for different options, York could speak the opening four lines to his army, announcing his arrival in England and calling for celebration of 'great England's lawful king'; then he could speak the remaining seven lines in an aside. In this scenario, York's Latin exclamation of anticipated satisfaction with the crown of England, 'Ah, *sancta majestas!*', would serve as a verbal transition.[51]

Editors attribute the Latin phrase to another poem of Ovid's, the *Ars amatoria* (Cairncross, ed. 139; Hattaway, ed. 199; Warren, ed. 268). There, in an astonishing passage, Ovid tells young women to reveal their beauty in public, including by 'visit[ing] three theatres' (those built in Rome by Pompey, Marcellus, and Balbus), for 'what is hidden is unknown; what is

---

[51] Hattaway comments, 'Although it is conventional to mark 23–31 [the Ajax speech] as an 'aside', there is little difference in kind between those lines and York's first speech [1–11]. Both could be taken as direct addresses to the audience, with the rhetorical question at 12 creating a bond between player and spectator' (ed. 199).

unknown none desires' (3.394–7). This advice to women leads Ovid to address his own vocation as a poet, along with its goal, poetic fame:

What is sought by the sacred bards save fame alone? toil we ne'er so hard, this is all we ask. Poets once were the care of chieftains and of kings, and choirs of old won great rewards. Sacred was the majesty and venerable the name of the poet (*Sanctaque maiestas et erat venerabile nomen / Vatibus*). (Ovid, *Ars amatoria* 3.403–8)

Ovid's linkage of poetry and theatre occurs elsewhere in his canon. Yet his verse discourse here does not simply dilate on the poet's power of fame; it migrates into the political sphere, claiming the utility of the poet to 'chieftains and … kings', citing Ennius' role in the career of Scipio (409–10). Thus, it is Ovid's combination of poetry, theatre, and politics that undergirds York's quotation of the *Ars amatoria* in *2 Henry VI*. Effectively, York wrenches Ovid, replacing the telos of renown with that of the crown, an Ovidian abstraction with a Marlovian concretion.[52]

The opposition between *fame* and *crown* turns out to be one of the most important frames of reference in *2 Henry VI*. Shakespeare's history play meditates on the goal not just of national leadership but of national renown. In *3 Henry VI*, the two topics will fuse in a single phrase, 'laurel crown' (4.6.34), intimating that whatever York imagines his goals to be, his author presents the duke as a 'self-crowned laureate', a political leader refracting authorship.

York's self-crowning theatricality continues in his last great soliloquy in *2 Henry VI*:

> Scarce can I speak, my choler is so great.
> O, I could hew up rocks and fight with flint,
> I am so angry at these abject terms;
> And now, like Ajax Telamonius,
> On sheep or oxen could I spend my fury.
> I am far better born than is the King;
> More like a king, more kingly in my thoughts;
> But I must make fair weather yet a while,
> Till Henry be more weak and I more strong.[53]
>
> (*2 Henry VI* 5.1.23–31)

---

[52] More precisely, York gives voice to Ovid by imitating Marlowe, esp. the Guise in *The Massacre at Paris*; see, e.g., Riggs 122.

[53] According to Hattaway, 'After his defeat by Ulysses in the contest for Achilles' armour, Ajax, son of Telamon, fell into such a fit of madness that he slaughtered the sheep of the Greek army under the illusion that they were his enemies. He then committed suicide' (ed. 200). Warren adds, 'This Ajax is a different one from the Ajax who appears in *Troilus and Cressida*' (ed. 269).

Ovid does not mention this myth in the *Metamorphoses*, but he does rehearse it the *Amores*, where Marlowe made it available in *Ovid's Elegies*, the first translation of the Roman poet's inaugural work into any European vernacular.[54] In Elegy 1.7, Ovid narrates how he had insanely abused Corinna in a fit of anger, which proceeds in Marlowe's translation, 'Why, Ajax, master of the seven-fold shield, / Butchered the flocks he found in spacious field' (*OE* 1.7.3–8). Here, Ovid and Marlowe deliver a 'mock-epic, mock-heroic comparison by the speaker of himself to Ajax'.[55] As with Meleager, then, Ovid and Marlowe use the Ajax myth of anger and madness as a self-reflexive myth of authorship.

In York's aside, Ovid's and Marlowe's erotic dynamic disappears, but the authorial one remains, as York struggles to control his 'choler' at Henry for surveilling his military return from Ireland, and in the process compares himself with Ajax, who did not control his anger, but went mad, performing acts of atrocity when he mistook 'sheep and oxen' from the pastoral domain for the commanders of epic, Agamemnon and Menelaus. As in his opening soliloquy in Act 1, York turns to an Ovidian myth of authorship to fashion his identity as an English political leader. Unlike earlier, however, he does not turn the Ovidian (and Marlovian) poetic book into a Machiavellian (and Marlovian) form of historical theatre, but instead uses the discourse of these authors to muster up his will to control his temper.[56] For reasons to which we are not privy, Shakespeare rehearses the problem of anger and the difficulty political leaders have controlling it. The story of Ajax among his sheep and oxen, made available to the Elizabethans by Ovid and Marlowe, mythologizes the problem on the new stage. Notably, Shakespeare transposes the problem of temperance to the inventive sphere of artistic expression.[57]

Only by understanding York's theatrical Ovidianism can we approach his most unusual Ovidian reference in *2 Henry VI*. The scene itself is unusual. If it begins with York in his characteristic mode, speaking an aside of Ovidian theatricality, it moves swiftly to his abandonment of that mode. First Buckingham and then Henry convince York that Somerset has been imprisoned, leading York to disband his army. Next, Somerset arrives, arresting York for treason. Outraged, York takes off his Ovidian

---

[54] Hattaway (ed. 200) follows Cairncross in citing Douglas Bush, who back in 1927 had identified the sixteenth-century sources for Shakespeare's reference to this version of the Ajax myth.

[55] Striar's gloss in *The Collected Poems of Christopher Marlowe*, ed. Cheney and Striar.

[56] In this literary ploy, York differs from Gloucester, who in Acts 1–3 repeatedly deals with anger simply by *exiting*.

[57] See *Hamlet*, when the Prince tells the players, 'use all gently, for in the very torrent, tempest, and, as I may say, whirlwind of your passion, you must acquire and beget a temperance that may give it smoothness' (3.2.5–8).

mask and declares his intent to usurp Henry's crown. Whereas most usurper figures in Shakespeare work surreptitiously to assassinate their rivals (as Richard III, Henry IV, and Macbeth do), York drops his mask, betraying his Ovidian identity in open indictment of his sovereign:

> That head of thine doth not become a crown:
> Thy hand is made to grasp a palmer's staff
> And not to grace an aweful princely sceptre.
> That gold must round engirt these brows of mine,
> Whose smile and frown, like to Achilles' spear,
> Is able with the change to kill and cure.
> Here is a hand to hold a sceptre up.   (*2 Henry VI* 5.1.96–102)

As we saw in chapter 1, Shakespeare is indebted to Ovid for his representation of Achilles' spear as able to both 'kill and cure'. And as editors remind us, the allusion is to the myth of Telephus: 'The spear of Achilles … was reputed to strike a mortal wound and then heal the wound with its rust. The source of the line is probably Ovid's *Metamorphoses* 13.171–2, where Ulysses mentions the spear's double power in the course of a debate over Achilles' arms with the Ajax Telamonius already mentioned by York at l. 26; but the spear's qualities became a proverbial commonplace (Dent S731)' (Warren, ed. 273). As we now know, that last point about a commonplace is misleading, since it neglects Ovid's recurrent appropriation of the myth for the power of his own authorship, although the detail about 'Ajax Telamonius' is useful for connecting York's two Ovidian speeches. Since both are speeches about the same event in the story of Achilles, we here become privy to Shakespeare's Ovidian strategy of characterization. York's reference to Achilles when indicting Henry makes clear that he abandons his Ovidian theatrical policy. It also lays bare Shakespeare's critique of Spenser, for York criticizes Henry as a 'palmer' with his 'staff' – a gesture that conjures up Guyon's faithful guide in the Legend of Temperance. In York's discourse of 'hands', Henry is a Spenserian palmer fit only to grasp a religious staff, while he himself uses his hand 'to hold a sceptre up'. Here at the end, the sudden concentration of hand-instrument imagery may gesture to the name of Shake-speare.

'ETERNIZ'D IN ALL AGE TO COME'

In the final two scenes of the play, Shakespeare introduces two competing models of immortality, both of which set up the same event in *3 Henry VI*: Young Clifford will exact revenge on the Duke of York (1.4). In Act 5, scene 2, of *2 Henry VI*, York kills Old Clifford in a chivalric duel;[58] the details inaugurate what we have called the Shakespearean literary eternal. In this model, Shakespeare stages a climactic scene of literary immortality occurring on the cusp of the Last Judgment, as he does memorably at the end of *King Lear*, when Kent asks, witnessing the corpse of Cordelia, 'Is this the promis'd end?', and Edgar offers, 'Or image of that horror?' (5.3.264–5), the word 'image' drawing attention to the literary representation being staged.

At the end of *2 Henry VI*, Shakespeare scripts perhaps his earliest version of this apocalyptic terrain, after Young Clifford finds his father dead:

> O, let the vile world end,
> And the premised flames of the last day
> Knit earth and heaven together!
> Now let the general trumpet blow his blast.
>
> (*2 Henry VI* 5.2.40–3)

Beholding the fallen corpse of his beloved father, Clifford imagines that he occupies the end of history. In this apocalyptic domain, however, the young man does not pray for deliverance but turns to poetry to perform political action – not once but twice: the first to transact (Marlovian) revenge, modeled on Ovid's Medea from the *Tristia* (Knowles, ed. 359), the second to fulfill (Spenserian) destiny, modeled on Virgil's Aeneas (Knowles, ed. 359):

> Henceforth I will not have to do with pity.
> Meet I an infant of the house of York,
> Into as many gobbets will I cut it
> As wild Medea young Absyrtus did;
> In cruelty will I seek out my fame.
> [*He takes him up on his back.*]
> Come, thou new ruin of old Clifford's house:
> As did Aeneas old Anchises bear,
> So bear I thee upon my manly shoulders;
> But then Aeneas bare a living load –
> Nothing so heavy as these woes of mine.   (*2 Henry VI* 5.2.56–65)

By turning to works of literature to prepare for the Christian apocalypse, Young Clifford fulfills the idea emerging in his father's final utterance, when the old man attempts to turn his life into a literary monument: '*La fin couronne les [oeuvres]*' (28) ('the end crowns the work').

---

[58] On the folio's chivalry, absent in the quarto, see Hodgdon 66–7.

To conclude the play, in Act 5, scene 3, Warwick offers a competing model of immortality when he celebrates the Cliffords' arch-enemy, York, as the action's premier epic hero:

> Now, by my [faith], lords, 'twas a glorious day.
> Saint Albans battle won by famous York
> Shall be eterniz'd in all age to come.
> Sound drum and trumpets, and to London all,
> And more such days as these to us befall!   (*2 Henry VI* 5.3.29–33)

Warwick's tribute looks like a conventional classical celebration of an epic victor and his ensuing fame. Yet the intensification of three terms designating the immortality of York's achievement – 'glorious ... famous ... eterniz'd' – might give us pause. So especially might the third term, and not simply because Shakespeare uses the word only here in his canon (Knowles, ed. 363): 'eterniz'd' has a distinct Christian connotation. The verb *eternize* means 'To make eternal, i.e. everlasting or endless' (*OED*, Def. 1). Warwick seems to locate York's immortality as a form of classical fame on earth, yet he gestures to the Christian eternal. Given the ominous sound of the play's last word, 'befall', and a tragic destiny the Elizabethan audience knew very well, Shakespeare can be seen to explode York's attempt to bridge the divide between classical fame and Christian glory.[59] Yet Warwick's speech rehearses a further complication, because it succeeds in building the bridge we witnessed at the outset in Gloucester's speech on fame.[60] Out of the projected ashes of York's imminent fall, Shakespeare illuminates how English political history refracts his own authorship of English literary history for the new London stage.

Epilogue: *'Tygers hart wrapt in a Players hyde'*

We know that Shakespeare's project of authorship succeeded in *2 Henry VI*, as in the first tetralogy generally, because our first recorded reference to Shakespeare in the London literary scene shows Robert Greene attacking

---

[59] Riggs refers to Talbot's speech at *1H6* 4.7.18–22 for a version of the bridge (110), and he quotes Warwick here to document Shakespeare's 'disillusionment with the tradition of fame' (148): 'the characters who succeed [Talbot] ... drift further and further towards the Machiavellian premise that fame is the creature of earthly fortune' (149).

[60] As Garber explains, 'Warwick ... imagines the "eternizing" as an act of historical memory, borne out in Shakespeare's day by the various chronicle sources ... From the perspective of a theatrical audience or reader in the ever-shifting present that is literature's "now", the act of "eternizing" will be accomplished by Shakespeare's play, and the "all age" to whom he refers is the time of reading and of playing, as well as the eternal future' (*Shakespeare After All* 115).

the 'upstart crow' for his literary plagiarism. Greene (perhaps really Henry Chettle) deftly dresses York's final Marlovian indictment of Margaret in *3 Henry VI* – 'O tiger's heart wrapp'd in a woman's hide' (1.4.137) – in terms of Shakespeare's own literary profession: 'his *Tygers hart wrapt in a Players hyde*, supposes he is as well able to bombast out a blanke verse as the best of you: and beeing an absolute *Iohannes fac totum*, is in his owne conceit the onely Shake-scene in a countrey'.[61] As the references to the poetic 'conceit' and the medium of 'blanke verse' suggest, Greene indicts Shakespeare for his role not simply as an actor but also as an author. Equally to the point here, Greene uses a *Henry VI* play to specify the indictment, and the figure of York in particular, drawing on the military name 'Shake-speare' to equate the ambitious military-bent duke with the aspiring writer from Stratford. If we look at the terms of the indictment, we see that what really gets the university-trained Greene is the grammar-school trained Shakespeare jumping the gap between the high literary calling of the poet and the professional vocation of the new Elizabethan playwright.

[61] Repr. *Riverside* 1959. See D. A. Carroll, 'Greene's "Upstart Crow" Passage'; Knowles, ed. 106–11; Warren, ed. 60–1.

CHAPTER 6

Halting sonnets: The comedy of Petrarchan desire in Much Ado about Nothing

Much Ado about Nothing appears to have little to do with *2 Henry VI*, yet recent scholarship helps us bring the late 1590s comedy into alignment with the early 1590s history play. As textual scholarship has suggested, Shakespeare was likely revising *2 Henry VI* in preparation for a stage revival at about the time he was composing *Much Ado*.[1] Curiously for such different plays, both are set against the backdrop of civil war: *2 Henry VI*, the War of the Roses in England; *Much Ado*, the civil broil in Italy between Don Pedro, Prince of Arragon, and his 'bastard brother', Don John (dramatis personae). Yet if the history play concludes with the first battle of the English war, St Albans, the comedy opens with the end of an Italian war near Messina. 'How many gentlemen have you lost in this action?', the governor of Messina, Leonato, asks a messenger in the initial conversation (5–6). 'But few of any sort, and none of name', the messenger replies (7), evidently to assure the audience of a comedic turn from martial conflict. Whereas *2 Henry VI*, then, begins with the climactic event of comedy, the 'marriage' of Henry to Margaret of Anjou (1.1.99), and concludes with a historic tragic battle, *Much Ado* opens with the resolution to tragedy in preparation for the double marriage of Don Pedro's two military friends, Benedick to Beatrice, and Claudio to Hero. If in the history play Petrarchan (and Spenserian) eros forms simply a momentary and troubling respite to the intestine broil of civil war, principally in the secretive affair of Margaret with the Earl of Suffolk, in the comedy eros forms the play's principal 'action'.[2]

---

[1] For a probable original date of 1591–2 for *2 Henry VI*, see Warren, ed. 74; for a probable date of late 1598 for *Much Ado*, see Humphreys, ed. 4; Zitner, ed. 5; Mares, ed. 8. For the 1598–9 revision of the *Henry VI* plays for a stage revival, including a reference to them in the Epilogue to the 1599 *Henry V* (13–14), see Warren, ed. 73–4. Warren adds that scholars have noticed a high percentage of feminine line-endings in the rose-plucking scene of *3 Henry VI*, and he quotes Gary Taylor: 'we do not find anything like so high a percentage until we come to *Much Ado*' (ed. 73).
[2] On eros as the animating spirit of Shakespearean comedy, see Frye, *A Natural Perspective* 82–3.

Shakespeare's theatrical art may 'mature' between the early 1590s and the late 1590s, but the poet-playwright continues to manipulate generic conventions in ways that speak to his literary ambitions, well after many believe he passed through a 'bookish' or 'lyric' phase. At the height of his comedic prowess, he constructs a romantic plot about erotic desire in the sphere of civic politics that lays bare his own literary authorship, including its religious or metaphysical dynamic. Thus, in the final scene *Much Ado* prepares for its double marriage by rehearsing two moments of revelation: the first (more famous), about theatre; the second (less discussed), about sonneteering. In the first revelation, Friar Francis and his newly formed acting troupe (Beatrice, Margaret, Ursula, Benedick, and Leonato), put on the play of Hero's resurrection before Don Pedro and Claudio: 'The former Hero! Hero that is dead!' (5.4.65). In the second revelation, Claudio, newly reconciled with Hero, pulls a 'halting sonnet' from Benedick's pocket, while Hero herself plucks 'another' from the 'pocket' of Beatrice (87–9). As Benedick remarks, 'A miracle! here's our own hands against our hearts' (91–2). This double revelation in the final Act intimates that Shakespeare's comedy might be processing more than simply the politics of gender difference.[3] *Much Ado* might also be processing a dynamic of authorship between two literary forms, often kept separate in mainstream Shakespeare scholarship on this comedy: poetry and theatre, sonneteering and plays, including their shared literary telos, immortality.

We can explain Shakespeare's use of sonneteering as an integral part of his dramatic fiction here, as in his plays as a whole, by recalling his unusual standing among contemporaries: during the English Renaissance, he is the only man of the theatre to produce a sonnet sequence, published in 1609 as *Shake-speares Sonnets*.[4] While critics between Charles Gildon in 1710 and David Schalkwyk in 2002 have studied the connection between the Sonnets and the plays, most neglect the professional template of authorship underwriting the connection.[5] By looking further into this dynamic, we may discover how Shakespeare *professionalizes* the organizing topic of comedy, desire, that emotional bond between man and woman, and thus the emotional spring to the institution of marriage that concludes Shakespearean comedy as a literary form.[6]

[3] For variations on this model, see C. Cook, '"Sign and Semblance of Her Honor"'; Howard, 'Renaissance Antitheatricality and the Politics of Gender and Rank in *Much Ado about Nothing*'; Gay, '*Much Ado about Nothing*'; Paster, '*Much Ado about Nothing*'; Berger, '"Against the Sink-a-Pace"'; Suzuki, 'Gender, Class, and the Ideology of Comic Form'.
[4] On this phenomenon, see *SNPP*, ch. 7.
[5] Schalkwyk, *Speech and Performance in Shakespeare's Sonnets and Plays*; on Gildon, see Canaan, 'Early Shakespeare Criticism'.
[6] On the classical, early Christian, and medieval traditions linking desire to writing, see, most recently, R. R. Edwards, *Flight from Desire*, esp. 2–9. Working from such early theorists of desire as Plato,

SHAKESPEARE'S THEATRE OF SONNETS

While most critics ignore Shakespeare's staging of sonneteering in *Much Ado*, a few refer to it in passing.[7] In our most sustained and recent study of 'Shakespeare's Sonnets and Plays' (from book title), Schalkwyk offers the following brief discussion:

> Beatrice and Benedick's mutual engagement in the world of the sonnet – despite their shared ironical stance towards Petrarch – is decisive in breaking their solitary poses. Their alignment of hands and hearts reminds us that the sonnet is a form of action, something produced through and by the body towards the union of both bodies and souls ... Beatrice and Benedick require the publication of sonnets written separately to the beloved to attest to feelings that neither can finally deny. (Schalkwyk, *Speech and Performance* 69; see 136)

Schalkwyk identifies two important features to Shakespeare's narrative. First, the playwright makes sonneteering a crucial 'action' in the plot, the very device that 'breaks' the 'solitary poses' of the play's two most celebrated characters: once the sonnets are published, Benedick and Beatrice can no longer deny their love for each other. Second, and following from the first, Shakespeare presents the lovers' sonnets as material evidence for the mutuality of their emotions.

From Schalkwyk's brief analysis, we can discern an idea that taps into an important conversation in Shakespeare studies today: only through the material publication of sonnets does an individual's emotional character become visible.[8] The sonnets, in other words, serve as written manifestations of an interior identity that is emotional in quality. Through his fiction, we might speculate, Shakespeare confronts and overcomes a primary limitation to theatre, which often depends on the stage to perform an external action (or 'show'): through sonneteering, the playwright permits the audience to become privy to what we cannot see, the hidden recesses of a character's emotional subjectivity.

Aristotle, Cicero, and Augustine, and such modern theorists as Denis de Rougemont, R. Howard Bloch, Irving Singer, and Jonathan Dollimore, Edwards focuses on desire as 'a passionate yearning based on absence' (4), as 'a necessary condition of language' (3), and finally on 'representation as itself a form of desire': 'In the process of rhetorical invention that underlies writing in medieval literary culture, desire serves the ambitions of authorship no less than the practical aims of composing texts' (9). We can profitably carry Edwards's project forward to the early modern period; see, e.g., Belsey, *Desire*.

[7] Howard 182; Neely, *Broken Nuptials in Shakespeare's Plays* 56; Lewalski, 'Love, Appearance, and Reality' 245.

[8] For recent work on the passions, see esp. Paster, *Humoring the Body*. On the emotions in *Much Ado* with reference to comedy, see Everett, '*Much Ado about Nothing*' 71, 76.

In our most important recent study of Shakespeare's poems, Colin Burrow finds Shakespeare characteristically doing just the opposite, including in the 1609 Sonnets and in its companion poem, *A Lover's Complaint*. In this narrative poem, the country maid throws 'deep-brain'd sonnets' (209) in a river, leading Burrow to conclude that 'in Shakespeare's poems objects do not reveal emotions; they encrypt them intriguingly, and start his readers on a quest for mind. An object is held up as something which offers a point of access to an experience, but the experience which it signifies … is withheld from us.'[9] If this occlusion of emotional identity is characteristic of Shakespeare when he represents sonnets as objects, we might attend all the more to his use of sonnets in *Much Ado*, where sonnets do encrypt the passions. In fact, the dramatic scene concluding the comedy takes us into intriguing emotional territory, precisely where the divide between body and mind, hand and heart, 'physiology and interiority' ends.[10]

The phrase 'halting sonnet' serves as a clear signpost. Editors typically do not gloss the key word, 'halting'. The recent *Folger* edition offers 'lame, limping', while David and Ben Crystal in *Shakespeare's Words* add 'hesitating … faltering'.[11] Although providing a start, these glosses miss the pun on metric *foot*, a unit of rhythmic measure in poetry; a halting sonnet is a poem with a limp or lame meter: a bad sonnet.[12] In Sonnet 89, Shakespeare presents his speaker, named Will in Sonnet 136, resorting to this self-conscious poetic pun when addressing the young man: 'Speak of my lameness, and I straight will halt' (3). The line may not identify Shakespeare himself as lame, but it portrays his narrator as lame in the exercise of his metric foot.[13]

Will's maneuver has Ovidian origins. For the *Amores*, Ovid's inaugural volume of verse, begins with the pun: 'Both verses were alike till Love (men say) / Began to smile and took one foot away' (1.1.7–8). Christopher Marlowe had made the first translation of the *Amores* into any European vernacular, a sequence of forty-eight poems on erotic and poetic topics that becomes 'in a sense, Marlowe's sonnet sequence'.[14] When Marlowe's Ovid personifies Elegy as a lady, he makes her walk with a limp: 'And one, I think, was longer of her feet; / … / By her foot's blemish greater grace she

[9] C. Burrow, 'Life and Work in Shakespeare's Poems' 28.
[10] Quoted from the subtitle of Schoenfeldt, *Bodies and Selves in Early Modern England*.
[11] Mowat and Werstine, ed., *Much Ado* 194; Crystal and Crystal, *Shakespeare's Words* 211.
[12] Cf. Zitner, who does gloss 'halting' as 'metrically awkward' (ed. 200).
[13] See Booth, ed. 293: 'Presumably the line is only one of the many stock witticisms that derive from juxtaposing traditional idioms (metrically clumsy verses are called lame or said to halt) with the fact that metric units are called feet'. See also Duncan-Jones, ed. 288; Evans, ed. 196; C. Burrow, ed. 558.
[14] Orgel, ed., *Christopher Marlowe* 233. On Shakespeare's debt to *Ovid's Elegies* in his own sonnet sequence, see Stapleton, *Harmful Eloquence*.

took' (3.1.7–10). To write a halting sonnet, then, is technically to write a comedic Ovidian form of poetry. In Act 3, scene 2, of *As You Like It*, a comedy that refers to 'honest Ovid' (3.3.8) and alludes to Marlowe as the 'dead shepherd' (3.5.81), Shakespeare pauses to insert a dialogue on a poem's halting metric feet. After Celia reads Orlando's poem, Rosalind agrees provisionally with her cousin that 'the feet might bear the verses', except that 'the feet were lame, and could not bear themselves without the verse, and therefore stood lamely in the verse' (3.2.167–71).

As the presence of this metric discourse about poems in a play intimates, Shakespeare could assign to the idea of halting verse not merely 'poetic' but also theatrical significance. Thus, in *Hamlet* the Prince responds to news about the arrival of the players at Elsinore with some animated wit: 'He that plays the king shall be welcome ... and the [actor playing the] lady shall say her mind freely, or the blank verse shall halt for't' (2.2.319–25).[15] Hamlet reminds us that not just sonnets but plays can speak in halting verse. The rhymed iambic pentameter of a sonnet and the blank verse or unrhymed iambic pentameter of a play can both exhibit the same stylistic failure.

It is the fiction of this failure that Shakespeare moves to center stage, in the Sonnets as in *Much Ado*, as well as in such plays as *Love's Labor's Lost*, *As You Like It*, *Hamlet*, and even *Othello*, where Iago tries to produce a poem on Desdemona (2.1.148–58), only to have Desdemona playfully retort, 'O most lame and impotent conclusion' (161). The phrase 'halting sonnet', then, forms a useful metonymy or syntactical model for Shakespeare's practice of yoking poetry to theatre. A sonnet halting is a sonnet in action, poetry performed before the theatre audience.

In *Much Ado*, the metonymic failure is not merely stylistic; the discourse of the halting sonnet certainly evokes questions of professional language or form but also questions of the body or physiology, and of the emotions or interiority. Benedick makes the connection explicit when he wittily identifies the revelation of the sonnets as a 'miracle': 'here's our hearts against our hands'. We shall return to the language of miracle later, but for now we may emphasize the form the miracle takes: the two sonnets inscript the truth of the lovers' (concealed) 'hearts', and thus contradict (work 'against') the evidence of their 'hands', which previously have been at 'merry war' (1.1.62). Once the sonnet evidence is produced, Benedick is compelled to tell Beatrice, 'Come, I will have thee, but by this light, I take thee for pity' (5.4.92–3). In Shakespeare's theatrical staging, Benedick and Beatrice's mutual composition of 'sonnets' becomes the spring to the comic denouement leading to their

---

[15] The *Riverside* supplies this gloss: 'the verse will not scan if she omits indecent words' (1204).

marriage. Benedick's humorous expression of 'pity' draws attention to the empathic quality of emotion bonding male and female throughout the Shakespeare canon, from *Titus Andronicus* (5.3.161) to *The Tempest* (5.1.17–32), including most famously in *Othello*, when the Moor locates the origin of Desdemona's love in this human capacity, produced when she hears Othello's epic romance 'story' (1.3.158): 'She lov'd me for the dangers I had pass'd, / And I lov'd her that she did pity them' (167–8; see 158–61).

STAGING SONNETEERING IN *MUCH ADO*

Let us look more closely, then, at Claudio's full speech on Benedick's 'halting sonnet':

> And I'll be sworn upon't that he loves her,
> For here's a paper written in his hand,
> A halting sonnet of his own pure brain,
> Fashion'd to Beatrice.   (*Much Ado about Nothing* 5.4.85–8)

Claudio begins with an oath ('I'll be sworn') to support his claim that Benedick 'loves' Beatrice. He produces the evidence as a 'paper' document written by and in his friend's 'hand'. The phrase 'of his pure brain' describing the sonnet anticipates the 'deep-brain'd sonnets' in *A Lover's Complaint* (*SNPP*, ch. 8), suggesting how consistently Shakespeare imagines sonneteering as a practice inscripting the mind, whether deeply or purely. Claudio's final phrase, 'Fashion'd to Beatrice', is resonant. Rarely glossed, the word 'Fashioned' means 'addressed' (*Norton* 1442), as well as 'form, shape, make [into]' (Crystal and Crystal, *Shakespeare's Words* 170). Benedick both addresses his halting sonnet to Beatrice and shapes his pure brain to her, creating a form wherein they – or their 'hearts' – meet. The sonnet is a purifying site for the mutual greeting between male and female: brains, hearts, hands.[16]

Here is Hero's full revelation of Beatrice's sonnet:

> And here's another
> Writ in my cousin's hand, stol'n from her pocket,
> Containing her affection unto Benedick.
>   (*Much Ado about Nothing* 5.4.88–90)

---

[16] As Greenblatt remarks in his *Norton* introduction to the play, the word 'fashioned' evokes Renaissance self-fashioning: 'the play's term for the social system in which all the characters … are involved is "fashion"'. Shakespeare deftly uses the term … both to designate the images that elicit emotions and to describe the process that shapes these images' (ed. 1385). We shall return to Greenblatt at the end of this chapter.

Like Benedick's sonnet, Beatrice's is 'Writ' in her own 'hand' and produced against her will ('stol'n'); it testifies against her public claims to warfare with her rival wit, 'Containing her affection' for him. The sonnet is a container, or receptacle, for female affection, a passionately written inscription of emotional attachment.

While the word 'affection' may be Shakespeare's best-known word for the bond of endearment between humans (*WT* 4.4.481; *Temp* 5.1.18), the word 'pocket' is rarely if ever glossed (including, surprisingly, by the Crystals). According to the *Oxford English Dictionary*, a pocket for Elizabethans was 'A small bag or pouch worn on the person; spec. one inserted in or attached to a garment, for carrying a purse or other small articles' (Def. 2a). Thus, both Beatrice and Benedick have been carrying their sonnets around in small bags or purses attached to their clothing. Critics often remark on the importance of 'fashion' and clothing in the play; the word 'fashion' occurs significantly more in *Much Ado* than in any other Shakespearean work (twenty-one times with cognates).[17] Thus we may determine the significance of this dramatic climax: a 'sonnet' concealed within a 'pocket', a hidden document 'Containing … affection', becomes the play's final image for the affective heart, at once pure and deep, within a social exchange between male and female. The comedy treats this exchange playfully, for a halting sonnet is also an 'impotent' one, a sign especially of the male's lack of sexual vigor and thus the occasion for his cuckolding.[18]

PETRARCHAN THEATRE

If Claudio can pull a 'halting sonnet' out of Benedick's pocket, we might wonder how it got there. In Act 5, scene 2, Shakespeare supplies an answer. In this romantic comedy, Benedick, 'the Prince's jester' (2.1.137), is a theatrical man who is caught in the throes of sexual desire, and tries to write Petrarchan love poetry.[19] The scene begins playfully, when Benedick asks Margaret for 'help' in writing a 'speech of Beatrice' (2–3). As soon as Benedick is convinced

---

[17] According to Cook, the 'characters talk a good deal about how they dress'; she goes on to align 'dressing well' with 'talking well', suggesting that both 'modes of decorous behavior serve similar functions': 'to cover their emotional nakedness and to avoid exposure' (189).

[18] On the importance of cuckoldry in the play, see Paster, '*Much Ado*'.

[19] This analysis extends my work on Petrarch in Shakespeare from 'Shakespeare's Sonnet 106, Spenser's National Epic, and Counter-Petrarchism', which responds to Braden, 'Shakespeare's Petrarchism'. On desire and subjectivity in Petrarch, see T. M. Greene, *Light in Troy* 81–146; Frecerro, 'Fig Tree and the Laurel'; Mazzotta, *Worlds of Petrarch*, esp. 58–79; Kennedy, *Authorizing Petrarch*, esp. 235–54, and *Site of Petrarchism* 163–81; as well as Braden, *Petrarchan Love and the Continental Renaissance* 1–60. Thanks to William J. Kennedy.

that he loves Beatrice, he turns to the Elizabethan convention of composing Petrarchan sonnets on her (Howard 182). Just as Desdemona will ask Iago to compose a poem to her, Margaret suggests to Benedick, 'write me a sonnet in praise of my beauty' (5.2.4–5). In this play, women join men in the production of Petrarchan verse, which is programmed for (and by) men to 'praise' female 'beauty'. Benedick greets the prospect enthusiastically – too enthusiastically it turns out, since he claims with confidence, 'In so high a style, Margaret, that no man living shall come over it' (6–7). Here Benedick betrays a paradox at the center of the Petrarchan enterprise: even though penning his intimate affection for the female, the sonneteer competes with other 'm[e]n' in an economy of poetic fame.[20] Margaret quickly sees through the exaltation of Benedick's 'high … style', punning on his word 'over': 'To have no man come over me?' (9). Wickedly bawdy, her question speaks to the hierarchical fantasy at the heart of the Petrarchan tradition, where the male wishes to be 'over' or above the female, on top of her (sexually). This pun then reroutes the conversation from sonneteering to repartee, ended only when Benedick tells Margaret to bring Beatrice to him.

As soon as Margaret exits, Benedick, alone on stage, breaks into song – an unusual form in Shakespeare that we might term a lyric soliloquy:

> The god of love,
> That sits above,
> And knows me, and knows me,
> How pitiful I deserve –
> *(Much Ado about Nothing* 5.2.26–9)

This may not appear much of a song, but that is what Shakespeare's fiction makes evident.[21] The great wit of the Men's Club of Messina (in Harry Berger's phrase) turns out to deserve only pity when it comes to producing sonnets on his lady, as Benedick himself confesses (30). Indeed, the contents of the song trope the convention of pity central to the Petrarchan tradition (e.g., *RS* 1.8), betraying the lover's self-absorption: Cupid, god of love, sits above the lover, knows the condition of his desire – and knows him – only

---

[20] On Petrarch's Laura as both a beautiful lady and a figure for the poet's fame, see Durling, ed. 27. On Shakespeare's competition for literary fame around 1598, see esp. the Rival Poet sonnets (78–86), as discussed by M. P. Jackson, 'Frances Meres and the Cultural Contexts of Shakespeare's Rival Poet Sonnets'.

[21] According to Humphreys, Benedick sings the opening lines 'of a song by the actor and balladist William Elderton, printed in 1562 and often quoted or imitated' (ed. 236). In other words, the song is not even Benedick's own invention; it is as if he sings it in order to inspire himself, but comes up empty.

to pity him. Nonetheless, we might acknowledge that Benedick's failure makes for excellent drama.

His final speech before the arrival of Beatrice advances his failure in terms specific to the literary tradition, and brings that tradition up to date for Elizabethans:

> in loving, Leander the good swimmer, Troilus the first employer of pandars, and a whole bookful of these quondam carpet-mongers, whose names yet run smoothly in the even road of a blank verse, why, they were never so truly turn'd over and over as my poor self in love. Marry, I cannot show it in rhyme; I have tried. I can find out no rhyme to 'lady' but 'baby', an innocent rhyme; for 'scorn', 'horn', a hard rhyme; for 'school', 'fool', a babbling rhyme: very ominous endings. No, I was not born under a rhyming planet, nor I cannot woo in festival terms. (*Much Ado about Nothing* 5.2.30–41)

Here Shakespeare uses a soliloquy to stage failed sonneteering in considerable detail. The scene captures Benedick in the very throes of sonnet invention. He compares himself to two famous lovers from classical culture: Leander, who loved the original woman named Hero but then died while swimming the Hellespont to visit her; and Troilus, who met Cressida through her uncle, the go-between Pandarus, only to be betrayed by her. Scholars are not sure what specific literary works Shakespeare evokes, but probably he refers to Ovid's two verse letters between Hero and Leander in the *Heroides* (Poems 18 and 19) and Marlowe's famous Ovidian epyllion, *Hero and Leander*, as well as to, if not his own play *Troilus and Cressida*, then Chaucer's brief epic, *Troilus and Crisyede*.[22]

Although Benedick is not specific, Shakespeare probably evokes a 'Renaissance' literary tradition: the Englishing of classical epic narratives of love poetry. Both Leander and Troilus are tragic lovers in this tradition, which becomes part of Benedick's comedic failing. He imagines both Leander and Troilus as exemplary: Leander, for being a 'good swimmer'; Troilus, for being the 'first employer of pandars'. Not simply is Benedick a failed sonneteer; he is a failed reader of the Western epic tradition of love poetry. Unsurprisingly, he criticizes the 'whole bookful' of lovers as mere 'carpet-mongers': they are not real but false (mere armchair lovers). He, not they, is the true lover because he suffers – 'truly turn'd over and over … in love'. The word 'turn'd' fuses the literary process of invention to the Ovidian idea of change or metamorphosis.[23] Benedick does not mention the author of his own poetry book, but

[22] See Humphreys, ed. 207. On the relation between Shakespeare's Hero in *Much Ado* and Marlowe's Hero in *Hero and Leander*, see Mowat and Werstine, ed., *Much Ado* 203–4; Suzuki 130–3.

[23] In the *OED*, Def. 5 for 'turn' reads: 'fig. To shape, form, or fashion artistically or gracefully: a. a material object: usually into a rounded form, as if shaped on a lathe.' See Spenser, *Aug* 191; Wall, *Imprint of Gender* 36–7 on *LLL* 1.2.184; *TGV* 3.2.92.

no doubt it is his own 'self'. As soon as he vaunts his success, however, he confesses his failure: 'I cannot show it in rhyme.' The word 'show' is Shakespeare's favorite word for theatre, and here Benedick employs it to identify his attempt at rhyme as merely a show, an outward appearance, not a true work of poetry. He has 'tried', but he can only produce a series of silly rhymes, each having a simplistic meaning, whether 'innocent', 'hard', or 'babbling', and all are 'ominous'. His failure at rhyme leads to a measured conclusion: he has 'not been born under a rhyming planet' – a fascinating phrase that does not simply refer to astral determinism but speaks directly to a poetic universe. Benedick has not been born a poet, and he is not destined to become one. Indeed, Shakespeare refers to a major question in Renaissance poetics: just whether a poet is born or made.[24] Candidly, Benedick decides he is neither. Accordingly, he will not use sonneteering to 'woo in festival terms' – bring about the marital conclusion of Shakespeare's 'festive comedy'.[25] Quite the opposite occurs: that conclusion is brought 'against' him through the publication of a halting sonnet he claimed he could not write.

THE PRINCE'S JESTER

Shakespeare's presentation of Benedick as a failed sonneteer at the end of the play is important, because at the beginning this witty lover is the consummate theatrical man.[26] In Act 2, scene 1, during the meta-theatrical Masque, Beatrice, herself wearing a mask, tells her rival wit, also masked, that he is 'the Prince's jester, a very dull fool; only his gift is in devising impossible slanders' (137–8), primarily against her. Later in the scene, Benedick expresses his dismay to Claudio: 'that my Lady Beatrice should know me, and not know me! The Prince's fool' (203–4). Yet a third time Benedick complains, this time to Don Pedro, 'She told me, not thinking I had been myself, that I was the Prince's jester, that I was duller than a great thaw, huddling jest upon jest with such impossible conveyance upon me that I stood like a man at a mark, with a whole army shooting at me' (242–7). Such hyperbolic dramaturgy helps classify Benedick not just as a clout or target but as a professional fool, a man of the theatre, kinsman to Feste in *Twelfth Night*, the Fool in *King Lear*, and Autolycus in *The Winter's Tale*.[27]

In Act 3, scene 2, however, Claudio records a decisive – and little-discussed – character-change in Benedick: 'his jesting spirit ... is now crept into a

---

[24] In his memorial poem on Shakespeare, Jonson answers the question with respect to his colleague: 'For a good Poet's made, as well as borne, / And such wert thou' (64–5).
[25] Barber, *Shakespeare's Festive Comedy*.   [26] A fuller reading would attend further to Beatrice.
[27] On 'clout' as the centre of a target, see *KL* 4.6.91–2.

lute-string' (59–60). This seemingly innocuous remark announces a career change, with reference to the laureate instrument of Apollo (chapter 2): Benedick has turned from his role as the Prince's jester to become a lutenist. Effectively, he has turned from being a professional man of the theatre to assume the part of 'laureate' poet – or more aptly, counter-laureate. When Don Pedro replies, 'Indeed that tells a heavy tale for him' (61), Shakespeare draws attention to the narrative of Benedick's professional career change.[28] Let us look into the details of this heavy tale.

Just prior, the audience has witnessed the moment of change. To open Act 2, scene 3, Benedick tells the Boy, 'In my chamber-window lies a book, bring it hither to me in the orchard' (2–3). Seemingly a trivial detail, the directive alerts us to a critical contour in this comedy: Benedick turns from stage to page, theatre to print shop, performance to books.[29] Hence, during his subsequent monologue, Benedick displaces his own change to a change in Claudio, delivering a detailed analysis of his friend's 'conversion' at falling in love with Hero, only to refer to his own falling in love with Beatrice:

I have known when there was no music with him but the drum and the fife, and now had he rather hear the tabor and the pipe … [N]ow is he turn'd orthographer – his words are a very fantastical banquet, just so many strange dishes. May I be so converted and see with these eyes? I cannot tell; I think not. I will not be sworn but love may transform me to an oyster. (*Much Ado about Nothing* 2.3.12–24)

On the surface, Shakespeare rehearses no more than an Elizabethan convention: a soldier turns from warfare to wooing, exchanging one kind of 'music' for another. Yet the terms evoke musical instruments in the Renaissance hierarchy of genres, specifically associated with the Virgilian genres of epic ('the drum and the fife') and both amorous lyric and pastoral ('the tabor and the pipe').[30] Like Claudio, Benedick is moving down the Virgilian path, from higher to lower forms, undergoing Ovidian 'transform[ation]'. Hence, Benedick speaks the lines in the pastoral locale of the epic city, the 'orchard', indicating that here Shakespeare localizes his familiar comedic pattern of court and country.[31]

The young men's turn from warfare to wooing, from military to erotic attachments, explains the precise design of the next event: Benedick 'hide[s] … in the arbor' (36) to overhear Don Pedro and Claudio persuading

---

[28] Cf. W. N. King, 'Much Ado About Something' 144n5, 153–5.

[29] On this 'curious small scene', wherein the book is 'a symbol of the solitary', see Everett 82.

[30] For the pastoral association of these musical instruments, see *WT* 4.4.182–3. See also Spenser, *Maye* 20–2; *Epithalamion* 129–31.

[31] For a recent discussion of this pattern in Shakespearean comedy, see Sullivan, 'Geography and Comedy'. On *Much Ado*, see Lewalski 237; Krieger, 'Social Relations and the Social Order' 54.

the professional musician Balthasar to sing a song he sang to them earlier
(43). If the singer is not reluctant to sing, he is at least modest. 'O good my
lord', says Balthasar to Don Pedro, 'tax not so bad a voice / To slander music
any more than once' (44–5). Yet in Balthasar's vocational modesty, Don
Pedro finds the mark of excellence: 'It is the witness still of excellency / To
put a strange face on his own perfection' (46–7). The phrasing relies on a
theatrical metaphor for disguise familiar throughout the Shakespeare
canon: the singer puts a mask on his 'face' as 'witness' to his 'perfection'
(*SNPP* 135–9). Everywhere we look, Shakespeare does not separate poetry
and theatre; here he uses theatre as a metaphor for poetry.

Such playful banter on the theatrical vocation of the singer leads to the
pun at the center of a play called *Much Ado about Nothing*, marking this
scene at the structural mid-point the pivotal one of the comedy:

D. PEDRO.	Do it in notes.
BALTHASAR.	Note this before my notes:
	There's not a note of mine that's worth the noting.
D. PEDRO.	Why, these are very crotchets that he speaks –
	– Note notes, forsooth, and nothing.

$\qquad\qquad\qquad\qquad\qquad\qquad$ (*Much Ado about Nothing* 2.3.54–7)

As critics observe, the comedy that makes much ado about 'nothing' puns
on the concept of 'noting', which lies at the heart of the dramatic action,
the use of language to make observations on others.[32] Long ago, Harold
C. Goddard wrote: 'in all of Shakespeare's immense vocabulary, there are
few more interesting words ... Nothing is ... practically a synonym for
creativity'.[33] As Goddard helps us see, the halting sonnets produced at the
end of the play from the recesses of the two lovers' pockets evoke the
'creativity' of making musical notes, placing lyric song literally in the title
of this play: *Much Ado about Nothing* / *Much Ado about Noting*. This is a
dramatic comedy about the theatrical art of Petrarchan lyric song.[34]

Consequently, it is right at this moment – hovering around the play's
central pun – that Benedick speaks a theatrical aside about the Orphic
power of lyric:

Now, divine air! now is his soul ravish'd! Is it not strange that sheep's guts should
hale souls out of men's bodies? (*Much Ado about Nothing* 2.3.58–60)

---

[32] See P. Holland, ed. xxxii. On 'misprision' as the core idea in the play, see Rossiter, '*Much Ado*' 54.
On the 'Problems of Knowing' (chapter title), see R. Berry, *Shakespeare's Comedies* 154–74.
[33] Goddard, *Meaning of Shakespeare* I: 273; cf. Bloom, *Shakespeare: The Invention of the Human* 200.
[34] In his *Norton* introduction, Greenblatt links 'nothing' and 'noting' only with theatricality (ed. 1383).

Benedick does not just wittily detach himself from the art of the singer. He uses inspired discourse (as if against his will) to participate in that art. He evokes the Orphic power of music to ravish the soul, to draw the soul out of the body to experience the joyful condition of transcendence, and he refers to the material practice of stringing musical instruments – here the lute – with 'sheep's guts'.[35]

At the heart of Benedick's wit, then, is a paradox: such a seemingly low body part of a dead animal can produce the most 'divine air' from a human. This is what Benedick finds 'strange'. The mystery of the material gives birth to the spiritual; an animal's organ can elevate the soul to the highest mystery of exaltation. Yet we may be even more precise. Through the material process of Orphic music, the interior organ of a dead sheep can metamorphose the interior organ of a human being into a state of religious ecstasy.

On the surface, Benedick may be mocking the idea of Orphic poetry to ravish the soul, but Shakespeare prepares to deliver one of the most remarkable lyric songs in his theatrical canon:

> Sigh no more, ladies, sigh no more.
>   Men were deceivers ever,
> One foot in sea, and one on shore,
>   To one thing constant never.
> Then sigh not so, but let them go,
>   And be you blithe and bonny,
> Converting all your sounds of woe
>   Into hey nonny nonny.
> Sing no more ditties, sing no moe,
>   Of dumps so dull and heavy,
> The fraud of men was ever so,
>   Since summer first was leavy,
> Then sigh not so, etc.   (*Much Ado about Nothing* 2.3.62–74)

A surprising dearth of commentary exists on this song.[36] As readers will recognize from previous quotations in this chapter, even though the song is not a sonnet, 'songs and sonnets' were closely linked both as a phrase during the English Renaissance and as lyric forms, including by Shakespeare (*MW* 1.1.198–9; chapter 3).[37] The close connection between songs and sonnets in Shakespeare, as in his culture, helps explain the allied discourse of songs and

---

[35] For the Orphic significance of the image, see *TGV* 3.2.74-80. For Orphic transcendence, see Spenser, *Oct* 25–30.

[36] For brief commentary, see Paster, '*Much Ado*' 217. P. Holland sees the song standing as 'the play's meaning' (ed. xxxvi).

[37] At this time, the word 'sonnet' could thus mean any short lyric.

sonnets in *Much Ado*. The two forms are kinds of lyric, and both operate as a separate or lyric space, important to distinguish from theatrical 'show'.

For up to this point in the play, theatre has been fully in the hands of Don Pedro and his brother, Don John, as has been widely discussed.[38] The play begins with Don Pedro, and focuses immediately upon his authority and agency: 'I learn in this letter', says Leonato, 'that Don [Pedro] of Arragon comes this night to Messina' (1.1.1–2). By turning down the path from Virgilian war to Ovidian wooing, Don Pedro prepares for a different kind of 'action' (6) – and one that formally organizes the plot until Act 3, scene 2. For, at the Masque scene of 'reveling' (1.1.320), Don Pedro uses theatrical costume to woo Hero on Claudio's behalf: 'I will assume thy part in some disguise / And tell fair Hero I am Claudio … / In practice let us put it presently' (321–8).

In the first half of the play, this theatrical 'practice' turns out to be much ado about noting, and it undergoes a strange afterlife, as characters recurrently report that they have overheard the plan. In Act 1, scene 2, Antonio's servant overhears Don Pedro's plan and tells his master of it; Antonio then tells Leonato he has some 'news' to report:

the [event] stamps them [= the news], but they have a good cover; they show well outward. The Prince and Count Claudio, walking in a thick-pleach'd ally in mine orchard, were thus much overheard by a man of mine. The Prince discover'd to Claudio that he lov'd my niece your daughter, and meant to acknowledge it this night in a dance. (*Much Ado about Nothing* 1.2.7–13)

It is not clear whether the servant or Antonio misconstrues the plan, but immediately we become privy to the vulnerability of Don Pedro's comedic theatre of courtly wooing. In the tightly woven community of Messina, theatre is subject to 'noting' – to overhearing and thus to misconstruing. To introduce the 'news' about this particular noting, Antonio relies on an intricate metaphor, which splices terms from book culture ('stamps', 'cover') with theatre culture ('show').[39] The outward show of the news is good, the conceit runs, because it prints an inner truth. While seemingly incidental, the discourse of book and theatre opens up a channel of professional communication that the play will extend.

Subsequently, in Act 1, scene 3, Borachio reports to Don John that he, too, has overheard the plan. But his terms suggest that he also misconstrues the details, even though he catches the drift: 'I whipt me behind the arras, and there

---

[38] Howard; Paster, '*Much Ado*' 225–6. On 'social' and 'linguistic performance', see Greenblatt, *Norton* introduction 1382–4.

[39] As the *Riverside* glosses lines 7–8: 'Antonio uses the figure of news printed and bound in a book' (370). Zitner adds that '"Stamp" and "cover" continue the book metaphor of 1.1.296' (ed. 109).

heard it agreed upon that the Prince should woo Hero for himself, and having obtain'd her, give her to Count Claudio' (60–4). Then, in Act 2, scene 1, Leonato tells Hero that Don Pedro will court her for marriage: 'Daughter, remember what I told you. If the Prince do solicit you in that kind, you know your answer' (66–8). It is in this scene that we witness the plan in operation. During the wooing, the masked Don Pedro wants to know when Hero will 'walk' with him in 'company' (90–1). She replies, 'When I like your favor, for God defend the lute should be like the case' (94–5). The vocational comparison is important; Hero likens the masked suitor and his desiring heart to a lute in its musical case. By comparing a theatrical agent with a lyric instrument, Shakespeare implicitly likens theatre to poetry.

Later in this scene, we see the anti-theatre of Don John set in, when the villain tells Claudio of Don Pedro, 'He is enamor'd on Hero … I heard him swear his affection' (164–8). Then in Act 3, scene 2, the formal moment of crossover in the authority of masculine theatre occurs, when Don John and Claudio extend their theatre of comedic wooing to their plot against Benedick and Beatrice (76–9), only to be interrupted by the dramatic entry of Don John, who says of Hero: 'The lady is disloyal' (104). Don John deploys his villainous theatre in order to break marriage apart, bringing his brother and Claudio to Hero's window to witness a set playlet, with Margaret disguised as Hero making love to Borachio (2.2).

Initially, then, the plot's focus on a double theatrical action shows a conflict between the two brothers for the rights to patriarchal authority. While Don Pedro uses theatre to bring about marriage, Don John uses theatre to break marriage up. At its center, however, the plot shows a succession from the one to the other. The succession operates through a shared patriarchal attitude toward the female: both brothers use theatre to target the female, betraying the goal of festive comedy, companionate marriage.

Once we recognize this theatrical design, we see what is so radical in Balthasar's lyric. The dramatic context of his song presents another paradox: the leading patriarch of the play, the theatrical Don Pedro, asks Balthasar to sing 'Sigh no more, ladies' ('again'); yet as this opening line reveals, the song addresses ladies (who in the actual performance are absent). The paradox is no doubt amusing, revealing that even the arch-patriarch is instinctively sympathetic to a song opposing his project. But the paradox also has an edge; its address to 'ladies' removes the audience of the song out of the fiction to include ladies in the theatre. In other words, Balthasar's song constitutes a visible moment of authorship. If it is true that 'we long to listen to

Shakespeare's own voice and rarely are offered it',[40] in the lyric song of Balthasar we might come to hear at least a version of the author's voice.

The contents of the song thus introduce a counter-voice into the play: the voice of lyric poetry. A male song encourages ladies to turn away from the authority of men to find authority in themselves. The song criticizes masculinity for its deceptive agency ('Men were deceivers ever') and unfaithful desire ('One foot in sea, and one on shore, / To one thing constant never'), and in the end it invites women to 'let them go'. The song advises women to locate their love and faith elsewhere, other than in men, and to be happy on their own: 'be you blithe and bonny'. Women should turn from love of and faith in the deceptive theatre of men to their own lyric voice. While several recent critics have expressed unwillingness to find here a feminist manifesto, we might alternatively discover a lyric manifesto, critiquing masculine theatre for its deceptive agency and unfaithful desire, and relocating authority in a feminine-based song: in music, in lyric poetry, 'Converting all your sounds of woe / Into hey nonny nonny'.

The word 'nonny' is not merely enigmatic; it is gnomic. Yet the *Oxford English Dictionary* suggests only one primary meaning: 'Used in songs as (part of) a refrain ... Often with allusion to Shakespeare' (Def. 1a). The word 'nonny' is therefore a vocational term for the art of song itself; interestingly, it becomes a Shakespearean signature for song. We might then see a verbal connection between the key word for lyric in the song, 'nonny', and the lyric pun on 'noting' in the key word in the play's title, 'nothing'.[41] Balthasar's song is a mournful song of loss, of separation, of women choosing to detach themselves from men, but it also constructs a new female identity and voice, in which women learn to live independently of men and find happiness without them – on their own, through their own art form: the feminine lyric of song. In other words, Shakespeare selects lyric, not theatre, as a private space for an intimate, premarital phase in the formation of (female) identity.

'THE STORY ... IS PRINTED IN HER BLOOD': READING
THE PETRARCHAN BOOK

The opposition between lyric poetry and staged theatre in Acts 1–3 sets up this very opposition in the potentially tragic catastrophe of Act 4. As we

---

[40] Bloom, *Hamlet: Poem Unlimited* 46.

[41] Is it then coincidental that 'nonny' and 'nothing' turn out to share a second meaning: the vulva, first recorded by the *OED* in 1611? P. Holland cites the Elizabethan meaning of 'nothing' as 'the female genitals' (ed. xxxii).

should expect, Claudio's calumny of Hero at the church in scene 1 depends on a particular charge. Not simply has she falsified her desire; she has falsified masculine theatre:

> Behold how like a maid she blushes here!
> O, what authority and show of truth
> Can cunning sin cover itself withal!
> Comes not that blood as modest evidence
> To witness simple virtue? Would you not swear,
> All you that see her, that she were a maid,
> By these exterior shows? But she is none:
> She knows the heat of a luxurious bed;
> Her blush is guiltiness, not modesty.
>
> *(Much Ado about Nothing* 4.1.34–42)

Readers are often irritated at Hero; she has so little to say, including for herself. Yet, as Claudio's first line indicates, what absorbs Shakespeare, here and throughout his canon, should not surprise us: the idea that the masculine 'conception' of the female causes tragic suffering and death.[42] Nowhere is this idea on more concentrated display than in *Much Ado*, and most concentrated in this scene.

In his calumnizing speech, Claudio directs the viewers on stage (and thus the audience) to focus on Hero's face, and to interpret the blush suffusing her cheeks. Himself a man of theatre, he reads into his beloved's blush a 'show of truth', an 'exterior show' of modesty 'cover[ing]' her 'guiltiness' – the words 'cover' and 'show' recurring from the second scene of the play, with their terms balancing print and theatre culture. Importantly, Claudio assigns theatrical and bookish agency to Hero's blush – her inwardness – convinced that she controls her very 'blood' for the purpose of deceiving men.

As Claudio's assault on her integrity continues – intensified when her father wishes to commit suicide (109) – Hero faints. Seeing this as further evidence of her guilt, Don Pedro, Don John, and Claudio march swiftly off. To his credit, Benedick remains behind. In doing so, he performs a moment of masculine separation, the breaking up of the Messina Men's Club: 'How doth the lady?' (113). Similarly, Beatrice depends not on the objective theatrical proof offered by men but on her own inward authority: 'O, on my soul, my cousin is belied!' (146). A community of men and women then hovers over the fallen body of a lady, with two men stepping forward to deliver

---

[42] For the pun on 'conception' as betraying this tragic problem, see *KL* 1.1.12–16. Occurring as it does in the opening scene to arguably Shakespeare's greatest work, the problem of 'conception' may be seen to dilate the precipitating idea of Shakespearean tragedy.

readings of her facial blush. First, the humiliated father exclaims decisively: 'The story ... is printed in her blood ... O she is fall'n / Into a pit of ink, that the wide sea / Hath drops too few to wash her clean again' (122–41). Perhaps only after *Macbeth* can we recognize how darkly we stand on the threshold of Shakespeare's most tragic territory. For Macbeth uses a similar image when confronting the horror of his crime against his king: 'Will all great Neptune's ocean wash this blood / Clean from my hand? No; this my hand will rather / The multitudinous seas incarnadine, / Making the green one red' (2.2.57–60).

Unlike Macbeth, however, Leonato selects a metaphor from Elizabethan print culture. Not simply a convention, the metaphor draws attention to a particular masculine economy, rooted in the material condition of the book. In particular, Leonato gives voice to the 'stigma of print', through which 'Gentlemen ... shunned print' because it was beneath their dignity. Yet Leonato also betrays what lies beneath the stigma: the effeminized falsification of manly identity.[43] Leonato imagines his daughter's face as a book that men may read in order to discover the truth about female 'virginity' (47). The father looks at his daughter's face to see a blush stamped on her unconscious form, and he is convinced that the outward blush reveals her inner truth. The 'blood' in her cheeks 'print[s]' the 'story' of her whoredom. The key to the feminine narrative is the blood suffusing the face; a blush manifests the truth of emotional character, revealing an inwardness we cannot otherwise see.

Yet Friar Francis intervenes, delivering a different interpretation of the textualized female:

> By noting of the lady ... I have mark'd
> A thousand blushing apparitions
> To start into her face, a thousand innocent shames
> In angel whiteness beat away those blushes,
> And in her eye there hath appear'd a fire
> To burn the errors that these princes hold
> Against her maiden truth. Call me a fool,
> Trust not my reading, nor my observations,
> Which with experimental seal doth warrant
> The tenure of my book; trust not my age,
> My reverence, calling, nor divinity,
> If this sweet lady lie not guiltless here
> Under some biting error.   (*Much Ado about Nothing* 4.1.158–70)

Noting of the lady. By punning on the key word in the title of the play, 'nothing', Friar Francis centralizes this moment of interpretation,

---

[43] Saunders, 'Stigma of Print' 140. See also Wall, *Imprint of Gender* 227–78.

transposing the action of 'noting' from the theatre of the two Dons to his own theologically purified reading of the female. As a member of the clergy, the Friar experiences nothing less than a religious epiphany, which he witnesses in the face of an unconscious girl, a dramatic metaphysical action beyond human agency.[44]

First, the Friar sees a 'thousand blushing apparitions … start into her face', the word 'apparitions' identifying the rush of red blood as a militant, ghostly presence. Next, a second set of spirits, equal in number, arrives on the scene, but with a different character, color, and action: 'a thousand innocent shames / In angel whiteness beat away those blushes'. In this metaphysical war in heaven, the thousand white angels beat away the thousand red apparitions, as the forces of innocence defeat the invading army of evil. Miraculously, the Friar peers into Hero's closed 'eye' to see something apocalyptic, a burning 'fire' that purifies the 'errors' of the 'Princes'. This fire is righteous indignation itself, an interior (Christian) armor protecting the female from patriarchal corruption.[45]

The Friar calls his interpretation of Hero's innocence a 'reading' of a lady's 'book'.[46] Unlike the angry Leonato, this visionary clergyman does not suffer from the stigma of print, and thus he voices a masculine integrity having clear access to the metaphysical truth about female interiority. If the lady is a book, we might wonder who the author is. Here Shakespeare's representation of agency is striking. On the one hand, only Hero can be her own author (as Coriolanus says memorably of himself [5.2.36]); on the other, she has fainted. Yet even in her unconscious state Hero continues to author her own integrity, and this is the book that the Friar discovers and reads. Shakespeare does not locate metaphysical truth outside of Hero's psyche; but neither does he reduce that psyche to mere psychology. Rather, he invests the psyche with the glow of metaphysics, and that is the story printed in Hero's blood.

Shakespeare's concern with printed books as a metaphysical form of emotional identity marks a unique version of the Petrarchan blazon. Instead of inventorying the parts of a female body, he concentrates on her face, but discovers her outward form to be the 'print' of an emotional 'story'.

---

[44] In *Shakespeare's Comedies*, R. Berry connects the Friar's principle of noting the lady with Dogberry's method for catching a thief ('take no note of him … let him show himself what he is, and steal out of your company' [3.3.28, 58–60]): 'a hypothesis must be checked against a sufficient body of confirmatory data' (165).

[45] On the Friar as a 'good Platonist' who 'takes the lady's physical beauty as a sign of her inner virtue', see Lewalski 249. I side with Lewalski (and others such as Everett) in seeing *Much Ado* as a 'serious' play with compelling emotional and metaphysical significance.

[46] In his phrase 'tenure of *my* book', the Friar evidently imagines ownership of the feminine book he reads.

The scene constitutes a bold counter-Petrarchan moment, and its imagery of an eroticized book with metaphysical power coheres both with Balthasar's song about female identity and with Benedick's haplessly acquired interest in the feminine art of lyric.

Shakespeare's discourse of the book also identifies Hero rather technically as a figure of extemporal intertextuality, for the scene gestures to texts by his two chief 1590s rivals, Marlowe and Spenser. As is well known, in *The Faerie Queene* Spenser's story of Phedon, his beloved Claribell, and his faithless friend Philemon (2.4.17–32) serves as one of the source-texts for *Much Ado*: Philemon tricks Phedon into thinking he sees Claribell making love with Philemon, when in fact he sees only her maid, Pyrene, dressed in her mistress's clothes.[47] Two years before Shakespeare wrote *Much Ado*, Spenser published Book 6 of *The Faerie Queene*, in which the hero of courtesy tracks his arch-enemy, the Blatant Beast, a figure for slander, turning the fault of Philemon's faithless friendship into a major cultural problem, including for the poet and his 'homely verse' (*FQ* 6.12.41). In *Hero and Leander*, Marlowe had made his heroine not simply a sexy young woman poised for lovemaking that culminates tragically in exposure and shame, but an icon of literary form, the feminized body in which the Ovidian genres of erotic poetry, epic, and tragedy powerfully meet.[48] By making the calumny of a Marlovian figure named Hero the central event in a Spenserian plot, Shakespeare turns *Much Ado* into a play about the authorial problem of slander in literary texts, that most biting social telos of theatrical art.

EPITAPHS, LYRIC SONGS, AND THEATRE

Through excavating Shakespeare's intertextual narrative about poetry and theatre, books and performance in Acts 1–4, we prepare ourselves to return to Act 5. In scene 3, the newly reformed Claudio, repentant about the (supposed) death of Hero, and willing to listen to Leonato's advice about

---

[47] On the Spenser connection, see Humphreys, ed. 5; Zitner, ed. 12; Mares, ed. 3; esp. Gough, '"Her Filthy Feature Open Showne"'.

[48] On Hero's generic significance, see Cheney, *Profession* 243–5, including on Ovid's use of the female to represent the genres of Elegy and Tragedy in *Am* 3.1, translated by Marlowe (*OE* 3.1); on Hero's exposure and shame, see *Profession* 253–6. In his continuation of Marlowe's *Hero and Leander* – about that other 'Hero' – Chapman appears to echo Shakespeare's passage about the faint, with his ekphrasis confirming Hero's significance as a figure of literary form: 'On it a scarf she wore of wondrous frame, / In midst whereof she wrought a virgin's face, / From whose each cheek a fiery blush did chase / Two crimson flames, that did two ways extend' (4.37–40, noted Cheney and Striar, ed. 235).

marrying the (fictional) daughter of Antonio – 'Almost the copy of my child that's dead' (5.1.289) – visits Hero's tomb in command not of theatre but of poetry. The term 'copy' here, also from print culture (see Son 11.14), communicates Claudio's changed attitude, including toward printed poetry. Accordingly, Shakespeare presents the new Claudio as a poet, the author of a funeral 'epitaph', which he reads out loud before hanging it on Hero's tomb:

> 'Done to death by slanderous tongues
> Was the Hero that here lies.
> Death, in guerdon of her wrongs,
> Gives her fame which never dies.
> So the life that died with shame
> Lives in death with glorious fame.'
>
> (*Much Ado about Nothing* 5.3.3–8)

In this epitaph, Claudio accepts blame for his beloved's death but finds consolation in Hero's virtue. Through her 'Death', she achieves 'glorious fame'. As such, the epitaph recalls Shakespeare's Sonnets, which deeply probes the idea of poetic immortality.[49]

The last line of Claudio's epitaph, 'Lives in death with glorious fame', only looks to be an expression of traditional fame. For 'Lives in death' should give us pause, evoking the miracle of the Resurrection in the Gospel, as Spenser expresses it in his Legend of Holiness, when the Redcrosse Knight remembers 'his dying Lord, / For whose sweete sake that glorious badge he wore, / And *dead as living* ever him ador'd (*FQ* 1.1.2; emphasis added). As Spenser's language of Christian immortality indicates, Shakespeare's word 'glorious' has deep Christian significance. In a single line, he both tropes classical fame and gestures toward Christian glory. While critics often indict Claudio for his shallowness, the artistic quality of his lyric epitaph lends access to a profound interiority.[50]

The earliest editions of *Much Ado* do not identify the singer of the following 'Song', but Claudio's directive in line 11, 'Now, music, sound, and sing your solemn hymn', prompted Edward Capell (and subsequent editors, such as A. R. Humphreys [ed. 210]) to assign the lyric to Balthasar. It is another stunning poem within a play:

---

[49] According to Frye, 'For Shakespeare, the subject matter of poetry is not life, or nature, or reality, or revelation, or anything else that the philosopher builds on, but poetry itself, a verbal universe. That is one reason why he is both the most elusive and the most substantial of poets' ('Argument of Comedy' 173).

[50] On Claudio's final process of religious purification, see Lewalski 248–50.

> Pardon, goddess of the night,
> Those that slew thy virgin knight,
> For the which, with songs of woe,
> Round about her tomb they go.
>> Midnight, assist our moan,
>> Help us to sigh and groan,
>>> Heavily, heavily.
>> Graves, yawn and yield your dead,
>> Till death be uttered,
>>> Heavily, heavily.
>
> *(Much Ado about Nothing* 5.3.12–21)

Addressed initially to Diana, classical goddess of the moon and of virginity, the song is at once both pagan and Christian, as intimated perhaps in the phrase 'solemn hymn' – for this audience, a classical genre with Christian resonance. Rather than erasing death, the song confronts its darkness head-on: 'Midnight, assist our moan'. Shakespeare takes the tragic tenor of lyric to its limit when the singer concludes by addressing 'Graves', evoking the superb disturbance of pagan resurrection on the cusp of the Last Judgment: the dead 'yawn' and the tombs 'utter' the word 'death, / Heavily, heavily' (as if in preparation for *Hamlet* 1.1.114–25). Here Shakespeare uses lyric as a haunting theatrical space to mark the male's change in attitude toward the female, even as he gestures to the eternizing power of the author's art.[51]

'STRIKE UP, PIPERS'

The playlet next staged by Friar Francis and his acting troupe (which intriguingly combines male with female characters) introduces a model of theatre radically opposed to the one that begins the play. In the earlier theatre of Don Pedro, the Don was the principal playwright and lead actor, performing with his friend Claudio, while Hero was both their target and a silent actress unaware she was rehearsing their script. At the close, however, Hero becomes the lead actor, while Don Pedro and Claudio are reduced to being members of her audience:

HERO.   [*Unmasking.*] And when I liv'd, I was your other wife,
           And when you lov'd, you were my other husband.
CLAUDIO.   Another Hero!
           …
DON PEDRO. The former Hero! Hero that is dead!
           (Much Ado about Nothing 5.4.60–5)

---

[51] See Zitner's gloss on 'Graves ... uttered': 'the uttering as ejecting ... of death itself, which would occur when the graves yielded their dead at the Day of Judgement' (ed. 195).

The language evokes the miracle of resurrection, Hero come back from the grave, in a theatrical staging that literalizes the contents of Balthasar's final song. In a sense, Shakespeare can be seen to recast the story of Scripture, which presents a male messiah undergoing a bodily resurrection in the afterlife. Throughout his dramatic canon, the playwright discovers fresh ways to relocate redemption in the female, her power to redeem the male, from Romeo's dream of Juliet reviving her dead lover through her kiss (5.1.1–11), to the resurrection of Hermione in *The Winter's Tale* (5.3.98–121). In Shakespeare's mid-career comedy, 'Hero that is dead' enacts a powerful emotional theatre that affects the hearts of its on-stage audience: men who need it.[52]

This theatrical revelation gives way to the final discovery, in which Claudio and Hero pull the halting sonnets out of the pockets of Benedick and Beatrice. In perhaps the most authoritative statement on this discovery, Stephen Greenblatt finds an incident of Renaissance self-fashioning:

> Near the play's close, we see Benedick struggling to compose the required sonnet to Beatrice – an entirely conventional exercise performed to fulfill the theatrical role in which he has been cast [by Don Pedro] ... And in the final moments, when the deception is revealed, it is this exercise, rather than any feelings of the heart that confirms the match ... When a similar sonnet by Beatrice is produced, Benedick cries, 'A miracle! Here's our own hands against our hearts' ... Many readers of the play, and most performers, have tried to reverse this formulation ... But what if we do not dismiss their own words? ... Beatrice and Benedick would not in that case 'love' each other ... They are tricked into marriage against their hearts. (Greenblatt, introduction to *Norton*, ed. 1385–6)

The present argument has tried to find a way out of this interpretive impasse, neither asserting the romanticism of 'love' in the amusing sonnet-eering nor reducing 'marriage' to a 'social conspiracy' cemented by two sonnets that lack 'authentic inward feelings' (Greenblatt, introduction, ed. 1386, 1385). Instead, we have discerned a Shakespearean fiction of English Renaissance authorship, cut along the divide between outward practice and inner feeling. In a move we might find surprising for such a consummate man of the theatre, Shakespeare creates a dramatic plot that moves from theatre to poetry, fictionalizing a succession from plays to sonnets. Possibly, then, the author validates rather than simply mocks the art of the sonnet as an important cultural institution.

---

[52] Cf. Lewalski on how 'Hero's masquerade' alludes to 'Christ's death, burial, and resurrection', rehearsing 'the archetype of sacrificial love' (250–1). According to Frye, Hero's resurrection also fulfills the design of comedy as a literary form: 'The fact that the dying and revising character is usually female strengthens the feeling that there is something maternal about the green world, in which the new order of the comic resolution is nourished and brought to birth' ('Argument of Comedy' 171).

Newly exposed as the author of a bad sonnet, Benedick steps forward to bring the play to its conclusion (rather surprisingly, not Don Pedro, the highest-ranking official), after learning that Don John has been captured:

Think not on him till to-morrow. I'll devise thee brave punishments for him. Strike up, pipers. *Dance.* (*Much Ado about Nothing* 5.4.127–9)

The intrusion of Don John into the play's final line is structural. From the outset, this 'villain' (1.3.32) has declared, 'I have decreed not to sing in my cage' (34).[53] Don John is a theatrical man devoid of lyric; he is the dark antithesis to the lyric comedian who becomes his witty judge. At the close, Benedick revises judicial affairs in the counter-terms of artistic invention ('devise', 'brave'), to become the comedy's master of ceremonies. The jesting sonneteer uses his new cultural authority to address the pastoral pipers of the city, and to strike up their instruments for the performance of dance. Reminiscent of his creator, Benedick becomes a man of the theatre who composes halting sonnets to conclude an emotional comedy of Petrarchan desire.

In *Much Ado about Not[h]ing*, then, Shakespeare uses the Elizabethan comedic stage to fictionalize the complexities of his own compound form of counter-laureate authorship. The author's recurrent literary representations – Petrarchan sonneteering and stage performance, books and theatre, fame and immortality, as well as his practice of extemporal intertextuality with the texts of Marlowe and Spenser – indicate that in 1598 Shakespeare continues to refine a metaphysics of reputation as the goal of a literary career.

---

[53] On the bird in its cage in the Petrarchan sonnet, esp. Spenser's *Amoretti* 65.5–8, see Cheney, *Flight* 175–6.

CHAPTER 7

The profession of consciousness: Hamlet, tragedy, and the literary eternal

Since scholars tend to date *The Tragedy of Hamlet, Prince of Denmark* between 1600 and 1601, we cannot expect much to have changed since *Much Ado about Nothing*, composed just few years before.[1] Indeed, the literary features we have been tracing, especially Shakespeare's fiction of authorship, continue apace, with a combined discourse of books and theatre, including poetic books and performed theatre, as well as extemporal intertextuality and the passion for immortality. With one qualification: in a work renowned for rehearsing 'a model for the new mind of Europe',[2] the tragedy outstrips the comedy by intensifying its literary project. It is the precise literary character of the new Shakespearean 'mind' that we shall pursue in this chapter.

For instance, in his famed speech on 'the purpose of playing' in Act 3, scene 1, the Prince creates a chink in the armature of *Hamlet* as Shakespeare's arch-theatrical drama, drawing quietly on terms from Elizabethan print culture. That this speech should contain a verbal echo of *Much Ado* makes it especially apt as our point of departure here:

the purpose of playing, whose end, both at the first and now, was and is, to hold as 'twere the mirror up to nature: to show virtue her feature, scorn her own image, and the very age and body of the time his form and pressure.[3] (*Hamlet* 3.2.20–4)

This speech is justly famous as 'metadrama', for a character inside the fiction articulates the goal of the art that the audience watches. According to Hamlet, the playwright holds up a 'mirror' to the audience to 'show' not simply universal 'virtue' and 'scorn' their 'image[s]' but also the historical

---

[1] On dating *Hamlet*, see Thompson and Taylor, eds. 43–59; on the three texts – Q1 (1603), Q2 (1604–5), and FF (1623), see 8–13. They identity Q2 as having the most 'authority' (eds. 11), and believe that Shakespeare gave his 'consent' to its publication (eds. 12). On the 'literariness' of Q2 and Shakespeare's composition of it as a work to be printed and read, see Erne, *Shakespeare as Literary Dramatist* 220–44: 234.

[2] Kermode, introduction to *Hamlet*, *Riverside* 1184.

[3] Thompson and Taylor gloss 'Scorn her own image' with '*MA* 3.1., where Beatrice overhears Hero and Ursula deliberately discussing her scorn for men' (eds. 297).

203

'age' its 'form and pressure'. While critics have long discussed Hamlet's speech as a major statement on English Renaissance theatre (including as a violation of Shakespeare's own practice), we might attend alternatively to the curiosity emerging in his concluding phrase. In 'form and pressure', the Prince relies on print culture to describe the 'purpose of playing'.[4]

According to the *Oxford English Dictionary*, the word 'pressure' can be used figuratively to mean the 'mark, form, or character impressed; impression, image, stamp' (Def. 4). As an example, the *OED* cites an earlier speech in *Hamlet*, when the Prince reacts to the Ghost's tragic narrative by promising to 'wipe away all trivial fond records, / All saws of books, all forms, all pressures past' (1.5.99–100).[5] This first instance of 'pressure' comes from 'book' culture, meaning 'imprints' (P. Edwards, ed. 122). While editors observe that the word derives from the 'impression' made by a 'stamp' in 'wax' (Hibbard, ed. 248), we need to recall that a stamp is also a print term; Definition 5b in the *OED* reads: 'To print (a book)'. As its conjunction with 'pressure' indicates, 'form' is also a term from print culture; Definition 20 in the *OED* is from 'Printing': 'A body of type, secured in a chase, for printing at one impression'. While Hamlet's phrase 'form and pressure', then, generally means 'likeness and impression' (Thompson and Taylor, ed. 298), it simultaneously evokes the specific operation of the printing house, wherein the mechanics of likeness and impression print books.

Yet 'form and pressure' is also a hendiadys, and is identified as such by George T. Wright in his seminal essay.[6] This particular hendiadys is so important that Wright concludes his essay with it: the phrase 'surely means "the imprint, or stamp, of his form", though we may also be justified in hearing a more complex meaning: "his form and the stamp of his form"' (182). As Wright points out, Hamlet's hendiadys is preceded syntactically by another, 'the very age and body of the time', which has prompted considerably more speculation, from Dr Johnson forward. Wright determines that Hamlet's first hendiadys means 'not *age* and *body* but *age* and *body of the time*' (182; his emphases). Together, then, the two hendiadys form part of a larger utterance: 'The very age – that is to say, the period of time, conceived as a body – will find the imprint of its figure in the mirror of stage

---

[4] Kiernan, *Shakespeare's Theory of Drama*, notes: 'It is a commonplace of *Hamlet* criticism that the Prince's advice to the Players is completely at odds with his creator's practice' (126). On the play's metadrama, see Mack, 'World of *Hamlet*' 245–7; Calderwood, *Negation and Metadrama in 'Hamlet'*.
[5] Modern editors tend to follow the *OED* in linking the language of 'form' and 'pressure' in the two passages (Jenkins, ed. 288; Hibbard, ed. 248; P. Edwards, ed. 165).
[6] Wright, 'Hendiadys and *Hamlet*' 187.

representations' (182). What might catch our eye is a concrete verbal locution that complicates the play's famed theatrical economy. Through a double hendiadys, Hamlet implicates the purpose of playing in the 'two different and in some sense fundamentally opposed forms of production [in Shakespeare's professional career]: theatrical performances and printed books'.[7]

Moreover, Hamlet's 'form and pressure' acquire dramatic importance once we see Shakespearean hendiadys as an arch-trope for theatre itself. In Wright's formulation, a 'miniature stylistic play within the play, hendiadys holds its mirror up to Hamlet and … enforces our awareness of the drama's central action. For in hendiadys, as in the play, we experience an encounter between two mismatched and incommensurable forces, in open and yet obscure relation to each other, joined yet disparate, one pair in the sentence and one in life' (181). Hendiadys is especially at home in *Hamlet* because Shakespeare uses it to 'express the mystery of things' (171), and in particular to 'explore the problematical depths of thought and feeling' (173) – in other words, consciousness, that interior, subjective depth of the socialized mind, groping toward eternity.[8]

For Shakespeare, hendiadys becomes an arch-figure not simply for a theatre of consciousness but also for an authorial profession of consciousness: a literary career devoted to the mystery of consciousness. Furthermore, the double hendiadys in Hamlet's speech on theatre encourages us to discern a kind of conceptual hendiadys, which brings into collision the terms of theatre and book culture. In Hamlet's complete utterance, we discover a formulation of some importance to the conversation today about Shakespearean authorship: the purpose of playing is to show the age its

---

[7] Bristol, *Big-Time Shakespeare* 30.
[8] One of Mack's influential 'three … attributes' in 'World of *Hamlet*' is 'mystery' (235–6). From Wilson Knight to Garber, critics routinely use the term 'consciousness' when discussing *Hamlet*'s historical achievement; see, e.g., Knight, '*Hamlet* Reconsidered'; Mack, 'World of *Hamlet*'; Frye, '*Hamlet*', in *Northrop Frye on Shakespeare*; de Grazia, 'Soliloquies and Wages in the Age of Emergent Consciousness'; Bloom, *Shakespeare: The Invention of the Human* and *Hamlet: Poem Unlimited*; Greenblatt, *Will in the World*; Garber, *Shakespeare After All*. Rhodes, '*Hamlet* and Humanism', writes: 'The modern term "consciousness" did not exist in Shakespeare's day. Instead, he seems to be extending the meaning of "conscience" in that direction by associating it with the humanist concept of selfhood as something constituted by a sense of inward truth' (127). See also Maus, *Inwardness and Theater in the English Renaissance*, who responds to Belsey, *Subject of Tragedy*, and Barker, *Tremulous Private Body*, by locating 'inwardness' as an important early modern phenomenon. Most recently, Lee, *Shakespeare's 'Hamlet' and the Controversies of Self*, offers a history of the terms for and models of the Prince's inward identity, yet without attending much to the term 'consciousness'. Relying on evidence from Shakespeare's day, Lee refutes the New Historicist and Cultural Materialist model, which 'argue[s]' that neither the Prince nor any other English Renaissance dramatic person has a self-constituting sense of self, but are instead socially produced subjects lacking any meaningful sense of interiority' (1).

imprint; the aim of theatre is to print the image of its age.[9] By including the concept of print culture in the Prince's definition of theatre, Shakespeare counteracts any simplistic notion that Hamlet is merely 'the English Renaissance's greatest tribute to theatrical man', or that he himself is simply a man of the theatre.[10] Hamlet's discourse of book and theatre recurs throughout the play, opening up a fiction about the relation between page and stage.

As we might expect from previous chapters, *Hamlet* also presents dramatic characters on the stage who *talk* about one particular kind of book: the book of poetry, especially in its relation to theatre. Often, that is, characters like the Prince perform set-lyrics as a memorable part of the story. While not all books are either printed books of poetry or of drama, this chapter will show how books, theatre, and poetry are an enduring part of the 'story' told in *Hamlet* (5.2.349). By conjoining poetic books with staged theatre, Shakespeare processes the 'pressures' of the new, sixteenth-century 'form' of authorship that he inherited from Christopher Marlowe, and that he and Marlowe bequeathed to Ben Jonson, when they responded to the 'laureate' art of Edmund Spenser: the author as English poet-playwright. In *Hamlet*, Shakespeare's fictional conjunction of printed poetry and staged theatre creates a new language, important historically because it explores consciousness so profoundly. In Shakespeare's hands, books, poetry, and theatre join to form a signature *profession of consciousness*. For Shakespeare, consciousness is not just psychological but literary; and it is Shakespeare's literary consciousness that becomes arguably his greatest legacy.[11] The objects rattling around in Shakespearean consciousness turn out to take the material form of books, poetry, and plays. In Shakespeare's theatre, consciousness is fundamentally intertextual.[12]

---

[9] In a personal communication, Joseph Loewenstein suggests an even more precise interpretation: Hamlet is saying that the aim of theatre 'is to represent the self-representational impression of the age. The age impresses (in wax or on page) and the theatre reflects that impression': 'theater reflects, or maybe even reflects on, the way in which culture asserts itself as a culture of printed books'. On sealing in 'form and pressure', see Loewenstein, 'Shakespeare's Stamp'.

[10] Helgerson, *Self-Crowned Laureates* 159.

[11] This argument transposes Adelman's influential analysis of 'emergent selfhood' from the methodology of psychoanalysis ('*Hamlet* and the Confrontation with the Maternal Body' 273) to that of authorship. Cf. de Grazia, 'Emergent Consciousness', who resists the notion that Shakespeare uses soliloquies to depict 'consciousness', arguing that he represents 'mind' as material objects (81). De Grazia traces the concept of consciousness to Hegel, Marx, and Burckhardt, emphasizing that Foucault resists the nineteenth-century invention of the 'Renaissance' as the birth of modern consciousness (70–3). As we shall see, 'profession' becomes an important term at the end of *Hamlet*.

[12] De Grazia is on the verge of this idea twice: when she identifies the 'sources' of Hamlet's 'To be or not to be' soliloquy, speculating about how we have 'mistaken an obvious citation for Shakespeare's

The sections below trace a distinct literary under-plot in *Hamlet*. The Prince's speech immediately following his audition with the Ghost inaugurates the conjunction between a discourse of theatre and a discourse of the book, representing an idea important perhaps to literary history: a figure of Western epic in the stage genre of tragedy (chapter 1), the Ghost disrupts Hamlet's education at Luther's Wittenberg University in the divine comedic book of Scripture. Then, in Acts 2 and 3 Hamlet turns first to Petrarchan poetry and then to Machiavellian theatre to solve the conundrum he inherits from the Ghost: the Prince enacts a literary response to the politics of metaphysical evil poisoning Elsinore, a response that tragically fails. While this part of the under-plot focuses on Hamlet as an author-figure resorting to literary agency, the next part, on Act 4, scenes 5 and 7, discovers Ophelia transposing the topic of failed masculine authorship to the vehicle of female madness: Ophelia's acute fusion of theatrical performance and lyric song leads to a haunting, self-crowning suicide. Finally, in Act 5 Hamlet's conversation with the song-making Gravedigger, and then the Prince's last utterances after being wounded in the fencing match with Laertes, suggest what is at stake in Shakespeare's profession of consciousness: a new model of the *literary eternal*, located on the conceptual borderland between Christianity and modernity.[13]

'IN THIS DISTRACTED GLOBE' / 'THE BOOK AND VOLUME OF MY BRAIN'

In Act 1, scene 5, after Hamlet inherits the 'dread command' (3.4.108) from the Ghost, with its impossible edicts – killing Claudius, leaving Gertrude alone, keeping his mind untainted, and remembering the Ghost (1.5.25–91) – the Prince delivers a soliloquy that probes a conundrum of consciousness. Yet his probe relies on two distinct forms of professional discourse, the theatrical and the bibliographical:

> And shall I couple hell? O fie, hold, hold, my heart,
> And you, my sinows, grow not instant old,
> But bear me [stiffly] up. Remember thee!
> Ay, thou poor ghost, whiles memory holds a seat
> In this distracted globe. Remember thee!

representation of consciousness' (79); and when she says that the 'words of others are subsumed into Hamlet's original thought' (86). Notably, the material objects de Grazia foregrounds in Hamlet's consciousness are 'table and posy' (81).
[13] This literary version of the new author-figure differs from that in J. Knapp, 'What Is a Co-Author?': 'the literary paradigm of single authorship' (Abstract) that Knapp terms 'the player-author' (12).

> Yea, from the table of my memory
> I'll wipe away all trivial fond records,
> All saws of books, all forms, all pressures past
> That youth and observation copied there,
> And thy commandment all alone shall live
> Within the book and volume of my brain.   (*Hamlet* 1.5.93–103)

Here Hamlet's combined discourse of the theatre and the book *represents* the 'brain' in its capacity to record events from real life, to remember them, and to act on them. Let us unpack the two strands of discourse before observing their conjunction.[14]

The Prince's reference to the theatre is complicated through metaphor and wordplay. The phrase 'holds a seat' uses theatre as a metaphor for memory – memory is a theatre – in order to intimate an equation between the place of the stage and a ventricle of the mind. This equation leads to the memorable phrase 'this distracted globe', which scholars believe has three meanings: (1) metaphorically, the globe-shaped earth; (2) also metaphorically, the orb-shaped mind; and (3) allusively, the Globe Theatre, where the play was first performed.[15] Thus, Hamlet says that he will remember the Ghost as long as his memory remains within both his mind and the world, while for his part Shakespeare speaks through his character to say that his play will remember the Ghost as long as playgoers come to the Globe Theatre. Whereas Hamlet uses theatre to trope memory as a cognitive and social phenomenon, the author uses theatre to allude to his own theatrical practice. We come to understand the theatrical operation of the brain in its social setting, but we also witness Shakespeare communicating with his audience about his literary profession. Through this strategy of triple-voice, the playwright advertises the continued marketing success of his play and projects its literary fame, but he does something else. He identifies his tragedy at the Globe Theatre as a play *about* the 'distracted globe' – about 'consciousness'.

For 'theatre' or 'performance' critics accustomed to see Shakespeare committed to the stage as actor, playwright, and shareholder in the Globe Theatre, the Prince's speech becomes a showpiece for a man of the theatre. What the theatrical part of Hamlet's soliloquy points to is the theatricality

---

[14] In *Fools of Time*, Frye helps me identify this speech as the birth-moment of the tragedy: 'Hamlet is forced to strike everything out of his "tables" that represent … thought and feeling and observation and awareness, and concentrate solely on hatred and revenge, a violent alteration of his natural mental habits' (39).

[15] See Gurr, *Hamlet and the Distracted Globe* 9–10.

of the Ghost as a metaphysical – and Catholic – agent.[16] Thus, out on the castle platform Horatio addresses the Ghost with a term that critics identify as the quintessential principle of theatre: 'illusion' (1.1.127).[17] Seconds before, Horatio refers to ghosts as a 'prologue to the omen coming on' (123) – the term *prologue* always being theatrical in Shakespeare's vocabulary, including in this play, which formally stages one (3.2.140–54). Later, Hamlet uses a key Shakespearean verb for the role of an actor when he fears that the Ghost 'assume[s his] ... noble father's person' (1.2.243).[18] In Act 1, scene 5, as Hamlet swears Horatio and the soldiers to silence, the Prince quips, 'you hear this fellow in the cellarage' (151) – drawing the audience's eyes to the space beneath the stage trapdoor, from which the actor playing the Ghost speaks. The playwright's presentation of the Catholic spirit of the father as a specter of theatre may appear disturbing, but it anticipates the Ghost's most haunting moment: his evaporation 'out at the portal' during the Bedroom Scene (3.4.136), never to be heard from again (chapter 1). Clearly, Shakespeare's tragedy will deal with a new model, paradoxically beyond the supernatural, beyond the reach not merely of Catholicism or of Protestantism but of Christianity itself.[19]

Yet for those interested in bibliographical criticism, Hamlet's speech becomes an invaluable site for 'books' that inscribe 'saws': the so-called 'Tables', 'Table-books', or 'commonplace books' used for collecting 'pieces of poetry, noteworthy epigrams, and new words; recording sermons, legal proceedings, or parliamentary debates; jotting down conversations, recipes, cures, and jokes; keeping financial records; recalling addresses and meetings; and collecting notes on foreign customs while traveling'.[20] Such criticism becomes particularly interested in Hamlet's statement in lines 98–101, that he will erase the contents of this type of book: 'tables did not require the use of ink', for the writer could use a metal-point stylus, not an ink-quill, to write on a 'specially coated paper or parchment' that allowed for easy erasure (Stallybrass, *et al.* 405, 408). While this research is invaluable – it tells us a good deal about the table-books Hamlet holds – it tells us very little about the speech itself.

Although Hamlet refers to table-books, not printed books, we might recall that 'poetry' forms an important content of the commonplace books

---

[16] See Greenblatt, *Hamlet in Purgatory*: Hamlet, 'a young man from Wittenberg, with a distinctly Protestant termperament, is haunted by a distinctly Catholic ghost' (240).

[17] See Goddard, *Meaning of Shakespeare* 1: 55.

[18] See *MA* 1.1.321, where Don Pedro says to Claudio about wooing Hero on his behalf, 'I will assume thy part in some disguise.'

[19] For support, see Frye, '*Hamlet*' 87.

[20] Stallybrass, Chartier, Mowery, and Wolfe, 'Hamlet's Tables and the Technologies of Writing in Renaissance England' 380, 402–3.

in the inventory just quoted.[21] In this light, Hamlet's simple use of the term 'books' becomes more complicated than we might think. He will erase the maxims he has copied from printed books, including printed poetry, and he will replace them with the theatrical commandment of the Ghost. Such a replacement constructs – and may work uncannily to predict – a historic trajectory: from a (Spenserian) culture of books to a (Shakespearean) culture of theatre. Yet Shakespeare's particular formulation suggests that Hamlet will *contain* theatre within the contents of a book, thus making the two media part of a larger literary economy.[22] Paradoxically, the Prince's vow to wipe away both 'forms' and 'pressures' that he has 'copied' in his table-book draws on the terminology of print culture to represent manuscript composition. Here Hamlet's climactically elongated phrase (another hendiadys emphasized by Wright) takes on resonance: 'within the book and volume of my brain'. The phrase means 'voluminous book' (Hibbard, ed. 191), suggesting that the phrase could evoke both printed and non-printed material.

That Shakespeare represents the book of poetry here becomes clearer when we discover that Hamlet's phrase 'the table of my memory' is virtually a quotation from the period's most famous literary treatise. First published in 1595, Sidney's *Defence of Poesie* uses the phrase to refer to an epic poem of some importance to Hamlet: 'Only let Aeneas be worn in the tablet of your memory.'[23] Later, Shakespeare will show Hamlet enacting Sidney's epic poetics when the Prince asks the First Player to 'act' a 'speech' from 'an excellent play' on 'Aeneas' [tale] to Dido' about 'Priam's slaughter' by ' "The rugged Pyrrhus" ' (2.2.434–52).

Yet the Player's speech is more complicated than the Virgilian and Sidneian dynamic suggests, for it contains one of the most extraordinary moments of extemporal intertextuality in the Shakespeare canon. The speech's most memorable image turns out to originate both in Marlowe and in Spenser, and more precisely in a process we might describe as typological. For here the text's most obvious allusion (to the *Aeneid*) targets the texts of his chief rivals.[24] Thus, to describe the climactic event of the speech, the death of Priam by the sword of Pyrrhus, the First Player rehearses how

---

[21] Hibbard glosses the word 'saws' as 'maxims copied from books' (ed. 191).

[22] On the cover of *Shakespeare as Literary Dramatist*, Erne includes a painting of this principle, by Sir Anthony Van Dyck: the seventeenth-century English lyric poet Sir John Suckling holds a book containing Shakespeare's plays, conveniently open at *Hamlet*.

[23] Sidney, *Defence of Poesie*, in G. G. Smith, ed., *Elizabethan Critical Essays* I: 179. Lees-Jeffries, *England's Helicon*, argues that 'Sidney's image of the "tablet" of the memory here recalls the strongly material textuality of the *Hypnerotomachia*, the way in which it is at once text-as-story, landscape-as-experience, book-as-object' (90).

[24] For my 'typology of intertextuality', see *SNPP* 38–46.

> Unequal match'd,
> Pyrrhus at Priam drives, in rage strikes wide,
> *But with the whiff and wind of his fell sword*
> Th' unnerved father falls.   (*Hamlet* 2.2.471–4; emphasis added)

Typically, editors gloss the italicized 'Virgilian' line with Marlowe's *Dido, Queen of Carthage*, which had put the Virgilian Fall of Troy on the stage (Furness, ed., *Ham* 1: 182–6; Hibbard, ed. 229; P. Edwards, ed. 150):

> Which he [Pyrrhus] disdaining whisked his sword about,
> And with the wind thereof the King fell down.
> (Marlowe, *Dido, Queen of Carthage* 2.1.253–4)

Yet a few editors also cite Spenser's *Faerie Queene*, Book 1, canto 7, when Orgoglio defeats the Redcrosse Knight (ed. Jenkins, ed. 480–1; Thompson and Taylor, eds. 269):

> And lightly [the knight] lept from underneath the blow:
> Yet so exceeding was the villeins power:
> That with the wind it did him overthrow.
> (Spenser, *Faerie Queene* 1.7.12)

Almost certainly, Marlowe responds to Spenser.[25] Yet in a single line Shakespeare responds to Marlowe and Spenser, replaying the death of Priam from Virgil's epic poem. Through this specific typology of intertextuality, Shakespeare complicates the notion of Hamlet's table-book as simply a prose manuscript commonplace book. The Prince vows to erase the printed book of 'past' epic poetry in service of the nation in order to script a new tragic epic theatre foregrounding the bookish self: 'Within the book and volume of my brain'.

Hamlet's initial reference to 'books' unleashes the discourse of textuality that Shakespeare stages so prominently in this play. For instance, in Act 2, scene 2, the Prince comes on stage '*reading on a book*', prompting his mother to exclaim, 'look where sadly the poor wretch comes reading' (168 and SD preceding). Analogously, in Act 3, scene 1, Polonius sets Ophelia up as a decoy to spy on Hamlet by instructing her, 'Read on this book' (43). In both cases, the actors read printed books on stage, making the process of printing and reading part of the fiction. In the case of the book Hamlet 'read[s]', we know it is printed because Polonius asks the Prince what its 'matter' is, prompting Hamlet to retort, 'Slanders, sir; for the satirical rogue says here that old men have grey beards' (191–7). The Prince's wry reference to the

---

[25] For details on Marlowe's response to Spenser throughout *Dido*, see Cheney, *Marlowe's Counterfeit Profession* 99–114.

author of the book as a 'satirical rogue' indicates that most likely he reads a volume of printed poetry from the genre of satire, and long ago William Warburton even identified a particular poetic book: Juvenal's tenth *Satire*.[26] We may not learn such information about Ophelia's book, but scholars assume that it is a devotional book, in keeping with early modern women's reading practices.

In both cases, Shakespeare associates books with theatre. As is well known, Hamlet reads on a book as part of his 'antic disposition' (1.5.172), the performed role of madness that he 'put[s] … on' before Claudius' court. Similarly, Polonius' full instruction to Ophelia runs, 'Read on this book, / That show of such an exercise may color / Your [loneliness]' (3.1.43–5) – the word 'show' being one of Shakespeare's most recurrent terms for his theatrical profession (3.2.143–5). In fact, all uses of the word 'book' in this play are intimately connected to theatricality. Thus, Hamlet's climactic phrase about the textuality of memory, 'the book and volume of my brain', reproduces the idea mentioned earlier for the 'distracted globe': in Shakespeare's 'brain', books also foreground consciousness.[27]

Equally to the point, the Prince *jumbles* the metaphors of book and theatre. His author does so to represent consciousness *in its state of distraction*. If Shakespeare uses books and theatre to represent mental distraction, we might infer that Hamlet's distraction is connected *to* this literary economy.[28] For instance, Hamlet's literary distraction results at *the* crucial moment in the play: precisely when Hamlet's interior moral arbiter, which he famously calls 'conscience' in his 'To be or not to be' soliloquy (3.1.82), confronts and resists the metaphysical command of the Ghost to commit revenge: 'And shall I couple hell?' Here Shakespeare speaks to the fundamental problem of the late sixteenth-century intellectual. Should he listen to his conscience as the primary voice of authority, as urged by Martin Luther, the famed theologian who began the Protestant Reformation at Hamlet's university, Wittenberg? Or should the intellectual listen to the metaphysically sanctioned voice of the 'father' exterior to his consciousness, lodged at the Vatican in the Roman Catholic Church, as the notorious detail about the Ghost in purgatory indicates (1.5.9–13)?[29] Shakespeare takes

---

[26] Furness, ed., *Ham* 1: 151.

[27] Stallybrass, *et al.*, begin their essay by quoting the 'distracted globe' passage, but they neglect the theatrical discourse, commenting only on the textuality. Like such theatre critics as Gurr, they attend to one discourse or the other but not both together.

[28] Cf. Findlay, '*Hamlet*: A Document in Madness': Hamlet's '"distracted" speeches suggest that it is language as much as female sexuality, neglected love, or grief that has made him mad' (194).

[29] Conscience was also vital to Catholics but it needed to work in compliance with the church, just as for Protestants conscience needed to work through Scripture.

the old Norse story from Saxo Grammaticus and Belleforest, and invests it with deep Reformation significance.[30]

While the opposition between Protestant conscience and Catholic metaphysics – interior versus exterior truth – is well recognized in *Hamlet* criticism, we might find more fresh the idea that Shakespeare represents this historic religious conflict through the terms of his own authorship, and further, that Shakespearean authorship combines the *poetical* with the *theatrical*. Intriguingly, in this play the theological is intimately bound up with the literary. Shakespeare uses his professional predicament as an author trying to combine page and stage to process his era's religious predicament about Christian faith. At stake in both problems is the question of authority, especially linguistic authority, and thus both agency and its afterlife. Effectively, Shakespeare suggests that his play, a tragedy written both for performance at the Globe Theatre and for publication at a London print-shop, operates at a decisive historical moment. He does so, we may speculate, to help the audience process the great spiritual crisis of the age: the crisis of faith that around 1600 overtakes the humanist exuberance of the English 'Renaissance', with *The Tragedy of Hamlet, Prince of Denmark* arguably its most profound testament.

HAMLET'S DUBIOUS POEM TO OPHELIA

In keeping with the play's literary under-plot, in Acts 2 and 3 Shakespeare presents Hamlet as a new author-figure, the writer of the two literary forms that occupied his own career: both poetry and drama.

Near the beginning of 2.2, Polonius reads to Claudius and Gertrude a love letter and a poem that Hamlet has composed to Ophelia:

POLONIUS. 'To the celestial and my soul's idol, the most beautified Ophelia' –
          That's an ill phrase, a vile phrase, 'beautified' is a vile phrase. But
          you shall hear. Thus:
          'In her excellent white bosom, these, etc'.
QUEEN.   Came this from Hamlet to her?
POLONIUS. Good madam, stay awhile. I will be faithful.

---

[30] Hamlet's discourse of the theatre appears in both Saxo and Belleforest but not his discourse of poetry and books. The latter becomes one of Shakespeare's most important contributions to the Hamlet story.

[Reads the] letter.
'Doubt thou the stars are fire,
Doubt that the sun doth move,
Doubt truth to be a liar,
But never doubt I love.

O dear Ophelia, I am ill at these numbers. I have not art to reckon my
groans, but that I love thee best, O most best, believe it. Adieu.
Thine evermore, most dear lady,
whilst this machine is to him, Hamlet'.

(*Hamlet* 2.2.109–24)

Hamlet is not the only one who is ill at these numbers. Routinely, critics
dismiss the poem as doggerel verse, without recognizing the dramatic utility
of such a poetic rehearsal.

Philip Edwards, editor of the recent Cambridge edition, is genuinely
perplexed: 'Hamlet's letter to Ophelia is a great puzzle; it is so affected,
juvenile and graceless. We should be glad to take it as part of Hamlet's
recent heartless treatment of Ophelia but it is very firmly said that Ophelia,
in obedience to her father, has refused to receive his letters (2.1.109; 2.2.144).
If this is one of Hamlet's real love-letters, why did Shakespeare make him
write like Don Armado in *Love's Labour's Lost?*' (ed. 135). Such perplexing
moments of poetic representation, however, afford a more productive site
for analysis than such criticism allows.

In context, Polonius joins Claudius and Gertrude in using Hamlet's
letter and poem to interpret the motives of his antic disposition. In other
words, Polonius produces the letter containing the poem to plumb
Hamlet's interiority, to discover the motive for his histrionic conduct. As
Polonius boasts, 'I will find / Where truth is hid, though it were hid indeed /
Within the centre' (157–9). The truth Polonius later claims to discover is
that of a young man's erotic melancholy, caused when his beloved, listening
to the authority of her father, repels her lover's devotion (146–51). Yet the
audience becomes privy rather to Polonius' folly. In the artifact of Hamlet's
poem, we discover a 'centre' that remains 'hid', a 'truth' that continues to be
opaque: a work of art that puts the hunters off the scent. In this regard, the
dramatic scene of poetry stages the central problem this play rehearses. In
response to a ghostly call to revenge, Hamlet re-scripts tragic inwardness,
performing his troubled consciousness.

Consciousness is indeed the topic of Hamlet's letter and poem. In
particular, the document identifies the prince as a Petrarchan lover and
poet – a tragedic correlate to the Petrarchist Benedick. The scraps of
discourse Polonius teasingly quotes from Hamlet's letter participate in the

conventions of Elizabethan Petrarchism.[31] Specifically, Hamlet addresses
Ophelia in the language of Petrarchan idolatry, describing his beloved first
as 'celestial' – a divine body gloriously above his own decaying 'machine' –
and then as 'my soul's idol' – the object of his interior adoration. By evoking
Petrarchism, Shakespeare draws a historical genealogy for the invention of
inwardness, with himself in the role of counter-Petrarchan heir. Equally
Petrarchan is Hamlet's (or is it Polonius'?) singling out of a female body
part: 'In her excellent white bosom, these, etc'. In the history of
Petrarchism, it might be difficult to find not simply a briefer blazon but a
more splendid representation of female interiority as physiological vacancy
and absence – something truly interior. Gertrude finds this poetic conceit so
repulsive she instinctively recoils ('Good madam, stay awhile').

For his part, Polonius recoils from another of Hamlet's words: 'beautified'. Critics have long observed that Hamlet attaches to Ophelia the word
that Robert Greene used when criticizing Shakespeare back in 1592 as an
'upstart crow, beautified with our feathers'.[32] If correct, we have here a
rather unusual historical moment. Shakespeare presents his Petrarchan
prince being maligned in public for his erotic poetic diction, while the
author himself airs his own public maligning by a colleague. If Shakespeare
laughs at himself, and perhaps returns the laugh to the dead Greene as part
of a public hearing, he therefore signs the scene with his own authorial 'form
and pressure'. Such a moment might suggest some of the sophisticated art
that Shakespeare uses to reckon the Petrarchan numbers he makes so
patently ill.

Consciousness also lies at the heart of the four-line verse Hamlet composes to Ophelia, as the quadruple anaphora of 'Doubt' and the climactic
word 'love' record. The contents again are formally Petrarchan; this
Petrarchan lover attempts a Petrarchan poem. The concrete images of
'stars', 'fire', and 'sun' both brighten and heat up the erotic beat of the
verse, but they also help set up a characteristic Shakespearean interlock
between an exterior show and an interior truth. Belying the simplicity (and
vacuity) of the verse is its deep philosophical, theological, and scientific
resonance.

Long ago, Levin placed Hamlet's poem in the dubitative tradition of
Western philosophy – what he calls 'the philosophical outlook of skepticism'
(54). He quotes Sir Walter Ralegh, who said, 'The Skeptick doth neither
affirm, nor denie any Position; but doubteth it' (54), and more famously

---

[31] See *RJ* 2.4.38–9: 'Now is he for the numbers that Petrarch flow'd in.'
[32] See Levin, *Question of Hamlet* 63–4; Greenblatt, *Will in the World* 215.

John Donne, 'The new philosophy calls all in doubt' (54). According to Walter N. King, who follows up on Levin, the decisive historical event underwriting Hamlet's poem is the 1543 publication of Copernicus' *De revolutionibus orbium coelestium*, which rejected the Ptolemaic theory of a geocentric universe to posit a heliocentric theory: 'The stars, Hamlet asserts, may not be igneous planetary bodies, as they appear to be to the naked eye. The earth may orbit about the sun. If so, the traditional moral and metaphysical truth regarding man's centrality in the universe may be a lie. Nevertheless, Hamlet's love need not be doubted.'[33]

More recently, Stanley Cavell suggests that 'the advent of skepticism as manifest in Descartes' *Meditations* is already in full existence in Shakespeare'.[34] The 'skeptical problematic' that Cavell finds in Shakespeare's plays 'is given philosophical refinement in Descartes' way of raising the questions of God's existence and of the immortality of the soul': 'The issue posed [in Shakespeare, as in Descartes] is … how to conduct oneself best in an uncertain world … how to live at all in a groundless world' (3). In his short chapter on *Hamlet*, Cavell does not mention the Prince's poem to Ophelia, but he well could have, to find in it a potently bad artifact of philosophical skepticism, a 'poetic' advent to what Cavell calls modern philosophy.[35]

Levin had outlined the skeptical problematic in Hamlet's Petrarchan poem as a poetic 'mix[ing of] cosmology with intimacy', in order to place it in 'the Metaphysical School' of Donne (54). As a classification, this may be inaccurate, because it does not account for Hamlet's Petrarchism, and especially his bad Petrarchism. Nor should we try simply to make sense of the poem as a puzzle in the Prince's personality. While reading it as a function of character leads to a dead end, we may see the poem as an unusual register of the author's own counter-Petrarchism, everywhere on display in Shakespeare's Sonnets. Shakespeare's disproportionate loading of deep philosophy onto a 'juvenile' quatrain becomes a wry but patent sign of Shakespearean authorship. Often, this author inserts a *bad poem* in order to create *great drama*.

The central word in Hamlet's poem, 'Doubt', has been seen to have at least three different meanings: '(1) to be skeptical (as about the ancient truths about the stars and the sun); (2) to suspect (that, e.g., truth might be a

---

[33] W. N. King, *Hamlet's Search for Meaning* 52.
[34] Cavell, *Disowning Knowledge in Six Plays of Shakespeare* 3.
[35] Garber, '*Hamlet*: Giving up the Ghost', calls Hamlet 'the poet of doubt' and his poem 'a paean to negation' (301). In *Tragedy and Scepticism in Shakespeare's England*, Hamlin offers a historicist response to Cavell, concentrating on Pyrrhonism and Montaigne as influential texts for the English dramatists, including Shakespeare in *TC*.

liar); (3) to disbelieve e.g., Hamlet's love'.[36] As David Leverenz puts it, Hamlet sends Ophelia 'an ambiguous poem that can be read as "Never doubt that I love" or "Never suspect that I love." '[37] However doggerel the verse may be, Shakespeare is careful to enclose in it Hamlet's famous penchant for wordplay and ambiguity.

As such, we cannot tell if Hamlet's poem is a verse testament to his faith to Ophelia – his spiritual care for her – or merely another form of antic disposition. The question over the Prince's motives lingers, and in so doing raises the dynamic central to the play as a whole: that between inner truth and outer appearance. To borrow Hamlet's own vocabulary from his first appearance in Act 1, scene 2, does the poem to Ophelia 'denote' him 'truly' or does it perform an 'action that a man might play'? Does it merely 'seem' or does it 'have that within which passes show' (83–5)? Shakespeare uses the poem to Ophelia to represent not merely the question of Hamlet's interiority, poised as it is on the threshold between medieval Christianity and modern philosophy, but also his own fundamental theatricality.[38]

In case we missed it, Shakespeare powerfully rehearses Hamlet's Petrarchan theatre earlier, when Ophelia describes to her father the prince's histrionic entry into her closet. Ophelia's portrait of Hamlet's dress and state of mind – 'with his doublet all unbrac'd, / No hat upon his head, his stockins fouled … / Pale as his shirt' (2.1.75–8) – depicts with 'excruciating vividness' (Knight, 'Embassy of Death' 21) not simply 'the typical lover' (Hibbard, ed. 201) but more precisely the Petrarchan lover.[39] Accordingly, Ophelia's description of Hamlet's subsequent behavior literalizes the 'hall-mark' of Petrarchan lyric poetry, the blazon, which displays 'intense attention to the female countenance' (Kerrigan 66):

> He falls to such perusal of my face
> As 'a would draw it. Long stay'd he so.
> At last, a little shaking of mine arm,
> And thrice his head thus waving up and down,
> He rais'd a sigh so piteous and profound
> As it did seem to shatter all his bulk
> And end his being.   (*Hamlet* 2.1.87–93)

[36] Mowat and Werstine, eds., *Hamlet* 88.   [37] Leverenz, 'Woman in Hamlet' 119.
[38] For 'the Platonic presumption that the reality of anything is other than its apparent self,' see Booth, 'On the Value of *Hamlet*' 58.
[39] The following is indebted to Kerrigan, *Hamlet's Perfection* 66–7.

Ophelia's simile, 'As 'a would draw it', comes from painting, but in Sonnet 24 Shakespeare uses the art of the painter to represent the art of the Petrarchan poet, and in the process connects it linguistically with both theatre and book, including the very discourse we have been examining: 'Mine eye hath play'd the painter and hath [stell'd] / Thy beauty's *form* in *table* of my heart' (1–2; emphasis added). Like Hamlet in Ophelia's closet, Will here 'play[s]' the role of the artist who *stells* – portrays – the 'form' of the beloved's beauty in the 'table' of his emotional faculty.[40] In both cases, Shakespeare voices the idiom of Petrarchan poetry to represent an aesthetic process. A male envisions the face of a beautiful beloved, and relies on the metaphor of painting to depict a process of erotic writing. In both cases as well, Shakespeare fuses the discourse of theatre and the discourse of the book to present the authorial figure as a theatrical Petrarchist.

Often, productions and films veer from the three early texts of the play (Q1, Q2, FF) by turning Ophelia's description of her closet encounter with Hamlet into a 'dumb-show' (Thompson and Taylor, eds. 233). In the text, a female character simply narrates a dumb-show about a Petrarchan poet. In this 'mirror' refraction, we acquire access to something rare in the Petrarchan tradition, especially on the London stage: it is the female who perceives the Petrarchan poet as a distracted lover. Through the agency of Ophelia, we discern a 'poetical' version of the purpose of playing concluding Act 2. If Hamlet will use 'the play' to 'catch the conscience of the king' (2.2.604–5), here the Prince uses the poem to catch the conscience of his beloved. In our zeal to embrace the Prince's theatricality, perhaps we have underestimated his commitment to the art of poetry.[41]

HAMLET, JEPHTHAH'S DAUGHTER, AND THE PLAYERS

Elsewhere in Act 2, scene 2, Hamlet relies on a combined literary discourse that he shares with his author. It is remarkable to discover that during this memorable 'theatre' scene the Prince appears nearly as committed to poetry as he is to drama; this was sometimes a paradox, but the story is extant, and writ in choice English. For instance, Hamlet routinely lapses into popular song, as in his famous snippets on Jephthah's daughter:

---

[40] For annotation on Sonnet 24, citing the *Hamlet* passage, see C. Burrow, ed. 428; in lines 10 and 14, Will uses the word 'draw' as the verb for his Petrarchan painting of the beloved.

[41] Jenkins remarks: 'Deliberately or not, the eyes that "bended their light" on her [Ophelia] echo Ovid's description of Orpheus, *flexit amans oculos* (*Met.* X.57), at the moment of his losing Eurydice, when coming back from hell' (ed. 462). Effectively, Shakespeare stages Hamlet also as an Ovidian Orphic poet.

HAMLET.   O Jephthah, judge of Israel, what a treasure hadst thou!
POLONIUS.   What a treasure had he, my lord?
HAMLET.   Why –

    'One fair daughter, and no more,
    The which he loved passing well'.

POLONIUS   Still on my daughter.
[ASIDE].
HAMLET.   Am I not i' th' right, old Jephthah?
POLONIUS.   If you call me Jephthah, my lord, I have a daughter that I love
    passing well.
HAMLET.   Nay, that follows not.
POLONIUS.   What follows then, my lord?
HAMLET.   Why –

    'As by lot, God wot',
    and then, you know,
    'It came to pass, as most like it was' –

                   (*Hamlet* 2.2.403–18)

The artistic paradigm here is complex, as Hamlet relies on his antics to refer to the biblical story of Jephthah and his daughter in the Book of Judges and then to quote three passages from a popular ballad on the story. Hamlet and Shakespeare combine theatre with popular song to situate the action of the scene in the context of Scripture, compelling the audience (but evidently not 'old Jephthah') to understand the rashness underlying the patriarch's selling of his daughter. As with Hamlet's verse to Ophelia, the topic is again one of betrayal, removed from the marital or erotic sphere to the parental or filial one.

The snatches from the Jephthah ballad link Hamlet's earlier conversation with Polonius on 'The best actors in the world' (396) to the entrance of the Players themselves. For Hamlet's line immediately following the passage quoted above reads:

the first row of the pious chanson will show you more, for look where my abridgment comes. (*Hamlet* 2.2.419–20)

Hamlet's remark is more than a stage cue to the actors playing the players. It is a register of an intimate link between the 'chanson' and the art of theatre. Indeed, the syntax of the cue literally represents this link: '*chanson* will *show ... abridgment*'. The song will show the performing players. Perhaps no formulation in the Shakespeare canon more intriguingly exhibits this author's habitual interlink between song and show, poetry and theatre.

What is notable here is the presence of two rare Shakespearean literary words within a single utterance, 'chanson' and 'abridgment', with 'chanson' spanning the divide of performed and printed poetry, and 'abridgment' the divide of bibliographical and theatrical discourse.[42] Hamlet's gnomic utterance draws attention to his antic songs on Jephthah being interrupted by the arrival of the players, for he tells his listeners to read the opening stanza of this pious ballad if they want to hear more, even as he announces the arrival of the players to the stage.

Once the players enter, Hamlet entreats the First Player to deliver the speech out of Virgilian epic on Pyrrhus' slaughter of old Priam. While most editors believe that Shakespeare evokes Marlowe's *Dido*, it seems important that Hamlet's prized speech 'was never acted' (2.2.435). Curiously, it is more bibliographical than theatrical, as the intertextuality with Spenser (and Sidney) noted earlier also perhaps intimates. As in Hamlet's poem to Ophelia and the snippets from the Jephthah ballad, the topic is based on gender. Now, however, the heroic fidelity of the wife, Hecuba, emerges amid the most heart-rending of circumstances: the brutal murder of old Priam by the son of Achilles. Shakespeare economizes the poetry-drama paradigm in terms of the larger play and its probing of faith.

Immediately following, Hamlet asks the First Player about altering 'The Murther of Gonzago' (537–8), which the Prince has requested for playing before the King and Queen: 'You could for need study a speech of some dozen or sixteen lines, which I would set down and insert in't, could you not?' (540–3). We are not sure which 'dozen or sixteen lines' Hamlet writes for *The Mousetrap*, but Shakespeare intriguingly presents the Prince as more than a learned commentator on the art of acting in the theater (2.2.421–546, 3.2); Hamlet is also a writer of a dramatic speech. Thus, in the full portrait of Acts 2 and 3, Hamlet becomes an author of both drama and poetry.[43]

OPHELIA, LYRIC PERFORMANCE, AND MADNESS

Shakespeare's presentation of Hamlet in the professional terms of his own authorship compels us to reconsider the much-discussed relationship

---

[42] According to the *OED*, 'chanson' is unusual in English. Under Def. 1, 'A song (French, or of France)', the *OED* cites the 1602 *Hamlet*. Edwards notes that 'A "row" is more properly a line, but, as this does not make much sense, some editors suggest, without much authority, "stanza" – i.e. "you'll have to read the first stanza of this pious ballad [the one about Jephthah] if you want more" ' (ed. 147). The word 'abridgment' is also unusual; according to the *OED*, it has only three meanings – *shortening, entertainment, abstract* – the first two exemplified in Shakespeare, who uses the word four other times. While Hamlet's usage pertains most directly to the first meaning, it also evokes the second and third ones, which pertain to the *theatrical* and the *bibliographical*.

[43] The linguistic economy of book and theatre shows up repeatedly in Acts 2 and 3. See 2.2.502–6 ('the players … are the abstracts and brief chronicles of the time. After your death you were better have a bad epitaph than their ill report while you live'); 3.2.130–5 (on the theatrical 'hoby-horse' and the poetic 'epitaph'); 3.2.152 ('Is this a prologue or a posy of a ring?').

between the Prince and Ophelia. We need to do so because of the unusual way in which Shakespeare displaces his tragic character's masculine professionalism on to his tragic heroine. Thus, after Hamlet both writes a Petrarchan poem to Ophelia and sits in her lap during the performance of a Machiavellian tragedy, the Prince's beloved becomes the theatrical performer of her own lyric art. Specifically, in Act 4, scene 5, she relies on lyric songs to perform the 'distracted' (SD) voice of female madness. Shakespeare identifies the condition of Ophelia's consciousness through the same word he had used to identify Hamlet's mental state in his speech on the 'distracted globe'.

Most critics agree that the relationship between Hamlet and Ophelia is built on a *mirroring* principle: 'Through her impossible attempt to obey contradictory voices, Ophelia mirrors in her madness the tensions that Hamlet perceives: her suicide embodies what Hamlet ponders in his soliloquies … She herself is a play within a play … The songs [she sings] mirror every level of the play' (Leverenz 117, 120). Despite this curious characterization, critics still view Ophelia exclusively as a female character who goes mad with song.

Unlike Hamlet's lyrics, Ophelia's have been the subject of much scrutiny, especially during the past twenty years. Typically, critics approach her songs through one of two interrelated lenses: that of music, and that of madness. Those interested in musicology place Ophelia's songs within the context of Renaissance notions of musical art. More frequently, feminist critics locate Ophelia's songs within the context of Renaissance attitudes toward female madness as a signal disorder of patriarchy.[44] We may complement this important research by situating Ophelia's performance of lyric song within the context of Shakespearean authorship.

Leverenz writes influentially on 'the woman in Hamlet', yet we might also be intrigued by *the man in Ophelia*. This approach is not as far-fetched as it might at first sound. For instance, Shakespearean theatre repeatedly reminds us that a boy actor performs the role of female characters, and we might specify this principle with respect to Hamlet's beloved.[45] In such

---

[44] The classic feminist work remains Showalter, 'Representing Ophelia'. Often, critics discuss music and madness together. In addition to Findlay, see L. Bate, 'Which Did or Did Not Go to the Grave?'; Seng, 'Dramatic Function of the Songs in *Hamlet*'; Bishop, 'Elizabethan Music as a Cultural Mode'; Dane, 'Reading Ophelia's Madness'; Dunn, 'Ophelia's songs in Hamlet'; Fox-Good, 'Ophelia's Mad Songs'; Hartsock, 'Major Scenes in Minor Key'; Klein, '"Angels and Ministers of Grace"'; Lindley, 'Shakespeare's Provoking Music'; Lyons, 'Iconography of Ophelia'; Ranjini, 'Shattered Glass'; Fienberg, '"She Chanted Snatches of Old Tunes"'.

[45] Shakespeare gestures to the boy actor playing Ophelia in the Nunnery Scene when Hamlet indicts her for wearing cosmetics; see Garber, *Shakespeare After All* 473. Lindley, *Shakespeare and Music*, notes that Ophelia in two of her songs 'seems to adopt … a male position' (158). De Grazia, '*Hamlet*'

works as *The Rape of Lucrece* and *A Lover's Complaint*, Shakespeare joins his colleagues in 'taking on the voice of a fallen woman' to worry about the masculine shame of publication. In *Hamlet*, Shakespeare uses the theatrical songs of Ophelia to gesture to the trauma of the new English poet-playwright.

Almost certainly, Shakespeare derives his representation linking madness with poetry from the ancient tradition of Platonic *furor*. The *locus classicus* is the *Phaedrus*, where Socrates delineates four kinds of madness: divine, prophetic, poetic, and erotic. Of 'the third form of possession or madness', Socrates identifies 'the Muses' as 'the source':

> This seizes *a tender, virgin soul and stimulates it to rapt passionate expression, especially in lyric poetry*, glorifying the countless mighty deeds of ancient times for the instruction of posterity. But if any man come to the gates of poetry without the madness of the Muses, persuaded that skill alone will make him a good poet, then shall he and his works of sanity with him be brought to nought by the poetry of madness, and behold, their place is nowhere to be found. [46]

Socrates' opening phrasing is particularly resonant for Shakespeare's representation of Ophelia, a 'virgin soul' stimulated to 'rapt passionate expression' in 'lyric poetry'.[47]

The notion of poetic *furor* was a commonplace of Elizabethan poetics. In *The Shepheardes Calender*, for instance, E. K. refers to it when glossing Cuddie's high-flying discourse in the *October* eclogue: 'he seemeth here to be ravished with a Poetical furie. For (if one rightly mark) the numbers rise so ful, and the verse groweth so big, that it seemeth he hath forgot the mean-enesse of shepheards state and stile' (255–7). In *A Midsummer Night's Dream*, Shakespeare makes his most famous reference to the Platonic theory, when Theseus speaks of 'the lunatic, the lover, and the poet' (5.1.7; see chapter 2). What is perhaps surprising in *Hamlet* is Shakespeare's transposition of the Platonic idea of poetic fury to the tragedy of lyric desire within a virginal girl played by a boy actor.[48]

---

without Hamlet, quotes Lacan, who sees Ophelia's name signifying " 'O-phallus' " (154). This superb book appeared too late for me to make full use of it here; it incorporates her essay 'Soliloquies and Wages', cited earlier.

[46] Plato, *Phaedrus* 245a; emphasis added. On Shakespeare and Plato's *Phaedrus*, see, e.g., Carnes, 'Mind, Imagination, and Art in Shakespeare's *The Tempest*'; Everett, 'Shakespeare, Plato, and the Plotting of the Sonnets'. Aldus, *Mousetrap*, discusses the role of the *Phaedrus* in *Hamlet* but neglects its relevance to Ophelia.

[47] Thanks to Nicholas Repsher for this idea (personal communication).

[48] Two recent studies of madness in Shakespeare, *Hamlet*, and Ophelia underscore the connection between madness and theatricality: K. Jackson, *Separate Theaters* 70–155; Neely, *Distracted Subjects* 23–67.

At the beginning of the scene, the Gentleman indicates something of the theatricality of Ophelia's songs when telling Gertrude, 'Her speech is nothing, / Yet the unshaped use of it doth move / The hearers to collection' (7–9). As the entire scene dramatizes, Ophelia does not sing her songs in melancholy isolation but instead seeks out an audience. The opening lines indicate that Ophelia seeks an audience with the Queen:

QUEEN.   I will not speak with her.
GENTLEMAN.   She is importunate, indeed distract.   (*Hamlet* 4.5.1–2)

Once Gertrude consents to speak with her, Ophelia abandons prose and breaks into song. When Gertrude interrupts by asking, 'what imports this song?' (27), Ophelia countermands her authority, 'Nay, pray you mark' (28), repeating the command twice more (35, 46). Later, when Ophelia returns to the stage to give flowers to the Queen, the King, and her brother, and to sing songs for them, she makes the public performance of her art a striking feature of the action. In the place of the stage, not just in the fiction, she moves the hearers to collection.

The dramatic details surrounding Ophelia's lyric performance are complex, for two interlocked reasons. First, as the Gentleman reports, she 'speaks things in doubt, / That carry but half sense' (6–7). The first reference to these 'things', prefacing Ophelia's entry, compels us to listen carefully to what she says. We strain to decipher a kind of symbolic language, taking the cue of the 'hearers' mentioned by the Gentlemen:

> they yawn at it [her speech],
> And botch the words up fit to their own thoughts,
> Which as her winks and nods and gestures yield them,
> Indeed would make one think there might be thought,
> Though nothing sure, yet much unhappily.   (*Hamlet* 4.5.9–13)

Second, the 'meaning' of Ophelia's song is not simply 'hidden'; in keeping with her mental state, it is *fragmented*, as her lyric ' "explanations" go from Hamlet to Polonius and back again' (P. Edwards, ed. 207) – to Laertes as well. In other words, Ophelia's lyric art uses the feminine voice to process her distracted relations with the three chief men in her life: her father, her lover, and her brother. Like the Queen, we want to know what the song imports.

While Ophelia is distracted, clearly her author is not. He draws her art of lyric performance along the divide between the Christian urge toward transcendent grace and the material constraints of physical desire. Indeed, the contents of Ophelia's songs are remarkable. They present the singer as a person of deep Christian spirituality reacting to the double trauma of sudden death and sexual betrayal. What is especially shocking is that Shakespeare's exquisite lyric form should give voice to such explicit sexuality (often graphic during performance), as emerges in Ophelia's Valentine's Day song:

> 'Young men will do't if they come to't,
> By Cock, they are to blame.
> 'Quoth she, "Before you tumbled me,
> You promis'd me to wed."'
>
> (*Hamlet* 4.5.60–3)

Ophelia's song is about the loss of female virginity, and the male's subsequent betrayal of her innocent faith:

> 'Then up he rose and donn'd his clo'es,
> And dupp'd the chamber-door,
> Let in the maid, that out a maid
> Never departed more.'
>
> (*Hamlet* 4.5.52–5)

Ophelia's song expresses a tragic recognition about male identity: young men use the sacred day of lovers to 'daff' the 'white stole' of a virgin's 'chastity' (*LC* 297). What Laertes says about Ophelia's flower-giving, we could say of her songs: 'A document in madness, thoughts and remembrance fitted' (178–9). Shakespeare presents Ophelia as a tragic book of lyric performance.

Accordingly, her songs accrue generic resonance. Most obviously, they function as erotic lyric poems in an elegiac key.[49] Yet Shakespeare also presents Ophelia as a figure from the genre of pastoral, best witnessed in her floral ceremony, a self-conscious trope for poetry during the period, which Shakespeare reprises in the great pastoral scenes with Perdita in *The Winter's Tale*.[50] Unlike Perdita, however, Ophelia performs her floral associations in the royal court of Elsinore, and thus she acquires an association with the other Renaissance Virgilian genre, epic, especially as Spenser had made the Virgilian progression important to Elizabethan poets.[51] Shakespeare appears to map the Spenserian career coordinate of pastoral and epic on to an insane young female singer. If so, not long after the New Poet's death in 1599, Shakespeare may use the icon of the deranged female to foreclose the idea of a Spenserian literary career. In Ophelia, Shakespeare intimates something like the tragic death of the Virgilian career model for post-Spenserian authors. Perhaps he believed that the corruption of the Elizabethan court,

[49] Bloom calls them 'a lyrical splendor' (*Hamlet: Poem Unlimited* 42).
[50] See Cheney, 'Perdita, Pastorella, and the Romance of Literary Form'. Cf. Neill on 'the pastoral sweetness briefly evoked by Ophelia's herbal emblems' (*Issues of Death* 249).
[51] Lyons identifies Ophelia with Flora, who for the Renaissance had a 'double' meaning, one as 'pastoral', the other as 'urban', citing Spenser's *FQ* (67).

with the Queen aged and dying, precluded an author's serious engagement not only with pastoral but also with epic. In Ophelia, we find a miniature for the birth of Shakespearean tragedy itself.

In her death scene of 4.7, narrated famously by Gertrude, Shakespeare identifies Ophelia's pastoral character explicitly, bringing a staple of the pastoral tradition, the tragedic elegy, to center stage (see, e.g., Spenser's *November* eclogue). In her last moments, Ophelia performs three interrelated actions. First, she 'make[s]' 'fantastic garlands' out of various flowers, including 'long purples, / That liberal shepherds give a grosser name, / But our cull-cold maids do dead men's fingers call' (168–71). Second, she hangs the 'crownet weeds' (172) on the branches of 'a willow' tree that 'grows askaunt the brook' (166). Third, after falling into the brook, 'mermaid-like' she 'chaunted snatches of old lauds' (176–7).[52] In this pastoral death by water, in which the poet-figure slips narcissistically into the source of her own inspiration, Shakespeare creates one of the most delicate icons on record of the tragically doomed, self-crowning laureate.[53]

'[A] SINGS IN GRAVE-MAKING': HAMLET AND THE LITERARY ETERNAL

Like Ophelia's mad lyric performance, Hamlet's failed literary profession – his reading and writing of books (printed and commonplace), his writing and singing of lyric poems, and his writing and performing of plays – all map out a tragic form of early modern consciousness. Recurrently, Shakespeare shrouds Hamlet's profession as a poet-playwright in the complex mystery of causality and immortality on which this tragedy so famously centers.[54]

In the graveyard of Act 5, scene 1, Hamlet meets Horatio after returning from the sea voyage, and they overhear the conversation of the 'two Clowns', including the immortal songs of the First Clown. When Hamlet quips, ''a sings in grave-making' (66), Shakespeare voices a compelling equation between the making of graves and the making of songs. Accordingly, the conversation

---

[52] On the mermaid as 'the quintessential figure for poetry', see de Vroom, 'Mediating Myth' 437.

[53] See Witmore, *Culture of Accidents*, on Ophelia's death as 'coded ... artificial when it is delivered in an elegy, a formal piece of verse that stands out from the rest of the play as a kind of miniature of craft' (190n59). *The Return from Parnassus* alertly records Spenser's use of the waterfall as his signature trope: 'the waters fall he tun'd for fame, / And in each barke engrav'd Elizaes name' (7: 279–80). See Spenser, *Apr* 33–6; *June* 7–8; *Aug* 153–6; *Dec* 1–4; and the woodcuts to *Apr* and *Dec*.

[54] The following discussion departs from Gross's engaging emphasis on 'The Rumor in *Hamlet*' (chapter title in *Shakespeare's Noise*); and allies itself with Fernie, 'Last Act', esp. Fernie's emphasis on 'eschatological presentism' (188) and 'the novel spirituality of immanence that *Hamlet* develops' (201).

between the two Clowns foregrounds the concept of a 'profession'. The first mentioned is 'Adam's profession', which the 'grave-makers ... hold up': 'The Scripture says Adam digg'd' (30–7). From this inaugural profession, the Clowns mention a whole host of professions: that of the coroner, the gardener, the gallows-maker, the mason, the shipwright, and the carpenter, but also the courtier, the lawyer, the tanner, the doctor, the emperor, and finally the jester. The Clowns also assign an action to the profession, which they identify as *making*. Thus, the answer to the First Clown's riddle, 'Who builds stronger than a mason, a ship-wright, or a carpenter' (50–1), is ' "a gravemaker": the houses he makes lasts till doomsday' (58–9).

The scene in the cemetery also meditates deeply on lyric poetry, represented in the Gravemaker's songs, and on theatre, represented in the Gravemaker's and Hamlet's recollections of the court jester, Yorick. Since the Gravemaker is a maker of both graves and songs, he is a gravemaker-poet, and accordingly he throws up a self-image. 'That skull had a tongue in it, and could sing once', says Hamlet of Yorick's skull (75–6). This is not just any skull, not just a *memento mori*; it is an icon of the poet's death. Yet this bony lyric singer was once also 'the King's jester' (181), a performer – Elsinore's theatrical man:

Alas, poor Yorick! I knew him, Horatio, a fellow of infinite jest, of most excellent fancy ... Where be your gibes now, your gambols, your songs, your flashes of merriment, that were wont to set the table on a roar? (*Hamlet* 5.1.184–91)

As with Feste in *Twelfth Night* or the Fool in *King Lear*, Shakespeare presents Yorick as a poet-playwright figure, whose songs express 'flashes of merriment', himself a performer of 'gibes' and 'gambols'.

Yet for the first time in the play Shakespeare does not rely on the performance of lyric song to express madness in its association with death. Now song expresses a wry merriment about the prospect of 'Christian burial' and 'salvation' (1–2). While the contents of the Gravemaker's song meditate on the question of death, they do so in a robust voice emanating confidence:

> 'In youth when I did love, did love,
>   Methought it was very sweet,
> To contract – O – the time for – a – my behove,
>   O, methought there – a – was nothing – a – meet.
> ...
> 'But age with his stealing steps
>   Hath clawed me in his clutch,
> And hath shipped me into the land,

As if I had never been such.

…

'A pickaxe and a spade, a spade,
   For and a shrouding sheet:
O, a pit of clay for to be made
   For such a guest is meet'.   (*Hamlet* 5.1.61–97)

This song is a 'garbled version of a poem by Thomas Lord Vaux, entitled 'The Aged Lover Renounceth Love', first printed in *Tottel's Miscellany* in 1557 (*Riverside* 1226). It traces the lover's life from an idealistic youth eager for love to an aged man clawed by death. Yet at the end the song reaches a balanced resignation about this sad, mortal fate: it is 'meet' that our decaying body should be buried in a 'pit of clay'.[55] Shakespeare reiterates this robust resignation when the Gravemaker sings the last two lines as his refrain (120–1). What seems unusual is Shakespeare's evident urge in this deeply religious scene to get a private lyric poem from the English past on to the stage, in a play that would be printed in quarto and folio editions for the reading public. Rather than locate authorship simply in the tragic hero, *Hamlet* disperses authorship across a wide spectrum not merely of gender but also of class.[56]

During Act 5, scene 1, in the last lines Hamlet utters before the funeral procession enters, the Prince shifts out of prose to produce a *second* poem, another four-line verse, this time in rhymed couplets:

Imperious Caesar, dead and turn'd to clay,
Might stop a hole to keep the wind away.
O that that earth which kept the world in awe
Should patch a wall t' expel the [winter's] flaw.

         (*Hamlet* 5.1.213–16)

In terms similar to those of the Gravemaker, Hamlet registers his primary understanding about the body's end. Even dust from the body of Julius Caesar is destined to plug up the hole in a beer barrel. In a poem, in other words, Hamlet summarizes what he learns in this bony locale: the human body is destined for dust. Whether Alexander or the jester Yorick, we are going to die. It is out of this stark recognition that Hamlet plucks his final discovery, recorded in the spiritual affirmations of the final scene.

Momentously, Act 5, scene 2, crafts out the defining features of the play's model for the new mind of Europe. We may discern the coordinates of this

---

[55] On Shakespeare's 'significant changes in meaning' to Vaux's lyric, see Jenkins, ed. 550.
[56] On the Gravemaker not as a republican poet but as an egalitarian philosopher, see Bristol, ' "Funeral Bak'd Meats" '.

model by taking the cue of the Gravemaker: the songs he makes last 'till doomsday'. According to this lyric performer, human artistic making on the tragic topic of death lasts 'till doomsday' – but evidently not beyond.[57]

The Gravemaker's profession bears uncanny resemblance to that of the poet, as identified in Sonnet 55, when Will says to the young man,

> Not marble nor the gilded [monuments]
> Of princes shall outlive this pow'rful rhyme,
> But you shall shine more bright in these contents
> Than unswept stone, besmear'd with sluttish time.
> When wasteful war shall statues overturn,
> And broils root out the work of masonry,
> Nor Mars his sword nor war's quick fire shall burn
> The living record of your memory.
> 'Gainst death and all-oblivious enmity
> Shall you pace forth; your praise shall still find room,
> Even in the eyes of all posterity
> That wear this world out to the ending doom.
>   So till the judgment that yourself arise,
>   You live in this, and dwell in lovers' eyes.   (Sonnet 55)

Lines 1–11 clearly voice a classical idea of literary fame, derived from Virgil and Ovid: the poet can make the individual famous along a *horizontal* axis: on earth, in time, 'in the eyes of posterity'.[58] Yet lines 12–13 clearly insert an Augustinian model of immortality, or Christian glory, referring not once but twice to the Christian endpoint of human history, the Last Judgment. In this Christian model, Christ can make the individual immortal along a vertical axis: not on earth but in heaven, not in time but in eternity, not in the eyes of posterity but in the eyes of God, the Virgin, and the Saints.[59] Sonnet 55, however, inserts the distinct presence of a *third* model, which we might call Shakespearean. This model differs from the classical one because it includes the Christian endpoint, yet it differs from the Christian model

---

[57] De Grazia, '*Hamlet' without Hamlet*, includes a chapter titled 'Doomsday and Domain' (129–57), but she does not do much with the Last Judgment (140–2). She does emphasize 'the eschatological setting' of Act 5, concluding that 'the graveyard scene conjoins concern about Last Things with issues of entitlement' (142), and arguing that 'Domain looms large in the shadow of Doomsday' (156).

[58] Critics writing on Sonnet 55 almost always see no more than a classical model of fame. See, e.g., Leishman, *Themes and Variations in Shakespeare's Sonnets* 22. Recently, Greenblatt ends *Purgatory* with a note on 'the afterlife' in Sonnet 55: 'We know that he [Shakespeare] entertained the idea of posthumous existence ... Through the incantatory power of the poet's verse, the fair young man will defy mortality and walk the earth' (313n1). Similarly, in 'Ovid, Petrarch, and Shakespeare's Sonnets', Braden discusses Sonnet 55 only through the notion of 'poetry's ability to defy time' (108).

[59] On classical fame and Christian glory, see Cheney, *Spenser's Famous Flight* 7–10, following Braudy, *Frenzy of Renown*.

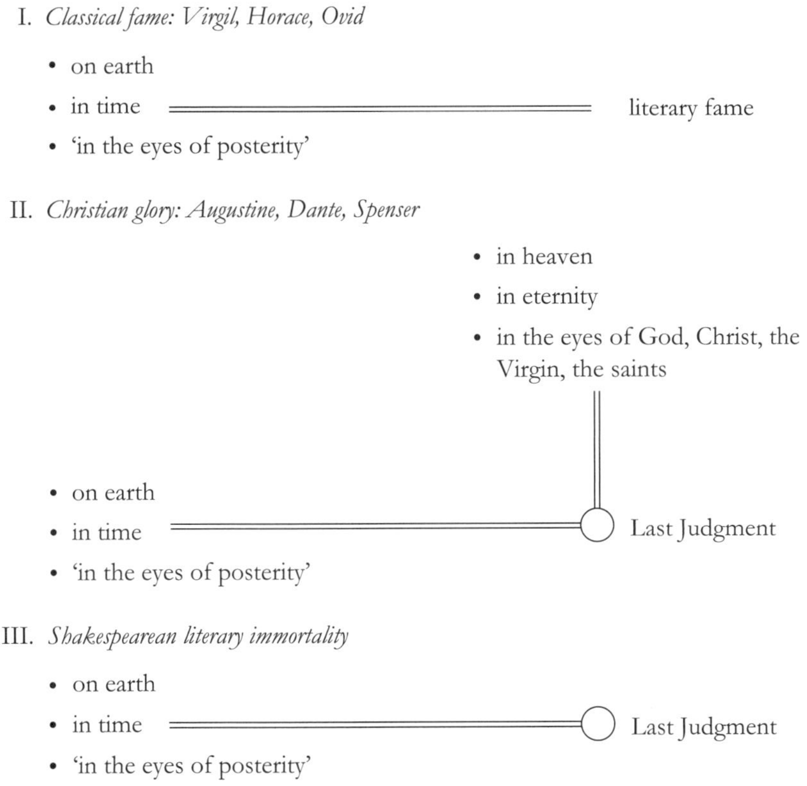

I. *Classical fame: Virgil, Horace, Ovid*

- on earth
- in time ═══════════════════════════════════ literary fame
- 'in the eyes of posterity'

II. *Christian glory: Augustine, Dante, Spenser*

- in heaven
- in eternity
- in the eyes of God, Christ, the Virgin, the saints

- on earth
- in time ═══════════════════════════════════○ Last Judgment
- 'in the eyes of posterity'

III. *Shakespearean literary immortality*

- on earth
- in time ═══════════════════════════════════○ Last Judgment
- 'in the eyes of posterity'

Figure 9. The Shakespearean literary eternal

because it does not go beyond that endpoint. If we look carefully, in the Shakespearean model of fame we witness a virtual *blackout* along the *Christian vertical* (see Figure 9).[60]

Whereas Virgil and Ovid vaunted poetry's power to secure fame along a horizontal axis, both Dante and Spenser vaunted poetry's power to secure Christian glory along a vertical axis.[61] By contrast, Shakespeare appears to craft out an intermediate space and power for poetry, between Virgilian earthly fame and Spenserian Christian glory. Shakespeare's poetry cannot get the individual into heaven to secure grace and salvation, but it can get

---

[60] The word 'arise' in line 13 is the only gesture to the moment of resurrection, but the gesture remains characteristically oblique.
[61] On how Sonnet 55 responds to Spenser, see Hieatt, 'Genesis of Shakespeare's Sonnets' 807–8.

the individual *to* 'the ending doom'. The conceit of an art that can sound to the Day of Judgment occurs in a related form throughout the Shakespeare canon, in both poems and plays, including three times in the Sonnets.[62] In the history of fame, Shakespeare's tiny words 'to' and 'till' acquire dramatic significance, bridging the relation between classical Virgilian fame and Spenserian Christian glory. Will dramatically writes a verse in which the young man steps forth with great authority in the eyes of posterity 'to' the 'ending doom' – 'till' the 'judgment'. Shakespeare is not as bold as Dante or Spenser, but he is bolder than Virgil or Ovid. The final telos of Shakespearean poetry, we may speculate, is to prepare the individual's soul for such a momentous occasion. This may well be the 'promised end' (*KL* 5.3.264) of Shakespeare's profession of consciousness, not merely in the Sonnets but in *Hamlet*, and beyond.[63]

Only by understanding Shakespeare's staging of the limitations and breakdown of Catholic external authority, Protestant internal authority, and the bridging power of theatre as the art of conscience, and finally 'godlike reason' itself (4.4.38), can we prepare ourselves to see Shakespeare's major staging in this play: 'I do not know / Why yet I live to say, "This thing's to do"' (4.4.43–4). When Hamlet leaves Denmark, he charts unknown intellectual and spiritual waters, beyond the known limits, in the wake of the primary cultural authorities available to sixteenth-century individuals. All of the available voices, wisdoms, authorities, and institutions have failed him. He is now fully on his own, truly alienated, not just from the world of Elsinore but from the sum of Western religion, philosophy, and art.

On the sea voyage, for the first time in the play Hamlet *abandons his will*, his *agency*, and 'give[s] himself up to destiny':[64] 'There's a divinity that shapes our ends, / Rough-hew them how we will' (5.2.10–11). Instead of trying to control his destiny through learning and will, Hamlet submits his learning and will to destiny. His experience on the sea voyage is the perfect vehicle for this event, because Hamlet is not the pilot of the ship but its

---

[62] Sonnet 116.12 and 122.4, as well as, e.g., *RL* 924; *LLL* 4.3.270; *R3* 3.1.78; *H5* 4.1.137. See esp. Wittreich, '"Image of That Horror"'; Lascelles, '*King Lear* and Doomsday'. On the Last Judgment in the romances, see Marshall, *Last Things and Last Plays*. To my knowledge, critics do not discuss the Last Judgment and authorship.

[63] The words 'to' and 'till' indicate that Shakespeare imagines the decisive event of consciousness to be the moment when eternity intersects with time, as if he wishes us to understand that the event is always occurring, or always possible. For prompting this thought, thanks to Ewan Fernie, who sees the 'Shakespearean metaphysics' foregrounding 'the potentially infinite fullness of any embodied moment', with 'human life fully triggered and fulfilled in the cross-hairs' of time and eternity (personal communication).

[64] Coleridge, *Lectures*, in Hubler, ed., *Ham* 194. Cf. Bradley's 'fatalism' (*Shakespearean Tragedy* 116).

imprisoned passenger. And yet through 'rashness' (5.2.7) he discovers Claudius' plot to have him murdered, and is set free when pirates capture the ship.

Back home in Denmark, he makes a brilliant discovery. During his conversation with Horatio before the fencing match, he moves beyond Christian conscience as the arbiter of faith:

> Not a whit, we defy augury. There is special providence in the fall of a sparrow. If it be [now], 'tis not to come; if it be not to come, it will be now; if it be not now, yet it [will] come – the readiness is all. Since no man, of aught he leaves, knows what is't to leave betimes, let be. (*Hamlet* 5.2.219–24)

The 'augury' Hamlet defies is conscience itself, mentioned last when he tells Horatio of Rosencrantz and Guildenstern, 'They are not near my conscience' (58), and subsequently when he asks about Claudius: 'is't not perfect conscience / [To quit him with this arm?]' (67–8). In place of conscience as the shield to corruption, Hamlet discovers that the individual needs to make his mind *ready* for death, and use his remaining time on earth to scour out his interior faculty in preparation for the crushing event of annihilation. *Not ready for resurrection, but ready for death.* Hamlet reroutes spiritual preparedness from the mind's fixation on the next life to this one. The sum of such intellectual preparedness is: 'Let be.'

This phrase is a profound articulation, hard to capture. Hamlet has just used a technical Christian phrase, 'special providence', yet he goes on to voice a thought that critics often label as secular.[65] Initially, the phrase 'Let be' grants final authority to some mysterious, faceless divinity that shapes our ends, rough-hew them how we will. Yet finally that divinity operates tragically against the individual, as an occult external force: the 'special providence' is only about the individual's 'fall'. If we look carefully, by *letting be*, Hamlet turns away from worrying about an external force of annihilation to concentrate on his mind, his inward character, his subjectivity: his profession of consciousness.

---

[65] Bloom calls the concept 'quietism', 'disinterestednous' (*Shakespeare: the Invention of the Human* 428–9). Lander, *Inventing Polemic*, traces Hamlet's 'disinterestedness' to R. G. Hunter, *Shakespeare and the Mystery of God's Judgments*: 'It is precisely this distinterestedness, Hunter insists, that guarantees the play's status as art: not an "imaginative presentation of theology", *Hamlet* is the realization of Shakespeare's "artistic purposes" ' (Lander 140). See also Fernie 199, 201, 204–5. Watson observes: it 'looks less like a happy declaration of faith than like an agnostic yielding to fate' (*Rest is Silence* 93). The more recent work of Trevor, *Poetics of Melancholy*, supports this line of thought by seeing Shakespeare in *Hamlet* distancing himself from 'the Neoplatonism of Spenser' through 'the decidedly materialist [Galenic] outlook of the Prince' (64).

The rest is silence. Death *is* annihilation, writes Robert N. Watson (book title), and this is what Hamlet comes to see. Yet Shakespeare presents the Prince as concentrating on an internal process for beating death, discovering it in his ability to ready his psyche for annihilation, and then to act out his readiness theatrically.[66]

Not merely does Shakespeare usher his 'audience' into a new modern era. He ushers his fellow writers into a new modern era of authorship. This model combines poetry with theatre, but also human agency with something like *cosmic construction*. The whole project aims to help authors and audiences learn to live with 'purposes mistook / Fall'n on th' inventors' heads' (5.2.384–5): with a life beyond agency, in a distracted globe.

No fewer than three times in his final seconds Hamlet uses language to prepare for such a state by committing himself to a literary rather than to a Christian afterlife:

> Report me and my cause aright
> To the unsatisfied.   (*Hamlet* 5.2.338–9)

> O God, Horatio, what a wounded name,
> Things standing thus unknown, shall I leave behind me.
>   (*Hamlet* 5.2.344–5)

> And in this harsh world draw thy breath in pain
> To tell my story.   (*Hamlet* 5.2.348–9)

In his dying moment, Hamlet's use of the word 'story' to designate his preferred form of legacy should give us pause. He does not tell Horatio, 'Perform my play', just as he does not say, 'Read my poem'. The word 'story' appears to lift free of the poetry-theatre model, to designate a purely *narratival* afterlife. Yet recent work on narrative in both Shakespeare's plays and his poems suggests that the term 'story' may well be a veritable bridge between poetry and theatre, a formal avenue for both.[67]

While *Hamlet* does not explicitly end his life by locating the narrative profession of literary consciousness at the crossroads of classical fame and Christian glory, the way *King Lear* and *Antony and Cleopatra* will go on to do, *Hamlet* does include five further references to the Last Judgment.[68] Moreover, when Horatio offsets Hamlet's narratival, literary profession of

---

[66] Neill, *Issues of Death*, emphasizes the late sixteenth-century English turn to theatre and performance 'to render oneself immune to the unshaping hand of death' (36).

[67] See, e.g., Dubrow, ' "These So Differing Twins" '. On 'Hamlet's story', see Lee 205–8. Watson emphasizes Hamlet's compulsion to turn his life into a 'story', a 'dramatic work of art', which can be infinitely 'repeatable' (96).

[68] *Ham* 1.1.118–20; 2.2.238; 3.4.48–51; 3.4.52–53; 5.1.59.

consciousness with the Christian model of grace and salvation, few believe we have reached the promised end: 'Good night, sweet prince, / And flights of angels sing thee to thy rest' (359–60).

Rather, *The Tragedy of Hamlet* inaugurates a bold new model of identity in which literary art – plays as well as poems – prepares human consciousness for the Christian Last Judgment. Shakespeare uses books, poetry, and theatre to make a case for the cultural, spiritual utility of his own art in the formation of early modern identity. In this tragedy, the author charts new psychic and spiritual territory: a new 'bourn' of the literary eternal (3.1.78).[69]

---

[69] In *Culture of Accidents*, Witmore emphasizes the play's 'structural … identity' between 'theatrical and providential consciousness' (106).

CHAPTER 8

Venting rhyme for a mockery: Cymbeline and national romance

> Will you rhyme upon't,
> And vent it for a mock'ry?   *Cymbeline* 5.3.55–6

After *Hamlet*, Shakespeare produces several world-class plays, reaching an artistic apex no doubt in *King Lear*, but every one of them experiments with and extends the literary authorship traced in this book. To look in on this authorship during the late or mythic phase of his career, we may turn to a romance that intersects remarkably with the other three plays we have examined in Part II. Recognizing that the intersections are legion, for a technical reason to be explained presently, we might start by noting that *Cymbeline* shares with *Hamlet* a male protagonist who chases the title of national theatrical poet into unusual apocalyptic territory, obsessed with the boundary between inner and outer; with *Much Ado about Nothing*, a stunning portrait of the resurrected female, who herself becomes an icon of national literary form; and, perhaps most remarkable of all, with *2 Henry VI*, an originary, contested site of English or British nationalism, Milford Haven.[1]

Cymbeline helps conclude a study of Shakespeare's literary authorship – his historic role as national poet-playwright – because it is the only late romance set formally in Britain. It therefore affords a unique opportunity to wed the political topic of nationalism to the literary topic of romance, especially since late in his career Shakespeare re-scripts this emergent stage-genre by fusing a discourse of theatre to a discourse of poetry.

Indeed, the epigraph to this chapter comes from a curious speech toward the end of *Cymbeline* about the theatrical art of poetry. Posthumus is replying to the Britain Lord about 'a strange chance' that has just occurred;

---

[1] Not simply is Milford Haven the climactic site of battle and resolution at the end of *Cymbeline*, it is also the landing harbor for Henry Tudor's triumphant return to England – the endpoint, in other words, of Shakespeare's first historical tetralogy (*R3* 4.4.532–4). On this dual dynamic of Milford Haven, see Sullivan, *Drama of Landscape* 135–7.

as the Lord himself narrates the event, 'A narrow lane, an old man, and two boys!' (5.3.52). He refers to Belarius, Guiderius, and Arviragus, in disguise as the cave-dweller Morgan and his two rustic sons, who have just marshaled considerable courage and prowess to rescue the British king, Cymbeline, from defeat by the Roman army. 'Nay, do not wonder at it' (53), Posthumus tells the Lord,

> you are made
> Rather to wonder at the things you hear
> Than to work any. Will you rhyme upon't,
> And vent it for a mock'ry? Here is one.   (*Cymbeline* 5.3.53–6)

He then extemporizes a two-line rhymed couplet, turning the 'strange' event into a miniature work of poetic art: '"Two boys, an old man (twice a boy), a lane, / Preserv'd the Britains, was the Romans' bane"' (57–8).

Posthumus performs this rhyme with fierce gusto, for the Lord responds by saying, 'Nay, be not angry, sir' (59), prompting Posthumus to continue his rage – in more rhymed couplets:

> 'Lack, to what end?
> Who dares not stand his foe, I'll be his friend;
> For if he'll do as he is made to do,
> I know he'll quickly fly my friendship too.
> You have put me into rhyme.   (*Cymbeline* 5.3.59–63)

Seeing that Posthumus continues to be 'angry', the Lord bids him 'farewell' (63). Left alone, Posthumus changes back into 'Roman costume',[2] intimating his interest in Hamlet-like theatricality: 'I have resum'd again / The part I came in' (75–6).

This scene is brief – it lasts only a few lines – but I would argue that it is paradigmatic, for *Cymbeline* as for the Shakespeare canon as a whole, because it self-consciously performs a fiction of authorship – in particular, of the theatrical art of poetry – and does so in bizarre fashion.[3] We shall return to the details of the scene later, but for now we may intimate its significance for a reappraisal of Shakespeare's role as an early modern author at the end of his career.

Partial grounds for this reappraisal emerge in Frank Kermode's recent spur to action: 'Every other aspect of Shakespeare is studied almost to death, but the fact that he was a poet has somehow dropped out of consideration.'[4]

---

[2] SD after line 73, in Butler, ed. 213.
[3] Cf. Palfrey, *Late Shakespeare*, for a de-idealizing approach to the play that eloquently matches its weirdness.
[4] Kermode, *Shakespeare's Language* vii.

By 'poet', Kermode means 'dramatic poet' or 'theatre poet', the author of 'dramatic verse' within plays for the London theatre (vii). Not surprisingly, when Kermode briefly examines *Cymbeline*, he focuses on its 'verse', which occasionally he finds 'venerated' (264) and 'rapt' (269) but most often 'overworked' and even 'over the top' (264), 'riddled with inexplicable complexities' (265). Yet Kermode does recall a second way in which we can consider Shakespeare a 'poet', even as he sidesteps it: 'He was an accomplished nondramatic poet, but his eminence depends on his work for the theatre' (vii). Once more, we need to pause over Shakespeare's accomplishment as a 'nondramatic poet', for right when Kermode was offering his reappraisal (in 2000), Shakespeare studies was entering a new phase of scholarship, signaled by a remarkable surge of editions, articles, and even monographs – not on Shakespeare's 'dramatic verse' but on his 'non-dramatic poe[ms]' (*SNPP* 4).

Cymbeline, I suggest, offers a bridging *third* way to speak of Shakespeare as a poet. Toward the end of his theatrical career, around 1609–10, when scholars think he wrote this dramatic romance, he uses the London stage to rehearse an important conversation about the art of poetry: its invention, its circulation, and its final effect, whether expressed as a form of spectral 'wonder' or as a form of redemptive work on behalf of 'Britain'. That is, if we look carefully at Posthumus' speech, we see that Shakespeare does not sever the art of poetry from the art of theatre but rather uses language to represent their interpenetration. Thus, Posthumus' question to a Lord from 'Britain', 'Will you rhyme upon't, / And vent it for a mock'ry', functions as a metonym for Shakespeare's signature mocking of national art – what we have called his counter-laureate authorship.

The word *vent* is a loaded term, meaning primarily 'To ... publish or spread abroad, by or as by utterance' (*OED*, Def. 5b); but it could also mean 'To give vent to (an emotion, feeling, passion, etc.)' (Def. 4a). The word derives from the Latin word for *wind*, *ventus*, so that the sense here (as often in Shakespeare) is 'literally "given out to the air"'.[5] As we shall see, the word *air* is important to the topic of poetry in this play, for it is at once a physiological, a meteorological, and finally a musical term. By contrast, the word *mockery* means 'Mimicry, imitation; a deceptive or counterfeit representation of something' (*OED*, Def. 3), and is one of Shakespeare's most intriguing (and recurrent) terms for theatre.[6] Thus, Posthumus asks

---

[5] Warren, ed. 228.

[6] As the Chorus to Act 4 of *Henry V* tells the audience, 'sit and see, / Minding true things by what their mock'ries be' (52–3). See also *Mac* 1.7.81; *WT* 5.3.18–20. As a formal term for a broader representational aesthetics, see *Tim* 1.1.36. For a fuller inventory of the various meanings of *mock*, see Crystal and Crystal, *Shakespeare's Words* 284.

the Britain Lord whether he will publish or perform the 'rhyme' with emotion. He draws our attention to the passions as at once the originator and the topic of (Shakespearean) poetry and theatre, as he speaks to the consonance between the performance of plays and the publication of verse.[7]

Cymbeline has been singled out as a unique work in the Shakespeare canon, but one neglected feature of its uniqueness lies in its extraordinarily detailed staging of the art of poetry late in the playwright's career.[8] To pursue the significance of this phenomenon, we may look at five principal scenes of poetry:

(1) the domestic scene of Imogen's bedchamber at 2.2 and 2.4, with its references to three central Ovidian myths (Philomela and Tereus, Lucrece and Tarquin, Diana and Actaeon), as well as a story from Plutarch that shows up briefly at the end of the *Metamorphoses*, that of Cleopatra and Antony;[9]

(2) the counter-domestic scene of Cloten and the musicians, including the incomparable lyric song 'Hark, hark, the lark at heaven's gate sings' (20);

(3) the pastoral scene of Arviragus and Guiderius singing another astonishing lyric song, 'Fear no more' (4.2.258), over the seemingly dead body of Imogen, followed immediately by Imogen's gripping counter-Petrarchan blazon on the headless corpse of Cloten;

(4) the scene foregrounded in the epigraph, between Posthumus and the Britain Lord about venting the rhyme for mockery; and

(5) the climactic scene of religious miracle, Posthumus' divinely produced dream of the Leonati – which we might imagine as the play's most spectacular fusion of the art of poetry to the art of theatre.

These scenes unfold an unusually rich representational conversation, focusing on questions of gender, art, performance, and theology, yet all funneled into the topic of nationalism. The final speech of the play, spoken by Cymbeline himself, rehearses the seminal word at issue in this whole conversation, as intimated in Posthumus' exchange with the Britain Lord, and formally resurrected from the last stanza of *The Rape of Lucrece* (1852): '*Publish* we this peace / To all our subjects' (5.5.478–9; emphasis added).[10]

---

[7] On *publish* meaning not merely *proclaim* but also *put in print*, see Barkan, *Gods Made Flesh* 347n8. Critics occasionally discuss 'books' in *Cymbeline* (e.g., Belsey, *Shakespeare and the Loss of Eden* 48–57), but they tend to emphasize 'Theatricality' (see Warren, ed. 1–15). R. King, *Cymbeline*, says she focuses on 'Shakespeare's skill as a dramatist rather than a poet' (3).

[8] Cf. Thorne, '"To Write and Read"', who examines Shakespeare's fiction of 'misreading' (185).

[9] Butler believes that Shakespeare called Imogen 'Innogen' (ed. 36). I retain 'Imogen' because the *Riverside* uses this traditional spelling. The same applies to other names, such as Iachimo (rather than Giacomo, adopted by Warren).

[10] On 'publish' in *Lucrece*, see *SNPP* 108–13.

As in the narrative poem at the beginning of his career, in this play at the end Shakespeare still broods over the very question of publication that continues to divide critics today, performed originally before an audience that could have included King James: what is the supreme theatrical man's attitude toward his nascent print culture? Or, to put the question so that we can reasonably address it: what attitude are we to take toward the representation of print in Shakespeare's plays?[11]

The above analysis of *Cymbeline* will allow us to select a final scene in this late national romance to conclude the present book: Imogen's conversation with Pisano about her plan for reuniting with Posthumus at Milford Haven. The conversation turns out to be about 'Britain', but it also combines an ancient trope for lyric poetry, the discourse of print culture, and theatre, and so forms a memorable miniature of Shakespeare's literary authorship near its close.

COUNTER-LAUREATE INTERTEXTUALITY/INTRATEXTUALITY

Critics have identified *Cymbeline* as the most perplexing play in the Shakespeare canon. It mixes various genres in seemingly gratuitous ways (comedy, tragedy, romance, along with pastoral and epic); it stages time-bending juxtapositions of national locale (ancient Britain and early modern Britain; ancient Rome and early modern Italy); it constructs a disunified plot through writing that critics find uneven; it relies on very odd characterization (especially the Queen, but also Cloten, Iachimo, Posthumus, and of course Cymbeline himself); it expresses irritation at contemporary society, especially British and Italian 'gentlemen'; it voices moments of fierce misogyny; and it yokes the grotesque and the lovely in unsettling ways. All of this perplexity (and more) has resulted in uncertainty about just how to place this work within Shakespeare's larger canon.[12]

[11] Underwriting this argument is Butler's 2005 Cambridge edition, which draws the following conclusions. Shakespeare most likely wrote the play 'either in May/June 1610 or shortly thereafter' (ed. 6). The play was first performed 'in December 1610, followed by a court performance in the Christmas season 1610–11' (ed. 6). The play exists only in the 1623 First Folio, and 'evidence points towards a literary transcript and has little to suggest preparation for playhouse use' (ed. 255), with further 'evidence of fossilized verbal revision' (ed. 263): 'revision must have taken place before the play was staged, since the performed version would have needed some technical adjustments and cutting' (ed. 264). Finally, '*Cymbeline*'s kingly families, masque-like revelations and praise of imperial peace make it seem more directly engaged with the circumstances of the new reign [of King James I] than any other [Shakespeare] play' (ed. 2).
[12] For instance, the usually sublime Bloom cannot conceal his irritation: 'Something … is askew in *Cymbeline* … The miasma of fatigue and disgust that hovers on the edges of the high tragedies and the problem comedies has drifted to the center of *Cymbeline*' (*Shakespeare: The Invention of the Human* 615–21).

For a play that scholars now believe Shakespeare wrote without a collaborator, *Cymbeline* exhibits a lot of problems; it may even be over the top. Yet that has not prevented critics from invading the play, especially during the past fifteen years, when most agree that '*Cymbeline* was produced by a dramatist working at the height of his powers' (Butler, ed. 1). Psychoanalytical critics fix on the 'phantasy' element.[13] Feminists attend to gender and sexuality.[14] Performance critics concentrate on theatricality.[15] And, most notably of late, historical critics probe nationalism, historiography, race, and geography.[16]

While all of these approaches have been important, we might organize them under a rubric that critics surprisingly neglect: authorship. When critics do mention the 'authorial', they tend to mean *Shakespeare the man*, the flesh and blood individual who possessed 'consciousness' between 1564 and 1616 and who (around 1610) produced a play of genuine perplexity – so much so that here he lapses into '[a]uthorial self-parody'.[17] While agreeing that *Cymbeline* is an unusual play, we might find a final occasion in it to redefine the authorial, not strictly as the biographical but also as the literary, and come to see its weirdness as one of Shakespeare's most visceral representations of counter-laureate authorship.

The notion of counter-laureate authorship helps account for the parodic cultural work that critics find *Cymbeline* performing: both detachment from the corruption of James's court and affirmation of a new national dispensation, modeled on the visionary poetics of Sidney and Spenser.[18] In *Cymbeline*, Shakespeare invents a strange art that subjects his canon to a

---

[13] See Adelman, *Suffocating Mothers* 193–38; Skura, 'Interpreting Posthumus' Dream from Above and Below'. For fantasy and empire, see Marshall, '*Cymbeline*: A Modern Perspective'. See also E. R. Sanders, 'Interiority and the Letter in *Cymbeline*'.

[14] Belsey, *Loss of Eden* 55–84; Wayne, 'Woman's Parts of *Cymbeline*'; Butler, ed. 24–36. The boundaries between the various types of criticism are at times not clear-cut, as the case of Adelman's feminist psychoanalytic approach testifies.

[15] Wayne, '*Cymbeline*: Patriotism and Performance'; Brockbank, 'History and Histrionics in *Cymbeline*'.

[16] Several of the following studies could nestle comfortably under the other critical approaches: R. King, '*Cymbeline*': Constructions of Britain; Griffiths, 'Geographies of *Cymbeline*'; Hadfield, *Shakespeare, Spenser, and the Matter of Britain* 160–8; Floyd-Wilson, *English Ethnicity and Race in Early Modern Drama* 161–83; Boling, 'Anglo-Welsh Relations in *Cymbeline*'; Redmond, '"My Lord, 1 Fear"'; Sullivan, *Drama of Landscape* 127–58; Mikalachki, *Legacy of Boadicea* 96–114; Jordan, *Shakespeare's Monarchies* 69–106; James, *Shakespeare's Troy* 151–88; Curran, 'Royalty Unlearned, Honor Untaught'; Parker, 'Romance and Empire'; Marcus, *Puzzling Shakespeare* 106–48; Miola, '*Cymbeline*: Shakespeare's Valediction to Rome'.

[17] Bloom 622. See also Kermode 266.

[18] For a version of the dual political vision, see James 152. In 'Cloten, Autolycus, and Caliban', Hartwig introduces parody to *Cymbeline* criticism (93–4), reminding us that the word *parody* during the Renaissance is a term from both theatre and lyric poetry: 'In Greek drama, the "parode" referred to a

powerful critique and sets its own self-effacement off as a *tour de force*: the scenes of poetry parody the art of poetry; they *vent rhyme for a mockery*. To attend to these scenes is to become attuned to the harmony of poetry, and its trauma; its power to idealize, and its failure; its authority to heal, and its impotence: in short, to discover a strange poetic space countering the disruptions of tragedy and in the process to invent a new form of national romance.[19]

As we have seen in previous chapters, the keystone to Shakespeare's counter-laureate authorship lies in his principle of extemporal inter-textuality. In *Cymbeline*, we can track this principle as before, through Shakespeare's engagement with classical and English authors who write the nation in an especially challenging way: Virgil and Ovid from antiq-uity; and Spenser and Marlowe from early modern England.[20]

Thus, in *Cymbeline* we can account for the remarkable concentration of poetry – especially poetry yoked with theatre – as a register of Shakespeare's ongoing predicament as an author. He continues to transact the complex exigencies of his theatrical profession while maintaining an interlocking interest in a literary career, including printed poetry. Critics routinely discuss the Ovidianism of Imogen's bedchamber, and they trace the matter of Britain to Shakespeare's equally acute Virgilianism.[21] Not surprisingly, critics tend to see in this romance the presence of Spenser. Usually, they recall that Spenser, like Geoffrey of Monmouth and Holinshed, narrates the Cymbeline story (*FQ* 2.10.50–2), and occasionally they introduce specific moments of intertextuality. Most recently, Martin Butler writes that the 1609 publication of *The Faerie Queene* 'affected Shakespeare profoundly', and not merely in *The Winter's Tale*: in *Cymbeline*, 'Spenser's presence is most directly felt in the Welsh scenes [of hard pastoral], which explore the antithesis between court and country in a manner very reminiscent of Book 6, the legend of courtesy' (ed. 11–12).[22] Observing that Spenser became attractive to disaffected intellectuals at James's court, Butler reminds us that

side entrance into the orchestra, as well as to the "first ode sung by the chorus after entrance" (*OED*)' (93). On 'Sidney and Spenser' in *Cymbeline*, see Butler's unit by this title (ed. 10–13) – the first in an edition of the play.

[19] On 'Tragedy and tragicomedy', see Butler, ed. 15–24. On 'Romance', see Warren, ed. 15–18; on 'Dramatic Romance', see Butler, ed. 13–15.

[20] James notes that 'Shakespeare's project in *Cymbeline* is particularly compatible with' Helgerson's model, in *Forms of Nationhood*, 'about the importance of literary form to the construction or "writing" of English nationhood' (252n1).

[21] On Ovid, see Barkan, *Gods Made Flesh* 247–51; Martindale and Martindale, *Shakespeare and the Uses of Antiquity* 54–6; J. Bate, *Ovid* 215–19; Belsey, *Loss of Eden* 55–6; Lyne, *Ovid's Changing Worlds* 265–7. On Virgil, see esp. Parker; James.

[22] I am grateful to Professor Butler for sharing his unit on Spenser with me before his edition was published. Usefully, he speaks of 'Spenserian dramaturgy' in the pastoral scenes (ed. 12).

the great Elizabethan poet of epic romance relied on a politics locating courtly critique within an affirmative visionary poetics (ed. 12–13). Less often, critics find Marlowe lurking in the play.[23]

Complementing the play's intertextuality is its much-discussed *intratextuality* – Shakespeare's engagement with his own work. Long ago, Harold C. Goddard called *Cymbeline* 'Shakespeare's most recapitulatory play' (*Meaning of Shakespeare* 2: 245), and recent critics agree.[24] Repeatedly, they link the play's theme of the jealous husband with *Othello* and *The Winter's Tale*; the courageous heroine in disguise as a male, with *Two Gentlemen of Verona*, *The Merchant of Venice*, *As You Like It*, and *Twelfth Night*; the matter of Britain, with *King Lear*, *Macbeth*, and the English history plays; the matter of Troy and Rome, with *Titus Andronicus*, *Julius Caesar*, *Antony and Cleopatra*, and *Coriolanus*; and the marvel and romance, with *Pericles* and *The Winter's Tale*. Thus, critics often see Imogen recapitulating Julia, Portia, Rosalind, and Viola, as well as Lavinia, Juliet, and Beatrice; with Posthumus recapitulating Othello and Leontes, Iachimo replaying Proteus, Iago, and Edmund, and Cymbeline remembering a long line of English or British kings, from Henry IV, V, and VI through Lear and Macbeth. Important to the present argument, *Cymbeline* is often seen recapitulating the Ovidian myths of the Athenian princess Philomela and the Roman matron Lucretia, who figure prominently in both *Titus* and *Lucrece*.

From this scholarship, we may draw the following inferences. First, *Cymbeline*'s unusual memory of previous Shakespearean works identifies it as a play about Shakespearean authorship. Second, the recapitulatory mode, together with the matter of 'Britain', suggests that *Cymbeline* is more specifically a play about the author's writing of Britain: an advertisement for the poet-playwright's contribution to the state, his national authority to affirm justice and to critique its violation. Third, the presence in *Cymbeline* of romance self-reflexivity within the recapitulatory mode indicates that this play reflects on Shakespearean art more broadly, both poems and plays,

Shakespeare's debt to Spenser in the late romances has long been a commonplace, although the topic has never been fully explored; see Alpers, *What is Pastoral?*, 204; Palfrey 14, 36–37, 109, 113–14; O'Connell, 'Experiment of Romance' 221; R. King 54, 70, 151. Kermode says that 'the pastoral tale of the King's lost sons is … close to the story of Child Tristram in Spenser's *Faerie Queene*, Book VI' (262–3); Goddard sees Shakespeare relying on Spenserian allegory in general (*Meaning of Shakespeare* 2: 257); and Butler specifies: 'In the encounter between the princes' natural civility and Cloten's courtly boorishness, there is more than a hint of Spenserean allegory' (ed. 12).
[23] J. Bate, *Shakespeare and Ovid*, observes the connection between the Diana/Actaeon myth in *Cymbeline* and Marlowe's *Edward II* (217); while Floyd-Wilson suggests that Shakespeare's romance 'resurrects some of the ethnological concerns of Marlowe's *Tamburlaine*' (161). On Iachimo's models, Iago and Edmund, as Marlovian figures, see Bloom 499–505.
[24] See Warren's unit on 'A Retrospective Play' (ed. 18–21).

from the beginning of his career to the end.[25] As a late national romance about Shakespeare's counter-laureate career, *Cymbeline* functions as a testament to his historic authorship.

While critics seem to have exhausted commentary on Imogen's bedchamber, perhaps our model of counter-laureate authorship can create a fresh lens. Indeed, we can learn a good deal about Shakespearean authorship here – not just about Iachimo as a character, or Imogen, or Posthumus. Usually, critics draw attention to the acute *bookishness* of the scene, viewing the contents of Imogen's bedchamber and the body of Imogen herself through the perspective of the voyeur Iachimo.[26] If Shakespeare presents Iachimo as a reader of the feminine book, he also presents the Italian villain as a writer of that book.[27]

When Iachimo slips out of the trunk, and approaches the sleeping princess, he imagines himself as 'our Tarquin' about to rape Lucrece (2.2.12–14). Then, when he addresses 'Cytherea', he imagines himself as a new Adonis (14–15). After describing Imogen's sleeping beauty in erotic detail, and 'writ[ing] ... all down' (24), Iachimo discovers something else: the princess 'hath been reading late / The tale of Tereus: here the leaf's turn'd down / Where Philomele gave up' (44–6). Later, in Act 2, scene 4, when he narrates 'the contents o' th' story' (2.2.27) to Posthumus to document Imogen's whoredom, Iachimo describes the bedchamber in detail, singling out a silk 'tapestry' depicting 'Cleopatra when she met her Roman' at 'Cydnus' (69–71), a 'chimney-piece' showing 'Chaste Dian bathing' (81–2), 'The roof o' th' chamber / With golden cherubins ... fretted' (87–8), and 'andirons' displaying 'two winking Cupids / Of silver, each on one foot standing, nicely / Depending on their brands' (88–91).[28] Thus,

---

[25] Cf. O'Connell: Shakespeare's romances 'appear to adumbrate a built-in critique of romance' (216): 'the self-critiquing character of romance elements in all four plays shows art willing to judge itself, to assert the truth of its claims and at the same time to preserve a skeptical awareness of itself as an imaginative construction' (228).

[26] Belsey concentrates on Iachimo's 'reading' of Imogen and her chamber, taking a cue from Cymbeline's question in Act 5, scene 4, 'Who is't can read a woman?' (48) – a question that 'might stand as an epigraph for the whole text' (57).

[27] See James: 'Iachimo reads and reinscribes Imogen as a renaissance Italian text in the line of Ovid' (174). Readings of Ovidian myths in this scene by Barkan, Bate, and Thompson ('Philomel in "Titus Andronicus" and "Cymbeline"') cohere with James's.

[28] See Simonds, *Myth, Emblem, and Music in Shakespeare's 'Cymbeline'* 95–123.

Iachimo both reads and writes a series of Ovidian myths: most importantly, that of Tarquin and Lucrece from the *Fasti*; and from the *Metamorphoses*, those of Venus and Adonis, Philomela and Tereus, and Diana and Actaeon (to a lesser extent, Cleopatra and Antony). Yet, as critics emphasize, Shakespeare does not merely re-embroider Ovid. He also *recollects* himself, including his two mid-1590s narrative poems, *Lucrece* and *Venus*, his first tragedy, *Titus*, a late Roman tragedy, *Antony*, and perhaps a mid-career comedy, *The Merry Wives of Windsor*, which centralizes the myth of Diana and Actaeon. Nonetheless, we might question the recent conclusion that Shakespeare's recapitulatory mode 'has no distinct function within the *Cymbeline* scene', and thus that the Ovidian 'intertextuality is a bit of a blind alley' (Lyne 267).

Within the scene: that has been the problem. We have tended to locate significance for Shakespeare's Ovidian intertextuality and intratextuality 'within' the fiction. Alternatively, what might we see when we stand back from the fiction? We see not simply Iachimo viewing a young princess in her bedroom but an author turning to literary texts, his own included, to compose the scene. Certainly, we can interpret the bedchamber by calling Iachimo a reader and writer of the feminine book, but the text suggests a complicating feature: Imogen is herself a reader of a masculine book – the book of Ovid, the favorite book of Shakespeare himself. The scene, then, presents a genuine paradox: an unconscious woman displays literary agency. In doing so, it stages one of Shakespeare's most innovative strategies of counter-laureate authorship.

Surprisingly, critics have not read the scene from the perspective of Imogen. The reasons for not doing so are clear: the audience encounters the scene primarily through the eyes of Iachimo, and she herself is unconscious. The male, not the female, appears to have agency here. As Iachimo determines, 'I will write all down' (2.2.24). Yet, in a vivid way, the scene displays the male as *subject* to the literary sensibility of the female. Iachimo reads and writes, but his entire system of *noting* (2.2.28) originates in the artwork of Imogen. This is *her* chamber. The myths tell us as much about her as they do about her intruder.

Why does Shakespeare present Imogen as a reader of Ovid's tragic tale of Philomela? Certainly, so that Iachimo can misinterpret the myth she takes to heart, when he calls it 'The tale of Tereus' and sees the book-leaf turned down 'Where Philomela gave up'. The book is on the stage not simply as a prop but as an authority, and if we open the book, as Lavinia does in *Titus*, we discover that the 'tale' is not 'of Tereus' but of Philomela, and further, that technically the virgin never 'gave up'. Iachimo, not Imogen, is a bad reader and inscriptor of Ovid. In contrast, we may infer, Imogen has taken an interest in the Ovidian tale to learn about the danger of masculine sexuality and thus to remain vigilant over her chastity. The Ovidian book becomes a stage prop for female consciousness – a material sign of her inward life.

The context of the scene suggests that Imogen is right to remain vigilant. Not merely has her husband been exiled, but right outside her door, as we learn in the next scene, Cloten positions himself. Left vulnerable in her room, she rightly feels threatened by masculine desire, and she turns to an author who powerfully expresses sensitivity to the female oppressed by masculine desire.[29] This helps explain why Imogen decorates her own intimate space with artwork depicting Cleopatra and Diana. Readers recognize the opposition in female icons here, but it is as easy to misread them as Iachimo misreads Ovid. Importantly, Imogen's artwork does not depict the male.[30]

The absence of the male in Imogen's bedchamber marks her domestic space as a literary site of feminine power, authority, and wisdom. This chaste young woman does not exclude the erotic but *presents* it. Her tapestry foregrounds Cleopatra at the Cydean harbor, where the river 'swell'd above the banks, or for / The press of boats or pride' (71–2). For Shakespeare, Cleopatra is a figure of feminine erotic power, and here she serves to balance with the chaste Diana, before Actaeon spies on her. In other words, Imogen's artwork shows the feminine on the threshold of masculine penetration, in her last or liminal moment of virgin consciousness. Reminiscent of the eunuchs presiding over Cleopatra in Shakespeare's tragedy (*AC* 2.2.191–218), in Imogen's bedchamber only prepubescent males appear: 'golden cherubins' and 'winking Cupids'. Viewed from this perspective, Imogen's bedchamber becomes a site of feminine agency, emptied of masculine corruption. Perhaps Imogen has read the *Metamorphoses* and decorated her room with its myths to *protect* her from abusive masculine power. If so, the bedroom scene juxtaposes two readings of Ovid: Iachimo's and Imogen's, the Italian male's and the British female's.

To this Ovidianism, we can add one of Shakespeare's most acute intertextual maneuvers. To conclude his surveillance work, Iachimo soliloquizes on his bookkeeping:

---

[29] On Philomela in *Lucrece* as a myth of feminist activism, see Newman, ' "And Let Mild Women" '.

[30] As James puts it, 'Ovid's Actaeon is nowhere to be seen', and 'Antony is not represented' (177).

> I have enough;
> To th' trunk again, and shut the spring of it.
> Swift, swift, you dragons of the night, that dawning
> May bare the raven's eye! I lodge in fear;
> Though this a heavenly angel, hell is here.   *Clock strikes.*
>
> One, two, three: time, time! *Exit [into the trunk].*
>
> (*Cymbeline* 2.2.46–51)

Modern editors have found Shakespeare evoking texts of two authors in particular: Ovid and the Ovidian Marlowe. For the image of the dragons in line 48, they cite Ovid's *Metamorphoses* 7.217–23, which refers to the chariot of Medea (Warren, ed. 132; Butler, ed. 121), along with Marlowe's *Hero and Leander* 1.107–8: 'Nor that night-wandring pale and watry star / When yawning dragons draw her thrilling car' (Nosworthy, ed. 52; Butler, ed. 121). In line 50, on Iachimo's references to Imogen as an 'angel' and to himself in 'Hell', editors cite Marlowe's *Doctor Faustus* 2.1.124–5: 'where we are is hell, / And where hell is must we ever be' (Nosworthy, ed. 52; see Warren, ed. 132). J. M. Nosworthy even wonders 'whether, in actual performance, the clock was sounded at regular intervals throughout the scene, as it apparently was at the end of *Doctor Faustus*' (ed. 52).

Yet we can be even more specific. While Faustus stands on the threshold of the Christian hell, with the clock striking, he utters 'perhaps the most extraordinary Ovidian allusion in Elizabethan drama' (J. Bate 45):

> *O lente, lente currite noctis equi!*
> The stars move still, time runs, the clock will strike,
> The devil will come, and Faustus must be damned.
>
> (Marlowe, *Doctor Faustus* A text 5.2.75–7)

Faustus' Latin quotation from Ovid's *Amores* 1.13, the great aubade to Dawn, is itself one of Marlowe's self-quotations, for he had translated Ovid's inaugural poem as *Ovid's Elegies*, Englishing Ovid's original 'lente currite, noctis equi!' (*Am* 1.13.40) as 'Stay night, and run not thus' (*OE* 1.13.40). Marlowe's translation is disappointing because it leaves out Ovid's reference to Night's horses, as if 'he is saving it up for the drama', even though in the process he creates one of his 'boldest strokes' (J. Bate 45).

Most likely, however, Shakespeare borrows the dragons from an earlier scene in Marlowe's tragedy, the Chorus to Act 3, when Wagner describes Faustus' cosmic journey, itself modeled on the Ovidian flight of Medea, as the image of the 'book' intimates:

> Learned Faustus,
> To know the secrets of astronomy,
> Graven in the book of Jove's high firmament,
> Did mount himself to scale Olympus' top,
> Being seated in a chariot burning bright,
> Drawn by the strength of yoky dragons' necks,
> He now is gone to prove cosmography.
>
> (Marlowe, *Doctor Faustus* A text 3.Ch.1–7)

Thus, Shakespeare conflates two different passages from Marlowe's play, one of which originates in a passage from a Marlowe poem. The effect is to present Iachimo as a Marlovian superhero, a literary figure of Ovidian 'lust', dabbling in a black art – here the erotic art of Marlovian poetry and theatre itself.

Shakespeare uses the opposition between the lustful overreacher Iachimo and the chaste beauty Imogen to process not just the aesthetics of Marlowe but of Spenser. For the depiction of Imogen as a chaste princess of great beauty is an instance of 'Spenserian dramaturgy'. In her purified, vulnerable chastity, Imogen recalls Britomart in Book 3 of the Legend of Chastity (James 178). In particular, Imogen's artwork balancing the sensual Cleopatra and the chaste Diana recalls Britomart's internalization of Venerean and Dianian principles: love and chastity (3.1.46). In this way, the scene of Imogen's bedchamber makes us privy to Shakespeare's own authorship. His *intertextual intratextuality* (as we might call it) comes to focus not just on Iachimo's reading of Imogen but on the author's literary representation of female consciousness and identity.

CLOTEN AND THE MASCULINE ART OF ORPHEUS

To bridge the two descriptions of Imogen's bedchamber (2.2 and 2.4), Shakespeare inserts the scene of Cloten among the musicians (2.3). Like the scene between Posthumus and the Britain Lord, this one is brief, yet it is also paradigmatic. The scene begins when Cloten and the First Lord enter, having just completed a game of dice – a game the boorish prince has lost. Cloten asks if it is yet 'morning' (9), but the Lord replies that 'Day' has arrived (10), prompting Cloten's impatience: 'I would this music would come. I am advis'd to give her music a' mornings; they say it will penetrate' (11–13).

Evidently, someone has advised Cloten how to use 'music' to play with Imogen (more successfully, perhaps, than he has played at dice). He is referring to the aubade, or morning song, sung at a beloved's window or door to awaken her, but his word 'penetrate' betrays his real goal, which equates the affective working of music with the male's sexual agency. Cloten redefines music cynically, from a civilizing power able to affect emotional inwardness, to a vicious force violating the sanctity of the female body.

When the musicians arrive, Cloten feverishly gives voice to this musical program:

Come on, tune. If you can penetrate her with your fingering, so; we'll try with tongue too. If none will do, let her remain; but I'll never give o'er. First, a very excellent good conceited thing; after, a wonderful sweet air, with admirable rich words to it – and then let her consider. (*Cymbeline* 2.3.14–19)

The indecent puns continue, debasing the art of music to that of pandering, and recasting the musicians' artful use of fingers and tongue with the male invading the protectively closed orifices of the female. After asserting his persistence against the likelihood of Imogen's rebuttal, he identifies a musical process for getting her to 'consider'. Scholars are not sure what makes up the process, but two general phases emerge: the 'First' is instrumental; the second, vocal.[31]

Cloten's distinction between prefatory instrumental music and a follow-up song with 'admirable rich words' forms an important frame for interpreting 'that incomparable lyric' (Goddard 2: 253):

> SONG
>
> Hark, hark, the lark at heaven's gate sings,
>   And Phoebus gins arise,
> His steeds to water at those springs
>   On chalic'd flow'rs that lies;
> And winking Mary-buds begin to ope
>   their golden eyes;
> With every thing that pretty is, my lady
>   sweet, arise:
> Arise, arise!   (*Cymbeline* 2.3.20–6)

Because our only text for the play, the First Folio, does not assign a speech-prefix to this song, some editors speculate that Cloten both authors and sings it, 'as in several modern productions' (Warren, ed. 133; cf. Butler, ed. 123). For critics, this routinely creates a problem. 'What', Goddard asks, 'did Shakespeare mean by connecting Cloten' with such a beautiful song (2: 253)? His tentative answer: 'Perhaps if this man had not had a crafty devil for a mother, some seed of celestial melody might have germinated even in him' (2: 253).

---

[31] According to Warren, by 'excellent good conceited thing' in the first phase, Cloten could mean either 'an elaborate piece of instrumental music' or 'simply an elaborate flourish introducing the song' (ed. 133).

Instead of explaining Cloten's lyric in terms of character, we might see a striking instance of Shakespeare's counter-laureate authorship, as the allusion to Ovid's myth of Orpheus suggests.[32] Just as later 'Cloten's clotpole [sails] down the stream / In embassy to his mother' (4.2.184–5), so in Ovid 'The poet's ... head and lyre, O Hebrus, thou didst receive, and (a marvel!) while they floated in mid-stream the lyre gave forth some mournful notes, mournfully the lifeless tongue murmured, mournfully the banks replied' (*Met* 11.50–3).

We have here, then, an unusual opportunity to specify the character of a counter-Orphic authorship, which operates through an unsettling disconnect: the Orpheus who sings (or at least commissions) incomparable music turns out to be a 'clotpole'. No wonder Goddard considers Cloten a genuine 'masterpiece' (2: 251): Cloten is himself a grotesque work of Orphic art. Not simply a superb character, Cloten lays bare the frame of Shakespearean parodic authorship. Such authorship refuses to give us what we want – the sublime portrait of a triumphant artist at work on his creation, such as Spenser depicts when Colin Clout conjures up the ethereal Graces on Mount Acidale. In Cloten, Shakespeare gives us something like Colin Clout's photographic negative.

Thus we might recall a specific historical context for Shakespeare's identification of Cloten as an Orphic poet of Ovidian amor: Spenser's career-long advertisement of himself as the 'Bryttane Orpheus'. The phrase comes from a *Commendatory Verse* to the 1590 *Faerie Queene* by the anonymous 'R. S.', whose discourse has intriguing application to *Cymbeline*:

> Fayre Thamis streame, that from Ludds stately towne,
> Runst paying tribute to the Ocean seas,
> Let all thy Nymphes and Syrens of renowne
> Be silent, whyle this Bryttane Orpheus playes:
> Nere thy sweet bankes, there lives that sacred crowne,
> Whose hand strowes Palme and never-dying bayes,
> Let all at once, with thy soft murmuring sowne
> Present her with this worthy Poets prayes.
> For he hath taught hye drifts in shepeherdes weedes,
> And deepe conceites now singes in Faeries deedes.
>
> (R. S., *Commendatory Verse* 4)

---

[32] Noted by Armitage, 'Dismemberment of Orpheus' 132. R. King sees the 'lark' in the song as 'the morning counterpart to the nightingale, the ravished ... Philomel in Ovid's *Metamorphoses* that Imogen had been reading before she fell asleep' (19), and King alertly recalls that 'Ovid was writing during the same historical period in which the story of *Cymbeline* takes place' (21).

Here, R. S. relies on Ovid's myth of Orpheus to present Spenser as England's Virgil, progressing from pastoral to epic in order to become renowned as a laureate poet.[33]

R. S.'s references to 'Bryttane', 'Ludds stately town', 'paying tribute', the geography of pastoral and epic, and the theatrical ring of 'Orpheus playes' might have caught Shakespeare's attention when putting Spenser's story of 'Kimbeline' (*FQ* 2.10.50) on the Jacobean stage. If so, we might wonder whether the name 'Cloten' could allude to Colin *Clout*.[34] Yet we might also wonder why Shakespeare would use Cloten to allude to Spenser's laureate persona. An answer exists in the nature of Shakespeare's counter-Spenserian art: not just a critique of the national poet but a homage to him, and therefore perhaps a critique of the Jacobean 'degeneration' of Spenser.[35]

Such an interpretation helps explain the lyric integrity of Cloten's song. As an aubade, the lyric performs the awakening of the beloved. In the 1595 *Epithalamion*, Spenser had adapted the tradition in his magnificent marriage poem, celebrating his wedding to Elizabeth Boyle:

> Wake, now my love, awake; for it is time,
> The Rosy Morne long since left Tithones bed,
> All ready to her silver coche to clyme,
> And Phoebus gins to shew his glorious hed.
> Hark how the cheerefull birds do chaunt theyr laies
> And carroll of loves praise.
> The merry Larke hir mattins sings aloft.
>
> (Spenser, *Epithalamion* 74–80)

The echoes of this passage in Cloten's aubade are remarkable. 'Phoebus gins' is a quotation from Spenser's line 77, while his repetition of 'Wake ... awake' in line 74 reappears in Shakespeare's 'arise, arise'. Instead of Morn's 'silver coche' climbing the sky, Phoebus' 'steeds' water at the 'springs' of Mount Helicon. The word 'hark', the act of *singing*, and of course the image of the *lark* singing in flight occur in both poems. Whereas Cloten hopes to use the Orphic power of song to penetrate Imogen, Spenser identifies himself as the Britain Orpheus for less violent purposes: 'So Orpheus did

---

[33] On R. S.'s allusion to 'Ovid, *Met.* 10.86–105', see A. C. Hamilton, ed. 723, although the word 'murmuring' probably picks up the concept from the Ovidian passage already quoted about the death of Orpheus.

[34] Critics often recall Cloten's commitment to clothing (e.g., James 158–9), while a 'clout' is 'a patch or piece of cloth' (*OED*, headnote). Palfrey is on the verge of identifying Cloten with Spenser: 'Cloten's background remains mysterious. There are hints at intervals throughout the play that Cloten is base born, son of a tailor or, as the paronomasia might hint, a 'Squire's Cloth' like his rival (II.iii.122)' (89). Spenser *was the son of a tailor*, and attended Merchant Taylors' School in London.

[35] When James calls Cloten the play's 'model of cultural degeneration' (159), she supplies a clue.

for his owne bride, / So I unto my selfe alone will sing' (16–17). Cloten thus parodies Spenser's Orphic self-presentation. A subtle student of the aubade, this royal sot nestles a series of womb-like images in his song's center, as his art invades the chastity of Imogen: her 'watry springs'; her cup in 'chalic'd flowers'; her exquisite 'winking Mary-buds' that 'begin to ope'; and even her 'golden eyes'. Cloten's song tries to see through the flowery form of Spenser's chaste poetics, laying bare the womb that this clown aims to target.[36]

Because Shakespeare in the scene with Iachimo has alluded to Ovid's aubade from the *Amores*, and thus perhaps Marlowe's translation of Elegy 1.13, in the Cloten scene we probably need to see a further allusion to both classical and English authors. It seems, however, that Cloten's erotic use of a song to awaken his beloved pertains more directly to Ovid's and Marlowe's aubade than it does to Spenser's. In any event, such detailed and complex intertextuality once more exposes the rib of Shakespeare's authorship, and in the image of the lark singing 'at heaven's gate' he quotes his own Sonnet 29 (Warren, ed. 133): 'and then my state / (Like to the lark at break of day arising / From sullen earth) sings hymns at heaven's gate' (10–12). Rather than present himself triumphantly as Britain's Orpheus, Shakespeare disperses authorship across several characters with varying ethical make-ups.[37]

IMOGEN'S COUNTER-ORPHIC AWAKENING

Shakespeare's scene of Cloten among the musicians, along with that of Iachimo in Imogen's bedchamber, prepares for 'the most incredible scene in Shakespeare' (Goddard 2: 255). Two parts of this scene (4.2) are especially important here. In the first, the lost princes, Guiderius and Arviragus, who live in the mountains with Belarius/Morgan as Polydore and Cadwal, deliver 'the finest of all the songs in Shakespeare's plays' (Bloom, *Invention of the thuman* 629).

The princes deliver this song over the body of Fidele, the boy page whom they believe to be dead but who is the really unconscious Imogen, recipient of her stepmother's sleeping potion. Before they sing, Guiderius and Arviragus engage in a lively conversation about their song. Guiderius, the more active of the two (3.3.86–95), does not want to linger over the

---

[36] A *clout* is also the (womblike) center of a target (*OED*, Def. 6), as Lear remembers (4.6.91–2).

[37] Long ago, Frye remarked that 'Orpheus is the hero of all four romances' (*A Natural Perspective* 147), and Armitage follows up with a clear articulation of Shakespeare's counter-Orphic authorship: 'The Orpheus who haunts the romances is a composite figure, a cluster of associations which can be seen accumulating across Shakespeare's work' (123).

burial: 'Prithee have done, / And do not play in wench-like words with that / Which is so serious' (4.2.229–31). Arviragus, the more contemplative, acknowledges his brother's feminizing of song but persists by suggesting a musical form for it: 'And let us, Polydore, though now our voices / Have got the mannish crack, sing him to th' ground, / As once to our mother; use like note and words' (235–7). The origin of Arviragus' interest in the art of music emerges in his first appearance, when he presents their hard pastoral life in the mountains: 'Our cage / We make a choir, as doth the prison'd bird, / And sing our bondage freely' (3.3.42–4). While conventional, the image of a man singing freely in his bird-like cage (chapter 6) identifies Arviragus' poetic sensibility. In contrast, Guiderius resists his brother's invitation to song: 'Cadwal, / I cannot sing. I'll weep, and word it with thee; / For notes of sorrow out of tune are worse / Than priests and fanes that lie' (4.2.239–42). The comparison is arresting yet opens up a religious underpinning to the song. Arviragus astutely sees the problem, and accords with his brother's wish: 'We'll speak it then' (242). They will speak the lyric they compose rather than sing it. After Belarius intercedes, reminding them of the dead Cloten, Arviragus remarks, 'If you'll go fetch him, / We'll say our song the whilst' (253–4). Such language marks the song as a lyric poem spoken aloud for a ritual purpose. When Arviragus tells his brother to 'begin' (254), the reticent Guiderius resists once more, making sure Fidele's head is laid 'to th' east' in accord with Morgan's instructions (255).

Finally, the princes *say the song*, four stanzas of six lines each, with the first three rhyming *ababcc* – sixains resurrected from Shakespeare's first narrative poem, *Venus and Adonis,* itself modeled on Spenser's *Januarye* and *December* eclogues. The stanzas produce an astonishing photograph of poetry's collaborative making, as the first two stanzas reveal:[38]

SONG

GUIDERIUS.   Fear no more the heat o' th' sun,
             Nor the furious winter's rages,
             Thou thy worldly task hast done,
             Home art gone, and ta'en thy wages.
             Golden lads and girls all must,
             As chimney-sweepers, come to dust.
ARVIRAGUS.   Fear no more the frown o' th' great,
             Thou art past the tyrant's stroke;
             Care no more to clothe and eat,

---

[38] In a personal communication, Valerie Wayne reminds me that 'the speech prefixes in the Folio text are the source (or proof) of the intertwined lyric'.

To thee the reed is as the oak.
The sceptre, learning, physic, must
All follow this and come to dust.

(*Cymbeline* 4.2.258–69)

In the third stanza, the brothers alternate lines, and they continue to do so in the fourth and final stanza, although there the meter changes from a pentameter to a tetrameter line and the rhyme scheme shifts to couplets, with the brothers voicing the final rhyme together: 'Quiet consummation have, / And renowned be thy grave' (280–1). Shakespeare had not staged the collaborative production of poetry since *Romeo and Juliet* (1.5.93–106). In the late romance, the intertwined lyric of Arviragus and Guiderius offers a brotherly, funereal form of lyric art, counterpointing the erotic sonnet that years before Romeo and Juliet had gracefully interwoven.

Whereas those young lovers express the romantic hope of eros in a collaboratively produced Petrarchan sonnet at the outset of their tragedy, in the late romance the young brothers enter the very register of tragedy. Twenty-two of the twenty-four lines brood darkly on the necessity of death, the relentless turning of the natural cycle. All that is 'golden' comes to 'dust'. Yet the rhetorical frame of the song works in the opposite direction – as an address to the body, as if it were still alive, and offering advice about the dark passage it is undertaking: do not fear the wrath of the sun or the rage of winter, for you have finished your worldly task, and returned 'Home' to receive your final reckoning; in this original earthly housing, you need not fear the scorn of superiors, the strike of tyrants, or your own poverty, for all power, knowledge, and achievement 'come to dust'; nor should you fear natural disasters or social calumny, magic, or supernatural harm: 'Nothing ill come near thee' (279). Only in the couplet does the song gesture formally toward consolation, for the dust of the grave will be 'renowned' for its earthly excellence.

Significantly, Shakespeare does not elsewhere present either Arviragus or Guiderius as a poet-figure. This feature of the song underscores what critics praising the lyric have wanted to see: not character but the author. The sudden appearance of the mountaineer-princes as poets capable of extemporizing stunning verse, and the intricate collaborative quality of their beautiful poem, make 'Fear no more' a set piece, a self-conscious dramatic moment.[39]

---

[39] Armitage briefly extends his principle of Shakespeare's Orphic authorship to the brothers (132). Bloom writes, 'I have no difficulty hearing in it ['Fear no more'] Shakespeare's own stance toward dying, and regard it as the *locus classicus* of Shakespeare upon death . . This poem is a dark comfort, but its extraordinary aesthetic dignity is the only consolation we should seek or find in Shakespeare' (630–1).

In the second part of the scene, the dead page Fidele, left alone on the stage, arises as the living princess Imogen, brooding on the dream phenomenon of her own resurrection. In a curious way, this moment lines up with that in Imogen's bedchamber; both scenes concentrate on the idea of female awakening. If in the earlier scene Cloten tries to use Orphic music to awaken Imogen from her night's rest, here the conversation and song performed over her unconscious body prepare for her actual awakening:

IMOGEN.　(*Awakes*.) Yes, sir, to Milford-Haven, which is the way?
　　　　　I thank you. By yond bush? Pray how far thither?
　　　　　'Od's pittikins! can it be six mile yet?

(*Cymbeline* 4.2.291–3)

The scene tells us that *Cymbeline*, like much else in the Shakespeare canon, strives to represent female consciousness – its social courtesy, even its earnestness about carrying on against odds.

Like the resurrection of Hero at the end of *Much Ado*, Imogen's resurrection is not real but staged. In his comedies and romances, Shakespeare marks the female's awakening into consciousness as a theatrical moment, represented visibly here in the costume Imogen wears. Even physiologically, her awakening is induced by art – the 'physic' originally supplied by the Queen's doctor, Cornelius. Hence, Imogen's awakening is about the *art-state*, and recollects most directly Cleopatra's dream of Antony in Act 5, scene 2: 'I dreamt there was an Emperor Antony. / O, such another sleep, that I might see / But such another man' (76–8). Two features of Cleopatra's dream reemerge in Imogen's discourse. The first is perhaps more obvious: the female delivers a blazon of the masculine body. Whereas the Eastern Star anachronistically relies on Revelation 10.1–2 (Kermode 228), simply to allude to Antony as the Colossus bestriding the ocean, as Jove shaking his 'rattling thunder', and as Arion riding his gleeful dolphin (5.2.82–90), Imogen refers directly to specific classical myths:

　　　　　　　The garments of Posthumus?
　　　I know the shape of 's leg; this is his hand,
　　　His foot Mercurial, his Martial thigh,
　　　The brawns of Hercules; but his Jovial face – Murther in heaven?

(*Cymbeline* 4.2.308–12)

In expressing the gap between Posthumus' real character and her perception of him, Imogen opens up the topic of Shakespearean authorship, which the comparison with Cleopatra underscores.

The second shared feature between Imogen's and Cleopatra's speeches is Shakespeare's exquisite language of dream reality. After delivering her blazon of the transcendent Antony, Cleopatra tries to convince Dolabella of its truth, since he has just denied the existence of 'such a man' as she has 'dreamt of' (5.2.93–4):

> if there be, nor ever were one such,
> It's past the size of dreaming. Nature wants stuff
> To vie strange forms with fancy; yet t' imagine
> An Antony were nature's piece 'gainst fancy,
> Condemning shadows quite.   (*Antony and Cleopatra* 5.2.96–100)

For Cleopatra, it is 'Nature', not 'fancy', which acquires the agency of imagination. For her, the truth about Antony's person is more real than anything imagination can create.[40]

In *Cymbeline*, Shakespeare returns to this topic, and once more when a grief-stricken figure of royal blood reflects on the loss of her beloved:

> I hope I dream;
> For so I thought I was a cave-keeper,
> And cook to honest creatures. But 'tis not so.
> 'Twas but a bolt of nothing, shot at nothing,
> Which the brain makes of fumes. Our very eyes
> Are sometimes like our judgments, blind. Good faith,
> I tremble still with fear; but if there be
> Yet left in heaven as small a drop of pity
> As a wren's eye, fear'd gods, a part of it!
> The dream's here still; even when I wake, it is
> Without me, as within me; not imagin'd, felt.
>
> (*Cymbeline* 4.2.297–307)

In Imogen's awakening, Shakespeare presents female consciousness imagining the relationship between dream and reality with more startling realism than perhaps anywhere else. His goal is to create a version of the real, which at once derives from imagination and exceeds it. Uncannily, Imogen discovers the contents of her dream before her waking eyes.

The familiar Shakespearean paradigm of *inner* and *outer* is crucial here to the discourse of the national romance, including its representation of subjectivity and performativity, but also the topic of poetry and its connection to theatre: 'it is / Without me, as within me'. This paradigm, explicitly articulated five times previously (1.1.8–10; 1.1.23–4; 1.4.9–10;

---

[40] See Ronald McDonald, 'Playing Till Doomsday' 94.

1.6.15–16; 2.2.35–6), is important because what is at stake is the very prospect of fusing *inner* and *outer*. If Iachimo deludes Posthumus into believing that his chaste wife separates what is fused here, the audience now (re)discovers outside the cave of Belarius Imogen's own articulation of her cardinal principle of chastity, at once a physiognomic feature and a spiritual condition. Yet, unlike the Egyptian Cleopatra, the British princess is patently mistaken about the object of her visionary awakening, for, unknown to her, the origin of her blazon is not her husband but Cloten. Thus, the scene is notable for the wedge it drives between inner and outer, between the creative visionary imagination and the object of its adoration. In this remarkable moment of counter-laureate authorship, Shakespeare maps the glory of vision on to the folly of error. Yet he does not simply mark the debilitating deflation of his character's integrity; simultaneously, he performs the mockery of his own art.

Repeatedly in *Cymbeline*, this author has used theatre to emphasize the separation between inner and outer. At the outset, Imogen calls the Queen 'Dissembling courtesy!' (1.1.84), while Iachimo maligns Posthumus as 'the Britain reveller' (1.6.61), and Posthumus himself furiously searches for 'The woman's part in me' (2.5.20) so he can eradicate it. In fact, Posthumus' belief that Imogen has separated her inner person from her outer character produces the discourse of theatre itself, which he transposes on to Imogen, as she herself discovers when reading his letter to Pisanio: 'Thy mistress … hath play'd the strumpet in my bed' (3.4.21–2). Hence, Posthumus orders Pisanio to 'act' a particular 'part' on his behalf (25–6): poison Imogen.

Moreover, Shakespeare uses the art of poetry to probe the integrity of inner and outer; nearly every expression of this art in the play circulates around Imogen. This helps explain why the play ends with the Soothsayer calling Imogen 'The piece of tender air' (5.5.446). When the author uses his familiar theatrical device of presenting his heroine as cross-dressing her identity – Imogen as Fidele – Shakespeare attempts not so much to *purify* theatre for its 'show of death' (1.5.40) as to put theatre to work for poetry.

POSTHUMUS AND THE MOCKERY OF RHYME

If Shakespeare portrays Imogen infusing theatricality with printed lyric, he presents her husband more formally as a counter-laureate poet-playwright. Critics remain divided over Posthumus' role in the play, even if they now tend to agree on his centrality.[41] Like Imogen, Posthumus dons disguise and thus becomes a figure of theatricality. Not merely does he vilify 'The woman's part' in himself, but he performs a costume change, in the speech that exhilarated Goddard: 'I'll disrobe me / Of these Italian weeds and suit myself / As does a Britain peasant; so I'll fight / Against the part I come with' (5.1.22–5). Unlike Imogen, however, Posthumus formally becomes a poet – in particular, a satirical poet. 'I'll write against them,' he declares to end his fiercely misogynistic soliloquy after he learns of his wife's whoredom (2.5.32).[42]

These verses present Posthumus as an actor-poet *performing* his art for an audience, and because his poetry writes the nation he becomes a theatrical epicist.[43] It seems characteristically Shakespearean that his poet-figure should produce an epic art that could be understood either as a low or a high genre, the ballad or the chronicle. When Posthumus produces a (Spenserian) 'rhyme' on the topic of the nation, he does so only in the diminutive form of a couplet:

> 'Two boys, an old man (twice a boy), a lane,
> Preserv'd the Britains, was the Romans' bane.'
>
> (*Cymbeline* 5.3.57–8)

Produced to satirize the Britain Lord, Posthumus' mini-epic qualifies as a late model of Shakespearean authorship.

Posthumus' reiterated term for the art of poetry supports this reading: 'rhyme'. In his works, Shakespeare uses this word and its cognates a total of fifty times. Although a potentially disparaging term (*AC* 5.2.215), *rhyme* can also signal the exaltation of poetry, as in Sonnet 55's 'pow'rful rhyme' (2). In particular, Sonnet 106 picks up Spenser's lexicon to define the achievement of national epic: 'When in the chronicle of wasted time / I see descriptions of the fairest wights, / And beauty making beautiful old rhyme / In praise of ladies dead and lovely knights' (1–4). Here Shakespeare equates 'chronicle'

---

[41] For Bloom, Posthumus is 'surely Shakespeare's most tiresome hero' (637). Yet Goddard finds Posthumus so worthy a creation that Shakespeare puts into his mouth 'one of the supreme spiritual utterances of England's supreme poet, and, by that fact, of England' (2: 259–60) – the soliloquy opening Act 5. James emphasizes Posthumus' centrality to 'the joint construction of national identity and heroic identity' (156).

[42] On Posthumus' 'changes in costume' as 'an index of his lost identity', see Wayne, 'Woman's Part' 296. On Posthumus as a satirical poet, see Nosworthy, ed. 73.

[43] As James reminds us, Posthumus has just told a 'stirring heroic narrative' about the 'tough native valor' required to 'seize the day' on behalf of the nation: 'Whether he is gathering samples of native wit suited for Camden's *Remains of Britaine*, or material for a ballad or broadside that he might "vent … for a mock'ry" – the lord is unresponsive to the techniques of heroic narrative – the speeches, the hyperbole, epic similes, and catalogues', which James reviews (181–2).

with (epic) 'rhyme' within a Petarchan sonnet gesturing to the Spenserian genre of national epic.[44] Yet Posthumus superbly overgoes Will in the Sonnets – and thus Spenser in *The Faerie Queene* – by condensing national epic into a mere two lines.

POSTHUMUS AND THE VISIONARY BOOK OF NATIONAL POETRY

Posthumus' standing as a 'surrogate' for the national poet-playwright helps account for the emergence of the supernatural during his dream of Act 5, scene 4, where we witness the play's most astonishing conjunction of poetry and theatre.[45] Yet this scene refuses to clarify the relation between psychology and metaphysics, unconscious dreaming and divine vision, human prayer and the immanence of the Godhead. Shakespeare harnesses not merely the latest in Jacobean stage mechanics, displayed in the descent of Jupiter astride an eagle, but also in a clearly marked poetic verse, used to give voice to the divine.

Shakespeare provides two points of entry to Posthumus' dream vision. The first is the soliloquy beginning Act 5 praised by Goddard, which concludes with 'the identical language of that unique and supreme sonnet, the 146th, which comes as close as anything Shakespeare ever wrote to being a personal religious creed', especially regarding 'the all-importance of the soul and its power to conquer death' (2: 260):

> Let me make men know
> More valour in me than my habits show.
> Gods, put the strength o' th' Leonati in me!
> To shame the guise o' th' world, I will begin
> The fashion: less without and more within.
>
> (*Cymbeline* 5.1.29–33)

This is a prayer – with attitude. Invoking the 'Gods' to infuse the spiritual strength of his deceased family 'in' him, Posthumus vows to 'shame' the 'world' for its commitment to 'guise' and to 'begin' a new 'fashion', as he changes his 'Italian weeds' to 'suit' himself in the 'part' of a 'Britain peasant' (23–5). Posthumus hopes to convince 'men' that he has more 'valor' in his soul than his 'habits show'. Yet the new fashion constitutes a new form of

---

[44] See Cheney, 'Shakespeare's Sonnet 106'.
[45] Cf. Bloom, who becomes especially gloomy here (633). Both Warren (ed. 57) and Butler (ed. 216) believe the scene to be Shakespeare's.

theatre: the world is a stage able to show 'less without and more within', one that locates judgment in subjectivity, not in cloutish clothes.

Posthumus attempts to put such theatre to work by defeating the chief actor of the old (Italian) theatre, Iachimo, only to suffer imprisonment when the Romans defeat Britain. While in jail, he makes his second prayer to the deities: 'and so, great pow'rs, / If you will take this audit, take this life' (5.4.26–7). After Posthumus goes to sleep, his prayer is answered. In a rare representation, Shakespeare stages the contents of a dream that his fiction shows to be supernatural in origin – in stark contrast to the dreams of Mercutio, Romeo, and Imogen herself, where we learn the divine origin only through the dreamer's description. Sometimes in Shakespeare, we witness a dream's metaphysical contents, as in the cases of Richard III, Brutus, and to some extent Macbeth, but in all three the ghostly presences are apparitions largely of conscience, as if we are witnessing the contents of a guilty mind. Shakespeare does stage the supernatural as a waking vision, as in Prospero's wedding masque in *The Tempest*. But in *Cymbeline* the supernatural vision is not a form of waking consciousness, the product of a guilty mind, or a dream description. Instead, Shakespeare represents an apocalyptic fusion of the mind with the afterlife. Not just Posthumus, but the audience, sees the ghosts of the Leonati – father, mother, brothers – as they rehearse their tragic history and that of their sole surviving son, calling on 'Jupiter' for 'Help' (91). Jupiter's descent on an eagle, '*throw [ing] a thunderbolt*' and causing '*The Ghosts [to] fall on their knees*' (SD after line 92), is the first and only appearance by the father of the classical pantheon in the Shakespeare canon. In the poetic verse of the vision, the author relies on the terms of the stage: 'show' (30), 'mock'd' (58), 'perform'd' (76), and 'perform' (122).

These professional terms suggest a contrast between the metaphysical theatrics of Jupiter with his ghosts of the Leonati and the false theatre of Iachimo (with the Queen and Cloten). Wondrously, the audience becomes privy to the 'fashion' that Posthumus has just described as existing only 'within'. Shakespeare's dramatic art represents both the inward truth of Posthumus' new theatre and its outward, material appearance. The moment of miracle occurs when Jupiter lays a 'tablet' upon Posthumus' 'breast, wherein / Our pleasure his full fortune doth confine' (109–10). By the time Posthumus awakes, the spirits have vanished, and he is left only to remember his 'dream'. But then he discovers a 'book' that inspires his theatrical prayer: 'O rare one, / Be not, as is our fangled world, a garment / Nobler than that it covers' (133–5).

Presumably, Shakespeare puts this moment on the stage to theatricalize St Paul's definition of faith: 'the grounde of things, which are hoped for, and

the evidence of things which are not sene' (Hebrews 11.1). Posthumus'
discovery of the book on his breast is the equivalent of – and may indeed
recollect – Arthur's awakening from his dream of the Faerie Queene in
Book 1, canto 9, of Spenser's national epic, when the Prince miraculously
discovers the 'pressed gras, where she had lyen' (15). The detail is not simply
one of the most memorable in the entire *Faerie Queene*; it may be unique in
the tradition of romance; and its rareness suggests that Shakespeare borrows
it from Spenser. Given that the image just happens to be of a book, we
might find here a staging of the Spenserian book itself.

As the *Riverside* glosses the *Cymbeline* passage, the book that Posthumus
discovers 'is an inscribed sheet within elaborate covers' (1602). Thus,
Shakespeare presents the *book* as a *garment*, the volume as a costume, fusing
the theatrical to the bibliographical. He mythologizes religious faith along
national, familial, and patrilineal lines; he psychologizes the supernatural;
and finally he theatricalizes the whole scene, as if to mock theatre pleasingly
as the art of imaginative grace, a new medium for redemption, a modern
theatrical consciousness, born in a British cell. Shakespeare's subsequent
phrase for this new metaphysical art form is memorably succinct: 'sprightly
show' (5.5.428).

PUBLISHING THE PIECE OF TENDER AIR

Shakespeare goes further, for he presents the actual contents of the book,
when Posthumus reads the prophecy contained within the garment of the
volume's covers, the first part of which reads, 'When as a lion's whelp shall,
to himself unknown, without seeking find, and be embrac'd by a piece of
tender air' (5.4.138–40). That last phrase is at once oblique and transparent,
relying on mysterious language to portray the princess of the British
realm.[46] As critics recall, the phrase reappears in the final scene, when the
soothsayer, aptly named Philharmonus (lover of harmony), deciphers the
prophecy of Jupiter's theatrical book:

> The piece of tender air, thy virtuous daughter,
> Which we call *mollis aer*, and *mollis aer*
> We term it *mulier*, [*to Posthumus*] which *mulier* I divine
> Is this most constant wife, who, even now,
> Answering the letter of the oracle,

---

[46] Thorne's reading is as clear a formulation of counter-laureate authorship as I have seen: 'Jupiter's
prophecy ... both invites and defeats interpretation' (188). And she goes on to see the soothsayer's
interpretation as 'no less flawed or provisional' (189).

Unknown to you, unsought, were clipt about
With this most tender air. *(Cymbeline* 5.5.446–52)

Editors reference the Latin etymology (false, it turns out) for the word *woman*, '*mulier*', *mul* (tender) and *ier* (air), and record Edward Dowden's words on the word 'piece': 'probably chosen because it was often used of persons, and often as indicating supreme excellence' (quoted in Nosworthy, ed. 161; Warren, ed. 238). As is well known, however, the word *piece* also means *masterpiece* and thus pertains to a work of art (*OED*, Def. 17a). Yet the word could mean 'Of something non-material, as *a piece of poetry*' (Def. 3e; see *TN* 2.4.1–7). Consequently, in *Cymbeline* the word 'piece' aligns with the word 'air', meaning *one of the four elements* and *human breath* but also *a type of song* (*OED*, Def. 4.18; see *MND* 1.1.183–4). Finally, the word 'piece' can also mean 'A dramatic work, a play' (Def. 14.e). The final word important to gloss, 'tender', locates the emotions, the affections, and the passions as the poetic substance of Shakespearean theatrical *air*. Imogen appears to be *Cymbeline*'s romance figure not merely of the lovely woman but of counter-laureate theatrical poetry itself.

Yet the word 'air' has a final meaning that carries over into the last two speeches of the play – that of publication (*OED*, Def. 11). In the play's final speech, Cymbeline lauds the gods (477) but also directs his country: 'Publish we this peace / To all our subjects' (478–9). Then he reiterates the word 'peace' to conclude the play – in the last line of a verse couplet: 'Never was a war did cease / (Ere bloody hands were wash'd) with such a peace' (484–5). In that last word, we might hear a pun on 'piece', not just because Shakespeare deploys the pun elsewhere, but because the play's penultimate speech, spoken by Philharmonus, self-consciously alludes to the soothsayer's name when he wraps the word in the air of music: 'The fingers of the pow'rs above do tune / The harmony of this peace' (466–7). *The harmony of this piece.* Here at the close, in arguably Shakespeare's most bizarre counter-laureate performance, the author stages the metaphysical air of romance nation-hood in order to publish the peace of Britain.

AFTERWORD: 'A SWAN'S NEST' AND 'TH' WORLD'S VOLUME'

Yet *Cymbeline* includes an even more notable imprint of Shakespeare's strange authorship, and we may bring the present book to a close through it. In Act 3, scene 4, Imogen responds to Pisano's advice about leaving 'Britain' to be reunited with her husband (3.4.135):

IMOGEN.　I' th'world's volume
　　　　　Our Britain seems as of it, but not in't;
　　　　　In a great pool a swan's nest. Prithee think
　　　　　There's livers out of Britain.
PISANO.　 I am most glad
　　　　　You think of other place. Th' ambassador,
　　　　　Lucius the Roman, comes to Milford-Haven
　　　　　To-morrow. Now, if you could wear a mind
　　　　　Dark as your fortune is, and but disguise
　　　　　That which, t' appear itself, must not yet be
　　　　　But by self-danger, you should tread a course
　　　　　Pretty and full of view.

　　　　　　　　　　　　　　　　　(*Cymbeline* 3.4.137–47)

Imogen's speech has been singled out as 'an important moment in the play':
not simply does it 'broaden out … the relations, and ultimately, the peace,
between Britain and Rome', but it 'expresses a more international view than
the Queen's narrow isolationism (3.1.14–33), regarding Britain as remote
from the rest of the world but still part of it' (Warren, ed. 174). In this
reading, Imogen's reference to Britain as 'a swan's nest' in 'a great pool'
forms a powerful trope of 'nationhood': 'The swan's nest may be peaceful,
but it preserves its separateness at the cost of marginality to the larger world,
the pool's edges from which it withdraws' (Butler, ed. 44; see 162).

　　Yet the swan's nest is also a literary trope. Editors identify similar political
conceits in the poetry of such authors as Samuel Daniel (Butler, ed. 44n1)
and Giles Fletcher (Butler, ed. 162), and they trace the nationalist concept
back to Virgil's Eclogue 1.66 ('penitus toto divisos orbe Britannos' ['the
Britons, wholly sundered from all the world']), concluding that, 'From this
more truly Virgilian perspective, which registers the costs as well as the
achievements of Augustan peace, Britain's isolation looks protective but
means exile to the global periphery' (Butler, ed. 44). Nonetheless, the
'Virgilian perspective' includes a specifically literary representation of nationhood, poised distinctively at the crossroads between lyric and epic.

　　In the literary tradition, the swan is most familiar as a figure of prophetic or
transcendent song, able to voice its impending death. Among Elizabethans,
Spenser relied on this representation in his laureate self-presentation as divine
poet in the *October* eclogue of *The Shepheardes Calender*:

　　　　　For Colin fittes such famous flight to scanne:
　　　　　He, were he not with love so ill bedight,
　　　　　Would mount as high, and sing as soote as Swanne.
　　　　　　　　　　　　　　　　　(Spenser, *October* 88–90)

Shakespeare makes use of this representation on a number of occasions, nowhere more powerfully than in *Othello* during the death-speech of Emilia, who is in mystical conversation with her dead mistress, the divine Desdemona: 'I will play the swan, / And die in music' (5.2.247–8). The word 'music' also means 'lyric', as Emilia's subsequent singing of Desdemona's 'willow' song makes clear (248), so that the conjunction of poetry with theatre ('play the swan') forms a striking refraction of Shakespearean authorship.

Unlike Emilia, however, Imogen does not refer to the transcendent meaning of the swan but rather to a less familiar meaning, emphasizing its nest-building power. In this alternative iconography, the swan is a figure for immanent literary making. Underlying it is Callimachus' *Hymn* 4, 'To Delos', which locates the origin of lyric poetry in the movement and song of the swan at the birth of Apollo:

> with music the swans, the gods' own minstrels, left Maeonian Pactolus and circled seven times round Delos, and sang over the bed of child-birth, the Muses' birds, most musical of all birds that fly. Hence that child in after days strung the lyre with just so many strings – seven strings, since seven times the swans sang over the pangs of birth. (Callimachus, *Hymn* 4, 'To Delos' 249–54)

Archaeological evidence from antiquity confirms the authority of this exquisite etiology of Apollonian lyric, for our earliest surviving harp is in the shape of a swan.[47] Shakespeare need not have known about either the swan-shaped harp or the Callimachean hymn to attach poem-making significance to the swan.

Strictly speaking, Imogen's swan-nest recapitulates one in Shakespeare's own *Lucrece*, which conveniently brings the two meanings above together:

> And now this pale swan in her wat'ry nest
> Begins the sad dirge of her certain ending.
>
> (*Rape of Lucrece* 1611–12)

Usually, editors gloss this 1594 image with reference to the swan song rehearsed in *The Merchant of Venice* (3.2.44–5), *Othello* (5.2.247), or 'The Phoenix and Turtle' (15; Roe, ed. 219; C. Burrow, ed. 327), without recalling the image in *Cymbeline*. Yet the moment of intratextuality linking the late play with the early poem does more than emphasize the different political choices made by the two heroines: Lucrece, the choice of suicide when giving birth to the Roman Republic; Imogen, the choice of life when joining Britain to Rome (Butler, ed. 43–4).

---

[47] For further detail and historical context, see Cheney, *Flight* 70–1; for a photograph of the swan-harp, see Figure 8 from that book.

For this intratextuality also scripts a moment of self-conscious author-ship, imping the political on to the literary. Not simply the 'swan's nest' but also the textualizing of the globe in the phrase 'world's volume': both poetry and book. While Imogen's bibliographical trope records that 'Britain is a page of the world's great volume' (Dowden, in Furness, ed., *Cym* 237), it also evokes the particular genre where this is so – chronicles like Holinshed's and romance epics like Spenser's. In this way, Imogen's conversation with Pisano writes and stages the nation. Yet it does so in a way consistent with Shakespeare's counter-laureate authorship, as the connection of poetry with theatricality implies. When Pisano suggests 'disguise' as a plan for going to Milford Haven, he completes the portrait of Imogen's counter-literary authorship of 'Britain', which here miniaturizes the conjunction of poetry, theatre, and books.[48] Such a conjunction forms an analogue to the one in *The Tempest* with which we began, from Prospero's Ovidian farewell to magic: 'printless foot' and 'demi-puppet' (5.1.34, 36; see Introduction).

Throughout this book, we have explored a new explanation for Shakespeare's authorial identity, which has long been characterized by self-concealment. We have found an explanation not only in his personal temperament or theatrical professionalism (the usual sites) but also in his self-conscious counter to the Western art of laureate self-presentation, on display from Homer to Marlowe, and prominent in Elizabethan England's first laureate poet, Spenser. In plays as in poems, from early till late, Shakespeare produces a counter-laureate authorship, which writes the nation without overt self-advertisement. Such self-concealing authorship often works by prismatic refraction, through which the terms of authorship appear, in a text nominally designed to reflect something else, such as politics, religion, or sexuality. Instead of following the laureate in penning prologues, prefaces, and other modes of self-presentation, the counter-laureate tells recurrent fictions of authorship that operate through the terms of the theater and the print shop, often conjoining a discourse of staged theatre with a discourse of printed poetry, epic as well as lyric. Such fictions, we have seen, speak to Shakespeare's standing as a sixteenth-century poet-playwright, the author of both poems and plays. Rather than being simply a man of the theatre, he is also an author with a literary career, in search not just of commercial success but of literary fame.

---

[48] Among modern editors, Nosworthy asks, 'Is it not possible that "swan's nest" incorporates Shakespeare's vision of Britain as a nest of singing birds, or poets?' (ed. 96). Not until Jonson's 1623 memorial poem in the First Folio may Shakespeare become the 'Sweet Swan of Avon' (71), but critics have long suspected a self-image in (for instance) 'the death-divining swan' of the 1601 'Phoenix and Turtle' (15; see *SNPP* 189).

Shakespeare's achievement as a counter-laureate author is so unique, decisive, and monumental that it ends up presiding over a powerful shift in the notion of English authorship for the ensuing centuries: from the ambitious Spenserian equation of the author with his art to a mocking counter to this equation.[49] Yet in countering Spenser's laureate authorship through a nonpareil canon of poems and plays, Shakespeare lends to English literature perhaps his defining legacy: the title of National Poet.

---

[49] On this topic, I am indebted to Helgerson, *Self-Crowned Laureates* 4. See also *SNPP* 47–8.

Works cited

Adelman, Janet. *Suffocating Mothers: Fantasies of Maternal Origin in Shakespeare's Plays, 'Hamlet' to 'The Tempest'*. New York: Routledge, 1992.
  '"Man and Wife Is One Flesh": Hamlet and the Confrontation with the Maternal Body'. Wofford, ed. 256–82.
Aldus, P. J. *Mousetrap: Structure and Meaning in 'Hamlet'*. University of Toronto Press, 1977.
Allen, Graham. *Intertextuality*. New Critical Idiom. London: Routledge, 2000.
Alpers, Paul. *What is Pastoral?* University of Chicago Press, 1996.
Apollodorus. *The Library*. 2 vols. Trans. Sir James George Frazer. Cambridge, MA: Harvard University Press, 1921.
Archer, John Michael. *'Love's Labour's Lost'*. Dutton and Howard, eds., *A Companion to Shakespeare's Works. The Comedies*. 320–37.
Aristotle. *The Basic Works of Aristotle*. Ed. Richard McKeon. New York: Random House, 1941.
Armitage, David. 'The Dismemberment of Orpheus: Mythic Elements in Shakespeare's Romances'. *Shakespeare Survey* 39 (1986): 123–33.
Baker, David J. *Between Nations: Shakespeare, Spenser, Marvell, and the Question of Britain*. Stanford University Press, 1997.
Baldwin, T. W. *William Shakspere's Small Latine and Lesse Greek*. Urbana: University of Illinois Press, 1944.
Barber, C. L. *Shakespeare's Festive Comedy: A Study of Dramatic Form and Its Relation to Social Custom*. Princeton University Press, 1959.
Barkan, Leonard. *The Gods Made Flesh: Metamorphosis and the Pursuit of Paganism*. New Haven: Yale University Press, 1986.
  'What Did Shakespeare Read?' De Grazia and Wells, eds. 31–47.
Barker, Francis. *The Tremulous Private Body: Essays in Subjection*. New York: Methuen, 1984.
Barthes, Roland. 'Theory of the Text'. *Untying the Text: A Post-Structuralist Reader*. Ed. Robert Young. London: Routledge, 1981. 31–47.
  'The Death of the Author'. *The Norton Anthology of Theory and Criticism*. Ed. Vincent B. Leitch, et al. New York: Norton, 2001. 1466–70.
Barton, Anne, ed. *The Tempest*. Harmondsworth: Penguin, 1968.
Bate, Jonathan. *Shakespeare and Ovid*. Oxford: Clarendon, 1993.

The Genius of Shakespeare. London: Macmillan-Picador, 1997.

Review of Brian Vickers, *Shakespeare as Co-Author*. *Times Literary Supplement* 18 April 2003: 3–4.

Bate, Jonathan, ed. *Titus Andronicus*. Arden Shakespeare. 3rd Series. London: Thomas Nelson, 1995.

Bate, Lucy. 'Which Did or Did Not Go to the Grave?' *Shakespeare Quarterly* 17 (1966): 163–5.

Bawcutt, N. W., ed. *Measure for Measure*. Oxford World's Classics. Oxford University Press, 1998.

Bednarz, James P. 'Imitations of Spenser in *A Midsummer Night's Dream*'. *Renaissance Drama* 14 (1983): 79–102.

Shakespeare and the Poets' War. New York: Columbia University Press, 2001.

Bellamy, Elizabeth Jane. *Translations of Power: Narcissism and the Unconscious in Epic History*. Ithaca: Cornell University Press, 1992.

Belsey, Catherine. *The Subject of Tragedy: Identity and Difference in Renaissance Drama*. London: Methuen, 1985.

Desire: Love Stories in Western Culture. Oxford: Blackwell, 1994.

Shakespeare and the Loss of Eden: The Construction of Family Values in Early Modern Culture. Basingstoke: Macmillan, 1999.

'Tarquin Dispossessed: Expropriation and Consent in *The Rape of Lucrece*'. *Shakespeare Quarterly* 52 (2001): 315–35.

Review of Patrick Cheney, *Shakespeare, National Poet-Playwright*. *Shakespeare Studies* 34 (2006): 170–6.

Benson, John, ed. *Poems: Written By Wil. Shake-speare. Gent.* London, 1640.

Bentley, Gerald Eades. *The Profession of Dramatist in Shakespeare's Time, 1590–1642*. Princeton University Press, 1971.

Berger, Harry, Jr. *Revisionary Play: Studies in the Spenserian Dynamics*. Berkeley: University of California Press, 1988.

Imaginary Audition: Shakespeare on Stage and Page. Berkeley: University of California Press, 1989.

'Against the Sink-a-Pace: Sexual and Family Politics in *Much Ado about Nothing*'. *Making Trifles of Terrors: Redistributing Complicities in Shakespeare*. Ed. Peter Erickson. Stanford University Press, 1997. 10–24.

Bergeron, David M., ed. *Reading and Writing in Shakespeare*. Newark: University of Delaware Press; Cranbury, NJ: Associated University Presses, 1996.

'Treacherous Reading and Writing in Shakespeare's Romances'. Bergeron, ed. 160–77.

Berry, Edward I. *Patterns of Decay: Shakespeare's Early Histories*. Charlottesville: University Press of Virginia, 1975.

Berry, Ralph. *Shakespeare's Comedies: Explorations in Form*. Princeton University Press, 1972.

Review of Brian Vickers, *Shakespeare as Co-Author*. *Review of English Studies* 54 (2003): 684–6.

Bevington, David, ed. *Henry IV, Part I*. Oxford World's Classics. Oxford University Press, 1987.

Bishop, T. G. 'Elizabethan Music as a Cultural Mode'. *Reconfiguring the Renaissance: Essays in Critical Materialism*. Ed. Jonathan Crewe. Lewisburg: Bucknell University Press, 1992. 51–75.

Shakespeare and the Theatre of Wonder. Cambridge University Press, 1996.

Blanpied, John W. *Time and the Artist in Shakespeare's English Histories*. Newark: University of Delaware Press, 1983.

Blayney, Peter W. M. 'The Publication of Playbooks'. Cox and Kastan, eds. 383–422.

Bloom, Harold. *The Anxiety of Influence: A Theory of Poetry*. 2nd edn New York: Oxford University Press, 1997.

Shakespeare: The Invention of the Human. New York: Riverhead-Penguin Putnam, 1998.

Genius: A Mosaic of One Hundred Exemplary Creative Minds. New York: Warner, 2002.

Hamlet: Poem Unlimited. New York: Riverhead, 2003.

Boling, Ronald J. 'Anglo-Welsh Relations in *Cymbeline*'. *Shakespeare Quarterly* 51 (2000): 33–66.

Bono, Barbara J. *Literary Transvaluation: From Vergilian Epic to Shakespearean Tragicomedy*. Berkeley: University of California Press, 1984.

Booth, Stephen, ed. *Shakespeare's Sonnets*. New Haven: Yale University Press, 1977.

'On the Value of *Hamlet*'. *New Casebooks: 'Hamlet'*. Ed. Martin Coyle. New York: St Martin's Press, 1992. 57–67.

Bradbrook, M. C. 'Shakespeare's Recollections of Marlowe'. *Shakespeare's Styles: Essays in Honour of Kenneth Muir*. Ed. Philip Edwards, Inga-Stina Ewbank, and G. K. Hunter. Cambridge University Press, 1980. 199–204.

Braden, Gordon. *Petrarchan Love and the Continental Renaissance*. New Haven: Yale University Press, 1999.

'Shakespeare's Petrarchism'. *Shakespeare's Sonnets: Critical Essays*. Ed. James Schiffer. New York: Garland, 1999. 163–84.

'Ovid, Petrarch, and Shakespeare's Sonnets'. Taylor, A. B., ed. 96–112.

Bradley, A. C. *Shakespearean Tragedy: Lectures on Hamlet, Othello, King Lear, Macbeth*. London: Macmillan, 1904.

Braudy, Leo. *The Frenzy of Renown: Fame and Its History*. New York: Oxford University Press, 1986.

Breitenberg, Mark. 'The Anatomy of Desire in *Love's Labor's Lost*'. *Shakespeare Quarterly* 43 (1992): 430–49.

Brink, Jean R. *Michael Drayton Revisited*. Boston, MA: Twayne, 1990.

Bristol, Michael D. '"Funeral-Bak'd Meats": Carnival and the Carnivalesque in *Hamlet*'. Wofford, ed. 348–67.

Big-Time Shakespeare. New York: Routledge, 1996.

Brockbank, J. P. 'History and Histrionics in *Cymbeline*'. *Shakespeare Survey* 11 (1958): 42–9.

Brooke, Nicholas. 'Marlowe as Provocative Agent in Shakespeare's Early Plays'. *Shakespeare Survey* 14 (1961): 34–44.

Brooks, Douglas A. *From Playhouse to Printing House: Drama and Authorship in Early Modern England*. Cambridge University Press, 2000.

Brooks, Harold F., ed. *A Midsummer Night's Dream*. Arden Shakespeare. 2nd Series. London: Methuen, 1979.

Brooks-Davies, Douglas. *The Mercurian Monarch: Magical Politics from Spenser to Pope*. Manchester University Press, 1983.

'Mercury'. *Spenser Encyclopedia*. 469–70.

Brower, Reuben A. *Hero and Saint: Shakespeare and the Graeco-Roman Tradition*. Oxford University Press, 1971.

Brown, Sarah Annes. *The Metamorphoses of Ovid: From Chaucer to Ted Hughes*. New York: St Martin's Press, 1999.

Bruster, Douglas. *Quoting Shakespeare: Form and Culture in Early Modern Drama*. Lincoln, NE: University of Nebraska Press, 2000.

Bryan, Robert A. 'Poets, Poetry, and Mercury in Spenser's *Prosopopia: Mother Hubberd's Tale*'. *Costerus* 5 (1972): 27–33.

Bulman, James C. 'Shakespeare's Georgic Histories'. *Shakespeare Survey* 38 (1985): 37–47.

Burnett, Mark Thornton, ed. *Christopher Marlowe: The Complete Plays*. Everyman Library. London: Dent; Rutland, VT: Tuttle, 1999.

Burrow, Colin. *Epic Romance: Homer to Milton*. Oxford: Clarendon, 1993.

'Life and Work in Shakespeare's Poems'. *Proceedings of the British Academy* 97 (1998): 15–50.

'The Sixteenth Century'. Kinney, ed. 11–28.

Burrow, Colin, ed. *William Shakespeare: The Complete Sonnets and Poems*. Oxford World's Classics. Oxford University Press, 2002.

Burrow, John A. 'Chaucer, Geoffrey'. *Spenser Encyclopedia*. 144–8.

Butler, Martin, ed. *Cymbeline*. New Cambridge Shakespeare. Cambridge University Press, 2005.

Cain, Thomas H. 'Spenser and the Renaissance Orpheus'. *University of Toronto Quarterly* 41 (1971): 24–47.

Cairncross, Andrew S., ed. *The Second Part of King Henry VI*. Arden Shakespeare. 2nd Series. London: Methuen, 1957.

Calderwood, James L. *Metadrama in Shakespeare's Henriad: Richard II to Henry V*. Berkeley: University of California Press, 1979.

To Be and Not To Be: Negation and Metadrama in 'Hamlet'. New York: Columbia University Press, 1983.

Caldwell, Ellen Cashwell. 'The Breach of Time: History and Violence in the *Aeneid*, *The Faerie Queene*, and *2 Henry VI*'. Diss. University of North Carolina at Chapel Hill, 1986.

Campana, Joseph. 'On Not Defending Poetry: Spenser, Suffering, and the Energy of Affect'. *PMLA* 120 (2005): 33–48.

Cannan, Paul D. 'Early Shakespeare Criticism, Charles Gildon, and the Making of Shakespeare the Playwright-Poet'. *Modern Philology* 102 (2004): 35–55.

Carnes, Valerie. 'Mind, Imagination, and Art in Shakespeare's *The Tempest*'. *North Dakota Quarterly* 35 (1967): 93–103.

Carroll, D. Allen. 'Greene's "Upstart Crow" Passage: A Survey of Commentary'. *Research Opportunities in Renaissance Drama* 28 (1985): 111–27.

Carroll, William C. '"The Form of Law": Ritual and Succession in *Richard III*'. *True Rites and Maimed Rites: Ritual and Anti-Ritual in Shakespeare and His Age*. Ed. Linda Woodbridge and Edward Berry. Urbana: University of Illinois Press, 1992. 203–19.

Cartelli, Thomas. *Marlowe, Shakespeare, and the Economy of Theatrical Experience*. Philadelphia, University of Pennsylvania Press, 1991.

'Jack Cade in the Garden: Class Consciousness and Class Conflict in *2 Henry VI*'. *Enclosure Acts: Sexuality, Property, and Culture in Early Modern England*. Ed. Richard Burt and John Michael Archer. Ithaca: Cornell University Press, 1994. 48–67.

'Suffolk and the Pirates: Disordered Relations in Shakespeare's *2 Henry VI*'. Dutton and Howard, eds., *A Companion to Shakespeare's Works. The Histories*. 325–43.

Cavell, Stanley. *Disowning Knowledge in Six Plays of Shakespeare*. Cambridge University Press, 1987.

Champion, Larry S. *Perspective in Shakespeare's English Histories*. Athens: University of Georgia Press, 1980.

Charnes, Linda. *Notorious Identity: Materializing the Subject in Shakespeare*. Cambridge, MA: Harvard University Press, 1993.

Chaucer, Geoffrey. *The Riverside Chaucer*. Ed. Larry D. Benson *et al*. Boston, MA: Houghton, 1987. Based on *The Works of Geoffrey Chaucer*, ed. F. N. Robinson, 2nd edn. Boston, MA: Houghton, 1957.

Cheney, Patrick. '"Secret Powre Unseene": Good Magic in Spenser's Legend of Britomart'. *Studies in Philology* 85 (1988): 1–28.

Spenser's Famous Flight: A Renaissance Idea of a Literary Career. University of Toronto Press, 1993.

Marlowe's Counterfeit Profession: Ovid, Spenser, Counter-Nationhood. University of Toronto Press, 1997.

'"O, Let My Books Be … Dumb Presagers": Poetry and Theater in Shakespeare's Sonnets'. *Shakespeare Quarterly* 52 (2001): 222–54.

'Shakespeare's Sonnet 106, Spenser's National Epic, and Counter-Petrarchism'. *English Literary Renaissance* 31 (2001): 331–64.

'"Novells of His Devise": Chaucerian and Virgilian Career Paths in Spenser's *Februarie* Eclogue'. Cheney and de Armas, eds. 231–67.

Shakespeare, National Poet-Playwright. Cambridge University Press, 2004.

'Biographical Representations: Marlowe's Life of the Author'. *Shakespeare, Marlowe, and Jonson: New Directions in Biography*. Ed. J. R. Mulryne and Takashi Kozuka. Aldershot: Ashgate, 2006. 183–204.

'Perdita, Pastorella, and the Romance of Literary Form: Shakespeare's Counter-Spenserian Authorship'. *Shakespeare and Spenser*. Ed. Julian Lethbridge. Manchester University Press, 2008.

Cheney, Patrick, ed. *The Cambridge Companion to Christopher Marlowe*. Cambridge University Press, 2004.

Cheney, Patrick, and Frederick A. de Armas, eds. *European Literary Careers: The Author from Antiquity to the Renaissance*. University of Toronto Press, 2002.

Cheney, Patrick, and Brian J. Striar, eds. *The Collected Poems of Christopher Marlowe*. New York: Oxford University Press, 2006.

Clayton, Jay, and Eric Rothstein. 'Figures in the Corpus: Theories of Influence and Intertextuality'. *Influence and Intertextuality in Literary History*. Madison: University of Wisconsin Press, 1992. 3–36.

Clements, Arthur L., ed. *John Donne's Poetry*. 2nd edn. New York: Norton, 1992.

Cook, Carol. '"The Sign and Semblance of Her Honor": Reading Gender Difference in *Much Ado about Nothing*'. *PMLA* 101 (1986): 186–202.

Cook, Elizabeth, ed. *John Keats*. Oxford University Press, 1990.

Cooper, Helen. *The English Romance in Time: Transforming Motifs from Geoffrey of Monmouth to the Death of Shakespeare*. Oxford University Press, 2004.

Cox, John D., and David Scott Kastan, eds. *A New History of Early English Drama*. New York: Columbia University Press, 1997.

Crewe, Jonathan. *Trials of Authorship: Anterior Forms and Poetic Reconstruction from Wyatt to Shakespeare*. Berkeley: University of California Press, 1990.

Crystal, David, and Ben Crystal. *Shakespeare's Words: A Glossary and Language Companion*. Harmondsworth: Penguin, 2002.

Curran, John E., Jr. 'Royalty Unlearned, Honor Untaught: British Savages and Historiographical Change in *Cymbeline*'. *Comparative Drama* 31 (1997): 277–303.

Dane, Gabrielle. 'Reading Ophelia's Madness'. *Exemplaria* 10 (1998): 405–23.

Daniel, Samuel. *Delia. Elizabethan Sonnets*. Ed. Maurice Evans; rev. Roy J. Booth. Everyman Library. London: Dent; and Rutland, VT: Tuttle, 1994. 58–80.

Samuel Daniel: Selected Poetry and 'A Defense of Rhyme'. Ed. Geoffrey G. Hiller and Peter L. Groves. Asheville, NC: Pegasus Press, 1998.

Daniell, David, ed. *Julius Caesar*. Arden Shakespeare. 3rd Series. London: Thomas Nelson, 2003.

Dante Alighieri. *The Divine Comedy*. Trans. Allen Mandelbaum. Everyman Library. New York: Knopf, 1995.

David, Richard, ed. *Love's Labour's Lost*. Arden Shakespeare. 2nd Series. London: Methuen, 1968.

Davidson, Clifford. 'Falstaff's Catechism on Honor'. *Neuphilologische Mitteilungen* 72 (1971): 283–6.

De Grazia, Margreta. *Shakespeare Verbatim: The Reproduction of Authenticity and the 1790 Apparatus*. Oxford: Clarendon, 1991.

'Soliloquies and Wages in the Age of Emergent Consciousness'. *Textual Practice* 9 (1995): 67–92.

'Hamlet' without Hamlet. Cambridge University Press, 2007.

De Grazia, Margreta, and Peter Stallybrass. 'The Materiality of the Shakespearean Text'. *Shakespeare Quarterly* 44 (1993): 255–83.

De Grazia, Margreta, Maureen Quilligan, and Peter Stallybrass, eds. *Subject and Object in Renaissance Culture*. Cambridge University Press, 1996.

De Grazia, Margreta, and Stanley Wells, eds. *The Cambridge Companion to Shakespeare*. Cambridge University Press, 2001.

De Vroom, Thersia. 'Mediating Myth: The Art of Marlowe's *Hero and Leander*'. *CLA Journal* 37 (1994): 425–42.

Dobson, Michael. *The Making of the National Poet: Shakespeare, Adaptation, and Authorship, 1660–1769*. Oxford: Clarendon, 1992.

Donaldson, E. Talbot. *The Swan at the Well: Shakespeare Reading Chaucer*. New Haven: Yale University Press, 1985.

Donne, John. *The Poems of John Donne*. Ed. Herbert J. C. Grierson. 2 vols. Oxford: Clarendon, 1912.

Dubrow, Heather. *Captive Victors: Shakespeare's Narrative Poems and Sonnets*. Ithaca: Cornell University Press, 1987.

　Echoes of Desire: English Petrarchism and its Counterdiscourses. Ithaca: Cornell University Press, 1995.

　'Twentieth-Century Shakespeare Criticism'. *Riverside Shakespeare*. 27–54.

　Shakespeare and Domestic Loss: Forms of Deprivation, Mourning, and Recuperation. Cambridge University Press, 1999.

　'Lyric Forms'. Kinney, ed. 178–99.

　'"These So Differing Twins": The Interplay of Narrative and Lyric in Shakespeare's Narrative Poems'. Unpublished paper.

　'What Imports This Song?' Unpublished paper.

Duncan-Jones, Katherine. *Ungentle Shakespeare: Scenes from His Life*. Arden Shakespeare. 3rd Series. London: Thomson Learning, 2001.

Duncan-Jones, Katherine, ed. *Shakespeare's Sonnets*. Arden Shakespeare. 3rd Series. London: Thomas Nelson, 1997.

Duncan-Jones, and Henry Woudhuysen, eds. *Shakespeare's Poems*. Arden Shakespeare. 3rd Series. Forthcoming.

Dunn, Leslie C. 'Ophelia's Songs in *Hamlet*: Music, Madness, and the Feminine'. *Embodied Voices: Representing Female Vocality in Western Culture*. Ed. Leslie C. Dunn and Nancy A. Jones. Cambridge University Press, 1994. 50–64.

Durling, Robert M. *The Figure of the Poet in Renaissance Epic*. Cambridge, MA: Harvard University Press, 1965.

Durling, Robert M., ed. and trans. *Petrarch's Lyric Poems: The 'Rime sparse' and Other Lyrics*. Cambridge, MA: Harvard University Press, 1976.

Dutton, Richard, and Jean E. Howard, eds. *A Companion to Shakespeare's Works*. 4 vols.: *The Tragedies*; *The Histories*; *The Comedies*; *The Poems, Problem Comedies, Late Plays*. Oxford: Blackwell, 2003.

Edwards, Philip, ed. *Hamlet, Prince of Denmark*. New Cambridge Shakespeare. Cambridge University Press, 1985, 2003.

Edwards, Robert R. *The Flight from Desire: Augustine and Ovid to Chaucer*. New York: Palgrave Macmillan, 2006.

　'Ricardian Dreamwork: Chaucer, Cupid, and Loyal Lovers'. *The Legend of Good Women: Context and Reception*. Ed. Carolyn P. Collette. Cambridge: D. S. Brewer, 2006. 59–82.

Engle, Lars. '"Afloat in Thick Deeps": Shakespeare's Sonnets on Certainty'. *PMLA* 104 (1989): 832–43.

Enterline, Lynn. *The Rhetoric of the Body: From Ovid to Shakespeare*. Cambridge University Press, 2000.

Eriksen, Roy T. 'Marlowe's Petrarch: *In Morte di Madonna Laura*'. *Cahiérs Elisabéthains* 29 (1986): 13–25.

Erne, Lukas. *Shakespeare as Literary Dramatist*. Cambridge University Press, 2003.
   'Print and Manuscript'. Cheney, ed., *Cambridge Companion to Shakespeare's Poetry*. 54–71.
   'Shakespeare for Readers'. *Alternative Shakespeares* III. Ed. Diana E. Henderson. London: Routledge. Forthcoming.

Evans, G. Blakemore, ed. *Romeo and Juliet*. New Cambridge Shakespeare. Cambridge University Press, 1984, 2003.

Everett, Barbara. '*Much Ado about Nothing*: The Unsociable Comedy'. *English Comedy*. Ed. Michael Cordner, Peter Holland, and John Kerrigan. Cambridge University Press, 1994. 68–84.
   'Good and Bad Loves: Shakespeare, Plato and the Plotting of the Sonnets'. *Times Literary Supplement* 5 July 2002: 13–15.

Faas, Ekbert. *Shakespeare's Poetics*. Cambridge University Press, 1986.

Fabiszak, Jacek. 'A Portrait of the Artist as a Shakespearean Character in *The Winter's Tale*'. *Studia Anglica Posnaniensia* 30 (1996): 149–57.

Farrell, Joseph. 'Greek Lives and Roman Careers in the Classical *Vita* Tradition'. Cheney and de Armas, eds. 24–46.

Fernie, Ewan. 'The Last Act: Presentism, Spirituality, and the Politics of *Hamlet*'. Fernie, ed. 186–211.

Fernie, Ewan, ed. *Spiritual Shakespeares*. London: Routledge, 2005.

Fienberg. ' "She Chanted Snatches of Old Tunes": Ophelia's Songs in Polyphonic *Hamlet*'. *Approaches to Teaching Shakespeare's 'Hamlet'*. Ed. Bernice W. Kliman. New York: Modern Language Association, 2001. 153–6.

Findlay, Alison. '*Hamlet*: A Document in Madness'. *New Essays on Hamlet*. Ed. Mark Thornton Burnett and John Mannery. New York: AMS Press, 1994. 189–205.

Fineman, Joel. 'Shakespeare's Will: The Temporality of Rape'. *Representations* 20 (1987): 25–76.

Floyd-Wilson, Mary. *English Ethnicity and Race in Early Modern Drama*. Cambridge University Press, 2003.

Foakes, R. A., ed. *A Midsummer Night's Dream*. New Cambridge Shakespeare. Cambridge University Press, 2003.

Foucault, Michel. 'What Is an Author?' *The Foucault Reader*. Ed. Paul Rabinow. New York: Pantheon Books, 1984. 101–20.

Fox-Good, Jacquelyn A. 'Ophelia's Mad Songs: Music, Gender, Power'. *Subjects on the World's Stage: Essays on British Literature of the Middle Ages and the Renaissance*. Ed. David G. Allen and Robert A. White. Newark: University of Delaware Press, 1995. 217–38.

Frecerro, John. 'The Fig Tree and the Laurel: Petrarch's Poetics'. Parker and Quint, eds. 20–32.

Freinkel, Lisa. *Reading Shakespeare's Will: The Theology of Figure from Augustine to the Sonnets*. New York: Columbia University Press, 2002.

Frye, Northrop. *A Natural Perspective: The Development of Shakespearean Comedy and Romance*. New York: Columbia University Press, 1965.

The Return of Eden: Five Essays on Milton's Epics. University of Toronto Press, 1965.

Fools of Time: Studies in Shakespearean Tragedy. University of Toronto Press, 1967.

'*Hamlet*'. *Northrop Frye on Shakespeare*. New Haven: Yale University Press, 1986. 82–100.

'The Argument of Comedy'. Kernan, ed. 165–73.

Furness, Horace Howard, ed. *A New Variorum Edition of Shakespeare: The Tempest*. Philadelphia, 1892.

A New Variorum Edition of Shakespeare: Much Adoe About Nothing. Philadelphia, 1899.

A New Variorum Edition of Shakespeare: Cymbeline. Philadelphia: J. B. Lippincott, 1913.

A New Variorum Edition of Shakespeare: Hamlet. 2 vols. New York: Dover, 1963.

Gallagher, Philip J. 'Prometheus'. *Spenser Encyclopedia*. 557–8.

Garber, Marjorie. 'Marlovian Vision / Shakespearean Revision'. *Research Opportunities in Renaissance Drama* 22 (1979): 3–9.

Shakespeare's Ghost Writers: Literature as Uncanny Causality. New York: Routledge, 1987.

'*Hamlet*: Giving up the Ghost'. Wofford, ed. 297–331.

Shakespeare After All. New York: Pantheon Books, 2004.

Gay, Penny. '*Much Ado about Nothing*: A King of Merry War'. *As She Likes It: Shakespeare's Unruly Women*. London: Routledge, 1994. 143–77.

Genette, Gerard. *Palimpsests: Literature in the Second Degree*. Trans. Channa Newman and Claude Doublinsky. 1982; Lincoln, NE: University of Nebraska Press, 1997.

Geneva Bible: A Facsimile Edition. Ed. Lloyd E. Berry. Madison: University of Wisconsin Press, 1969.

Giamatti, A. Bartlett. *The Earthly Paradise and the Renaissance Epic*. Princeton University Press, 1966.

Gibbons, Brian, ed. *Romeo and Juliet*. Arden Shakespeare. 2nd Series. London: Methuen, 1980.

Measure for Measure. New Cambridge Shakespeare. Cambridge University Press, 1991.

Gilbert, Miriam. 'Performance Criticism'. Wells and Orlin, eds. 550–67.

Gildon, Charles. *Works of Mr William Shakespear. Volume the Seventh. Containing, Venus & Adonis. Tarquin & Lucrece And His Miscellany of Poems*. London, 1710.

Gillett, Peter J. 'Vernon and the Metamorphosis of Hal'. *Shakespeare Quarterly* 28 (1977): 351–3.

Goddard, Harold C. *The Meaning of Shakespeare*. 2 vols. 1951; University of Chicago Press-Phoenix, 1960.

Golding, Arthur, trans. '*Metamorphoses*'. *Shakespeare's Ovid*. Ed. W. H. D. Rouse. New York: Norton, 1966.

Gough, Melinda J. "'Her Filthy Feature Open Showne" in Ariosto, Spenser, and *Much Ado about Nothing*'. *Studies in English Literature 1500–1900* 39 (1999): 41–67.

Goy-Blanquet, Dominique. *Shakespeare's Early History Plays: From Chronicle to Stage*. Oxford University Press, 2003.

Greenblatt, Stephen. *Renaissance Self-Fashioning: From More to Shakespeare*. University of Chicago Press, 1980.

'Murdering Peasants: Status, Genre, and the Representation of Rebellion'. *Learning to Curse: Essays in Early Modern Culture*. New York: Routledge, 1990. 99–130.

Hamlet in Purgatory. Princeton University Press, 2001.

Will in the World: How Shakespeare Became Shakespeare. New York: Norton, 2004.

Greenblatt, Stephen, ed. *'Much Ado about Nothing'*. Introduction. *Norton Shakespeare*. 1381–7.

Greene, Thomas M. *The Descent from Heaven: A Study in Epic Continuity*. New Haven: Yale University Press, 1963.

The Light in Troy: Imitation and Discovery in Renaissance Poetry. New Haven: Yale University Press, 1982.

Greenfield, Matthew. *'I Henry IV*: Metatheatrical Britain'. *British Identities and English Renaissance Literature*. Ed. David J. Baker and Willy Maley. Cambridge University Press, 2002. 71–80.

Griffiths, Huw. 'The Geographies of Shakespeare's *Cymbeline*'. *English Literary Renaissance* 34 (2004): 339–58.

Gross, Kenneth. *Shakespeare's Noise*. University of Chicago Press, 2001.

Guillory, John D. *Poetic Authority*. New York: Columbia University Press, 1983.

Gurr, Andrew. *Hamlet and the Distracted Globe*. Edinburgh: Scottish Academic Press, 1978.

Hackel, Heidi Brayman. "'The Great Variety of Readers" and Early Modern Reading Practices'. Kastan, ed., *Companion to Shakespeare*. 139–57.

Reading Material in Early Modern England: Print, Gender, and Literacy. Cambridge University Press, 2005.

Hadfield, Andrew. 'Was Spenser a Republican?'. *English* 47 (1998): 169–82.

'Michael Drayton's Brilliant Career'. *Proceedings of the British Academy* 125 (2002): 119–47.

Shakespeare and Renaissance Politics. Arden Shakespeare. New York: Thomson Learning, 2004.

Shakespeare, Spenser, and the Matter of Britain. Basingstoke: Palgrave Macmillan, 2004.

Shakespeare and Republicanism. Cambridge University Press, 2005.

Hamilton, A. C. *The Early Shakespeare*. San Marino: Huntington Library, 1967.

Hamilton, A. C., ed. *The Faerie Queene*. 2nd edn. New York: Longman, 2001.

Hamilton, Donna B. *Virgil and 'The Tempest': The Politics of Imitation*. Columbus: Ohio State University Press, 1990.

Hamlin, William M. *Tragedy and Scepticism in Shakespeare's England*. Basingstoke: Palgrave Macmillan, 2005.

Hammond, Antony, ed. *King Richard III*. Arden Shakespeare. 3nd Series. London: Thomson Learning, 2000.

Hardie, Philip. 'Ovid's Theban History: The First "Anti-*Aeneid*"?' *Classical Quarterly* 40 (1990): 224–35.

  Ovid's Poetics of Illusion. Cambridge University Press, 2002.

Hardie, Philip, ed. *The Cambridge Companion to Ovid*. Cambridge University Press, 2002.

Hardin, Richard F. 'Drayton, Michael'. *Spenser Encyclopedia*. 224–6.

Harris, Jonathan Gil. 'Materialist Criticisms'. Wells and Orlin, eds. 472–91.

Hartsock, Mildred E. 'Major Scenes in Minor Key'. *Shakespeare Quarterly* 21 (1970): 55–62.

Hartwig, Joan. 'Cloten, Autolycus, and Caliban: Bearers of Parodic Burdens'. *Shakespeare's Romances Reconsidered*. Ed. Carol McGinnis Kay and Henry E. Jacobs. Lincoln, NE: University of Nebraska Press, 1978. 91–103.

Hassel, Chris, Jr. 'Last Words and Last Things: St John, Apocalypse, and Eschatology in *Richard III*'. *Shakespeare Studies* 18 (1986): 25–40.

Hattaway, Michael. 'The Shakespearean History Play'. *The Cambridge Companion to Shakespeare's History Plays*. Ed. Michael Hattaway. Cambridge University Press, 2002. 3–24.

Hattaway, Michael, ed. *The Second Part of Henry VI*. New Cambridge Shakespeare. Cambridge University Press, 1991.

Helgerson, Richard. *The Elizabethan Prodigals*. Berkeley: University of California Press, 1976.

  Self-Crowned Laureates: Spenser, Jonson, Milton, and the Literary System. Berkeley: University of California Press, 1983.

  Forms of Nationhood: The Elizabethan Writing of England. University of Chicago Press, 1992.

Henderson, Diane E. *Passion Made Public: Elizabethan Lyric, Gender, and Performance*. Urbana: University of Illinois Press, 1995.

Hibbard, G. R., ed. *Hamlet*. Oxford World's Classics. Oxford University Press, 1987.

  Love's Labour's Lost. Oxford World's Classics. Oxford University Press, 1990.

Hieatt, A. Kent. 'The Genesis of Shakespeare's *Sonnets*: Spenser's *Ruines of Rome: by Bellay*'. *PMLA* 98 (1983): 800–14.

  'Shakespeare, William'. *Spenser Encyclopedia*. 641–3.

Hillman, David. 'Gastric Epic: *Troilus and Cressida*'. *Shakespeare Quarterly* 48 (1997): 295–313.

Hinds, Stephen. *The Metamorphosis of Persephone: Ovid and the Self-Conscious Muse*. Cambridge University Press, 1987.

Hobday, Charles. 'Clouted Shoon and Leather Aprons: Shakespeare and the Egalitarian Tradition'. *Renaissance and Modern Studies* 23 (1979): 63–78.

Hodgdon, Barbara. *The End Crowns All: Closure and Contradiction in Shakespeare's History*. Princeton University Press, 1991.

Holland, Norman N., Sidney Homan, and Bernard J. Paris, eds. *Shakespeare's Personality*. Berkeley: University of California Press, 1989.

Holland, Peter. 'William Shakespeare (1564–1616), Playwright and Poet'. *Oxford Dictionary of National Biography*. Oxford University Press, 2004–6. <www.oxforddnb.com/view/printable/25200>.

Holland, Peter, ed. *A Midsummer Night's Dream*. Oxford World's Classics. Oxford University Press, 1994.

Much Ado about Nothing. Pelican Shakespeare. Harmondsworth: Penguin, 1999.

Homer. *The 'Iliad' of Homer*. Trans. Richmond Lattimore. 1951; Chicago: University of Chicago Press-Phoenix, 1967.

The 'Odyssey' of Homer. Trans. Richmond Lattimore. 1965, 1967; New York: Harper Torchbooks, Harper & Row, 1968.

Honan, Park. *Shakespeare: A Life*. Oxford University Press, 1999.

Honigmann, E. A. J. *The Stability of Shakespeare's Text*. Lincoln, NE: University of Nebraska Press, 1965.

Honigmann, E. A. J., ed. *Othello*. Arden Shakespeare. 3rd Series. London: Thomson Learning, 1997.

Howard, Jean E. 'Renaissance Antitheatricality and the Politics of Gender and Rank in *Much Ado about Nothing*'. *Shakespeare Reproduced: The Text in History and Ideology*. Ed. Jean E. Howard and Marion F. O'Conner. New York: Methuen, 1987. 163–87.

Hubler, Edward, ed. *Shakespeare's Songs and Poems*. New York: McGraw Hill, 1959.

The Tragedy of Hamlet, Prince of Denmark. New York: Signet, 1987.

Hulse, Clark. *Metamorphic Verse: The Elizabethan Minor Epic*. Princeton University Press, 1981.

'Tudor Aesthetics'. Kinney, ed. 29–63.

Humphreys, A. R., ed. *The First Part of King Henry IV*. Arden Shakespeare. 2nd Series. London: Methuen, 1960.

Much Ado about Nothing. Arden Shakespeare. 2nd Series. 1981; London: Thomson Learning, 2002.

Hunter, Edwin R. *Shakespeare and the Common Sense*. Boston, MA: Christopher Publishing, 1954.

Hunter, Robert G. *Shakespeare and the Mystery of God's Judgments*. Athens: University of Georgia Press, 1976.

Hyland, Peter. *An Introduction to Shakespeare's Poems*. Basingstoke: Palgrave Macmillan, 2003.

Ide, Richard S. *Possessed with Greatness: The Heroic Tragedies of Chapman and Shakespeare*. Chapel Hill: University of North Carolina Press, 1980.

Jackson, M. P. 'Francis Meres and the Cultural Contexts of Shakespeare's Rival Poet Sonnets'. *Review of English Studies* 56 (2006): 225–46.

Jackson, Ken. *Separate Theaters: Bethlem ('Bedlam') Hospital and the Shakespearean Stage*. Newark: University of Delaware Press, 2005.

James, Heather. *Shakespeare's Troy: Drama, Politics, and the Translation of Empire*. Cambridge University Press, 1997.

Jenkins, Harold, ed. *Hamlet*. Arden Shakespeare. 2nd Series. London: Methuen, 1982.

Johnson, W. R. 'The Problem of the Counter-Classical Sensibility and Its Critics'. *California Studies in Classical Antiquity* 3 (1970): 123–51.

Jonson, Ben. *Ben Jonson*. Ed. C. H. Herford and Percy and Evelyn Simpson. 11 vols. Oxford: Clarendon, 1925–52.

Works of Ben Jonson. London, 1616.

Jordan, Constance. *Shakespeare's Monarchies: Ruler and Subject in the Romances*. Ithaca: Cornell University Press, 1997.

Jowett, John, ed. *Richard III*. Oxford World's Classics. Oxford University Press, 2000.

Kastan, David Scott. *Shakespeare and the Shapes of Time*. London: Macmillan, 1982.

Shakespeare and the Book. Cambridge University Press, 2001.

Kastan, David Scott, ed. *Critical Essays on Shakespeare's 'Hamlet'*. New York: G. K. Hall, 1995.

A Companion to Shakespeare. Oxford: Blackwell, 1999.

King Henry IV, Part 1. Arden Shakespeare. 3rd Series. London: Thomson Learning, 2002.

Keilen, Sean. *Vulgar Eloquence: On the Renaissance Invention of English Literature*. New Haven: Yale University Press, 2006.

Kennedy, William J. *Authorizing Petrarch*. Ithaca: Cornell University Press, 1994.

The Site of Petrarchism: Early Modern National Sentiment in Italy, France, and England. Baltimore: Johns Hopkins University Press, 2003.

Kermode, Frank. *Shakespeare's Language*. London: Allen Lane, Penguin, 2000.

Kermode, Frank, ed. *The Tempest*. Arden Shakespeare. 2nd Series. London: Methuen, 1954.

Kernan, Alvin. 'The Henriad: Shakespeare's Major History Plays'. Kernan, ed. 245–75.

'Shakespeare's Essays on Dramatic Poesy: The Nature and Function of Theater within the Sonnets and the Plays'. *The Author in His Work: Essays on a Problem in Criticism*. Ed. Louis L. Martz and Aubrey Williams. New Haven: Yale University Press, 1978. 175–96.

Shakespeare, the King's Playwright: Theater in the Stuart Court, 1603–1613. New Haven: Yale University Press, 1995.

Kernan, Alvin B., ed. *Modern Shakespearean Criticism: Essays on Style, Dramaturgy, and the Major Plays*. New York: Harcourt, Brace, & World, 1970.

Kerrigan, William. 'The Personal Shakespeare: Three Clues'. Holland, Homan, and Paris, eds. 175–90.

Hamlet's Perfection. Baltimore: Johns Hopkins University Press, 1994.

Kiefer, Carol Solomon, ed. *The Myth and Madness of Ophelia*. Amherst: Mead Art Museum, Amherst College, 2001.

'The Myth and Madness of Ophelia'. C. S. Kiefer, ed. 11–39.

Kiefer, Frederick. *Writing on the Renaissance Stage: Written Words, Printed Pages, Metaphoric Books*. Newark: University of Delaware Press; Cranbury, NJ: Associated University Presses, 1996.

Kiernan, Pauline. *Shakespeare's Theory of Drama*. Cambridge University Press, 1996.

King, Katherine Callen. *Achilles: Paradigms of the War Hero from Homer to the Middle Ages.* Berkeley: University of California Press, 1987.

King, Ros. *Cymbeline: Constructions of Britain.* Aldershot: Ashgate, 2005.

King, Walter N. 'Much Ado About Something'. *Shakespeare Quarterly* 15 (1964): 143–55.

Hamlet's Search for Meaning. Athens: University of Georgia Press, 1982.

Kinney, Arthur F., ed. *The Cambridge Companion to English Literature 1500–1600.* Cambridge University Press, 2000.

Klein, Joan Larsen. ' "Angels and Ministers of Grace": *Hamlet*, IV, v–vii'. *Allegorica* 1 (1976): 156–76.

Knapp, Jeffrey. 'What is a Co-Author?'. *Representations* 89 (2005): 1–29.

Knapp, R. S. *Shakespeare: The Theatre and the Book.* Princeton University Press, 1989.

Knight, G. Wilson. *The Wheel of Fire: Interpretations of Shakespearean Tragedy.* 1930; London: Routledge, 1989.

'The Embassy of Death: An Essay on Hamlet'. *Wheel of Fire.* 17–48.

'*Hamlet* Reconsidered'. *Wheel of Fire.* 338–66.

Knowles, Ronald. 'The Farce of History: Miracle, Combat, and Rebellion in *2 Henry VI* '. *English Studies* 21 (1991): 168–86.

Knowles, Ronald, ed. *King Henry VI, Part 2.* Arden Shakespeare. 3rd Series. London: Thomas Nelson, 1999.

Kreps, Barbara. 'Bad Memories of Margaret: Memorial Reconstruction versus Revision in *The First Part of the Contention* and *2 Henry VI* '. *Shakespeare Quarterly* 51 (2000): 154–80.

Krieger, Elliot. 'Social Relations and the Social Order in *Much Ado about Nothing*'. *Shakespeare Survey* 32 (1979): 49–61.

Krier, Theresa M. *Birth Passages: Maternity and Nostalgia, Antiquity to Shakespeare.* Ithaca: Cornell University Press, 2001.

Kristeva, Julia. 'Word, Dialogue, and Novel'. *The Kristeva Reader.* Trans. Alice Jardine, Thomas Gora, and Leon S. Roudiez. Ed. Toril Moi. New York: Columbia University Press, 1986. 33–61.

Kuskin, William. 'Recursive Origins: John Lydgate, Textual Culture, and Shakespearean Authorship in the 1594 *Contention*'. *Shakespeare and the Middle Ages.* Ed. John Watkins and Curtis Perry. Oxford University Press. Forthcoming.

Lamb, Mary Ellen. 'Ovid and *The Winter's Tale*: Conflicting Views toward Art'. *Shakespeare and Dramatic Tradition: Essays in Honor of S. F. Johnson.* Ed. William R. Elton. Newark: University of Delaware Press; London: Associated University Presses, 1989. 69–87.

Lander, Jesse M. *Inventing Polemic: Religion, Print, and Literary Culture in Early Modern England.* Cambridge University Press, 2006.

Lascelles, Mary. '*King Lear* and Doomsday'. *Shakespeare Survey* 26 (1973): 69–79.

Lateiner, Donald. '*The Iliad*: An Unpredictable Classic'. *Cambridge Companion to Homer.* Ed. Robert Fowler. Cambridge University Press, 2004. 11–30.

Lee, John. *Shakespeare's 'Hamlet' and the Controversies of Self.* Oxford University Press, 2000.

Leech, Clifford, ed. *Two Gentlemen of Verona*. Arden Shakespeare. 2nd Series. London: Methuen, 1969.

Lees-Jeffries, Hester. *England's Helicon: Fountains in Early Modern Literature and Culture*. Oxford University Press, 2007.

Leishman, J. B. *Themes and Variations in Shakespeare's Sonnets*. New York: Harper & Row, 1961, 1963.

Lethbridge, Julian B., ed. *Spenser and Shakespeare*. Manchester University Press, forthcoming, 2008.

Levenson, Jill L., ed. *Romeo and Juliet*. Oxford World's Classics. Oxford University Press, 2000.

Lever, J. W., ed. *Measure for Measure*. Arden Shakespeare. 2nd Series. London: Methuen, 1965.

Leverenz, David. 'The Woman in Hamlet: An Interpersonal View'. Schwartz and Kahn, eds. 110–28.

Levin, Harry. *The Question of Hamlet*. New York: Oxford University Press, 1959. 'Critical Approaches to Shakespeare from 1660 to 1904'. Wells, ed. 213–29.

Lewalski, Barbara K. 'Love, Appearance, and Reality: Much Ado about Something'. *Studies in English Literature 1500–1900* 8 (1968): 235–51.

Lindley, David. 'Shakespeare's Provoking Music'. *The Well Enchanting Skill: Music, Poetry, and Drama in the Culture of the Renaissance*. Ed. John Caldwell, Edward Olleson, and Susan Wollenberg. Oxford: Clarendon, 1990. 79–90.

Shakespeare and Music. Arden Shakespeare. London: Thomson Learning, 2006.

Lindley, David, ed. *The Tempest*. Arden Shakespeare. London: Thomson Learning, 2003.

Lodge, Thomas. *The Complete Works of Thomas Lodge*. 4 vols. New York: Russell & Russell, 1963.

Loewenstein, Joseph. 'Shakespeare's Stamp'. Unpublished paper.

Logan, Robert. *Shakespeare's Marlowe: The Influence of Christopher Marlowe on Shakespeare's Artistry*. Aldershot: Ashgate, 2007.

Lull, Janis, ed. *King Richard III*. New Cambridge Shakespeare. Cambridge University Press, 1999.

Lyne, Raphael. *Ovid's Changing Worlds: English 'Metamorphoses', 1567–1632*. Oxford University Press, 2001.

'Ovid, Golding, and the "rough magic" of *The Tempest*'. Taylor, A. B., ed. 150–64.

Lyons, Bridget Gellert. 'The Iconography of Ophelia'. *ELH* 44 (1977): 60–74.

McCabe, Richard A. *Spenser's Monstrous Regiment: Elizabethan Ireland and the Poetics of Difference*. Oxford University Press, 2002.

McDonald, Ronald. 'Playing Till Doomsday: Interpreting *Antony and Cleopatra*'. *English Literary Renaissance* 15 (1985): 78–99.

McDonald, Russ. *Shakespeare and the Arts of Language*. Oxford University Press, 2001.

The Bedford Companion to Shakespeare: An Introduction with Documents. 2nd edn. Boston, MA: Bedford, St Martin's Press, 2001.

Mack, Maynard. 'The World of *Hamlet*'. Hubler, ed., *Hamlet*. 234–56.

McKenzie, D. F. 'Printers of the Mind: Some Notes on Bibliographical Theories and Printing-House Practices'. *Making Meaning: 'Printers of the Mind' and Other Essays*. Ed. Peter D. McDonald and Michael F. Suarez, SJ. Amherst: University of Massachusetts Press, 2002. 13–85.

McKerrow, Ronald B., ed. *The Works of Thomas Nashe*. Rev. F. P. Wilson. 5 vols. Oxford: Blackwell, 1958.

Maclean, Hugh, and Anne Lake Prescott, eds. *Edmund Spenser's Poetry*. 3rd edn. New York: Norton, 1993.

Maguire, Laurie E. *Shakespearean Suspect Texts: The 'Bad' Quartos and Their Contexts*. Cambridge University Press, 1996.

Malone, Edmond, ed. *Plays and Poems of William Shakespeare*. London, 1790.

Manley, Lawrence. 'From Strange's Men to Pembroke's Men: *2 Henry VI* and *The First Part of the Contention*'. *Shakespeare Quarterly* 54 (2003): 253–87.

Marcus, Leah S. *Puzzling Shakespeare: Local Reading and Its Discontents*. Berkeley: University of California Press, 1988.

Mares, F. H., ed. *Much Ado About Nothing*. New Cambridge Shakespeare. Cambridge University Press, 1988, 2003.

Marotti, Arthur F. *Manuscript, Print, and the English Renaissance Lyric*. Ithaca: Cornell University Press, 1995.

Marshall, Cynthia. *Last Things and Last Plays: Shakespearean Eschatology*. Carbondale: Southern Illinois University Press, 1991.

'*Cymbeline*: A Modern Perspective'. *Cymbeline*. Folger Shakespeare. Ed. Barbara A. Mowat and Paul Werstine. New York: Washington Square Press, 2003. 289–302.

Martindale, Charles, and Michelle Martindale. *Shakespeare and the Uses of Antiquity: An Introductory Essay*. London: Routledge, 1990.

Masten, Jeffrey. *Textual Intercourse: Collaboration, Authorship, and Sexualities in Renaissance Drama*. Cambridge University Press, 1997.

Maus, Katharine Eisaman. 'Taking Tropes Seriously: Language and Violence in Shakespeare's *Rape of Lucrece*'. *Shakespeare Quarterly* 37 (1986): 66–82.

Inwardness and Theatre in the English Renaissance. University of Chicago Press, 1995.

Maxwell, J. C., ed. *Titus Andronicus*. Arden Shakespeare. 2nd Series. London: Methuen, 1968.

Mazzaro, Jerome. 'Shakespeare's "Books of Memory": *1* and *2 Henry VI*'. *Comparative Drama* 35 (2001): 393–414.

Mazzotta, Giuseppe. *The Worlds of Petrarch*. Durham, NC: Duke University Press, 1993.

Mikalachki, Jodi. *The Legacy of Boadicea: Gender and Nation in Early Modern England*. New York: Routledge, 1998.

Milton, John. *John Milton: Complete Poems and Major Prose*. Ed. Merritt Y. Hughes. Indianapolis: Odyssey, 1957.

Miola, Robert S. '*Cymbeline*: Shakespeare's Valediction to Rome'. *Roman Images*. Ed. Annabel Patterson. Selected Papers from the English Institute, 1982. Baltimore: Johns Hopkins University Press, 1984. 51–62.

Shakespear's Rome. Cambridge University Press, 1983.

Montrose, Louis Adrian. 'The Elizabethan Subject and the Spenserian Text'. Parker and Quint, eds. 303–40.

'*A Midsummer Night's Dream* and the Shaping Fantasies of Elizabethan Culture: Gender, Power, Form'. *Rewriting the Renaissance.* Ed. Margaret Ferguson, Maureen Quilligan, and Nancy J. Vickers. University of Chicago Press, 1986. 65–87.

'Spenser's Domestic Domain: Poetry, Property, and the Early Modern Subject'. De Grazia, Quilligan, and Stallybrass, eds. 83–130.

'Spenser's Political Imaginary'. *ELH* 69 (2002): 907–46.

The Subject of Elizabeth: Authority, Gender, and Representation. University of Chicago Press, 2006.

Mowat, Barbara A. 'Rogues, Shepherds, and the Counterfeit Distressed: Texts and Infracontexts of *The Winter's Tale* 4.3'. *Shakespeare Studies* 22 (1994): 58–76.

Mowat, Barbara A., and Paul Werstine, eds. *Hamlet.* Folger Shakespeare. New York: Washington Square Press, 1992.

Mowat, Barbara A., and Paul Werstine, eds., *Much Ado about Nothing.* Folger Shakespeare. New York: Washington Square Press, 1995.

Muir, Kenneth. *Shakespeare the Professional and Related Studies.* Totowa, NJ: Rowman & Littlefield, 1973.

Muir, Kenneth, ed. *Troilus and Cressida.* Oxford World's Classics. Oxford University Press, 1982.

Murphy, Andrew, ed. *The Renaissance Text: Theory, Editing, Textuality.* Manchester University Press, 2000.

Shakespeare in Print: A History and Chronology of Shakespeare Publishing. Cambridge University Press, 2003.

Neely, Carol Thomas. *Broken Nuptials in Shakespeare's Plays.* New Haven: Yale University Press, 1985.

Distracted Subjects: Madness and Gender in Shakespeare and Early Modern Culture. Ithaca: Cornell University Press, 2004.

Neill, Michael. *Issues of Death: Mortality and Identity in English Renaissance Tragedy.* Oxford: Clarendon, 1997.

Nelson, Alan H. 'Shakespeare and the Bibliophiles'. *Owners, Annotators, and the Signs of Reading.* Ed. Robin Myers, Michael Harris, and Giles Mandelbrote. New Castle, DE: Oak Knoll Press; London: British Library, 2005. 49–73.

Newdigate, Bernard H. *Michael Drayton and His Circle.* Oxford: Blackwell, 1941.

Newman, Jane O. ' "And Let Mild Women to Him Lose Their Mildness": Philomela, Female Violence, and Shakespeare's *The Rape of Lucrece*'. *Shakespeare Quarterly* 45 (1994): 304–25.

Norton Shakespeare: Based on the Oxford Edition. Ed. Stephen Greenblatt *et al.* New York: Norton, 1997.

Nosworthy, J. M., ed. *Cymbeline.* Arden Shakespeare. 2nd Series. London: Methuen, 1969.

O'Connell, Michael. 'The Experiment of Romance. *Cambridge Companion to Shakespearean Comedy.* Ed. Alexander Leggatt. Cambridge University Press, 2002. 215–29.

Ogilvy, J. D. A. 'Arcadianism in *1 Henry IV*'. *English Language Notes* 10 (1973): 185–8.

Orgel, Stephen. 'What Is a Text?' *Staging the Renaissance: Reinterpretations of Elizabethan and Jacobean Drama.* Ed. David Scott Kastan and Peter Stallybrass. New York: Routledge, 1991. 83–7.

Orgel, Stephen, ed. *Christopher Marlowe: The Complete Poems and Translations.* Harmondsworth: Penguin, 1971.

The Tempest. Oxford World's Classics. Oxford University Press, 1987.

The Winter's Tale. Oxford World's Classics. Oxford University Press, 1996.

Ornstein, Robert. *A Kingdom for a Stage: The Achievement of Shakespeare's History Plays.* Cambridge, MA: Harvard University Press, 1972.

Oruch, Jack B. 'Works, Lost'. *Spenser Encyclopedia.* 737–8.

Ovid. *Ovid.* 2nd edn. Trans. Frank Justus Miller; rev. G. P. Goold. Loeb Classical Library. 6 vols. Cambridge, MA: Harvard University Press; London: Heinemann, 1984.

Oxford Shakespeare. William Shakespeare: The Complete Works: Compact Edition. Ed. Stanley Wells and Gary Taylor. Oxford: Clarendon, 1988.

Paradin, Claude. *Devises Héroïques.* Aldershot: Scholar Press; Brookfield, VT: Gower, 1989.

Parfitt, George, ed. *Ben Jonson: The Complete Poems.* Harmondsworth: Penguin, 1975, 1988.

Paglia, Camille. *Sexual Personae: Art and Decadence from Nefertiti to Emily Dickinson.* New Haven: Yale University Press, 1990.

Palfrey, Simon. *Late Shakespeare: A New World of Words.* Oxford: Clarendon, 1997.

Parker, Patricia. 'Romance and Empire: Anachronistic *Cymbeline*'. *Unfolded Tales: Essays on Renaissance Romance.* Ed. George M. Logan and Gordon Teskey. Ithaca: Cornell University Press, 1989. 189–207.

Parker, Patricia, and Geoffrey Hartman, eds. *Shakespeare and the Question of Theory.* New York: Methuen, 1985.

Parker, Patricia, and David Quint, eds. *Literary Theory / Renaissance Texts.* Baltimore: Johns Hopkins University Press, 1986.

Paster, Gail Kern. '*Much Ado about Nothing*: A Modern Perspective'. Mowat and Werstine, eds., *Much Ado about Nothing.* 213–29.

Humoring the Body: Emotions and the Shakespearean Stage. University of Chicago Press, 2004.

Patterson, Annabel. *Pastoral and Ideology: Virgil to Valéry.* Berkeley: University of California Press, 1987.

Shakespeare and the Popular Voice. Oxford: Blackwell, 1989.

Patterson, Lee. *Chaucer and the Subject of History.* Madison: University of Wisconsin Press, 1991.

Pelican Shakespeare. Ed. Stephen Orgel and A. R. Braunmuller. New York: Penguin, 2002.

Pendleton, Thomas A., ed. *Henry VI: Critical Essays.* New York: Routledge, 2001.

Peters, Julie Stone. *Theatre of the Book 1480–1880: Print, Text, and Performance in Europe*. Oxford University Press, 2000.

Pettet, E. C. 'Shakespeare's Conception of Poetry'. *Essays and Studies: 1950*. Ed. G. Rostrevor Hamilton. London: John Murray, 1950. 29–46.

Pigman, G. W. 'Imitation and the Renaissance Sense of the Past: The Reception of Erasmus' *Ciceronianus*'. *Journal of Medieval Studies* 9 (1979): 155–77.

'Versions of Imitation in the Renaissance'. *Renaissance Quarterly* 33 (1980): 1–32.

Pitcher, John. 'Some Call Him Autolycus'. *In Arden: Editing Shakespeare: Essays in Honour of Richard Proudfoot*. Ed. Ann Thompson and Gordon McMullan. 3rd Arden Series. London: Arden Shakespeare, 2003. 252–68.

Plato. *The Collected Dialogues of Plato*. Ed. Edith Hamilton and Huntington Cairns. Princeton University Press, 1961.

Pope, Alexander, ed. *The Works of Mr William Shakespeare*. London, 1725.

Prince, F. T., ed. *The Poems*. Arden Shakespeare. 2nd Series. London: Methuen, 1960.

Pugh, Syrithe. *Spenser and Ovid*. Aldershot: Ashgate, 2005.

Pugliatti, Paola. ' "More Than History Can Pattern": The Jack Cade Rebellion in Shakespeare's *Henry VI, 2*'. *Journal of Medieval and Renaissance Studies* 22 (1992): 451–78.

Quint, David. *Epic and Empire: Politics and Generic Form from Virgil to Milton*. Princeton University Press, 1993.

Rabkin, Norman. *Shakespeare and the Common Understanding*. University of Chicago Press, 1967.

Rackin, Phyllis. *Stages of History: Shakespeare's English Chronicles*. Ithaca: Cornell University Press, 1990.

Ranjini, Philip. 'The Shattered Glass: The Story of (O)phelia'. *Hamlet Studies* 13 (1991): 73–84.

Redmond, M. J. ' "My Lord, I Fear, Has Forgot Britain": Rome, Italy and the (Re) construction of British Nation Identity'. *Shakespeare and Italy*. *Shakespeare Yearbook* 10. Ed. H. Klein and M. Marrapodi. Lewistown, ME: Edwin Mellon Press, 1999. 297–316.

Reese, M. M., ed. *Elizabethan Verse Romances*. London: Routledge & Kegan Paul, 1968.

Rhodes, Neill. '*Hamlet* and Humanism'. *Early Modern English Drama: A Critical Companion*. Ed. Garrett A. Sullivan Jr, Patrick Cheney, and Andrew Hadfield. New York: Oxford University Press, 2006. 120–9.

Ribner, Irving. 'Marlowe and Shakespeare'. *Shakespeare Quarterly* 15 (1964): 41–53.

Richards, Jennifer, and James Knowles, eds. *Shakespeare's Late Plays: New Readings*. Edinburgh University Press, 1999.

Ricks, Christopher. 'Allusion: The Poet as Heir'. *Studies in the Eighteenth Century*. Ed. R. F. Brissenden and J. C. Eade. University of Toronto Press, 1976. 209–40.

Riggs, David. *Shakespeare's Heroical Histories: 'Henry VI' and Its Literary Tradition*. Cambridge, MA: Harvard University Press, 1971.

Righter, Anne. *Shakespeare and the Idea of the Play*. London: Chatto & Windus, 1964.

Riverside Shakespeare. Ed. G. Blakemore Evans *et al.* 2nd edn. Boston, MA: Houghton, 1997.

Roe, John. *Shakespeare and Machiavelli*. Cambridge: D. S. Brewer, 2002.

Roe, John, ed. *The Poems*. New Cambridge Shakespeare. Cambridge University Press, 1992.

Rose, Mark. 'Othello's Occupation: Shakespeare and the Romance of Chivalry'. *English Literary Renaissance* 15 (1985): 293–311.

Rose, Mary Beth. *Gender and Heroism in Early Modern English Literature*. University of Chicago Press, 2002.

Rosenmeyer, Thomas G. *The Green Cabinet: Theocritus and the European Pastoral Lyric*. Berkeley: University of California Press, 1969.

Rossiter, A. P. *Angels with Horns and Other Shakespeare Lectures*. Ed. Graham Storey. New York: Theatre Arts Books, 1961.
  'Much Ado About Nothing'. *Shakespeare: The Comedies*. Ed. Kenneth Muir. Englewood Cliffs: Prentice-Hall, 1965. 47–57.

Rowe, Katherine. *Dead Hands: Fictions of Agency, Renaissance to Modern*. Stanford University Press, 1999.

Sanders, Eve Rachele. 'Interiority and the Letter in *Cymbeline*'. *Critical Survey* 12 (2000): 49–70.

Sanders, Norman, ed. *Othello*. New Cambridge Shakespeare. 1984; Cambridge University Press, 2003.

Santagata, Marco, ed. *Canzoniere of Francesco Petrarch*. Milan: Mondadori, 1996.

Saunders, J. W. 'The Stigma of Print: A Note on the Social Bases of Tudor Poetry'. *Essays in Criticism* (1951): 139–64.

Schalkwyk, David. *Speech and Performance in Shakespeare's Sonnets and Plays*. Cambridge University Press, 2002.

Schmidgall, Gary. *Shakespeare and the Poet's Life*. Lexington: University Press of Kentucky, 1990.

Schoenfeldt, Michael C. *Bodies and Selves in Early Modern England: Physiology and Interiority in Spenser, Shakespeare, Herbert and Milton*. Cambridge University Press, 1999.

Schwartz, Murray M., and Coppélia Kahn, eds. *Representing Shakespeare: New Psychoanalytic Essays*. Baltimore: Johns Hopkins University Press, 1980.

Scott, Charlotte. *Shakespeare and the Idea of the Book*. Oxford University Press, 2007.

Segal, Charles. *Orpheus: The Myth of the Poet*. Baltimore: Johns Hopkins University Press, 1989.

Seng, Peter J. 'Dramatic Function of the Songs in *Hamlet*'. *Hamlet*. Ed. Cyrus Hoy. 2nd edn. New York: Norton, 1992. 217–27.

Shakspere Allusion-Book: A Collection of Allusions to Shakspere from 1591 to 1700. Ed. C. M. Ingleby, L. Toulmin Smith, and F. J. Furnivall. Rev. edn. John Munro; pref. Edmund Chambers. 2 vols. 1909; Freeport, NY: Books for Libraries Press, 1970.

Shapiro, James. *Rival Playwrights: Marlowe, Jonson, Shakespeare*. New York: Columbia University Press, 1991.

A Year in the Life of William Shakespeare, 1599. London: Faber & Faber, 2005.

Showalter, Elaine. 'Representing Ophelia: Women, Madness, and the Responsibilities of Feminist Criticism'. Wofford, ed. 220–40.

Shuger, Debora. *Censorship and Sensibility: The Regulation of Language in Tudor-Stuart England*. Philadelphia: University of Pennsylvania Press, 2006.

Sidney, Sir Philip. *Sir Philip Sidney: Selected Prose and Poetry*. Ed. Robert Kimbrough. 2nd edn. Madison: University of Wisconsin Press, 1983.

The Defence of Poesy. Smith, G. G., ed. I: 148–207.

Simonds, Peggy Muñoz. *Myth, Emblem, and Music in Shakespeare's 'Cymbeline' and Iconographic Reconstruction*. Newark: University of Delaware Press, 1992.

Skura, Meredith. 'Interpreting Posthumus' Dream from Above and Below: Families, Psychoanalysis, and Literary Critics'. Schwartz and Kahn, eds. 203–16.

Smith, G. Gregory, ed. *Elizabethan Critical Essays*. 2 vols. London: Oxford University Press, 1904.

Smith, Hallett. *Elizabethan Poetry: A Study in Conventions, Meaning, and Expression*. Cambridge, MA: Harvard University Press, 1952.

Smith, M. Rick. '*Henry VI, Part 2*: Commodifying and Recommodifying the Past in Late-Medieval and Early Modern England'. Pendleton, ed. 177–204.

Spenser, Edmund. *The Poetical Works of Edmund Spenser*. Ed. J. C. Smith and Ernest de Sélincourt. 3 vols. Oxford: Clarendon, 1909–10.

Spenser Encyclopedia. Gen. Ed. A. C. Hamilton. University of Toronto Press, 1990.

Spevack, Marvin. *A Complete and Systematic Concordance to the Works of Shakespeare*. 6 vols. Hildesheim: Greg Olms Verlagsbuchhandlung, 1968–70.

Stallybrass, Peter, Roger Chartier, J. Franklin Mowery, and Heather Wolfe. 'Hamlet's Tables and the Technologies of Writing in Renaissance England'. *Shakespeare Quarterly* 55 (2004): 379–419.

Stallybrass, Peter, and Ann Rosalind Jones. 'Festishizing the Glove in Renaissance Europe'. *Critical Inquiry* 28 (2001): 114–32.

Stapleton, M. L. *Harmful Eloquence: Ovid's 'Amores' from Antiquity to Shakespeare*. Ann Arbor: University of Michigan Press, 1996.

Stern, Tiffany. *Making Shakespeare: From Stage to Page*. London: Routledge, 2004.

Still, Judith, and Michael Worton. *Intertextuality: Theories and Practice*. Manchester University Press, 1990.

Strohm, Paul. *Social Chaucer*. Cambridge, MA: Harvard University Press, 1989.

Sullivan, Garrett A., Jr. *The Drama of Landscape: Land, Property, and Social Relations on the Early Modern Stage*. Stanford University Press, 1998.

'Shakespeare's Comic Geographies'. Dutton and Howard, eds., *A Companion to Shakespeare's Works. The Comedies*. 182–99.

'Sleep, Epic, and Romance in *Antony and Cleopatra*'. *Antony and Cleopatra: New Critical Essays*. Ed. Sara Munson Deats. London: Routledge, 2005. 259–73.

Sullivan, Garrett A., Jr., and Linda Woodbridge. 'Popular Culture in Print'. Kinney, ed. 265–86.

Suzuki, Mihoko. *Metamorphoses of Helen: Authority, Difference, and the Epic*. Ithaca: Cornell University Press, 1989.

'Gender, Class, and the Ideology of Comic Form: *Much Ado about Nothing* and *Twelfth Night*'. *A Feminist Companion to Shakespeare*. Ed. Dympna Callaghan. Oxford: Blackwell, 2000. 121–43.

Tastpaugh, Patricia. 'Performance History: Shakespeare on the Stage, 1660–2001'. Wells and Orlin, eds. 525–49.

Taylor, A. B., ed. *Shakespeare's Ovid: The 'Metamorphoses' in the Plays and Poems*. Cambridge University Press, 2000.

Taylor, Gary. 'Forms of Opposition: Shakespeare and Middleton'. *English Literary Renaissance* 24 (1994): 283–314.

Teskey, Gordon. *Delirious Milton: The Fate of the Poet in Modernity*. Cambridge, MA: Harvard University Press, 2006.

Thompson, Ann. 'Philomel in "Titus Andronicus" and "Cymbeline"'. *Shakespeare Survey* 31 (1978): 23–32.

Shakespeare's Chaucer: A Study in Literary Origins. Liverpool University Press, 1978.

Thompson, Ann, and John O. Thompson. *Shakespeare, Meaning and Metaphor*. Brighton: Harvester, 1987.

Thompson, Ann, and Neil Taylor, eds. *Hamlet*. Arden Shakespeare. 3rd Series. London: Thomson Learning, 2006.

Thomson, Peter. *Shakespeare's Professional Career*. 1992; Cambridge University Press, Canto, 1994.

Thorne, Alison. '"To Write and Read / Be Henceforth Treacherous": *Cymbeline* and the Problem of Interpretation'. Richards and Knowles, eds. 176–90.

Tillyard, E. M. W. *The English Epic and Its Background*. Westport: Greenwood Press, 1976.

Trevor, Douglas. *The Poetics of Melancholy in Early Modern England*. Cambridge University Press, 2004.

Tudeau-Clayton, Margaret. *Jonson, Shakespeare and Early Modern Virgil*. Cambridge University Press, 1998.

Variorum Spenser. The Works of Edmund Spenser: A Variorum Edition. Ed. Edwin Greenlaw *et al.* 11 vols. Baltimore: Johns Hopkins University Press, 1932–57.

Vaughan, Virginia Mason, and Alden T. Vaughan, eds. *The Tempest*. Arden Shakespeare. 3rd Series. 1999; London: Thomson Learning, 2000.

Vickers, Brian. *Shakespeare as Co-Author: A Historical Study of Five Collaborative Plays*. Oxford University Press, 2002.

Vickers, Nancy J. '"The blazon of sweet beauty's best": Shakespeare's *Lucrece*'. Parker and Hartman, eds. 95–115.

Virgil. *Virgil*. Trans. H. Rushton Fairclough. Loeb Classical Library. 2 vols. 1916–18; Cambridge, MA: Harvard University Press; London: Heinemann, 1934–5.

Wall, Wendy. *The Imprint of Gender: Authorship and Publication in the English Renaissance*. Ithaca: Cornell University Press, 1993.

'Authorship and the Material Conditions of Writing'. Kinney, ed. 64–89.

Warren, Roger, ed. *Cymbeline*. Oxford World's Classics. Oxford University Press, 1998.

Henry VI, Part Two. Oxford World's Classics. Oxford University Press, 2003.

Watson, Robert N. *The Rest is Silence: Death as Annihilation in the English Renaissance*. Berkeley: University of California Press, 1994.

Wayne, Valerie. 'The Woman's Part in Cymbeline'. *Staged Properties in Early Modern English Drama*. Ed. Jonathan Gil Harris and Natasha Korda. Cambridge University Press, 2002. 288–315.

   '*Cymbeline*: Patriotism and Performance'. Dutton and Howard, eds., *A Companion to Shakespeare's Works. Poems, Problem Comedies, Late Plays*. 389–407.

Weil, Herbert, and Judith Weil, eds. *The First Part of King Henry IV*. New Cambridge Shakespeare. Cambridge University Press, 1997.

Weimann, Robert. *Author's Pen and Actor's Voice: Playing and Writing in Shakespeare's Theatre*. Ed. Helen Higbee and William West. Cambridge University Press, 2000.

Wells, Stanley. *Shakespeare: A Life in Drama*. New York: Norton, 1995.

   'By the Placing of His Words'. *Times Literary Supplement* 26 September 2003: 14–15.

   'Current Issues in Shakespeare Biography'. *In the Footsteps of William Shakespeare*. Ed. Christa Jansohn. Münster: Lit, 2005. 5–21.

Wells, Stanley, ed. *The Cambridge Companion to Shakespeare Studies*. Cambridge University Press, 1986.

   King Lear. Oxford World's Classics. Oxford University Press, 2001.

Wells, Stanley, and Lena Cowen Orlin, eds. *Shakespeare: An Oxford Guide*. Oxford University Press, 2003.

Whittier, Gayle. 'The Sonnet's Body and the Body Sonnetized in *Romeo and Juliet*'. *Shakespeare Quarterly* 40 (1989): 27–41.

Wilks, John S. *The Idea of Conscience in Renaissance Tragedy*. London: Routledge, 1990.

Wilson, John Dover, ed. *The Tempest*. Cambridge University Press, 1961.

Wilson, Richard. '"A Mingled Yarn": Shakespeare and the Cloth Workers'. *Literature and History* 12 (1986): 164–80.

   Secret Shakespeare: Studies in Theatre, Religion, and Resistance. Manchester University Press, 2004.

Wither, George. *A Collection of Emblems, 1635*. Menston: Scolar Press, 1968.

Witmore, Michael. *Culture of Accidents: Unexpected Knowledges in Early Modern England*. Stanford University Press, 2001.

Wittreich, Joseph. '"Image of That Horror": The Apocalypse in *King Lear*'. *The Apocalypse in English Renaissance Thought and Literature: Patterns, Antecedents, and Repercussions*. Ed. C. A. Patrides and Joseph Wittreich. Ithaca: Cornell University Press, 1984. 175–206.

Wofford, Susanne L., ed. *Hamlet*. Case Studies in Contemporary Criticism. Boston, MA: Bedford, St Martin's Press, 1994.

Worthen, William B. *Shakespeare and the Authority of Performance*. Cambridge University Press, 1997.

Wright, George T. 'Hendiadys and *Hamlet*'. *PMLA* 96 (1981): 168–93.

   Shakespeare's Metrical Art. Berkeley: University of California Press, 1988.

Wutrich, Timothy Richard. *Prometheus and Faust: The Promethean Revolt in Drama from Classical Antiquity to Goethe.* Westport: Greenwood Press, 1995.

Yachnin, Paul. *Stage-Wrights: Shakespeare, Jonson, Middleton, and the Making of Theatrical Value.* Philadelphia: University of Pennsylvania Press, 1997.

Zitner, Sheldon, ed. *Much Ado about Nothing.* Oxford World's Classics. Oxford University Press, 1993.

Index